The Political Economy of Managed Migration

The Political Economy of Managed Migration

Nonstate Actors, Europeanization, and the Politics of Designing Migration Policies

Georg Menz

OXFORD
UNIVERSITY PRESS

OXFORD
UNIVERSITY PRESS

Great Clarendon Street, Oxford OX2 6DP

Oxford University Press is a department of the University of Oxford.
It furthers the University's objective of excellence in research, scholarship,
and education by publishing worldwide in

Oxford New York

Auckland Cape Town Dar es Salaam Hong Kong Karachi
Kuala Lumpur Madrid Melbourne Mexico City Nairobi
New Delhi Shanghai Taipei Toronto

With offices in

Argentina Austria Brazil Chile Czech Republic France Greece
Guatemala Hungary Italy Japan Poland Portugal Singapore
South Korea Switzerland Thailand Turkey Ukraine Vietnam

Oxford is a registered trade mark of Oxford University Press
in the UK and in certain other countries

Published in the United States
by Oxford University Press Inc., New York

© Georg Menz 2009

The moral rights of the author have been asserted
Database right Oxford University Press (maker)

First published 2009

All rights reserved. No part of this publication may be reproduced,
stored in a retrieval system, or transmitted, in any form or by any means,
without the prior permission in writing of Oxford University Press,
or as expressly permitted by law, or under terms agreed with the appropriate
reprographics rights organization. Enquiries concerning reproduction
outside the scope of the above should be sent to the Rights Department,
Oxford University Press, at the address above

You must not circulate this book in any other binding or cover
and you must impose the same condition on any acquirer

British Library Cataloguing in Publication Data

Data available

Library of Congress Cataloging in Publication Data

Data available

Typeset by SPI Publisher Services, Pondicherry, India
Printed in the UK
on acid-free paper by
the MPG Books Group

ISBN 978–0–19–953388–6 (Hbk)

10 9 8 7 6 5 4 3 2 1

Preface

The often somewhat hysterical tone and nature of debates surrounding immigration to Europe may appear perplexing to an outside observer. It seems unsurprising that this prosperous and in parts economically dynamic subcontinent with generally high standards of living would appear attractive to newcomers. The wage gap between the northern and the southern shore of the Mediterranean exceeds 1:20. The income gap between Germany and Poland (roughly 1:8) is the highest of any directly adjacent countries worldwide, exceeding that between the United States and Mexico. Moving further east and outside of the realms of the European Union (EU), the wage and income gaps become even more starkly pronounced and obvious "push" and "pull" factors become visible.

But for many decades, immigration to Europe was limited to the prosperous northwest (see Table P.1) and heavily curtailed after the end to active labor recruitment in the early 1970s. This book examines the renaissance of immigration and the rediscovery of active labor migration recruitment that have unfolded since the 1990s. Nonstate actors played a crucial role in helping reshape policies in this domain. Employer organizations are eager to recruit liberally for positions that cannot be filled domestically, either because the jobs are unattractive to natives or because the required skill profile cannot be found at home. This means recruiting not only agricultural workers and staff for the gastronomy sector but also highly skilled information technology professionals. Trade unions have overcome their historical reticence towards immigration and approve of carefully managed migration, as long as the newcomers receive standard wages and enjoy standard working conditions. Governments across Europe are subscribing to the logic of the "competition state", having accepted a curious blend of neoliberal and neo-mercantilist logic that calls for the government to resign itself to creating conditions amiable and conducive to business and investment. Labor immigration is very much a component of such a strategy, though it remains uncertain whether the

Preface

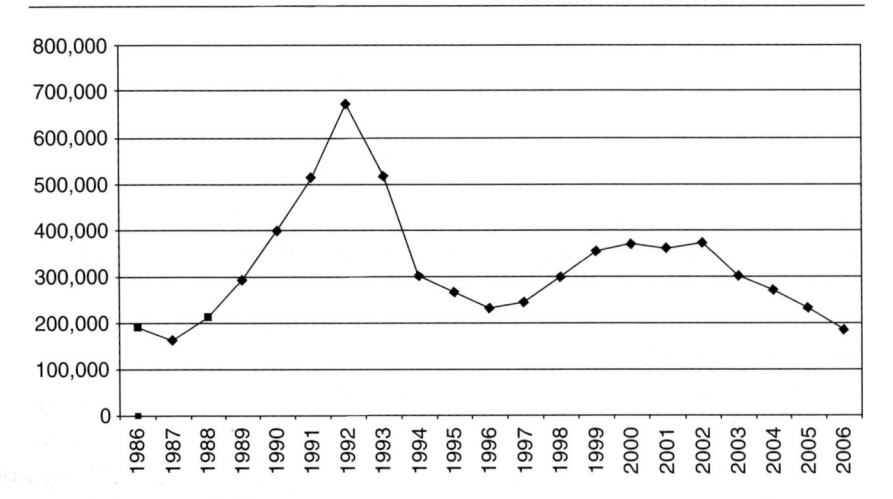

Figure P.1. First asylum applications in EU 1986–2006

Source: Eurostat

1986–2003 = applications in EU15; 2004–06 = applications in EU25

overpopulated Old Continent can ever hope to mimic successfully the policies of countries like Australia and Canada.

Similar notions prevail in Brussels. In European Union documents, labor migration is perceived as a vital component of the so-called Lisbon Strategy. According to this strategy, Europe shall turn itself into the "most competitive region" worldwide by 2010, again through competition state–style policies.

The flipside of the newly developed appetite for labor migration is an ever more restrictive approach to political asylum seekers and refugees. "Managed migration", a pan-European paradigm, involves the distinction

Table P.1. Total and foreign population as of January 1, 2006

	Total population	Non-nationals	Citizens of EU-27	TCNs
France	62,886	3,500	1,314	2,186
Germany	82,438	7,289	2,212	5,077
Ireland	4,235	314	215	99
Italy	58,752	2,671	539	2,132
Poland	38,157	700	16	684
United Kingdom	60,210	3,066	1,174	1,892

Source: Eurostat

between "useful" and "burdensome" migrants. Opening up the selected pathways to Fortress Europe seems to correlate with ever more tightly locked doors elsewhere (see Figure P.1). Humanitarian nongovernmental organizations actively lobby governments for more pragmatic, liberal, and accommodating policies towards migrants accepted for humanitarian reasons, principally refugees, asylum seekers, and beneficiaries of family reunion, but their organizational weaknesses are compounded by an unfavorable political and economic climate.

This book is the product of a research project originally entitled "Regressing towards the Mean? The Future of European Immigration and Asylum Policies". Financial support provided by Goldsmiths College, the University of London's Central Research Fund, and the British Academy is gratefully acknowledged. This funding proved invaluable as I spent countless hours during 2004-6 interviewing government officials, trade union and employer organization representatives, and staff representing nongovernmental organizations active in the migration field in six European countries. My thanks go to these individuals and their willingness to engage with me in discussing the finer points of political lobbying and interest positions regarding a highly sensitive and politicized policy domain. Researching immigration at a time when the subject regularly made headlines rendered elite interviewing not always a particularly simple enterprise. Though my interview requests eventually spawned more than three dozen extensive and in-depth explorations of policymaking processes in practice, organizational preferences for asylum and migration policy, and the distribution of power and its impact on lobbying efforts in Ireland, the United Kingdom, France, Germany, Italy, and Poland, these were often the fruit of repeated inquiries and considerable display of persistency. Additional background interviews with academic experts and not least with NGOs, trade unions, and employer organizations in Brussels as well as with representatives of the European Commission's Directorate-General for Justice, Freedom, and Security provided additional insights. On a more practical level, trekking across Europe, from Dublin to Warsaw and from Rome to Berlin, has not only meant spending an inordinate amount of time in airport lounges but more importantly has permitted several eye-opening experiences, which, though not always recorded specifically, have helped shape my thinking on the issue, as has living and working in sections of London with sizable immigrant communities. Special mention must be made of the Polish government's Office for Aliens and Repatriation, which

Preface

permitted me to visit one of its twenty reception centers for asylum seekers and refugees on the outskirts of Warsaw, a gesture of openness that was very far from the reception I received in certain other countries.

Research leave from Goldsmiths College during 2005–6 and a Jean Monnet Fellowship from the European University Institute's Department of Political and Social Studies permitted the necessary time away from teaching duties to assemble a first draft of the manuscript.

Some of the ideas and concepts developed in this book were also tried out on unsuspecting Goldsmiths College students and academic audiences on either side of the Atlantic, including at conferences of the US European Union Studies Association, the US Council for European Studies, the University of Alberta, Oxford University's COMPAS Centre, the British Political Studies Association, the workshop session organized by Virginie Guiraudon at the European University Institute's Robert Schuman Center, research conferences organized by Andrew Geddes in Manchester and Liverpool sponsored by the British University Association for Contemporary European Studies, and conferences organized by the Berlin Institute for Contemporary Social Research and sponsored by the European Union's Marie Curie Programme in Cecina and Florence. Some of the comments received in the course of these sessions have proven very valuable.

A number of friends and colleagues have assisted me with this project in one capacity or another. I would like to express my gratitude to Andrew Geddes, Virginie Guiraudon, Randall Hansen, Carl Levy, Adrian Favell, James Hollifield, Martin Rhodes, Gallya Lahav, Eleonora Lungu, Carlo Ruzza, Tanya Ward, Guillermo Ruiz, Anne Daguerre, of course, and Alberta Sbragia. Dominic Byatt at Oxford University Press has been a very competent and patient editor.

On a more personal note, I thank my mother and siblings for their support and encouragement.

Georg Menz

London, March 2008

Contents

List of Figures and Tables   x
List of Abbreviations   xi

1. Managing Migration: Political Economies, Nonstate Actors, and Multiple Arenas   1

2. Legacies of the Past and Currents of Change: Conundrums over Migration and Asylum   23

3. National Actors and European Solutions: The Contours of Conflict   76

4. Political Battles at Home and in Brussels: Labor Migration and Asylum Policy in Established Countries of Immigration: France, the United Kingdom, and Germany   125

5. Contested Areas of Sovereignty: Labor Migration and Asylum Policy in New Countries of Immigration: Ireland, Italy, and Poland   198

6. Managed Migration, Populism, and Pragmatism   257

Bibliography   269
Index   299

List of Figures and Tables

Figure

P.1. First asylum applications in EU 1986–2006 — vi

Tables

P.1.	Total and foreign population as of January 1, 2006	vi
2.1.	Developments in AMP since the 1970s	51
2.2.	Developments in AMP since 2000	54
3.1.	Conceptualizing top-down Europeanization	79
3.2.	Conceptualizing bottom-up Europeanization	85
3.3.	Organizational power of labor market interest associations	89
3.4.	The role of nonstate actors in shaping migration policy	90
4.1.	Sectoral composition and distribution of workforce in the UK, France, and Germany	126
4.2.	French immigration policy in the 1980s	127
4.3.	French immigration policy in the 1990s	128
4.4.	French immigration policy since 2000	130
4.5.	British immigration policy since the 1980s	155
4.6.	German immigration policy in the 1980s and 1990s	173
4.7.	German immigration policy since 2000	174
5.1.	Sectoral composition and distribution of workforce in Ireland, Poland, and Italy	204
5.2.	Irish immigration policy	210
5.3.	Polish immigration policy	222
5.4.	Developments in Italian migration policy	243
5.5.	Legalization campaigns in Italy	248

List of Abbreviations

AMP	Asylum and Migration Policy
ANAFE	Association Nationale d'Assistance aux Frontières aux Etrangers (National Association for the Aid of Foreginers at the Border: French Pro-Migrant NGO)
BDA	Bundesvereinigung der Deutschen Arbeitgeberverbände (German Employer Association)
BDI	Bundesverband der Deutschen Industrie (Association of Major German Business)
BGS	Bundesgrenzschutz (German Border Police)
CBI	Confederation of British Industry (British Business Association)
CFDT	Confédération Française Démocratique du Travail (French centrist Trade Union)
CGIL	Confederazione Generale Italiana del Lavoro (Italian center-left Trade Union)
CGT	Confédération Général du Travail (French Communist-influenced Trade Union)
CISL	Confederazione Italiana Sindacali Lavoratori (Italian center-left Trade Union)
Confindustria	Confederazione Generale del' Industria Italiana (Italian Employer Association)
DGB	Deutscher Gewerkschaftsbund (German Trade Union Association)
EU	European Union
IBEC	Irish Business and Employers Confederation
ICTU	Irish Congress of Trade Unions
LDH	Ligue des droits de l'homme (League of Human Rights: French Pro-Migrant NGO)

List of Abbreviations

MEDEF	Mouvement des entreprises de France (French Employer Association)
NSZZ	Niezależny Samorżadny Związek Zawodny (Polish Trade Union)
TUC	Trades Union Congress (Central Association of British Trade Unions)
UIL	Unione Italiana del Lavoro (Italian Trade Union)

1

Managing Migration: Political Economies, Nonstate Actors, and Multiple Arenas

> The great value of the employment of foreigners lies in the fact that we thus have a mobile labour potential at our disposal.
> Ulrich Freiherr von Gienanth, representative of German employer association BDA (*Der Arbeitgeber* 18 (20), March 1966: 153, cited in Castles and Kosack 1973: 98)
> The system should therefore primarily be focused on bringing in migrants who are highly skilled or to do key jobs that cannot be filled from the domestic labour force [...].
> Point 7 of the "executive summary" of Britain's "new" labor migration scheme (UK Home Office 2006)

Managed Migration as a New Paradigm

To study European history is to study migration. Over the course of the past three millennia, prolonged conflicts over borders, territory, resources, and the control of people have been fought, while throughout this period, population flows have been a constant feature. Immigration to Europe is clearly not a phenomenon of the late twentieth century. However, the direction of global migration flows has become more complex. Europe may still generate emigration, but it is now attracting significant numbers of immigrants, many from the subcontinent's unstable periphery, others from its former colonies, some from further afield.

Since the early 1990s, immigration has rapidly re-emerged as a highly contested, divisive, and explosive challenge for public policy across Europe. Active labor migration has been rediscovered after a prolonged hiatus. Under the influence of employer associations, governments once again contemplate and have quickly implemented new labor recruitment schemes across Europe. Recruitment of non-EU "third-country nationals" (TCNs) has been informed by concerns over skills shortages in select niches of sectoral labor markets and a common mismatch between the requirements of new professional opportunities and the skills portfolios of the domestic unemployed. Sectors experiencing recruitment problems include health care, finance, gastronomy, agriculture, and information technology. High-skill migration schemes exist in the Czech Republic, Austria, the United Kingdom, Ireland, Latvia, Estonia, and Sweden and are under debate or in genesis in France and Germany. Notwithstanding persistently high general unemployment rates and a political climate influenced by often hostile public opinion (Lahav 1998) and unease over existing social tensions as a result of past immigration (Joppke 1999), contributing to the electoral fortunes of the Far Right (Betz 1994; Hainsworth 2000; Heinisch 2003; Minkenberg 2000; Schain 1987), employer associations lobby governments for more permissive and pragmatic labor migration policy either openly or, given the less than amiable context, somewhat hidden from public scrutiny. European unions approve of these measures and support managed labor migration, provided immigrant workers benefit from standard wages and working conditions and do not contribute to a stratification of the labor market by feeding into either semi-legal or entirely illegal bottom tiers where exploitative circumstances are rife.[1]

Superficially, the return to labor migration may bear certain parallels to postwar policies, but the new paradigm of managed migration entails much more carefully regulated and restricted access channels. Managed migration reflects the pragmatic realization that in liberal societies immigration cannot be stopped or reversed (Joppke 1999), yet its core is managerial, economistic, and restrictive, focusing on the potential economic and social contributions by immigrants to host societies. Managing migration entails selecting newcomers based on their skills profile, reminiscent of policy approaches employed by some of the more established immigration countries, yet this concept also entails more rigorously restrictive aspects with respect to unwanted, unsolicited, and undesirable newcomers who seek alternative access paths. Given international legal obligations, notably the 1951 Geneva Convention relating to the Status of Refugees, and domestic policy entrepreneurship by courts (Guiraudon 2001; Hollifield 2006; Joppke 1999), de facto migration channels opened up for humanitarian reasons, including asylum and family reunion, are difficult to manipulate by the executive, despite their pivotal role in terms of the quantitative contribution to overall immigration levels, especially from the mid-1980s onwards. The regulation of both categories, especially political asylum, has therefore been a field of extensive and generally restrictive legislative activity since the 1990s, with attempts being made to construct new and inferior categories of temporary protection that do not bestow the full benefits of political asylum, while raising efforts to deport failed applicants and physically to prevent territorial access through the construction of buffer zones around the geographic territory of the European Union (EU) (Geddes 2000*b*). The regulation of political asylum is thus an important component of managed migration. Just as with labor migration, nonstate actors have endeavored to shape policy outputs through lobbying activities, yet not only are such efforts by humanitarian nongovernmental organizations (NGOs) hampered by the same unwelcoming political climate that labor market interest associations grapple with, but their own organizational deficiencies further impede effective lobbying efforts.

Analyzing managed migration and assuming this new paradigm to constitute more than mere clever rhetoric by zealous governments eager to be perceived as undertaking popular and populist action entails a highly skeptical stance regarding the claim submitted by a number of migration scholars who have questioned whether state sovereignty in this policy field is still sufficiently strong to implement effective regulatory policy (Heisler 1986; Sassen 2001; Soysal 1994). The question is not whether governments still can regulate migration flows, but rather what factors shape regulatory attempts at managing migration. In that sense, the state sovereignty debate (Lahav and Guiraudon 2000) needs to be recast to account for policymaking in liberal pluralist societies that permit access and voice to nonstate actors.

Nonstate Actors and Migration Policy

Who are the key actors in migration and asylum policy? In this book, I submit the claim that the migration literature, especially in political science, will profit immensely from building on an emerging strand that examines the activities of nonstate actors. Such analysis will help account for what Hollifield (1992) refers to as the control paradox, whereby Western nations promote economic liberalization in trade and capital

3

flow, but not with respect to the flow of people. The "gap" between restrictionist rhetoric and slightly more permissive practice (Hansen 2002) can thus equally be addressed. European migration policies are indeed "in flux" (Boswell 2003). But who drives these changes? Past scholarly efforts that emphasize the role of nongovernmental actors highlight courts (Guiraudon 2001; Hollifield 2001; Joppke 1998) or the media (Statham 1999), private actors such as security and transportation companies (Guiraudon 2002; Guiraudon and Lahav 2000; Lahav 1998), and, indeed, humanitarian interest groups (Favell 1998; Geddes 2000a; Koopmans and Statham 1999). Other endeavors stress the role of organized interest groups, though largely in the US context (Freeman 1995, 2001, 2002) and trade unions (Haus 2002; Watts 2002). Little recent work has examined the role of employer associations, though organized business played a pivotal role in earlier Marxist analytical contributions (Cole and Dale 1999; earlier: Castles and Kosack 1973; Castells 1975).[2] This book examines two principal avenues of immigration: labor migration and political asylum. It explores the role of two sets of domestic nonstate actors in influencing policy in these two fields, namely, trade unions and employer associations in migration policy and humanitarian NGOs in asylum policy. Interest groups matter in shaping domestic policy and much existing research in migration studies underestimates their impact. Labor market interest organizations represent their constituents and their concerns; new demands for labor migration will be colored by the contribution individual sectors make to the economy, the structure of the labor market, the predominant production system, and corporate strategies. Any attempt at influencing public debates hinges on internal policy consensus, which may not be present given different sectoral demands. Institutional coherence and strength also matter in successfully influencing public policy. Informed by recent advances in comparative political economy (Amable 2003; Hall and Soskice 2001; Hancké, Rhodes, and Thatcher 2007; Menz 2005a; Schmidt 2002), I argue that structural institutionalized differences between different models or "varieties" of capitalism, encapsulated by examining a number of relevant variables detailed below, are reflected in the preferences and claims that national labor market interest associations will make in seeking to shape labor migration policy. Therefore, to employ Hall and Soskice's typology (2001), the embedded environments of liberal and coordinated market economies shape the preferences of actors and will create different demands for different sets of labor migrants. Different national production strategies influence national migration management, though it is only relatively recently that such strategies have diverged sufficiently to produce substantially different policy outcomes.[3]

Henceforth, we would expect to note differences between national migration strategies in coordinated market economies such as Germany and liberal market economies such as Britain. In a CME, such as Germany, we would expect to see an employer preference for highly skilled top-tier labor migration. In addition, given the continuing importance of the secondary tier (Table 2.1), manufacturing sector employers may be particularly active. By contrast, in an LME like Britain, employers are likely to advocate recruitment of highly skilled labor *both* for select niches with labor shortages and for poorly paid sectors of the labor market that experience recruitment problems and high staff turnover due to low wages, poor morale and prestige, and unappealing working conditions.

The second set of actors who receive coverage are humanitarian NGOs operating at the national level focusing on asylum and refugee policy. The same analytical framework with regard to their institutional basis will be employed to assess their influence. Past scholarship on such groups has been skeptical about their leverage and influence (Statham and Geddes 2006), as various powerful opposition players counteract lobbying efforts for more liberal asylum policy, notably in the form of media actors and xenophobic far right political parties. In addition, as this study points out, institutional characteristics often impede effective lobbying, while links with government ministries are feeble or nonexistent.

Immigration is a sensitive issue. National governments are keen to minimize "interference" by nongovernmental actors, including courts, nongovernmental organizations and interest groups, and citizen initiatives. While it is important not to overstate the impact of the terrorist attacks of September 11, 2001 in New York and the subsequent attacks in Madrid and London, as immigration policy has long been managed by ministries of the interior and thus as a component of portfolios focused on organized crime, drugs, trafficking, and terrorism, rhetorical discourse and public policy in recent years have explicitly linked immigration and domestic security. The Copenhagen School (Buzan et al. 1993) concept of "securitization," influenced by the constructivist approach in international relations theory, highlights the construction of domestic security threats for political expediency. Jef Huysmans' work (2000: 752) has chronicled "how...migration [is] connected to representations of societal dangers" and how the "technocratic and politically manufactured spillover of the economic project of the internal market [has degenerated] into an internal security project." This trend potentially impedes lobbying efforts for pragmatic and liberal migration policy by any type of nonstate actor. However, as we shall argue in more detail below, such securitization needs to be amended to cover concerns over economic competitiveness, a central preoccupation of the European competition state of the early twenty-first century. These concerns can be stoked through skillful manipulation by employer associations, exploiting fears of being "outgunned" in a global battle for brains.

Playing with and in Europe

Adding to the complexity of analyzing contemporary European migration policy is the additional arena provided by the European Union (EU), which this book explores accordingly. Asylum and Migration Policy (AMP) at the EU level has been slow in the coming, yet all serious scholarship concurs on the remarkable giant leap forward since the mid-1980s (Geddes 2000*b*), especially since the Tampere Council meeting of 1999. AMP policymaking thus unfolds over several levels (cf. Marks and Hooghe 2002), notwithstanding the pronounced hesitancy of national governments to surrender control over this field to Brussels and permit Europeanization or *communautarization*. This does not only apply to Ireland, the UK, and Denmark, member states that have opted out of communal policymaking in this field altogether. When AMP making does ensue, governmental actors, especially the national ministries of interior affairs that administer the migration portfolio, prefer to meet often like-minded colleagues in the amiable and secretive environment of the Council of Ministers, avoiding the scrutiny often present at the national level. Where "venue shopping" (Guiraudon 2000*a*) is possible, governments will prefer this insulation "Brussels" affords. But ministers do not arrive in Brussels empty-handed; they are involved in complicated two-level games (Putnam 1988), seeking to "set the agenda" by presenting national policy as possible blueprints for EU AMP, while minimizing transaction costs of top-down initiatives in a politically highly sensitive policy area. Meanwhile, at the national level, nongovernmental actors clamor to shape national-level policy. Humanitarian NGOs may have limited success, facing governments that are often reluctant to consult with them, much less pay heed to their advice. Persistent though inaccurate conflation of asylum with welfare "scrounging," fraud and abuse, or, worse yet, "security threats" in media and public discourse does not facilitate effective lobbying. Labor market interest associations, such as trade unions and employer associations, are much more successful in communicating their preferences. As migration is increasingly being Europeanized, governmental actors find themselves engaging in two-level games, negotiating policy development both at the national level, where both policy implementation and agenda-setting for blueprints that can be taken to the EU level are politically embattled processes, and at the EU level, where the contours of AMP are being decided upon.

How will these actors attempt to set the agenda? Europeanization is a two-way avenue. In new areas of regulation, representatives of national governments that can propose policy blueprints that successfully imprint EU policy benefit from first mover advantages and minimal transaction costs (Héritier 1996). In other words, "goodness of fit" for them is optimal (Börzel and Risse 2003) and accommodation costs are insignificant. But bottom-up Europeanization in the AMP domain is an extremely arduous game to play, as other governments need to be successfully persuaded, given the *de jure* unanimity requirement for decision-making in the Council until 2004 and arguably de facto since.

Comparative Political Economy, Migration, and Europeanization

There are no compelling reasons why migration studies ought to be treated as a *sui generis* "subfield" of political science. This book combines insights from comparative political economy and migration studies as well as also the Europeanization approach in EU studies to study AMP in six European countries and at the EU level since the early 1990s. Drawing on these diverse bodies of literature to which it seeks to contribute in turn, it develops three principal arguments, which will be critically examined in light of the empirical evidence.

First, migration policy is strongly influenced by differences in systems of *political economy*, that is, the nexus of production strategies of corporations, the sectoral composition of the economy, and labor market regulation. Obviously, this applies particularly to labor migration policy, which is subject to the lobbying activities of trade unions and employer associations. These actors and their activities have been relatively neglected in the scholarly literature (for exceptions, see Haus 2002; Watts 2002).

Labor market interest associations call for labor recruitment schemes, while humanitarian NGOs lobby for more permissive approaches to asylum policy. These efforts partly account for the puzzle of European governments tolerating or even soliciting immigration despite largely hostile public opinion (Lahav 2004) and highly restrictive rhetoric by government officials. Freeman's pioneering work (1995, 2002, 2006) has emphasized the importance of client politics in liberal democracies, though principally the United States, where well-organized employer groups and ethnic advocacy groups combine efforts to press for liberal policies from which they benefit and whose costs are diffused. Though compelling in its empirical application and rightfully applauded for its introduction of a political economy angle, Freeman's work has been criticized for not being applicable to the European context (Joppke 1999), not addressing noneconomic forms of migration such as political asylum (but see Freeman 2006), and neglecting how immigration is framed and thus perceived by actors (Statham and Geddes 2006). Informed by Freeman and addressing the critiques leveled at his work, a unique framework for analyzing the impact of interest groups is developed that applies both to economic and noneconomic forms of migration. Correcting Freeman's analysis somewhat, it is maintained that employers will not simply lobby for "more liberal" policy, but rather the production system in which they are embedded conditions the quality and quantity of labor migration advocated. Addressing Statham and Geddes's concern (2006), it is argued that employer associations have successfully defined "competitiveness" as a central concern for national policymakers and have demonstrated how immigration can help provide the required human resources necessary to ensure economic competitiveness. National security is thus a more flexible term than most analysts of "securitization" have acknowledged (Bigo 2008; Buzan et al. 1993; Huysmans 2000, 2006) and need not be limited to associations with political extremism and terrorism.

But I do not simply seek to submit the claim that interest groups "matter," rather I explore how and why they influence governmental actors in the pursuit of their preferences. It is not their mere absence or presence that shapes governmental policy, but their relative power. These preferences are shaped by two diverging sets of logics. Humanitarian NGOs are most interested in asylum and refugee politics, their preference is for a liberal policy in this domain. Lobbying efforts are commonly hampered by weak organizational characteristics and poor links to the ministry of interior affairs, their main interlocutor at the governmental level. Labor market interest associations are usually organizationally stronger, though they need to create new links with ministries of interior affairs in addition to the existing and often well-established channels of influence to ministries of labor and social affairs.

Differences in systems of political economy have become more pronounced over the course of the past three decades, as the literature on comparative political economy reminds us (Amable 2003; Crouch and Streeck 1997; Hall and Soskice 2001; Katzenstein 1978; Shonfield 1965). During the postwar period of expansion under the aegis of a Keynesian-inspired macroeconomic policy mix, migration policy across West Europe was geared at filling labor market shortages mainly in unskilled Fordist manufacturing positions. The profile of the labor migrants recruited therefore did not vary dramatically across countries, despite differences in political "philosophies of integration" (Favell 2001) that are at the center point of comparative migration studies' efforts to chronicle past and present European migration policies (early: Castles and Kosack 1973; King 1993; Fassmann and Münz 1994; Hollifield, Cornelius, and Martin 2004; Uçarer and Puchala 1997; Angenendt 1999). The contemporary post-Fordist neoliberal competition state (cf. Cerny 1995; Hirsch 1995) seeks to maximize its "competitiveness" by assuring a business-friendly climate. In doing so, it is particularly prone to consider suggestions from employers on the design of its migration policy.[4] (Re)discovering migrants as potentially useful human resources, governments thus implement new labor migration policies that reflect the profile of the different production strategies and the structure of the labor market across Europe.

But not only do neoliberal governments perceive some types of immigrants as useful contributors, worth engaging into open competition over with other more established immigration destinations. Employer associations, themselves fairly neglected actors in migration studies, also have either rediscovered the benefits of reversing the total recruitment ban on labor migration of the 1970s in France, West Germany, and de facto Britain, a measure not necessarily to their liking in France and Britain in the first instance, or more recently discovered the benefits of a highly skilled, flexible, mobile, and dynamic addition to the domestic labor pool. A more transnationalized post-Fordist economy in which all employers stress "flexibility" of their work force as a core demand (cf. Caviedes 2006) has led to employers assuming an active stance in embracing economic migrants—one example is freshly designed forms of temporary migration to address seasonal labor market shortages that despite their recent provenance seem to resemble the philosophy of the 1960s guest worker approach. Despite common external pressures, European capitalisms continue to diverge and it would appear unwarranted to expect a convergence of labor migration policies (Hollifield 1992). There may be superficial similarities in certain sectors, as low-paid health care professionals such as nurses and carers for the elderly and frail are in short supply almost everywhere in Europe. But on closer inspection migration policy continues to differ across Europe in the wake of the rediscovery of actively solicited labor migration. Thus, labor migrants are recruited to compliment existing strengths in terms of the production strategy and address structural weaknesses and deficiencies. In liberal market economies (LMEs), where education is considered largely a private investment in one's own employability, there is potentially high interest in "poaching" migrants who have accumulated training and education elsewhere. In the aftermath of the neoliberal reforms of the 1980s, LME labor markets are fairly deregulated, creating a permanent low-skill low-pay secondary tier (cf. Piore 1979; Samers 2004) to which migrants are permitted if they are prepared to cope with the conditions offered. The added competition from native former recipients of welfare benefits who are pushed into the labor market under workfarist welfare state retrenchment policies (Peck 2001) leads to a further decline in the wages and working conditions offered for such jobs. Coordinated market economies (CME) may perceive migrants as agents to address perceived shortcomings such as a lack of rapid innovation in product development and the commercialization of research and development. Though neoliberal deregulation is affecting labor markets and the welfare state in CMEs, too, generating a segmentation and bifurcation of the labor market in certain economic sectors there as well, for example in construction (Menz 2001, 2005*a*), there is little interest in permanent low-skill migration. Using immigration as a deliberate tool to promote the segmentation of labor markets would be sufficiently politically controversial and costly as an overtly pursued strategy to dissuade CME governments from pursuing it. From a political economy perspective, it will be argued here that the employer interest in highly skilled migrants, which complements directly corporate production strategies, will strongly condition governmental policy.

The comparative political economy literature has thus far struggled to devise comprehensive analytical categories fully appropriate for southern and eastern Europe. This renders a political economy analysis of labor migration policies more challenging, though not impossible, as mixed regimes emerge that may defy the dichotomy proffered by Hall and Soskice (2001), as Mykhnenko (2005) and McMenamin (2004) among others have argued. Governments in central and southern Europe adopt labor migration policies that reflect similarities at the sectoral and sometimes regional levels with the more established and mature coordinated or liberal varieties of capitalism in Western Europe. Thus, for example, the Czech government is copying CME-style migration policies, seeking to attract highly skilled labor migrants for the service sector. But elsewhere in central Europe, notably in Poland, labor migration is not yet being actively pursued, as a sufficient pool of domestic workers satisfies labor needs in the primary and secondary sectors. Additional skill and labor demands are thus far met through a policy of tolerating undocumented migration into the primary and less so the tertiary sector and accepting limited numbers of highly skilled migrants often in the framework of intra-company transfers. Southern Europe defies easy categorization because of its eclectic mixture of high value-added high-skills CME "islands," both in services and in manufacturing, its still sizable agricultural sectors and predominantly low-skill services and manufacturing elsewhere. Often extensive informal and undocumented segments of the economy that absorb considerable numbers of immigrants complicate the picture further (Baldwin-Edwards 2002). This uneven economic structure is associated with labor migration policies that seek actively to recruit highly skilled employees, including self-employed entrepreneurs, while undocumented migration into the low-skill low-wage sectors of the economy is being tolerated.

The strategic use of labor migrants to address skills shortages, ensure flexibility in corporate strategic planning, and access new labor pools is a priority for employer associations, but given pervasive high unemployment and skeptical or outright hostile public opinion towards migration, business treads carefully in seeking to influence governmental actors. Lobbying in this highly charged and sensitive policy domain is a delicate process, likely to involve skillful rhetorical strategies invoking the danger posed to national competitiveness by skills shortages. The often very negative public perception of immigration in Europe is not exclusively informed by xenophobia, racism, and the rhetoric of the nativist Far Right. Much existing empirical research (for the United States: Borjas et al. 1992; Borjas 1994, 1995; for Europe: Gross 1999; Coppel et al. 2001) suggests that low-skilled native workers are likely to experience downward pressure on wages and labor conditions as migration increases the supply side pool of labor. A second factor influencing the negative public perception of immigration is the poor track record of the integration of the "second generation" or descendants of the postwar migrants into the labor market throughout Western Europe. The low-skill manufacturing jobs the postwar immigrants were recruited into no longer exist in Western Europe. Educational institutions have generally performed very poorly in preparing the second generation for highly skilled jobs (Crul and Vermeulen 2006; Menz 2006). There is predictably very little desire to add further numbers to this already disquieting phenomenon.

Such challenges are not insurmountable. Employers and unions embedded in different systems of political economy will seek to influence governments to adopt labor migration policies that reflect the profile of migrants deemed complementary to national production strategies.

Therefore, the first contention holds that different models of political economy will inform distinct types of labor recruitment strategies. Employers and unions will seek to influence governments, based on factors including the system of political economy and the relative size of components of the economy, but their ability to do so will be shaped by the degree of internal policy consensus and internal organization characteristics. Thus labor market interest associations will prefer certain groups of migrants over others, choosing those seen as complementing existing strengths and addressing perceived weaknesses or shortages in the domestic labor pool. Factors influencing labor market interest associations include the production strategy, the relative weight of component sectors of the economy, and labor market regulation.

Second, AMP is treated as a rapidly evolving case study of more general processes of Europeanization. As the European integration process attains maturity, more sensitive policy sectors, traditionally considered close or even essential to the very self-definition of a sovereign autonomous state, become subject to European influence. Indeed, "European" policymaking unfolds over several tiers of government, without entailing in this domain the degree of sovereignty loss the multilevel governance approach assumes, making it most appropriate to adopt what Marks and Hooghe (2002: 3) describe as the "state-centric" perspective according to which "national governments [are] constrained by political interests nested within autonomous national arenas." Thus policymakers are involved in multilevel games (Putnam 1988: 434): "at the national level, domestic groups pursue their interests by pressuring the government to adopt favorable policies, and politicians seek power by constructing coalitions among those groups. At the international level, national governments seek to maximize their own ability to satisfy domestic pressures, while minimizing the adverse consequences of foreign developments." Private actors are generally highly active in influencing both national migration regulation and the stance of their respective national governments. Proposals that governments seek to present to the EU level as a contribution to the future AMP as a form of bottom-up Europeanization are commonly the result of national-level solutions. Likewise, at the EU level, compromise solutions prevail in migration policy, given the requirement of unanimity in the Council of Ministers until 2004, which continues to shape outcomes informally.[5] In the meantime, member states may implement *anticipated* European solutions in a process I call *anticipatory obedience*.

Analyzing the process of migration policy formation as a case study of Europeanization, the dynamics of "top-down" and "bottom-up" Europeanization are explored. A common assumption underlying much of the rapidly emerging literature (Börzel and Risse 2000, 2003; Cowles, Caporaso, and Risse 2001; Héritier et al. 2001; Knill and Lehmkuhl 1999; Knill and Lenschow 1998; Mény, Muller, and Quermonne 1996; Radaelli and Featherstone 2003; Vink 2005) is that member states are responding by "accommodation." Indeed, this literature is somewhat akin to findings of the international political economy scholars in the late 1970s interested in exploring the international sources of domestic policy (Gourevitch 1978, 1986; Katzenstein 1978). However, in an indirectly market-related field such as migration, Wallace's contention (2000) that Europeanization is actively shaped, rather than encountered passively, is particularly relevant. Member states dread top-down Europeanization that requires costly and significant adjustment and will act accordingly in the Council of Ministers to avoid such an outcome. In other words, it is precisely the "central penetration of national systems of governance" (Olsen 2002: 923) that national governments are wary of, particularly given the sensitivity of the issue. Indeed, a recent study finds that true systemic change of Hall's third order is fairly rare in top-down Europeanization processes in this domain (Faist and Ette 2007). "Bottom-up" Europeanization is strongly shaped not only by past traditions and historical legacies but critically also through national-level interest groups, including employer associations, trade unions, and other NGOs. Particular attention is therefore being paid to the position, interests, and actions of these actors. Most of the existing literature on Europeanization provides analytical tools to assess the top-down impact. By contrast, the bottom-up role member states can play in actively shaping Europeanization by providing templates for future regulatory approaches has not received as much scholarly attention. Here, it is being demonstrated that member states attempt to "set the agenda" in EU policymaking and attempt to offer pan-European regulatory models that, if adopted, minimize their own transaction costs. One empirical example highlighted in a recent study (Geddes and Guiraudon 2004) is the EU antidiscrimination directive, drawing largely on Dutch and British inspiration. Considerations about transaction costs and implementation obviously also inform strategies of blockade and delay, as member states seek to avoid certain proposals. Héritier (1996) has argued that uneven or "patchwork" style regulation is the inevitable regulatory outcome of policy deliberations at the EU level because though individual states may endeavor to secure a "home run" by having their own regulations successfully uploaded to serve as the basis of European legislation, it is highly unlikely that any one state wins this competition consistently.

Top-down Europeanization is conditioned not only by the changes of the strategic position of domestic actors (Dimitrova and Steunenberg 2000; Knill 2001) but crucially by *these actors' preferences* (cf. Héritier et al., 2001). The conceptual weakness of the new literature on Europeanization is its slightly technocratic nature and its intellectual roots in the study of environmental policy (Börzel 2002, 2006; Jordan 2002; Knill 2001; Knill and Lenschow 1998) that do not always permit for the messy multidimensional and multicausal process of EU policymaking. Not only does Europeanization entail *coping with and (re-)regulating* European initiatives on the one hand (top-down) (Falkner et al. 2005; Menz 2005*a*), and not merely passively implementing EU directives, but active attempts by national governmental actors to *attempt proactively to shape policymaking* (bottom-up) either through positive policy entrepreneurship in the form of suggestions for blueprints or through strategies of blockade and delay. While the liberal intergovernmentalist approach (Moravcsik 1993, 1998) has emphasized the role of national governments during the "grand bargains" over major milestones of integration and Hooghe and Marks's work (2003) stresses the importance of conceptualizing European policymaking as straddling several interrelated and often interlocked arenas, this study suggests taking bottom-up avenues and strategies seriously as a field of scholarly inquiry and submits the analysis of migration and asylum policy as one example of such endeavors. Bottom-up Europeanization in policy-making is a neglected aspect of EU integration studies. With respect to top-down Europeanization, commonly at the center of scholarly attention, important amendments can be equally made to the existing literature. When considering interest groups and nonstate actors, it does not suffice to examine the absence or presence of "dominant actor coalitions" (Knill and Lehmkuhl 2002: 260 ff.) and "informal veto players" (Héritier et al. 2001). It is more promising to analyze *both* whether and how they can shape national migration regulation *and* to examine their preference. This latter point is embraced by analysts suggesting an examination of domestic actor beliefs (Kohler-Koch 1999). These nongovernmental actors may well prefer to retain the core of regulatory authority over migration at the national level, but to the extent that "venue shopping" and regulatory drift involves a movement of political authority to the European level, these groups will at the very least attempt to color the national position. As an influential US study of interest groups has argued:

On the one hand, they [interest groups] try to control the prevailing image of the policy problem through the use of rhetoric, symbols and policy analysis. On the other hand, they try to alter the roster of participants who are involved in the issue by seeking out the most favorable venue for consideration of their issues.

Baumgartner and Jones 1991, p. 1045

The second main contention is that domestic interest groups will seek to influence governments to shape national migration policy in their favor. They will do so in the anticipation that such regulation may serve as the blueprint for future EU level AMP, avoiding top-down Europeanization contrary to their interests.

Finally, valuable insights for the migration literature can be derived from studying the phenomenon from a political economy perspective. Much of this body of literature in political science attributes great importance to distinct national styles of migration regulation, flavored by national idiosyncrasies and traditions (Baldwin-Edwards and Schain 1994; Brochmann and Hammar 1999; Brubaker 1992; Cornelius et al. 2004; Geddes 2003; Hammar 1985). Castles and Miller (2003) helpfully distinguished between the postcolonial, the guest worker, and the universalist regulatory model in aiding an analysis of European migration policies. Such *legacies* in immigration and integration regulation continue to shape both politics and policies at the national level, yet despite a strongly path-dependent character, interest group activity may contribute to a punctured equilibrium. Thus, while "most policies are remarkably durable...Key features of political life, both public policies and (especially) formal institutions are change-resistant...formal barriers to reform are thus often extremely high...[given that the] institutional stickiness characteristic of political systems reinforces the already considerable obstacles to movement off on an established path" (Pierson 2003: 54–5). Indeed, increasing returns from particular institutionalized means for accomplishing tasks render jettisoning old institutional configurations and creating new ones more difficult. Though Krasner's model (1984) of punctured equilibrium may underestimate subtle, incremental changes in institutions, as Steinmo, Thelen, and Longstreth (1992) argue, it provides us with valuable inspiration for studying periods of rapid change. Following Baumgartner and Jones (2002: 297), it can be argued that "the punctuated equilibrium perspective directs our attention to how government institutions and policy ideas interact—sometimes yielding stability, sometimes yielding punctuations." But such analysis ought to take long-term developments into consideration and "bring history back in" as "most contemporary social scientists take a "snapshot" view of political life, [though]...there is often a strong case to be made for shifting from snapshots to moving pictures. This means systematically situating particular moments (including the present) in a temporal sequence of events and processes stretching over extended periods" (Pierson 2004: 1–2).

In light of recent developments, notably adverse demographic trends and restrictive asylum and refugee procedures being implemented across Europe, the question of convergence readily arises. In light of nontraditional regions of immigration, such as southern and eastern Europe, rapidly emerging as new destinations for immigrants, the suitability of older models must similarly be questioned. Are these models reasonably consistent over time or "path dependent" in the language of historical institutionalism, and, if so, how can we account for radical departures (cf. Hansen 2002)?

I do not wish to negate the importance of national diversity in migration regulation, but argue instead that recent change is gradually transforming the landscape of European migration policies, and a political economy angle seems particularly appropriate for assessing changes to this defrosted environment. But migration policy is also strongly influenced by differences in systems of political economy, that is, the nexus of corporate strategies, the sectoral composition of the economy, production cycles, and labor market regulation. During the postwar period of expansion under the auspices of a Keynesian-inspired macroeconomic policy framework, west European migration policy was geared at filling labor market shortages mainly in unskilled Fordist manufacturing positions. The profile of the labor migrants recruited therefore did not vary dramatically across countries, notwithstanding differences in political "philosophies of integration" (Favell 2001). The contemporary post-Fordist neoliberal competition state (cf. Cerny 1995; Hirsch 1995) seeks to maximize its "competitiveness" by assuring a business-friendly climate. In doing so, it is wont to accept suggestions from employers on the design of its migration policy.

Methodological Considerations

This book is a "small n" study (Peters 1999), employing the comparative method in exploring the recently Europeanized policy domain of migration policy. Though analytically distinct and subject to a very different and much more stringent international law regime, political asylum is often confounded with migration regulation, and is certainly related. While the main focus of this book lies in analyzing the politics of labor migration regulation in the more narrow sense of the term, due to the strong empirical and conceptual linkage, the regulation of political asylum will also be considered. The end to active labor recruitment of the mid-1970s has led to political asylum emerging as one of the few legal migration categories. Less attention will be placed on the regulation of migrant groups such as political refugees—often accepted under the obligations of international treaties—and family reunion. Though the historical origins of regulation philosophies will be traced, the analysis is primarily concerned with relatively recent policy developments, focusing on the period arguably witnessing the most fervent bout of design activity since 1990 in this field.

The case selection is informed by maximizing variance among the independent potential causal factors (Peters 1998) by sampling distinct national cases representing various national regulatory models, including three cases with long-standing traditions of managing immigration (France, Germany, the UK) versus three relative newcomers (Ireland, Italy, Poland), four Schengen signatories versus two nonadherents (the UK and

Ireland), as well as different systems of political economy: representative cases of the liberal (the UK and Ireland) and coordinated market economies (Germany, arguably France) as well as mixed cases (Italy and Poland).

Outline of this Book

The rest of this book proceeds in the following fashion. Past attempts to move towards the creation of an AMP are analyzed in Chapter 2. Past choices in the institutionalization of multilateral discussion arenas for asylum and migration issues have helped "securitize" this policy sector. Henceforth, from the early days of European coordination of migration policymaking in the mid-1970s onwards, migration policy has been negotiated as part of a portfolio comprising international crime and terrorism. However, even the more minimalist "competition state" of the twenty-first century, centrally concerned with providing market-friendly supply side policies, does not neglect asylum and migration issues. Member states therefore jealously guard their veto power over decision-making in the Council of Ministers. This pivotal institutional arrangement has hampered any overly ambitious policy projects to come to fruition and has encouraged "lowest common denominator" solutions in the past. It may very well continue to do so.

Drawing on empirical evidence from France, the UK, Germany, Ireland, Poland, and Italy, the argument that very divergent regulatory philosophies and historical trajectories of asylum and migration policy among the member states have further impaired progress is examined in closer detail. In light of the economic restructuring and reform of systems of welfare provision, we shall explore to what extent these different sociopolitical regulatory philosophies have been superseded by more pertinent structural economic factors and whether there has been a convergence on a more limited number of regulatory approaches. Few EU member-states are opposed to any form of migration; most are keenly interested in active labor recruitment. In light of the divergent production regimes across Europe, how pronounced can we expect differences in the regulation of migration management to be?

The politics surrounding the policy design of asylum and migration regulation are analyzed in Chapter 3. Both the national arena and the European level will serve as the focal points of conflict and interaction between actors. National governments may pre-empt European decision-making in creating national regulations, perceived to fit national modalities of production strategies, welfare state systems, and national political regulatory philosophies, also shaped, of course, by the influence of national-level interest groups. Such initiatives, including the Italian quota system with select third countries or the Irish skilled labor recruitment program, may then in turn be introduced to set the agenda at the European level. However, national governments also have to cope with and respond to top-down Europeanization, both of the "negative" nature—in the form of the deregulatory effects of European market-building, such as the freedom of labor mobility or the liberalization of service provision—and of the "positive" nature—the recent flurry of legislative activity in creating the structure of an AMP. One example of the somewhat unanticipated impact of top-down "negative" integration was the massive deployment of Portuguese subcontractors in the German construction industry under the auspices of the EU liberalization of service provision. As these workers could be legally employed on the terms, conditions, and pay scales of the sending country, this instance graphically demonstrates the collision between EU-induced liberalization of trans-European migration and the national regulation of labor markets. An example of top-down Europeanization is the implementation of existing EU regulations on migration, visa, border controls, and asylum, not always readily welcomed, especially by the 2004 newcomers not involved in their elaboration, yet obliged to implement the entire *acquis*, including the eastward extension of the *cordon sanitaire* of the Schengenzone, as part of the conditionality requirement. For Poland, this has meant cutting off the multiple informal commercial links between regions in the southeast and neighboring regions in Ukraine, with significant consequences for the local community.

Regardless of whether national governments passively encounter or actively influence Europeanization, they will engage other actors at the national level with a strong interest in influencing policymaking, notably trade unions, employers' organizations, and nongovernmental organizations focusing on migration and asylum policy.

Policymaking unfolds in several arenas. At the EU level, other governmental actors and the European Commission are being encountered. Given the institutional arrangements described in the previous chapter, national governments can hope to set the agenda, but cannot decisively color it without the agreement of all others.

From the European level, we proceed to the national level, examining the genesis of national initiatives in asylum and migration policy since

1990. This date is chosen as it represents the advent of renewed large-scale immigration in light of the disintegration of Yugoslavia and the Soviet Union, the "giant leap forward" in European integration, and the emergence of a powerful impetus for national regulation. Chapter 4 examines migration and asylum policymaking in the three largest European countries, which are also more "established" countries of immigration in the sense of having attracted immigrants previously. Applying the analytical framework set forth in the previous chapter, particular attention is being paid to the position, interests, and actions of trade unions, employers' associations, and other national-level actors in influencing migration and asylum policy initiatives.

From there, the focus shifts to an analysis of the genesis of asylum and migration policy in Ireland, Italy, and Poland. These countries have only very recently attracted immigrants and their regulatory framework is accordingly of very recent provenance. In Chapter 5, Ireland and Italy are both representative examples of the geographically more marginal countries that have mutated from countries of emigration to receiving countries in the light of greater prosperity and economic success in the 1990s. Meanwhile, despite popular fears of mass migration from central and eastern European applicant countries to current EU member states, in reality central Europe has long since become not only a transit territory for third-country nationals but is also attracting net immigration. Poland, the most populous and largest of the central European EU member states, is chosen as a representative case study of the "new" eastern immigration countries. Europeanization plays a particularly important role here, as applicant states are required to implement the EU migration and asylum regulation *acquis* as a precondition for membership.

Finally, Chapter 6 charts the path of future EU AMP based on a thorough examination of existing EU regulation and current policy developments and debates in the member states. Member states will remain hesitant to surrender control over asylum and migration policy to the EU wholesale. Successful AMP proposals will need to take into account past divergent regulatory philosophies, while proposing initiatives seen as embracing pan-European regulatory patterns. One of the more contested, yet also intriguing, questions concerning the future AMP is whether populists or pragmatists will decisively color policy development. It is argued that successful policy proposals will attempt to placate both. Thus asylum and migration policy will become less influenced by humanitarian factors, and more by economic rationale. Asylum and refugee policy will be relatively restrictive, while pragmatic programs aimed at attracting immigrants to fill labor market shortages, possibly coupled with national quotas or "preferred status" vis-à-vis select third countries, will flourish.

Notes

1. It is precisely for this reason that the Commission's proposal to extend the liberalization of service provision by introducing the so-called country of origin principle regarding wage levels and working conditions triggered such strong and sustained opposition. The so-called Bolkestein directive, named after the Dutch Commissioner Frits Bolkestein, would have permitted the employment of Latvian workers in high-wage countries such as Denmark or Germany at Latvian wages, currently averaging €1.84 per hour. Such radical liberalization of the European labor market would have produced new forms of feudalism. Large parts of the Barroso Commission actively supported this proposal, including Commissioner Peter Mandelson, who referred to this directive as "the way forward" and "Europe's future."
2. Interestingly, much of the Marxist-inspired analysis of immigrants and the labor market of the 1970s retains much of its bite (for Europe, see Castles and Kosack 1973; for the United States, see Gordon 1972 and Piore 1979). But it is worth adding that the critical Marxist perception of immigrants serving as a reserve army of workers, often used by employers to apply downward pressure on wages and working conditions, needs to be amended by the insight that immigrant labor is also used in high-skilled high-wage positions. The simple dichotomy in which immigrants always found themselves in the bottom tier of the labor market is no longer altogether accurate, but the value of the dual-tier labor market hypothesis is such that I employ it in this book.
3. During the *trente glorieuses*, labor shortages existed across all economic sectors, hence skill levels of potential migrants did not concern policymakers. However, in the wake of the decline of the primary and secondary sector in favor of the tertiary sector of the economy and the concomitant pursuit of divergent production strategies in coordinated versus liberal market economies, national labor recruitment strategies do diverge to a much greater degree. Of course, given the pan-European character of the structural metamorphosis of the economy, all national policymakers can be expected to solicit labor migrants for vacancies in the service sector, but to different degrees. However, in high-wage high-skill countries associated with coordinated market economies, particular emphasis is placed on highly skilled labor migrants, while liberal market economies attract migrants at both ends of the skill curve. They commonly possess significantly sized low-wage low-skill sectors,

which require labor demand, and will shape overall migration management accordingly.
4. Without, however, being completely captured by employer interests, as some of the cruder neo-Marxist accounts of the 1970s would have argued.
5. Until December 2004, this requirement was applicable to all areas of AMP with the role of the European Parliament limited to consultation. Since then, the asylum portfolio has been made subject to qualified majority voting, but not border control measures and labor migration.

2
Legacies of the Past and Currents of Change: Conundrums over Migration and Asylum

The regulation of migration involves considerations of widening or limiting access not only in the territorial, demographic, and societal sense but also in regard to economic and social issue areas, including access to labor markets as well as systems of social protection, provision, and redistribution. Migration therefore has pivotal implications in the political-economic sense. It interacts with broader mechanisms and institutions of labor market and social policy regulation. Therefore, broader trends of economic transnationalization, globalization of production strategies, and the increasingly apparent divergences between different European models of capitalism all shape migration management and labor recruitment strategies. Changes within the systems of politico-economic governance have led to the reconsideration of migration management policies and the rediscovery of labor migration in particular. Thus, the strongly path-dependent development of national and EU level migration policies is undergoing a phase of punctured equilibrium. Past legacies of migration regulation are important conditioning factors, obliging a detailed examination to be carried out in this chapter. But before doing so, the major structural changes to the European economies affecting migration policy need to be chartered. In particular, migration management serves the broader purpose of a business-friendly competition state agenda to broaden and deregulate access to "useful" human resources. Welfare state reforms aiming at the embrace of more punitive "workfarist" policies have not always increased the available pool of low-skill workers and migrants have also been recruited to be channeled into such low-skill and low-wage segments of the labor market. The often invoked term of securitization is conceived too narrowly and may well be stretched, notably by organized business and employers, to encompass the rhetorical emphasis on liberalized access to human resources as being of crucial import to the economic prosperity and security of a given polity.

The Present Power of Past Legacies

Past legacies continue to act as powerful factors, having molded past regulatory institutions, informing past decision making and institution-building as well as regulatory ideas about appropriate strategies for access and entitlement management. This chapter therefore examines these past legacies first at the EU level and subsequently at the national level, exploring the distinct regulatory approaches found in France, Germany, the United Kingdom, Ireland, Italy, and Poland. It is being argued that EU policy in particular has indeed been shaped by concerns over social and political instability induced by migration and by a legacy of negotiating migration regulation within a portfolio encompassing control, discipline, and punishment, alongside issues such as transnational crime, drugs, and politically motivated violence. But this does not amount to mere "securitization" in the narrow sense; relatively recent preoccupations with ensuring "competitiveness" are also strongly shaping EU policy developments, as the agenda of the competition state now also encompasses the ready and steady supply of human resources. Thus, both securitization and economic prerogatives combine to shape migration policy design. The competition state of the early twenty-first century welcomes migrants, provided they fit into a set of carefully delineated categories. Henceforth, some groups of migrants are seen as potentially making a useful contribution to alleviating labor market shortages, for example in IT, engineering, health care, tourism and gastronomy, agriculture, and construction. These two strands—security and the competition state agenda—are crucial in accounting for the growth and development of policies on migration and asylum at the EU level.

The communautarization of migration and asylum regulation is a relatively recent phenomenon. Traditionally, member states have been highly reluctant to surrender tight control over these domains to any supranational authority. This general pattern is still relevant and evident in the strong degree of institutionalized intergovernmentalism and the pronounced reluctance to abandon unanimous decision making in the Council of Ministers until 2004. Even since, qualified majority voting does not cover core areas such as labor migration. The refusal in principle of Ireland, the UK, and Denmark to partake in these efforts and only to "opt in" on a case-by-case basis are further testimony to the deep-seated concerns over loss of sovereignty in a highly politically sensitive policy area. Given the very distinct regulatory approaches to migration and asylum across Europe, the question why AMP development has most recently been so dynamic is more enlightening than querying why such development has not proceeded in greater strides. This chapter examines the historical development of EU AMP, tracing it from the early meetings of the TREVI group in the mid-1970s to the recent bout of EU legislative activity in the mid-2000s. As will be argued, developments have reached a critical juncture and a punctured equilibrium has now arisen. However, despite the consensus on the need for an AMP, clearly expressed at the 1999 Tampere European Council meeting, progress has been impaired by the differing interests related to diverse systems of political economy and the interventions of labor market interest associations with respect to labor migration and humanitarian nongovernmental organizations regarding asylum. The different traditions of migration regulation continue to shape national preferences, especially relating to noneconomic strands of migration, where employers and trade unions are unlikely to be active participants in lobbying efforts. These embedded differences have presented one of the key challenges to constructing an AMP. They do not necessarily create irreconcilable differences between interest positions; however, aside from implying a bias towards lowest common denominator solutions, these differences do certainly impede ambitious and progressive policy projects that would imply major change.

National Legacies and a Punctured Equilibrium

In much of the comparative migration studies literature (Fassmann and Münz 1994; Hollifield, Cornelius, and Martin 2004; Uçarer and Puchala 1997; Castles and Miller 2003; Angenendt 1999) and in single country studies (Green 2004; Marshall 2000; Weil 2005), the theme of path-dependent development of migration regulation emerges, though it is rarely explicitly mentioned. These "thick descriptions" chronicle continuity and the extremely slow tectonic shifts implying long-term changes at glacial pace. The historical institutionalist argument about self-reinforcing path-dependent developments, whereby initial choices shape future choices and decisions, applies particularly well to migration and asylum policies. As Pierson (2004: 54–5) has argued, "most policies are remarkably durable...Key features of political life, both public policies and (especially) formal institutions are change-resistant...formal barriers to reform are thus often extremely high...[given that the] institutional stickiness characteristic of political systems reinforces the already considerable obstacles to movement off on an established path." Drawing on this insight about path-dependent development, Hansen (2002) convincingly demonstrates the lock-in effects of early colonial policy with regard to immigration policy in France and Britain and asylum policy borne out of the collective memory of the Third Reich in postwar Germany. But such analyses are rare. Beyond the trite insight that "history matters," the historical institutionalist central focus on path-dependent developments, enhanced by Thelen's recent contributions on change (1999, 2004), can help us make sense of longevity and stability in European migration policies. Pierson's work has highlighted the characteristics of "self-reinforcing processes" (2000), while also drawing our attention to inertia (2004: 44) reinforcing the existence of multiple equilibria in initial conditions. Recent work in this vein (Pierson 2000; Streeck and Thelen 2005: 6; Thelen 2004) imports the concept of "increasing returns" from economics, arguing that positive feedback mechanisms help to consolidate, strengthen and reinforce past institutional choices. This argument has attracted criticism from Herman Schwartz (undated), who argues that political environments are more permissive than economic ones and the lock-in effects of past political choices tend to be overstated. The broad general claim about past choices weighing on current policy options, debates, and decisions, as advanced by Sewell (1996), can rightly be criticized for verging on the tautological (Peters 1998). It quickly becomes clear that the key insight historical institutionalism provides needs to be enhanced by a robust and analytically sophisticated understanding of change and the dynamics and driving forces behind it.

Past choices of migration regulation in Europe thus inform current policy design in terms of options, choices, debates, and perceptions of problems and possible regulatory solutions. Regulating access to the territory, and defining the characteristics of its subjects, has been at the core of modern state sovereignty. While citizenship did not emerge with the Westphalian state system, but much later, controlling the access to its geographical borders has been an important preoccupation of the postmedieval state, not least in order to exert taxation from its residents and charge road tolls of some nature to the entrants. Questions of citizenship and territorial access regulation thus inhabit a central status throughout Europe, yet the national traditions in dealing with issues of migration diverge considerably. These national traditions are deeply embedded in the historical trajectories of the growth of nations and the definition of conceptual boundaries of inclusion and exclusion and are directly related to the underlying defining ideological and mythological bricks and mortar of nationhood. These ideological structures of "invented communities" (Anderson 1983) provide an overarching framework for "a named human population sharing a historic territory, common myths and historical memories, a mass, public culture, a common economy and common legal rights and duties for all members" (Smith 1991: 14). But it is not simply the defining characteristics of citizenship which condition migration policies. While it is correct to assert the different ideological base of citizenship regulation and distinguish between ethnic citizenship criteria (*ius sanguinis*), historically used by Germany, and contrast it with the political-ideological commitment to core values and geographical location of birth (*ius solis*), historically used by France, as several scholars have done (Brubaker 1992), many EU countries combine both approaches. Other important historical and cultural factors informing and shaping migration policy include the presence or absence of colonial networks and the historical record of attracting immigration. The EU is composed of both countries that have traditionally solicited (labor) migrants and those that only most recently have experienced mutating in status from being predominantly a sending to being a receiving country. Britain, France, Germany, Austria, the Benelux, and the Scandinavian countries all possess some form of experience with inward migration, most, though not all of it, actively regulated and controlled. By contrast, Ireland, Portugal, Spain, Italy, Greece, and Finland have experienced very little, if any, immigration until the early 1990s, and until very recently were thought of as emigration countries, feeding substantial expatriate communities overseas. This is also true for the central and eastern European countries that joined the EU in 2004 and 2007, including notably Poland.

Citizenship regulation and national founding myths are intertwined with migration regulation and the (post-)colonial concept of British and French citizenship was thus open to inviting the new subjects back to the motherland, while the temporary labor migration recruitment agreements between German-speaking Europe and southeastern European countries were never intended as access channels to citizenship and long-term societal inclusion. National models of migration regulation are strongly shaped by different regulatory philosophies, which are crucial in helping to shed light on the regulation of immigration procedures, citizenship rights, and integration traditions across Europe.

Much emphasis has been placed on these often highly path-dependent national legacies in the existing literature. While their importance cannot be denied, it is crucial to realize that the conditions of punctured equilibrium accurately describe the current state of migration regulation in the European context. These conditions in turn permit access to the decision-making process for nonstate actors, as will be argued in Chapter 3. In exploring change, we heed Baumgartner and Jones's call (2002: 297) for "case studies of particular policy arenas cast within a framework that is sensitive to institutional constraints and incentives and the nature of ideas and arguments put forward by the participants." Scholars have grappled with change in different ways, realizing that "asserting that the social landscape can be permanently frozen hardly is credible [...] Change continues but it is bounded change." (Pierson 2004: 66–7). How do conditions of punctured equilibrium occur, alternatively referred to as "critical junctures" or instances of nonreproduction (Collier and Collier 1991; Katznelson 2003; Krasner 1989; Mahoney 2001; Pierson 2004; Streeck and Thelen 2005)? Another key assertion advanced by the historical institutionalist approach, namely, the historical contingency of stable equilibria, provides an important answer. The key structural change that is undermining the hitherto stable array of legacies is the socioeconomic change associated with the tertiarization of European economies and the transnationalization of production processes and strategies coupled with greater diversification among different European models of capitalism over the course of the past 30 years. During the *trentes glorieuses* of postwar economic expansion, labor shortages existed across all economic sectors; hence, skill levels of potential migrants were not a crucial concern for policymakers. However, in the wake of the decline of the primary and secondary sector in favor of the tertiary sector and the concomitant pursuit of divergent production strategies in coordinated versus liberal market economies, national labor recruitment strategies in the current period of renaissance of actively solicited and managed labor migration do diverge to a much greater degree. Of course, given the pan-European character of the structural metamorphosis of the economy, all national policymakers can be expected to solicit labor migrants for vacancies in the service sector. However, in high-wage high-skill countries associated with coordinated market economies, particular emphasis is placed on highly skilled labor migrants, while liberal market economies place somewhat less emphasis on skill levels. In fact, the latter commonly possess significant low-wage low-skill sectors, which generate quantitatively considerable labor demand, further enhanced by high staff turnover, low retention, and poor working conditions described as "dull, dirty and dangerous." Overall migration management will be shaped accordingly. Therefore, important differences emerge between national migration strategies in coordinated market economies such as Germany and liberal market economies such as Britain, with southern Europe adopting LME-style and eastern Europe CME-style policies. In identifying economic change as a major driving force, I stress the importance of a political economy angle, involving questions that have not received adequate scholarly attention thus far.[1]

National legacies and models (Castles and Miller 2003) of migration regulation are undermined by socioeconomic change, opening up additional room for maneuver for nonstate actors, rendering AMP more diverse, complex, and in some cases pluralist and messy. But these massive changes in terms of the structural composition of the European economies and the structures of politico-economic governance not only cast doubt upon the continued veracity and validity of regulatory models per se, as is acknowledged in a more recent contribution by Schierup et al. (2006: 15):

Politically powerful interest groups will, most probably, continue to have an interest in the immigration of menial labour and in an ethnically segmented labour market populated by "foreigners"... The racialized minorities of our time are socially and politically marginalized, but essential cogwheels serving the much-hailed *flexibility* of production and labour regimes and the new service economies characteristic of current processes of restructuring.

These conditions of a punctured equilibrium have also arisen due to the new economic prerogatives of the European competition state, which perceives of migration not only as a mere security threat but also as a valuable opportunity to avail oneself of attractive human resources with desirable skill portfolios and retain these immigrants exploiting their economic contribution. We will turn next to exploring the impact of this new competition state agenda.

The Competition State Needs Migrants

The Hague Program on future policy in the domains of freedom, security, and justice, adopted by the European Council on November 4–5, 2004, contains a passage stating that "legal migration will play an important role in enhancing the knowledge-based economy in Europe, in advancing economic development, and thus contributing to the implementation of the Lisbon strategy." The European Commission's stance is similar, as a 2005 communication argues that "while immigration should be recognised as a source of cultural and social enrichment, in particular by contributing to entrepreneurship, diversity, and innovation, its economic impact on employment and growth is also significant as it increases labour supply and helps cope with bottlenecks" (European Commission November 30, 2005, COM (2005) 621 final).

The explicit role of migration policy as a contributory factor and prerogative of economic competitiveness is thus acknowledged. Human resources are perceived as an invaluable contribution to national economies, and they are explicitly included in the 2000 Lisbon Agenda that established the goal of the EU becoming the world's "most competitive region" by 2010. I argue that the phenotype and chief concern of the European state is mutating to embrace the achievement and perpetuation of economic competitiveness.[2] This preoccupation now shapes migration management (Köppe 2003). An economistic fixation with migration as a constituent factor in ensuring continued patterns in accumulation and surplus extraction has spawned an obsession with managing migration proactively.

Philip Cerny (1995) argued that the contemporary state remains a pivotal agent in the process of globalization, but its central concerns now consist of providing a "relatively favorable investment climate for transnational capital... [including a] circumscribed range of goods that retain a national-scale... public character... [such as] human capital, [...] infrastructure [... and generally] maintenance of a public policy environment favorable to investment (and profit making)." But this comes at the expense of the much broader array of public service functions, which are simply abandoned, inspired by neoliberal ideology. Therefore, the competition state is residual in nature, it promotes flexibility and neoliberal response strategies to a changing economic global macroclimate, it endorses and enforces monetarist obsessions over inflation control at the expense of other macroeconomic goals, notably employment, and its extent of welfare provision is extremely limited, proceeding through a reliance on second-order effects of economic growth and private sector entrepreneurship. The competition state therefore merely promotes the "marketisation in order to make economic activities located within the national territory... more competitive in international and transnational terms." (Cerny 1997: 258). States thus engage in precisely the sort of neo-mercantilist competition previously declared anachronistic (Reich 1991) or simply misguided (Krugman 1996).

The emergence of post-Fordist production patterns, the abandonment of Keynesianism, and the embrace of neoliberalism as a dominant paradigm in macroeconomic policy design (Soederberg, Menz, and Cerny 2005) have reshaped the nature of the contemporary state with important repercussions for migration management. The reconfiguration of state activities to promote the agenda of economic competitiveness in the broadest sense aims to attract the attention of mobile international capital to retain this attractiveness in the eyes of long-term foreign direct investment, and to influence the rediscovery of labor migrants as potentially useful human resources. According to this ideology, states are gatekeepers over national arenas engaged in all-out global competition for investment and are favorably inclined towards the demands of business for favorable investment conditions, consisting ideally of a docile low-wage labor force, a low taxation regime, and permissive standards in labor market, social, and environmental policy. In this context, human resources matter greatly. Migrants are welcome, as long as they promise to contribute to the prerogatives of a business-friendly national economic growth strategy. The potentially pernicious outcome of such economistic conceptualization of migration and the focus of migration as a strategy for the lucrative solicitation of the best brains and the most willing helping hands from locations worldwide is the denigration of noneconomic channels of migration, including largely humanitarian avenues of access, such as family reunion and asylum. An emergent pan-European dichotomy erroneously distinguishes between "useful" migrants, accepted or even welcomed to the extent that they are conceived as filling labor market shortages in areas that natives do not want to or cannot occupy, creating new enterprises, and attracting inward foreign direct investment on the one hand and "burdensome" individuals, such as refugees and asylum seekers, who are exclusively viewed as imposing costs and drains on social security and public services on the other. Most concisely, if starkly, this line of reasoning was expressed by former Bavarian state minister of the interior Günther Beckstein: "We need to distinguish between people who will do us good and those who take advantage of us" ("...*Menschen, die uns nützen, und jenen, die uns ausnützen.*") (*Die Zeit* 2000). Consequently, managed migration as a new paradigm entails not only carefully delineated (labor) migration channels but also a more restrictive stance towards other avenues. This dichotomy is in itself flawed as it assigns—or indeed shoehorns—applicants for political asylum into a category that if combined with employment bans can easily turn into a self-fulfilling prophecy and may not only systematically discount skills but, in an ill-advised attempt to impede labor market participation, may also jeopardize economic and social integration in the long term. Failing to recognize the often significant professional skill levels of political refugees and being reticent to offer language courses and training may render lazy generalizations about useless and burdensome asylum seekers self-fulfilling.

While lip service is being paid to the international legal obligations European governments have entered into, notably the 1951 Geneva Convention on Refugees, amended by the 1957 New York Protocol, a restrictive approach towards such humanitarian forms of migration channels is evident.

Competition state ideology informs migration management design that explicitly copies aspects of active labor recruitment designed by classic countries of immigration, commonly administering point systems for language and professional skills, for example in Canada, Australia, and New Zealand.[3] European policymakers consciously enter into a competition with their former colonies. In doing so, they exploit existing patterns and flows of migration—documented or not—and often their recruitment efforts focus on countries that have functioned as sending countries in the past. Medical professionals for the British National Health Service are recruited in the Indian subcontinent and in sub-Saharan Africa, while Italy has concluded bilateral labor recruitment treaties with its North African and southeast European neighbors. Germany thought it could recruit Indians into its fledgling information technology (IT) sector, but most applicants for the so-called Green Card program came from southeastern Europe. Brain drain is an obvious problem, not always addressed in a satisfactory fashion.

Joachim Hirsch, influenced by the French regulation school as well as German state theory debates, argued that the competition state agenda was embraced precisely as a result of the transnationalization of production capacities. This new agenda does not, however, entail weakening of state capacity or a "powerless state" (Weiss 1998), but rather an internalization of corporate priorities and aims. Hirsch thus argues that the state's "primary goal is now to optimize the conditions for investing capital at the national level vis-à-vis the globalized accumulation process in perpetual competition with other national 'sites of investment'" (1998: 33), thus permitting "capital, which is acting ever more flexibly on a global scale, more amiable accumulation conditions in the competition with other states" (1995: 103, my translations from the German). Thus, domestic state activity is not declining. In fact, the repressive elements of what Jessop referred to as the Keynesian Welfare State are maintained or even augmented. In fact, the new Schumpeterian Workfare State (Jessop 1990) relies on punitive and highly interventionist state activity to maintain or even increase levels of labor market participation in the face of more precarious, short-term, insecure, poorly remunerated, and hazardous employment patterns and working conditions that would otherwise provide disincentives for the voluntary commodification of employees. The continuing crisis in the accumulation process, reflected in mass unemployment in continental Europe, partly camouflaged in countries such as the UK and the Netherlands through the extension of incapacity benefits, implies that raising labor market participation levels and encouraging "employability," as dictated by the Lisbon Strategy, requires a great deal of state interventionism in labor and social policy. While certain aspects of macroeconomic governance have thus been shed to independent quasi-public regulatory agencies in the aftermath of privatization and market re-regulation, labor and social policy remain areas in which state interventionism remains highly pronounced and supply-side measures are commonly implemented. Early efforts in the globalization literature were thus inaccurate in postulating the declining capacity for state action; instead, Epstein's observation (1996: 214) is more relevant that "short-term capital mobility undermines a country's ability to undertake policies that threaten investor confidence in its economy." Hence, the manipulation of the labor market through presumably tighter immigration control and more selective migration channels to meet pre-defined labor market needs dovetails with the competition state agenda of the contemporary European state. The embrace of the competition state paradigm does not, however, imply an end to politics, as Hirsch (1995: 81) advises that "ideological, authoritarian-populist, nationalist, and racist" influences continue to color political debates. The state is not receding nor does its phenotype cease to matter profoundly.

The comparative political economy literature has rejected simple claims of convergence and stressed the continued resilience of distinct varieties of capitalism (Amable 2003; Hall and Soskice 2001; Schmidt 2002; critical: Blyth 2003; Watson 2003). However, despite its analytical rigor, this body of literature may underestimate the neoliberalization of the macroeconomic agenda that an embrace of the competition state implies. Research in comparative welfare policy confirms the movement towards workfarism, "particularly where neoliberal economic orthodoxies are most heavily entrenched" (Peck 2001: 11). Jamie Peck (2001: 10) defines this trend: "The essence of workfarism...involves the imposition of a range of compulsory programs and mandatory requirements for welfare recipients with a view to *enforcing work* while *residualizing welfare*... the logic, structure, and dynamics of the system of poor relief are transformed so as to maximize work participation while minimizing 'dependence' on welfare." For migration and asylum policy, the implications are significant. The European competition state solicits migrants perceived to contribute to the promotion of competitiveness by possessing a profile conducive to rapid integration in the labor market and/or promotion of capacities deemed desirable and indeed vital in research and development, not least in areas including medicine, natural sciences, engineering, and information technology. As an added advantage, such efforts free-ride on other countries' educational facilities (a process often criticized as constituting "brain drain") and thus can serve as a substitute for necessary long-term fiscal policy efforts to raise standards of educational and training capabilities and facilities. Though its long-term sustainability may be highly questionable in terms of the socioeconomic implications for both sending and receiving countries, in the short terms, such policy may appear tantalizing. However, labor market niches may also exist and arise in low-pay low-skill niches of the economy as earlier work on dual labor markets has highlighted (Berger and Piore 1980; Gordon et al. 1982; Piore 1979), an insight of particular relevance to the LMEs. Such niches may be systematically unattractive to employees due to low status, low pay, unpleasant or even dangerous working conditions, often described as "3-D jobs" for dull, dirty, and dangerous. Piore (1979: 17) provides a useful description of these bottom tier jobs: "[They] tend to be unskilled, generally but not always low paying, and to carry or connote inferior social status; they often involve hard or unpleasant working conditions and considerable insecurity; they seldom offer chances of advancement toward better-paying, more attractive job opportunities...". He argues that this dual structure of the labor market is an inherent feature due to factors "ranging from the natural variation introduced by the seasons and the weather to the social variability of trends in fashion and taste and including the economic fluctuations of boom and depression" (1979: 36). Regardless of whether such labor market shortages are structural or temporary in nature, the import of short-term labor migrants may appear a more palatable policy option than either effecting higher pay and more amiable working conditions through legislation or prodding natives into these jobs through workfarist pressure—though, of course, workfarism and immigration recruitment are by no means exclusive of each other. Both strategies may well be pursued simultaneously to create a supply pool of docile, desperate, and dispirited labor competing against each other for employment in these sectors of the labor market. This bottom end has been identified as a structural feature of capitalist labor markets by the Marxist-inspired migration literature of the 1970s, akin to Marx's reserve army of labor (Castles and Kosack 1973; Cohen 1987; Mandel 1978). Neoclassically inspired empirical studies of the impact of migration on low-wage jobs confirm a slight adverse effect on wages and working conditions for native workers (Borjas 1999). The import of labor into positions in the bottom tier of the labor market is therefore very much congruous with the competition state agenda of securing a flexible and docile workforce.

Reconceptualizing and Broadening the Definition of Securitization

A recent insight formulated regarding the contours of national, but even more so EU-level immigration policy, is its "securitization," encapsulating the confounding of immigration with threats to the national security, defined not only in military and geographic, but also in ethno-cultural and "societal" terms, the latter implying "the sustainability, within acceptable conditions for evolution, of traditional patterns of language, culture, association, and religious and national identity and custom" (Waever 1993: 23). Jef Huysmans (2006: 7), an important contributor to this strand, describes the nature of securitization as follows: "It means that insecurity is not a fact of nature but always requires that it is written and talked into existence. [...] ... language does not simply describe an event, but [...] it mobilizes certain meanings that modulate them in rather specific ways." Influenced by the "Copenhagen School" (Buzan et al. 1993), a number of scholars in the tradition of critical security studies have made the case that migration policy, especially at the European level, though not exclusively, has become tainted by inappropriate conflation with measures aimed to curtail transnational criminal activity, including notably transnational terrorism. In that sense, the terrorist attacks of September 11, 2001 and subsequent attacks in Madrid and London further reinforced and added impetus and urgency to an already established trajectory of treating migration as a security threat (Buzan et al.

1998; Huysmans 1998, 2000, 2006; Koslowski 1998; Bigo 1992; Boswell 2007). This obsession with terrorist threats presumably precludes or at the very least impedes pragmatic migration policymaking. The conflation of migrants with criminals is then used to justify repressive measures and highly intrusive control and surveillance measures, which expand police powers and impinge on civil rights, including those of more established minority ethnic communities. Didier Bigo (2002, 2005) in particular is associated with an analysis and critical probing of these tendencies. The suspicion that such civil rights infringements are merely tested out on migrants as the most disenfranchised and socially and politically marginalized group prior to the introduction of similar measures for broader segments of the general population is of some concern and lent credibility given the Schengen Treaty and its inherent Schengen Information System enabling the exchange of personal data of asylum seekers being followed by the Prüm Treaty permitting yet broader remits of transnational data exchange among law enforcement agencies. Rudolph (2003, 2006) helpfully suggests broadening the conceptual boundaries of the migration-security nexus to include geopolitical interests, material production, and internal security. However, in light of the central concern over ensuring and promoting competitiveness that informs competition state policy, underlining the framing of immigration as a vital component of national strategies that ensure economic competitiveness by securing optimized access to crucial human resources appears even more analytically promising. Thus, as part of the agenda of the competition state, liberal immigration policy has been endorsed as an essential contribution to promoting the optimal conditions for business-friendly accumulation strategies. In that sense, the "framing" of immigration in terms of public discourse, highlighted by Statham and Geddes (2006), is indeed crucial. Rhetoric and of course the direct agency of employer associations, which will be examined in the next chapter, shape immigration policy. The internalization of the competition state agenda by European governments implies that ensuring "competitiveness" emerges as a central concern, including a liberal labor migration policy that incorporates employer associations' interests. The "leviathan of competitiveness" (Köppe 2003) heavily weighs on decision-makers. National security thus needs to be urgently conceptualized in broader terms and "securitization" can entail portraying unhindered access to foreign labor pools as essential to ensuring economic growth ahead of global competitors. Therefore, the claims about liberal states facing conundrums in controlling immigration (Freeman 1995; Hollifield 1992; Joppke 1998) need to be modified to reflect the highly influential competition state agenda that shapes migration policy design. In this policy domain, there is no "retreat of the state" (Strange 1996), as postulated in some of the more ambitious claims inherent in the globalization literature (Ohmae 2005), and claims about "transnationalization" in the sociological migration literature (Soysal 1994) ought to be regarded with some skepticism. Instead, a recast state with new priorities is playing an active role in engineering the construction of regulatory regimes ensuring a steady labor supply of desirable talent and skill portfolio.

Historical Development of AMP—Policing and Depoliticizing a Policy Sector

Proponents of the "securitization" argument (Buzan et al. 1993; Huysmans 2006) claim that control and surveillance of the state's physical boundaries and access to it have assumed new importance given the perceived or constructed security threats. Migration and asylum policy design were traditionally firmly established domains of competence of the European state throughout the postwar decades, notwithstanding the obligations arising out of international treaties such as the 1951 Geneva Convention.

One strategy to circumvent the protracted and often frustrating attempts at harmonization at the EU level has been the de facto undermining of existing national regulation through great strides forward and deregulation in the interest of pushing ahead the Single Market project. This approach of "negative integration" (Scharpf 1996) has come to dominate policymaking in sectors in which any such harmonization proved particularly difficult. The European project is marked by a liberal "market-building" structural bias, embedded in the Treaty of Rome, and revived in the relaunch of the Single Market in the 1980s. To the extent that migration could be construed as serving the purpose of this market-building project, it was encouraged. Henceforth, freedom of *labor* mobility, already contained in the 1957 Treaty of Rome (Arts. 48–66), was reiterated as one of the Maastricht "four freedoms." Indeed, with the partial exception of a bout of "positive integration" activism stemming from the 1970s Social Action Program, much of the EU's labor and social policy in the 1960s, 1970s, and again most recently (Geyer 2000) sought to foster trans-European migration flows (CEC 1977). It is worth noting that intra-EU migration was always conceived as being labor-oriented and related.

In practice, intra-EU migration did not assume significant quantitative dimensions prior to the early 2000s, however.[4] Instead, a steady flow of labor migration was ensured through reliance on bilateral treaties or preferential settlement agreements for residents of former colonies. Decolonization meant the return first of European settlers from British, Belgian, Dutch, and French colonies, followed then by members of the native ruling and middle classes. Indeed, colonization had forcefully disseminated European languages, customs, and traditions throughout Africa, Asia, and the Caribbean. Some of its denizens felt attracted to the prospects of life in Europe and the economic opportunities available in the favorable economic climate of the postwar expansion. In addition, alternative emigration destinations in the 1950s had either imposed national quotas heavily favoring European immigration, for example in the United States, or still explicitly excluded non-Europeans, as in the case of the "White Australia" policy, shadowed by New Zealand. Bilateral treatments were signed between the Scandinavian and German-speaking countries on the one hand and Southeastern Europe on the other. While Sweden could additionally rely on immigration from Finland and the Netherlands recruited in its former Asian colonies in addition to these bilateral treaties, West Germany lost its historical reservoir of cheap labor after the construction of the Berlin Wall in 1961. The OPEC crisis of 1973 and the subsequent end of the postwar boom provided a convenient economic rationale for curtailing active labor migration recruitment throughout Western Europe.

With the front door thus firmly shut, the two remaining legal access channels were family reunion and asylum. The former led to the perpetuation of existing migration patterns and the strengthening of existing immigrant communities: Turks settled in Germany and the Netherlands, Moroccans and Algerians turned to France and Belgium, while Pakistanis and Jamaicans sought residency in Britain. Asylum and refugee policies were shaped by the 1951 Geneva Convention and not least the historical legacy of collective failure in providing adequate refuge to refugees during the dark days of Nazi barbarism. In the spirit of rampant anti-Communism, refugees from Soviet-dominated Central and Eastern Europe were particularly welcomed. However, as the numbers of asylum seekers began gradually to increase throughout the 1970s and their countries of origin were no longer predominantly East European, the welcome they received became considerably less cordial.

Throughout the 1970s and until the 1990s, migration-related EU efforts focused on promoting intra-EU migration.[5] One of the lasting legacies of the 1970s, however, was a "securitized" coloring of intragovernmental coordination of what came to be known as justice and home affairs. The TREVI (Terrorism, Radicalism, Extremism, and International Violence) coordination group of 1975, part of the European Political Coordination framework, was an intergovernmental structure uniting ministers of the interior to counter political terrorist movements from the far left that grew largely out of the 1968 student revolts, including *Brigadi Rossi, Action directe, Rote Armee Fraktion*, neofascist groups in Italy and West Germany and regional separatist movements, such as the IRA and ETA. TREVI focused primarily on improving the cooperation of law enforcement agencies in light of transnationally active terrorist groups, but its portfolio included also migration. It may have helped socialize government officials in generating an environment "from which many of these officials active in the Third Pillar [created as part of Maastricht] received their education in intergovernmental coordination" (Levy 1999: 23).

Unlike the critical Copenhagen School, more conventional and conservative scholarly work has argued that non-traditional threats to national security may either arise due to natural adverse circumstances or be deliberately created by adversaries (Weiner 1993). Migration can thus become a serious challenge or indeed a security threat. The outflow of migrants may be purposefully engineered by ruthless governments intent on undermining domestic stability in adjacent geographical entities, as has been alleged of the East German government, when it permitted—or perhaps encouraged—refugees from the civil war in Sri Lanka to pass through the East Berlin airport to the western enclave of West Berlin in 1985 (Joppke 1999). However, the empirical cases are fairly limited and do not render this claim generally compelling. The Copenhagen School rejects such argument altogether and advances the proposition that security threats may be constructed for political purposes: governments will declare certain areas to be vital to their national security and thus "securitize" them (Buzan et al. 1993), without such shift in focus necessarily corresponding to objective empirical facts. Thus "securitization" may taint the language, ideology, and policy constructed to manage a certain policy domain, preclude the perception of alternative pathways and lead to the viewing of the policy domain through a tainted lens (cf. Huysmans 2006).[6] As Huysmans (2000: 770) has argued, Europeanization has "securitized migration, by integrating migration policy into an internal security framework." Bigo (1992, 1998) has similarly argued that the abolition of intra-EU border controls has been more than "compensated for" by the rise in police cooperation, surveillance, and control. Rather than treating migration alongside issue areas such as transnational crime and terrorism, more appropriately it could have been considered part of the labor and social affairs portfolio. However, the network channels created for the exchange of information among EU states had from very early on sought to compensate for the gradual abolition of internal border controls with closer cooperation in policing and customs (Kostakopolou 2000). This is a theme that was present as early as 1967 in the form of the Naples Convention that sought to address violations of customs regulations in cross-national commerce that marked the first such cross-national institution for the exchange of information on illegal transnational activity within the EU.

The Gradual Europeanization of a Sector

The 1985 Schengen Agreement (signed on June 14, but not implemented until June 19, 1990) was a multilateral extra-communitarian response to the impending completion of the Single Market and has its origins in a July 13, 1984 Franco-German bilateral agreement on the "gradual reduction of controls along the German–French border," which, together with the already existing passport union among the Benelux countries, laid the foundation for closer cooperation between police and customs authorities and created the Schengen Informational System and the European Automated Fingerprinting Regulation System (EURODAC) for the exchange of personal data. It also aimed at harmonizing visa policies, introduced a uniform tamper-proof visa, and led to greater cooperation in the enforcement of drug laws, joint police efforts in combating transnational crime and judicial cooperation in extradition. Later joined by Italy (1990), Spain and Portugal (1991), Greece (1992), Austria (1995), Denmark, Finland, and Sweden (1996), as well as non-EU member states Iceland, Norway, and Switzerland, Schengen created an extra-communitarian platform for designing blueprints for future EU AMP, despite its rejection by Ireland, the UK, and Denmark.

Politically, Schengen was very much a pet project of the West German government, especially Chancellor Helmut Kohl. Indeed, Kohl was a central actor in seeking to engineer an AMP, largely because West Germany attracted the largest number of immigrants in Europe in the 1980s. The Dublin Agreement was based on the West German government's initiative and the concepts of "safe country of origin" and "safe third country." German ideas originally introduced into the revised asylum legislation of 1993 attracted the interest of other European ministers of the interior during multilateral meetings in London in 1992 and gradually were introduced elsewhere. Throughout the 1980s, West Germany attracted increasing numbers of immigrants that entered under a variety of categories: ethnic Germans returning to the homeland of their ancestors under Art. 116 of the German Basic Law, political refugees commonly from the former Yugoslavia who were granted subsidiary protection and political asylum seekers who could base their claim on the relatively liberal Art. 16 of the Basic Law, and undocumented migrants.[7]

Concomitant to the multilateral commitment to creating migration policy, the Commission stepped up efforts to ensure the practical implementation of freedom of labor and unimpeded movement within the European Union. It strongly recommended measures to ensure such unobstructed movement in a January 23, 1985, communication (OJ 1985, C. 47/5), while the 1985 White Paper on the Completion of the Single Market repeats this recommendation (first section, paras. 24 ff.) and proposes an action program and a specific timetable for the abolition of any barriers. Indeed, the Single European Act defines freedom of movement in the amended Art. 8a and renders this area explicitly subject to EU jurisdiction.

Developments continued at the multilateral level. The British government was unwilling to sign up to Schengen, which caused Ireland to remain outside as well, unwilling to jeopardize the decades-old Common Travel Area or face the politically unpalatable prospect of introducing border controls along the frontier to Northern Ireland. However, the British were not averse to multilateral cooperation per se. Following a UK initiative, the Ad Hoc Group of Immigration Ministers was established in London on October 20, 1986. Two years later, this Ad Hoc Group oversaw the formation of the Intergovernmental Coordinators' Group on Free Movement of People, formed at the Rhodos European Council meeting, which was charged with coordinating measures aimed at phasing out intra-EU border controls. In a similar vein, the so-called TREVI 1992 Working Group was founded in 1988 to coordinate measures addressing migration management issues arising from the abolition of internal border controls. In 1989, the "Rhodos Group" issued a document at the Madrid European Council meeting calling for a coherent coordinated approach to regulating asylum and migration policy, known as the Palma document. Indeed, given the plethora of multilateral working and steering groups that had arisen by now, such a coherent approach seemed to be more needed than ever.

Continued pressure by the West German government to design a system capable of distributing and sharing the "burden" of increasingly less welcome refugees and asylum seekers finally led to at least partial fruition in the shape of the June 15, 1990 Dublin Convention (OJ C 254/1–12) ratified in 1997. While not as ambitious as the Kohl government had hoped for, the "Convention Determining the State Responsible for Examining the Applications for Asylum Lodged in one of the Member States of the European Communities" sought, as its lengthy official name implied, to prevent "asylum shopping," establish clear national responsibility for individual asylum seekers by requiring applicants to file applications in the first EU country of entry, and finally created the Dublin Committee to administer refugee and asylum issues. The Dublin Convention spawned the 1992 London meeting of national ministers of justice and home affairs that led to the creation of a common asylum information pool (CIREA = Center for Information, Discussion and Exchange on Asylum/*Centre d'information, de réflexion et d'échange en matière d'asile*), an agreement on a common resolution regarding "manifestly unfounded" asylum applications and a common list for "safe third countries" and "safe countries of origin." The former concept had been pioneered by the German government, which in the early 1990s concluded a number of readmission agreements with its eastern neighbors. Poland had become a transit country between the successor states to the Soviet Union and Western Europe by the early 1990s, as reflected in the increase of the total number of entries into Poland by foreigners from 8.2 million in 1989 to 87.5 million in 1996 annually (Koslowski 1999: 45–66). As part of its attempt to reduce immigration from eastern Europe, the German government concluded treaties on deporting undocumented migrants with Bulgaria, the Czech Republic, Croatia, Poland, and Romania (Ucarer 1997: 307). Meanwhile, bilateral labor treaties with these countries (Menz 2001) provided a quid pro quo. Not coincidentally, a readmission agreement between the entire Schengenzone and Poland had been concluded concomitantly in 1991.

The 1992 Treaty on European Union (TEU) created a new institutional framework for AMP and thus radically restructured the often somewhat overlapping intergovernmental working groups established earlier. However, in terms of *policy content*, the TEU changed remarkably little. The creation of the Third Pillar of Justice and Home Affairs (JHA) meant that many previous intergovernmental agreements became communitarized, notably the Schengen regime and Dublin Convention (Art. K7). Future policy developments could easily become communitarized (Arts. K7 and

K9) and a K4 Committee reporting to the Council of Ministers directly replaced the Rhodos Group and oversaw in turn the work of the new three Steering Groups, respectively responsible for Immigration and Asylum (thus replacing the Ad Hoc Group on Immigration), police cooperation (thus replacing functionally the TREVI Group), and judicial cooperation. However, most analysts concur that the net effect was less ambitious than expected, as decision-making remained largely intergovernmental in nature, with the power of the EP limited to consultation, and the ECJ enjoying no authority (Geddes 2000b; Levy 1999; Ucarer 1997).

While the TEU seemed to have cleaned up some of the previous organizational mess, its own organizational inadequacies, compounded by the awkward opt-out of three member states, soon led to calls for further organizational reforms that might in turn streamline and enhance the decision-making process. At the December 1995 European Council meeting in Madrid, the Reflection Group presented its final report, suggesting a communitarization of legislation on foreigners, refugees, displaced persons, and asylum. Most national governments were inclined to agree with this conclusion, with the notable exceptions of the UK and Denmark, while the Commission recommended the introduction of QMV in the third pillar and an extension of the power of the EP in a series of reports in the run-up to the 1996 Intergovernmental Convention (Levy 1999: 36).

While a shift of the entire JHA portfolio into the first pillar, implying increased powers for the Commission, EP, and even the ECJ, may have appeared as a radical step, this is precisely what the 1997 Amsterdam Treaty accomplished, seeking to establish an "Area of Freedom, Security and Justice," by modifying the now renumbered TEU Art. 2. The modified TEC includes a new title IV on "Visa, Asylum, Immigration and other policies related to free movement of persons." The relevant clause stresses that appropriate measures are to be taken regarding the protection of external borders and joint action regarding the combat of crime, while assuring unimpeded internal mobility. However, in practice, as will be outlined below, Amsterdam did not overcome member state hesitancy to introduce QMV throughout; member states retained the right to initiate policy in the council during the first five years, and the introduction of the cooperation procedure for the EP and a clear delineation of ECJ responsibility have both been successfully delayed by recalcitrant member states.

In many ways, the Amsterdam Treaty formalized the commitment to create an AMP, setting out an ambitious policy agenda for the immediate future. More specifically, it created a transition period of five years from the date of implementation, thus ending on May 1, 2004. During this period, the Council of Ministers is charged with implementing regulations on a number of AMP issues, including regarding criteria for the respective national responsibility for asylum-seekers (often referred to as "Dublin 2"), minimum standards regarding the reception of asylum seekers and the definition of refugees, minimum standards regarding the awarding and revoking of refugee status and minimum standards for so-called de facto refugees or "displaced persons from third countries who cannot return to their country of origin and for persons who otherwise need international protection" (63-3) (European Communities 1999: 131).[8] Such efforts go hand in hand with cooperation in policing (61e), the establishment of common policies regarding the management of visa applications from TCNs, including a common list of countries whose nationals are subject to a visa requirement (62-2) and common measures regarding illegal immigration and deportation (63-3). Not subject to the five-year limitation are the goal of setting forth common agreements on exchanging refugees, establishing residency rights for TCNs outside of the member state they have a legal residency in and conditionalities regarding long-term visa and residence permits, including family reunion matters (63-3).

Institutionally, during the five-year period, unanimity is required in the Council after a consultation with the EP, however, the votes of Denmark, Ireland, and the UK shall be disregarded as these states are not subject to the new title IV TEC. Both member states and the Commission have the right to propose policy. After the transition period, only the Commission has the right of initiative, but is obliged to examine requests by member states to submit a proposal to the Council. Under Art. 67 (2), the Council "acting unanimously, after consulting the European Parliament, shall take a decision with a view to providing for all or parts of the areas covered by this Title" to be covered by the co-decision procedure and also "adapting the provisions relating to the powers of the Court of Justice." However, no such steps have been taken yet. Indeed, as Lavenex (2001: 865) argues: "In the literature, this right [of initiative] is often seen as implying control over the negotiation agenda and facilitating the common interest. Nevertheless, in the event of unanimous voting in the Council, the Commission will anticipate the position of the most reluctant government, thus perpetuating harmonization with the lowest common denominator."

The next significant step in creating an AMP was the October 15–16, 1999 European Council meeting in Tampere, specifically and exclusively dedicated to the issue of migration and asylum policy planning. Discussions at Tampere emphasized a number of new elements, which indicated that migration was being recognized as related and integral to larger politico-economic trends. Hence, the final communiqué mentioned the need for developing a comprehensive approach to addressing migration issues, including the improvement of economic and political conditions in the countries of origin, creating "partnerships" with them to help identify questions of human rights and development policy that might be addressed cooperatively to reduce migration flows. At the same time, there was an emphasis on developing a Common European Asylum System with an explicit base in the Geneva Convention, the need to enhance the protection of foreign legal residents, and the general necessity of managing migration flows at all stages of the process. Member states also instructed the Commission to deliver a "scoreboard" or "checklist" with items in AMP affairs that required harmonization, without prejudice to the unanimity principle, of course (Commission Communication of March 24, 2000: Scoreboard to review progress on the creation of an area of "Freedom, Security, and Justice in the European Union" COM (2000) 167 final). Despite some of the progressive-sounding rhetoric, the parallel summit of NGOs, organized by the European Council on Refugees and Exiles (ECRE) criticized the routine invoking of now common concepts such as safe third countries and safe third countries of origin. Boesche (2003) mentions that the hotly contested issue of "burden-sharing" of refugees and asylum seekers was not mentioned at all in the final communiqué. A joint policy paper by the French, British, and German governments outlined some common positions, including a distinction between (labor) migration and asylum, a commitment to the Geneva Convention, and some form of burden-sharing scheme, taking into account historical and geographical particularities of the member states.

At the 2000 Intergovernmental Conference in Nice, very few new measures were taken. While member states may have seemed willing to concede to the introduction of the co-decision procedure after 2004, the unanimity requirement of the (then) larger Council of Ministers, encompassing the 10 EU newcomers, arguably rendered this decision less likely, which in any case was made contingent on the prior implementation of a common framework in asylum policy. Due to the resistance of the German *Länder* which felt that the German federal government negotiating on their behalf was undermining the delicate balance of power by stealth, once again no agreement could be found on "burden" sharing.

At the June 21–22, 2002 Council Meeting in Seville, migration and asylum once again dominated the agenda, though the general approach taken appeared to be strongly colored by the recent impressions created by the events of September 11, 2001. The thrust of the conclusions was much more restrictive and heavy emphasis was placed on closing, reinforcing, and guarding borders. There was also notably more pressure applied on third countries to partake in EU migration management as junior management partners with the explicit threat of sanctions in case of refusal. Thus Art. 33 states that "any future cooperation, association or equivalent agreement [...concluded] with any country should include a clause on joint management of migration flows and on compulsory readmission in the event of illegal immigration," while Arts. 34–36 indicate that "a systematic assessment of relations with third countries which do not cooperate in combating illegal immigration" will be carried out, which may result in sanctioning in the EU's foreign policy stance towards such a country with significant ramifications in terms of trade, aid, and developmental assistance.

The final communiqué of Seville explicitly distinguishes between "an integration policy for lawfully resident immigrants" and restrictive policy aimed at "combat[ing] illegal immigration" (Art. 28). This latter policy includes common lists of third countries requiring entry visas, a common identification system for visa data, the negotiation of readmission agreements, common deportation and repatriation policies (with reference to the Commission Green Paper (COM 2002, 175, April 10) and common policies regarding human trafficking (Art. 30). In addition, blueprints are drawn up for the eventual creation of European border police with the planned implementation of joint operations of border guards, the creation of a network of liaison officers among the national border police forces, and the creation of a common curriculum for future border guard training (Art. 32). The document is also explicit about applying a carrot-and-stick policy towards third countries, pressurizing third countries into accepting readmission agreements (Arts. 33–35).[9] Finally, Seville imposed a number of deadlines for the implementation of AMP measures, including the Dublin II Regulation by December 2002, directives concerning minimum standards for qualification and refugee status, modalities of family reunion, and the status of long-term TCNs by June 2003 and a directive regarding common standards for asylum procedures by December 2003.

Compelled by the imperative of the Tampere summit to create the basic framework of an AMP, a flurry of legislative activity unfolded over

Legacies of the Past and Currents of Change

the course of 2003 and 2004. Chapter 3 examines the political genesis of three of these directives. This includes the so-called minimum standards for reception of asylum seekers directive (2003/9/EC of January 27, 2003), asylum procedures (COM 2004, 503 final, July 15, 2004), creating the same minimum standards and presumably ensuring conformity with international treaty obligations with the included right for prompt processing of asylum claims and judicial review and the asylum qualification directives (2004/83/EC of April 29, 2004), establishing the standards for the categories of "refugee" and "asylum seeker," including the recognition of persecution by nonstate actors and persecution based on gender and sexual orientation, but limiting the rights of those considered posing a potential security threat to the EU. In 2003, a directive on Family Reunification of Third-Country Nationals (2003/86/EC of September 22, 2003) was passed by the Council. Other major activities worth mentioning included agreeing on uniform formats for visas (EC 334/2002), creating a European Agency for the "management of Operational Coordination at the External Borders of the Member States," headquartered in Poland, and the development of directives on students, researchers, and long-term residents. Labor migration was a much more contested issue, as will be analyzed in Chapter 3.[10]

Concerned about the somewhat lackluster progress by mid-2004, on November 4–5, 2004, the European Council of Ministers passed the Hague Program, outlining ten priority areas for the next five years. In AMP terms, these were based on declaring the period between Tampere and the Hague (1999–2004) the "first phase" and promising more active and prolific policy development during the "second phase" (2005–10), including the following: the adoption of the asylum procedures directive, an evaluation of legal instruments designed during the first phase and its implementation by member states, the development of a proposal on long-term resident status for refugees, studies on joint processing of asylum applications both within and outside the EU during 2006, the establishment of a European Asylum Office assisting in the operation of the Common European Asylum System, and the establishment of a European Refugee Fund (2005–13), charged with helping member states with processing and reception. In (labor) migration matters, assessment and monitoring of first phase legal instruments was promised, along with the presentation of a policy plan on legal migration, including admission procedures, in December 2005, focusing in the first instance on scientific researchers (Council Directive 2005/71/EC of October 12, 2005), skilled and seasonal workers, intra-corporate transferees, and remunerated trainees and interns. In addition, the launching of actions for financial support for deportations was promised, with the establishment on May 23, 2007 of a "European Return Fund" for the period 2008–13 including a total funding of €676 billion.[11] There is a relatively significant number of measures regarding border protection and deportation, including joint flights (Council Decision 2004/573/EC of April 29, 2004), the creation of an immigration liaison officers' network (Council Regulation (EC) No. 377/2004 of February 19, 2004), and a number of bilateral readmission agreements, including Macau and Sri Lanka. This is undertaken alongside efforts to establish so-called Regional Protection Programs for potential migrants and the establishment of a "European Neighbourhood Policy" to cooperate with sending and transit countries.[12] This should also be considered in conjunction with ongoing efforts to coordinate border guard training and create a comprehensive plan for the protection of external borders. The final result of these deliberations is the program "Solidarity and Management of Migration Flows" for 2008–13. The Commission is charged with developing a proposal for minimum standards on deportation. The introduction of biometrics into both visa and identity documents for EU citizens is considered.

In sum, the Hague program revisits most of the themes already expounded in the Seville document—and to some extent in Tampere—but develops them further. The strong emphasis on control, monitoring, deterrence, and surveillance is even more pronounced and the more progressive references to partnership in cooperation with third countries no longer feature quite as prominently.

This element of repression and surveillance is also apparent in the multilateral so-called Schengen III or Prüm Treaty signed on May 27, 2005 by the governments of Germany, Spain, France, Luxembourg, the Netherlands, Austria, and Belgium, not yet part of EU *acquis*. The treaty creates the legal basis for the automated and routine access by police to biometric information such as DNA and fingerprints as well as vehicle registration data held by other national police forces. Arts. 13–15 also permit the routine exchange of "black lists" on individuals considered a threat to public order, usually due to previous political activity. Informally already used in the run-up to the demonstrations against the G8 summit in Genoa in 2001, this treaty now permits regular exchange of personal data on political activists, facilitating refusal to entry or even detention at the border.[13] The treaty also contains passages on the employment of armed undercover government agents on commercial airline flights (Arts. 17–18). Finally, the treaty reiterates two measures already in use:

Legacies of the Past and Currents of Change

the detachment of European "document advisors" to countries of origin, where they "consult" transportation companies on entry requirements for the EU (Arts. 20–21) and the practice of joint deportation flights from Europe (Arts. 23–24).

Aside from the newly established program for "Solidarity and Management of Migration Flow," spawning four subsidiary funds, covering external borders, integration, return, and the European Refugee Fund, 2006 and 2007 saw somewhat modest genuinely new development. There were agreements on the mutual exchange of information on new national legislative measures (Council Decision 2006/688/EC of October 5, 2006), the establishment of a European Fund for the Integration of third-country nationals for 2007–13 (Council Decision 2007/435/EC of June 25, 2007) and some clarification on the implementation of asylum management and control systems (Commission Decision 2006/400/EC of January 20, 2006). A somewhat more ambitious program was the establishment of the European Refugee Fund adopted on December 8, 2006. But progress on labor migration remained extremely slow and very little emerged from the December 14–15, 2006 European Council meeting in Brussels aside from general declarations on the desirability of well-managed migration policies that respect national autonomy in this domain and continue cooperation efforts with third countries, while some frustration over the slow and cumbersome progress seems to be implied (Council of the European Union, Brussels European Council Presidency Conclusions December 14–15, 2006, February 12, 2007). One notable exception, however, was the formal establishment of a coordination unit for external border policing named Frontex in Warsaw, itself the product of earlier legislation, however, and the creation of "rapid border intervention teams."[14] Also, by June 2007, the Commission had issued a Green Paper on future asylum policy to which it solicited input, organizing a public hearing on October 18. The issues raised in this paper concern subsidiarity, degrees of harmonization in procedures, administration, recognition, and labor market access, EU level coordination of financial transfer payments and exchange of expertise, and the future of regional protection programs and border protection where it affects access to asylum status.

The Commission is expected to draft directives on intra-corporate transferees, remunerated trainees, and seasonal workers in September 2008. By the end of 2007, the Commission felt confident enough to press ahead with *communautarization* on labor migration and the establishment of a comprehensive "Blue Card" for highly skilled migrants along with further facilitation of intra-EU migration for third-country nationals. On

October 23, two draft directives were sent to the Council. The first seeks to assure "a single application procedure for a single permit...to reside and work" in the EU and "a common set of rights" (COM 2007, 638 final). It aims to create a one-stop shop for all third-country nationals who are not yet considered long-term residents; bars governments from imposing additional permit requirements; does not affect family reunion rights; and stipulates a number of rights regarding, among other issues, labor market access. The slightly more contentious draft directive on high-skill migration followed prolonged discussions and detailed questionnaire-based work in the CIA, including a Commission study of existing national level schemes (interview EU-COM-1). The directive stresses its contribution to "competitiveness, flexibility of labour markets, improving adaptability," and creates fast-track processing of highly skilled migrants, defined as possessing a work contract, rather than a form of self-employment, with a salary offer above three times the gross monthly minimum wage, professional qualifications in the form of a tertiary degree or a minimum of three years of "equivalent" professional experience. It offers immediate family reunion rights, an exemption for family members from obligatory integration measures prior to arrival, the accumulation of long-term residence status after five years through periods in several EU member states, and, most crucially, a two-year work and residency permit. Particularly favorable treatment can be afforded to university graduates of less than 30 years of age. Individual member states, not the Commission, can set national quotas. The so-called EU Blue Card is currently under discussion, but has already provoked strong negative reactions from German employer association BDA (BDA December 5, 2007). Pre-empting these initiatives, the May 16, 2007 directive on illegal employment of third-country nationals (COM 2007, 249 final) sought to impose sanctions on undocumented forms of migrant employment, more motivated by reducing undocumented migration than by improving migrant rights, however.

In the June 2007 Green Paper for Common European Asylum System, the Commission demonstrates its commitment to move further towards harmonization in years to come, rather than set minimum standards as it did in drafting the reception, conditions and procedures directives. Some of the more ambitious initiatives flouted include significant amendments to past directives to move towards harmonization, especially regarding national treatment, recognition, details including labor market access, the possible extension of the long-term residence directive to beneficiaries of subsidiary protection, and a common agency for processing applications (interview EU-COM-1) (Tables 2.1 and 2.2).

Table 2.1. Developments in AMP since the 1970s

Year	Event
1975	Establishment of the Terrorism, Radicalism, Extremism, and International Violence (terrorisme, radicalisme, extrémisme, violence internationale" = TREVI) group, bringing together the national ministers of interior affairs, aimed at coordinating efforts aimed at politically motivated terrorism, but also including immigration within its remit.
1985	Schengen Agreement (signed June 14, implemented in the Convention of June 19, 1990; available at: www.unhcr.bg/euro_docs/en/_schengen_en.pdf); originally signed by France, (West) Germany, and the Benelux countries, based on already existing passport union among the Benelux countries and the July 13, 1984 Franco-German bilateral agreement on the "gradual reduction of controls along the German–French border," established the cooperation between police and customs authorities, created Schengen Informational System and the European Automated Fingerprinting Regulation System (EURODAC) for the exchange of personal data, aimed at creating common visa policies; later refined through the Council Decision of May 20, 1999 concerning the definition of the Schengen *acquis*, Council Decision of May 20, 1999 determining the legal basis for each of the provisions or decisions which constitute the Schengen *acquis* (1999/435/EC and 1999/436/EC), additional clarifications were issued regarding the membership of Iceland and Norway (1999/437/EC and 1999/139/EC); (europa.eu.int/scadplus/leg/en/lvb/l33022.htm); later joined by Italy (1990), Spain and Portugal (1991), Greece (1992), Austria (1995), Denmark, Finland, Sweden (1996).
1985	Commission proposal recommends free movement of EU citizens across intra-EU borders (OJ 1985, C. 47, February 19, 1985, p. 5), White Paper on the Completion of the Single Market (europa.eu.int/scadplus/leg/en/lvb/l22022.htm) makes similar recommendations, proposes action program, and timetable.
1986	Single European Act (implemented July 1, 1987) defines freedom of movement (amended Art. 8a) and explicitly includes this area within EU jurisdiction.
1986	Establishment of Ad Hoc Group of Immigration Ministers (October 20) in London, following British initiative.
1988	Rhodos European Council meeting leads to formation of Coordinators' Group on Free Movement of People ("Rhodos Group") (December 2–3), coordinates activities on border control relaxation for EU citizens.
1988	TREVI 1992 Working Group founded to design measures addressing control deficit arising out of the abolition of intra-EU border controls (europa.eu.int/scadplus/leg/en/lvb/l33022.htm).
1989	Intergovernmental Coordinator Group proposes coordinated approach to regulating asylum and migration at the Madrid European Council meeting (June 26–27) in the so-called Palma document.
1990	Dublin Convention (OJ C 254, August 19, 1997, p. 1–12) (ratified in 1997) limited asylum application to one, created obligation for asylum seekers to apply for asylum in first EU country entered, obligation for member state to process claims of these claimants, created Dublin Committee to administer refugee and asylum issues.
1991	(May 1) Readmission Agreement between the Schengen zone and Poland.

(cont.)

Table 2.1. (Continued)

Year	Description
1991	Maastricht European Council (February 9–10) agrees on Treaty.
1992	Treaty on European Union signed in Maastricht (February 7), implemented November 1, 1993, creates three pillar structure and declares asylum, migration, and treatment of TCNs as matters of common interest in Article group K (europa.eu.int/en/record/mt/title6.html), creates article K cooperation instruments and regulations, Art. K7 incorporates Schengen regime and Dublin Convention and permits further policy development even without the consent of all EU member states; Art. K8 defines financial responsibility, Art. K9 permits rapid *communautarization* of policy developments, esp. in asylum and refugee policy, Art. K.
1992	London meeting of national ministers of justice and home affairs (November 30 to December 1); creates common asylum information pool (CIREA = Center for Information, Discussion and Exchange on Asylum/Centre d'information, de réflexion et d'échange en matière d'asile); agreement on common resolution regarding "manifestly unfounded" asylum applications, common list for "safe third countries" and "safe countries of origin."
1995	Council of Ministers adopts resolution 95/C262/01 "on burden-sharing" (September 25) "with regard to the reception and residence of the displaced persons on a temporary basis" (JO C262 October 7, 1995, p. 1–3).
1995	European Council meeting in Madrid (December 15–16, 1995) Reflection Group created at the Corfu Council meeting presents final report, suggesting a communitarization of legislation on foreigners, refugees, displaced persons, and asylum.
1996	Council Decision 96/198/JHA "on an alert and emergency procedure for burden-sharing with regard to the reception and residence of displaced persons on a temporary basis" (OJ L063, October 13, 1996, pp. 10–11).
1997	Treaty of Amsterdam signed (October 2), implemented May 1, 1999, established the "Area of Freedom, Security and Justice," by modifying the now renumbered TEU Art. 2—appropriate measures are to be taken regarding the protection of external borders and joint action regarding the combat of crime, while assuring unimpeded internal mobility. The modified TEC includes a new title IV on "Visa, Asylum, Immigration and other policies related to free movement of persons," thus moving this policy into the first pillar and communitizing it. A transition period of five years from the date of implementation of the Amsterdam Treaty is being established, during which period the Council of Ministers is charged with proposing regulations regarding criteria for the respective national responsibility for asylum-seekers (often referred to as "Dublin 2") minimum standards regarding the reception of asylum seekers and the definition of refugees, minimum standards regarding the bestowal and revocation of refugee status and minimum standards for so-called de facto refugees or "displaced persons from third countries who cannot return to their country of origin and for persons who otherwise need international protection" (63-3). (European Communities 1999: 131). Such efforts go hand in hand with cooperation in policing (61e), the establishment of common policies regarding the management of visa applications from TCNs, including a common list of countries whose nationals are subject to a visa requirement (62-2), and common measures regarding illegal immigration and deportation (63). All of these policies are "aimed at ensuring the free movement of persons … in conjunction with directly related flanking measure."

(new Art. 61, formerly Art. 73i). Not subject to the five-year limitation are the goal of setting forth common agreements on exchanging refugees, establishing residency rights for TCNs outside of the member state they have a legal residency in and conditionalities regarding long-term visa and residence permits, including family reunion matters (63-3). During the five-year period, unanimity is required in the Council after a consultation with the EP, however, the votes of Denmark, Ireland, and the UK shall be disregarded as these states are not subject to the new title IV TEC. Both national member states and the Commission have the right to propose policy. After the transition period, which expires on May 1, 2004, only the Commission has the right of initiative, but is obliged to examine requests by member states to submit a proposal to the Council. Under Art. 67 (2), the Council "acting unanimously, after consulting the European Parliament, shall take a decision with a view to providing for all or parts of the areas covered by this Title" to be covered by the co-decision procedure and also "adapting the provisions relating to the powers of the Court of Justice." However, no such steps have been taken yet.

1998   Joint Council and Commission "Action Plan" (December 3) on "how best to implement the provisions of the Treaty of Amsterdam on the creation of an area of freedom, security and justice," available at: www.europa.eu.int/scadplus/leg/en/lvb/l33080.htm. European Council meeting in Vienna (December 11–12) endorsed this action plan and emphasized the need for a common policy in this area.

1999   European Council meeting in Tampere (15–16 October) results in an invitation to the Commission to produce a scoreboard on measures necessary to be taken within the next five years and reviewing progress regularly (Commission Communication of March 24, 2000: Scoreboard to review progress on the creation of an area of "Freedom, Security, and Justice in the European Union" COM 2000, 167 final).

2000   Treaty of Nice (Intergovernmental Conference held on December 7–8): Member states seem willing to introduce the co-decision procedure (Art. 251 TEC), but the introduction, originally anticipated for May 1, 2004, is extremely limited in immigration policy and made contingent on the implementation of a common framework in asylum policy.

2004   (November 4–5) The Hague Program sets forth EU policy priorities for 2004–09.

2005   (May 27) Prüm Treaty on automatic exchange of DNA, fingerprint and vehicle registration data between signatory states, also sharing of data on political activists prior to major demonstrations, armed police on joint deportation flights on commercial airlines.

2007   (October 23) EU commission sends draft directives on highly skilled migration and rights of TCNs to Council; promises more legislative activity on labor migration by late 2008.

Table 2.2. Developments in AMP since 2000

EU Asylum and Migration Policy since 2000

Responsibility for asylum applications ("Dublin II")
Commission proposal for Regulation, July 2001: COM (2001) 447
Council Regulation (EC) No. 343/2003 of February 18, 2003, establishing the criteria and mechanisms for determining the Member State responsible for examining an asylum application lodged in one of the Member States by a third-country national OJ L 050 (February 25, 2003) (Dublin II).
Commission Regulation (EC) No. 1560/2003 of September 2, 2003, laying down detailed rules for the application of Council Regulation (EC) No. 343/2003 establishing the criteria and mechanisms for determining the Member State responsible for examining an asylum application lodged in one of the Member States by a third-country national OJ L 222 (September 5, 2003).
Green Paper on the Future Common European Asylum System (COM 2007, 301 final)

Reception conditions for asylum seekers
Commission proposal for Directive, April 2001: COM (2001) 181
Council "general approach" agreed, April 25/26, 2002: doc. 8351/02
Council Directive (2003/9/EC) laying down minimum standards for the reception of asylum seekers

Asylum procedures (see discussion in Chapter 3)
Commission proposal for Directive, April 2001: COM (2000) 578
Council conclusions on future of Directive: doc. 15107/1/01
Revised Commission proposal, June 2002: COM (2002) 326
Final directive on minimum standards for qualification and status of third-country nationals or stateless persons as refugees or as persons who otherwise need international protection and the content of the protection granted (2004/83/EC)

Temporary protection
Commission proposal for Directive, May 2000: COM (2000) 303
Directive agreed by Council, July 2001: *Directive 2001/55*

Family reunion (see discussion in Chapter 3)
Commission proposal, December 1999: COM (1999) 638
Revised Commission proposal, September 2000: COM (2000) 624
Council reaction, May 2001: *doc. 9019/01*
Revised Commission proposal, May 2002: COM (2002) 225
Final directive 2003/59/EC on the right to family reunion

Long-term residents
  Commission proposal for Directive, March 2001: COM (2001) 127
  Directive 2003/109/EC of November 25, 2003 concerning the status of third-country nationals who are long-term residents

Labor migration
  Commission proposal for Directive, July 2001: COM (2001) 386
  Council working party began discussions March 2002
  Long stalemate in Council
  Italian proposal to introduce EU level quotas is rejected by French, Germans, and Austrians
  January 11, 2005 EU Commission Green Book on labor migration (COM 2004, 811 final)
  Consultation with national governments, social partners, NGOs
  Policy plan of December 21, 2005 promises four future directives, focusing on highly skilled and seasonal workers, intra-corporate transferees and remunerated trainees and interns
  Council Directive 2005/71/EC of October 12, 2005 on a specific procedure for admitting third-country nationals for the purposes of scientific research (OJ L 289 of November 3, 2005, p. 15) addresses one of the least contentious groups of economic migrants, following in the spirit of Council Directive 2004/114/EC of December 13, 2004 on the conditions of admission of third-country nationals for the purposes of studies, pupil exchange, unremunerated training or voluntary service (OJ L 375 of December 23, 2004, p. 12)
  Proposed Council Directives on the conditions of entry and residence of third-country nationals for the purposes of highly qualified employment (EU "Blue Card") (COM 2007, 637 final) and on a single application procedure for a single permit for third-country nationals to reside and work in the territory of a Member State and on a common set of rights for third-country workers legally residing in a Member State

Regulatory Philosophies and Historical Trajectories of Migration Regulation

We shall turn next to a more detailed examination of the distinct regulatory philosophies and past historical trajectories of migration and asylum policy that continue to shape national policies and government preferences in the creation of AMP. These philosophies are commonly a curious amalgam of past active migration recruitment, partly discontinued and abandoned, but often partly reconfigured, citizenship concepts and migration channels that were shaped by colonial and postcolonial legacies and contributed to the creation of preferential treatment of certain ethnic groups over others, and, to a more limited degree, humanitarian motives, either pertaining to the relations of (labor) migrants as concessions often made in response to judicial intervention or filtered through the obligations arising explicitly out of the Geneva Convention, collective memories of past injustices or recent emigration experiences.

As will become apparent, the two basic categories proposed by Castles and Miller (2003) who distinguishes between "postcolonial" and "guestworker" philosophies for France and Britain and German-speaking Europe respectively, provide a valid descriptive typology for the postwar decades, though significant regulatory change since and the increasing importance of different economically motivated preferences in migration management render these forms of categorization less accurate today. The dynamics of relatively new immigration countries are obviously too complex to be captured by them. In addition, a bias shared by the comparative immigration policy literature is the exaggeration of differences among the three largest European immigration countries France, Germany, and Britain that may cloud the very similar timeline in imposing an end to active labor recruitment in the early 1970s, when the end of the postwar economic boom, the oil shocks, and first signs of surfacing xenophobic backlashes coincided, just as all three countries reconsidered this policy in the late 1990s, under pressure from organized business and demographic challenges. Similarly, analysts employing stark dichotomies between the Germanic guest worker approach and the presumably more encompassing postcolonial Franco-British model (Brubaker 1992; more nuanced: Weil 2002) risk losing sight of the de facto blurring of these two categories in practice: in France, the residency permits offered were *de jure* temporary in nature and employer initiatives to recruit workers in North Africa resembled the business-driven recruitment efforts of German officials soliciting labor migrants in southeastern Europe. In

Britain, bureaucratic restrictions de facto significantly impaired the theoretical rights of subjects of the crown to settle freely anywhere in the UK. The functional similarities among the recruitment teams of Renault in action in small Algerian villages, German officials inviting Anatolian peasants to work the assembly lines of Mercedes-Benz, and London Underground recruiting staff in Barbados are striking. From a political economy angle, then, the similarities in labor migration regulation are remarkable.

France

The mortar of the ideological construction of the French republic was the construction of a common political identity based on the universal "republican" values of freedom, equality, civil rights, and democracy, values that were deliberately free of any notion of ethnicity which would have undermined any claim to universality and may have posed problems in the cultural integration of a regionally diverse country and the fairly aggressive formation of a linguistically homogeneous French nation during the Third Republic (Favell 2001; Feldblum 1999; Weil 1991, 2005). Encompassing and universal public institutions, such as the army and the schools, were charged with the mission of disseminating knowledge of and policing adherence to the common language and cultural and political values. Newcomers were expected to adapt and adhere to this ideal. Such conception of self-identity facilitated the integration of migrants arriving from Belgium, Italy, and Poland in the slowly industrializing East and Northeast in the late nineteenth century (Le Moigne 1986). In fact, only after 1917 did arriving noncitizens have to apply for a residency permit (*carte de séjour*). Citizenship was based on a combination of ethnically based (*ius sanguinis*) and territorially based (*ius solis*) characteristics. Indeed, first restrictive efforts were imposed in the aftermath of the global recession of the late 1920s. In 1927, deportation became possible: an August 10, 1932 law legalized national quotas for foreign employees in companies, while in the mid-1930s deportations, especially of Polish migrants, were implemented. The most repressive period came during the fascist Vichy regime, which spawned the October 4, 1940 law permitting the internment of "foreign residents of the Jewish race" (*les rassortissant étrangers de race juive*) and the surveillance and limited mobility of non-Jewish "foreigners of excessive numbers in the national economy" (*étrangers en surnombre dans l'économie nationale*) in accordance with legislation implemented on September 27, 1940.

Immigration control was relatively lax before World War I, not least because the unfolding wave of industrialization permitted and even necessitated the easy integration of migrants into the ranks of the industrial working class. Nevertheless, in direct contradiction to the ambitious theoretical ideal of a color-blind republic—to employ a slightly anachronistic term—backlashes against the Italian and Belgian immigrants during times of economic slump were not unheard of, while the Dreyfus affair of 1871 uncomfortably revealed deep-seated antisemitism among many of the Third Republic's elite.

The postwar boom (*trente glorieuses*), subsequent large-scale industrialization, and postwar reconstruction exhausted domestic labor supplies. In 1945, the National Office for Migration (*Office National d'Immigration*) was established (Ordonnance nr. 45-2658 of November 2, 1945 "*relative aux conditions d'entrée et de séjour des étrangers en France*") to recruit foreign workers needed to reconstruct a devastated economy and compensate for demographic deficiencies, immediately setting up recruitment offices in Italy. Work and residency permits for 1, 3, and up to 10 years were issued, while citizenship regulations were liberalized following an October 18, 1945 *ordonnance*. Since Algeria was still considered part of France for political purposes until independence in 1962, Algerian residents were automatically considered French citizens and could thus easily enter mainland France. This legal particularity created "involuntary" French citizens who could pass on this status given the ethnic component of citizenship regulations. To stimulate additional labor migration, the French government concluded bilateral labor treaties with Spain (1961), Portugal (1963), and Morocco (1963).

Though formally labor recruitment occurred through the bilateral treaties administered by the ONI, in practice migrants that had arrived outside of any controlled framework commonly received work permits once they had secured employment in France (Le Moigne 1986: 9). Conceptually, such guest worker programs sit fairly uneasily with the ambitious republican ambition of *integration*. Nevertheless, the ONI officially only issued temporary work permits. Post hoc *régularisation* especially of low-skill employees stopped after a July 29, 1968 *circulaire* of the Ministry of Social Affairs to that effect, although important exceptions were made for family reunion, Portuguese nationals, domestic employees, and certain highly skilled workers. Active labor recruitment had not ended, as the signing of a bilateral labor treaty with the Algerian authorities in December 1968 demonstrates. However, as elsewhere in Western Europe, the early 1970s witnessed the end to such active recruitment: the

Legacies of the Past and Currents of Change

so-called Marcellin and Fontanet circulaires (February 23 and September 15, 1972 respectively) established the requirement of employment as a condition for a residency permit and permitted the revocation of these permits in case of job loss. While a 1973 *circulaire* by Minister of Labor Gorse permitted one last regularization of undocumented resident migrants, on July 5, 1974 the official recruitment of migrants ended. In 1970, the free mobility of labor for EU citizens became possible, but by then migration from Portugal, Spain, Morocco, and Tunisia had long surpassed the numbers of Italian migrants. Indeed, though French authorities had actively recruited Italians and tolerated Portuguese and Spaniards arriving (with Europeans still constituting the majority of resident foreigners in 1975) by 1990, non-Europeans had overtaken them in quantitative terms (Hargreaves 1995: 22). In the late 1970s, the French government encouraged voluntary repatriation by offering assistance to migrants (payments of up to 10,000 French francs, know as the "million Stoleru"), targeted primarily at migrants from the Maghreb countries. While family reunion had recommenced after 1975 and limited labor recruitment after 1977, the main emphasis of public policy remained on limiting immigration and expanding the legislative repertoire, notably through the modification of the original 1945 legislation through the 1980 *loi Bonnet* (80-9) which facilitated deportations. Though presumably cushioned by integration measures, improvement of housing and education, the 1980 legislation elicited considerable protest and public demonstrations, not least in response to State Secretary of Labor Stoleru's statement that "it is out of the question to accommodate a single foreigner in France" on October 15, 1980.

Since the end of active labor recruitment, the French approach to designing immigration policy has been somewhat inconsistent, moving, often rapidly, back and forth between the two poles of promoting integration and regularizing the status of resident undocumented migrants post hoc on the one hand and enforcing more rigid border controls, carrying out deportations, limiting access to citizenship, and implementing draconian measures against irregular forms of employment on the other. These two poles are largely adhered to by the political Left and Right respectively, though despite rhetorical pronouncements that suggested more pronounced divergences, there has been a commonly shared adherence to a restrictive framework, within which differences in the application and the micro-management of migration remain contested. To the extent that political power has shifted from the right to the left and, most recently, back to the right, French migration policy over the years oscillated between more liberal policies, including the *régularisation* of *sans-papiers* (as we have seen, very much in the tradition of the postwar years) by the Left (Siméant 1998), and measures aimed at impeding access to citizenship by the Right.

Commencing in the early 1980s, the electoral rise of the National Front and a very vivacious and often polemical debate about the philosophical contours and practical modalities of French citizenship have affected its regulation, albeit with some delay.

The self-assertion of the second generation of immigrants with roots in the Maghreb, giving rise to *Radio Beur*, a pirate Paris radio station, in 1981, was not so much motivated by separatism, as by an anti-racist movement (*Ne touche pas à mon pote*). The expression *beur* was coined to escape the often derogatorily used term *arabe*. By contrast, the attempt at a self-constructed identity by parts of the current fourth generation, particularly young males, isolated in the *banlieues*, composed of a simplistic and imaginary conception of Islam, extreme misogynist imagery, and *faux* self-identification with the spillover of the Algerian civil war into France, is not primarily a result of the failure of French integration as such, but has more to do with the socioeconomic exclusion from the labor market of a generation of young, male, low-skill adolescents. The low-skill manufacturing jobs enabling a living to the previous generation are no longer available, and the service sector prefers to attract skilled employees, many of them now female. Their fathers worked at Renault, but Renault now produces in the Czech Republic.

The reason why France was hesitant to endorse Europeanized migration policy went beyond the specifically Gaullian concerns over shedding national autonomy to any European superstate, particularly over such a crucial domain dear to the core of the nation-state. Though French self-identity and the ideological construct of the republic and the nation are conceptually receptive to newcomers willing to integrate (Favell 2001; Hargreaves 1995), it is precisely this open and nonethnically based character which is exposed to sustained and often vicious attacks both from the moderate right, as outlined above, and from an openly xenophobe and racist far-right. Multiculturalism is often criticized in France as promoting the growth of ethnic enclaves and self-imposed segregation into rigid "communities" (*communautarisme*) that impede integration. It is thus often rhetorically construed as yet another Anglo-American concept whose import ought to be avoided.

We might note that the citizenship ideal seems to have no concrete implications for migration policy. The Left and Right have embraced a very different rhetoric and engaged in some modest symbolic gestures, but more fundamentally the extent to which migration was tolerated and legitimized in a post hoc fashion seems to have been influenced by the business cycle, while conversely migrants serve as scapegoats in times and/or regions of economic downturn. It needs to be noted that official grandstanding rhetoric notwithstanding, migration policy had been historically strongly informed by perceived economic motives.

Germany

Germany turned from being a country of emigration to one of immigration in the late nineteenth century. In the wake of the industrial revolution, the heavy industries of the Ruhr area in particular attracted Polish workers, while political repression and economic instability led many Russians, many of them Jewish, to settle in Berlin and Frankfurt. Though forcefully united in 1871 under the Prussian aegis, individual regions maintained their own regulations on citizenship, until the genesis of the 1913 law on citizenship (*Reichs- und Staatsangehörigkeitsgesetz*) (Nathans 2004). This legislation, remaining in effect in (West) Germany until 1998 with a reversal of the racist Nazi modification of 1936, was heavily colored by the Prussian tradition, itself based on an ethnic conception (*ius sanguinis*).

In the literature, such ethnically defined conception of citizenship is often attributed to nineteenth-century Herderian notions of *völkisch* nation-state construction (Brubaker 1992), though a commonly neglected practical reason was the relatively late unification of Germany and the continuing allegiances to particular *Länder* that were only superseded by the 1913 law. Given the traditional plethora of German mini-states with often contested boundaries, a territorial definition would have created multiple instances of repeatedly changing citizenship statutes.[15]

Postwar West Germany adopted a curious mixture of migration policies. On the one hand, the self-righteous ambition to speak on behalf of all of Germany and the only belated official recognition of Polish and Soviet sovereignty over the eastern regions compelled the architects of the Basic Law to devise a very inclusive ethnic concept of citizenship. Art. 116a of the Basic Law permitted access to citizenship not only for residents of the 1937 (i.e. pre-World War II) territory but also for ethnic descendants of German emigrants to eastern Europe, some of whose links dated back to the late nineteenth century, including the settlers invited by Catherine the Great to Russia and forcefully resettled to Kazakhstan under Stalin.[16]

Similarly generous in principle was the constitutionally guaranteed right to political asylum, enshrined in Art. 16 of the Basic Law, itself an expression of accepting the political legacy of a regime that had engendered the political persecution and execution of millions.

Yet these liberal traits always compared unfavorably with a highly restrictive managerial approach to limiting permanent access to German territory and indeed the labor market.

During the postwar decades, admitting ethnic German refugees from East Germany, Russia, Poland, and Romania was deemed both politically desirable and even economically necessary as long as the "economic miracle" implied their simple absorption into the labor market. The construction of the Berlin Wall in 1961 cut off the West from its traditional labor pool. Not coincidentally, West Germany concluded its first bilateral labor agreement in 1955 (Italy), followed by Spain and Greece (1960), Turkey (1961 and 1964), and later Morocco, Portugal, Tunisia, and Yugoslavia (Herbert 2001; Marshall 2000). Meanwhile, the new citizenship law of the eastern German Democratic Republic of February 20, 1967 defined an independent citizenship, an important modification of its 1949 constitution that still contained the commitment to one pan-German citizenship concept.

Unlike the somewhat lofty self-proclamation of the French republic, the ideological foundation and the citizenship concept of the West German Federal Republic were not intended to be as universal and was strictly limited to geographic residents with some allowance made to ethnic descendants scattered throughout eastern Europe. Since Germany had lost its colonies in 1918, there were neither returning settlers in large numbers nor postcolonial ties to any significant degree. Migration was therefore conceived to be temporary and not intended to lead to long-term—much less, to permanent—settlement; it was also exclusively aimed at employment. These notions came together to shape the installation of presumably temporary labor recruitment of *gastarbeiter* (Herbert 1986; Miller and Martin 1982; Morris 2002).

While the oil shocks of 1973 were used to justify an end to active labor recruitment (*Anwerbestopp*), it had become readily apparent, yet was not acknowledged, that the *gastarbeiter* concept had failed. While some Italians of the first migrant wave might have returned, most of the Yugoslavian and Turkish migrants stayed and were developing social ties to their adopted country of residence.

The fall of the Berlin Wall and the civil war in Yugoslavia precipitated an unprecedented wave of migration to Germany. Not only could ethnic

Germans enter from Russia, Kazakhstan, Romania, Poland, and eastern Germany: figures rose from 42,788 in 1986 to 202,673 in 1988 and 4,000,000 in 1989 (Marshall 2000: 9). Strong existing ethnic communities and historical ties turned Germany into the preferred destination of Polish and Yugoslav migrants. The relatively liberal asylum regime had constituted the only gateway to West Germany in the 1980s. This, along with existing ethnic communities, accounts for the rise in asylum applications from countries experimenting in authoritarian and repressive regimes in the 1980s, including notably Turkey, Iran, Iraq, and Poland (Bade 1994). While in the 1960s and early 1970s political asylum attracted no more than a few thousand Eastern European applicants annually, by the early 1980s this figure had increased to an annual average of 100,000 where it was to remain throughout the decade. By the late 1980s, it had increased to 121,318 in 1989, 193,063 in 1990, and reached an all-time high of 438,191 in 1992, according to government statistics (Statistisches Bundesamt, Statistisches Jahrbuch).

In response to the regional electoral successes of the far right, notably *Die Republikaner*, and repeated instances of violent attacks on foreigners and asylum-seekers, notably in northeastern Rostock and Lübeck, the Kohl government severely limited the right to asylum in a 1993 revision of the Basic Law. Given the introduction of a zone of so-called safe third countries to which migrants arriving in transit could be immediately deported plus carrier sanction for airlines, physical access to Germany for potential claimants was rendered extremely difficult (Bade 1994). At the same time, Kohl backed strongly the nascent European initiatives of Dublin and Schengen and would have undoubtedly lent his support to restrictive European-level migration comanagement. Such enthusiasm for European initiatives was nourished by the perception that the country was disproportionately affected by migration from eastern and southeastern Europe.

An important modification to German migration policy was the 1998 reform of the 1913 citizenship law instigated by the Schröder government, facilitating access to citizenship after seven years of residence, and permitting the acquisition of citizenship for native-born descendants of migrants (Nathans 2004). The red–green coalition government implemented additional legislation on migration in 2004, placing the labor recruitment of migrants in niche sectors of the economy experiencing labor shortages into a broader legislative framework, though failing to create a substantial labor migration channel. It is fairly modest compared to the original ambitions. While a fairly pragmatic stance was pursued regarding economic migration, the new law seeks to reduce the category of family reunion. These previous attempts to recruit high-skill migrants in information technology, only modestly successful in filling about one-fifth of the annual quota, in some sense continued the temporarily limited labor contracts for workers from Central and Eastern Europe, signed in the early 1990s for the construction sector, hotels and catering (Menz 2001), and since then also for personal care.

Past efforts in the comparative migration policy literature have emphasized the importance of Germany's ethnically defined concept of citizenship (Brubaker 1992; skeptical: Joppke 1999; Weil 2002), highlighting the importance this paradigm has played in informing a refusal to acknowledge immigration as such and impede access to citizenship. Recent legislative changes notwithstanding, the main emphasis remains on ethnicity. Given the tainted nature of identity in light of Nazi racism, authoritarianism, and militarism, the contours of any such concept proved contested. East Germany sought to construct a national identity based on a radical rejection of fascism and on a stylized version of Marxist-Leninist ideology. The Bonn Republic possessed a feeble core of self-identification. Habermas's unconvincing attempt (1992) to call for constitutional patriotism (*Verfassungspatriotismus*) did not resonate outside the ivory tower.

However, attempts to construct a nonethnic cultural or political-ideological identity have not been particularly successful in postwar Germany. The imposed state socialist identity of eastern Germany failed to gain solid support. The mortar of the Bonn republic, rampant materialism, has been more successful in creating a Mercedes-Benz identity, which was first rejected, but has since been embraced with a vengeance by the 1968 generation.

While the Left failed to construct a republican French-style identity, the right traditionally had very little to offer as well.[17] The ill-inspired attempts by the Christian Democrats in 2001 to call for a German "dominant culture" (*Leitkultur*) to which migrants should aspire provoked little positive resonance (Nolte 2001).

United Kingdom

Though the political and ideological self-constitution process had been completed much earlier in Britain than elsewhere in continental Europe, migration access channels to Britain were not exclusively or indeed explicitly constructed for economic purposes. It could be argued that

Legacies of the Past and Currents of Change

economic considerations did play a role in permitting access on ostensibly humanitarian grounds, as in the case of East European Jewish migrants that arrived in the late nineteenth century and again in the 1930s (Schuster and Solomos 1999). Since citizens of commonwealth countries were legally considered British subjects, they were permitted unrestricted right to access and abode until the stringent 1962 and 1968 Commonwealth Immigrants Acts imposed "working voucher" requirements on noncitizens (Hansen 2000; Layton-Henry 1984). Subsequent reforms in the 1971 Immigration Act separated working permits from residence rights and rights to family reunion. The relatively early end to liberal positions should not be exclusively attributed to the politics of domestic race relations and the early politicization of nonwhite immigration, as is commonly argued (Layton-Henry 1984; Paul 1997; Rose et al. 1969), as the much more lackluster economic growth patterns played a very important role as well (Peach 1968) in helping account for an early end to theoretically strongly liberal migration policies regarding the Commonwealth, coupled with active labor solicitation primarily from Italy and Poland (Miles and Kay 1992), and, of course, Ireland (Jackson 1963).

While even during the intervening years there was a pronounced gulf between the theoretical right for New Commonwealth citizens to use their claim to British nationality and practical avenues of exercising such rights to migrate to Britain, subsequent citizenship reforms sought to curtail such rights to ever more limited circles, helping carve out the contours of a distinctively British and thus postcolonial citizenship concept, most explicitly in the shape of the 1981 British Nationality Act. The ethnic component of previous curtailment that continued to apply preferential treatment towards Old Commonwealth countries might be interpreted as a functional equivalent to the German basic Law's channels for ethnic Germans. Indeed, decolonization in the 1960s led to a wave of returning settlers. From a brief window of nearly unparalleled liberalism, British migration policy went to applying a highly restrictive set of rules, especially towards the New Commonwealth countries, many of which found themselves at the receiving end of visa requirements in 1986, the introduction of carrier sanctions in 1987 and the curtailment of family reunion rights in 1988. Similarly, over the past two decades, British asylum policy, once relatively generous, has been rendered more restrictive, with legislative initiatives in 1993, 1996, and 1999, as asylum seeker numbers exceeded 30,000 annually in the early 1990s and peaked at 44,000 in 1995 (Hansen 2000).

While the colonial concept of imposing political and cultural rule without the desire to assimilate the colonized fully-fledged into British culture as in the French case *theoretically* permits greater tolerance for multiculturalism, understood as the parallel existence of several cultures, and does not generate calls for assimilation, *in practice* the repercussions of the Salman Rushdie affair and more recently the 2005 attacks carried out on the London Underground spurred often heavily polemical debates about the rights and responsibilities of citizenship and highlighted unpalatable questions of integration regarding Muslims. The anxieties caused by perceived cultural Americanization (Gamble 2002), increasing movements towards regionalization and an uncertain postimperial self-concept taint and complicate attempts to map out decisively a distinct British identity.

It is somewhat intellectually lazy and dishonest to attribute British reticence about embracing the move towards a European migration policy exclusively to presumably deeply ingrained Euroskepticism. Ostensibly, the British refusal to adopt the Schengen agreement even after it became part of the *acquis*, following the Maastricht Treaty, and to opt out of Amsterdam's Title IV can be interpreted in this light. Insular, isolationist, and parochial strands in British political thinking, combined with delusions of grandeur nourished by now slightly anachronistic imagery of empire spawn a "go it alone" attitude, are reflections of this. Indeed, the British government, particularly during the 1980s, has always been highly skeptical of supranational authority over this policy domain. However, there are important modifications to be made to such facile interpretations of British migration policy: first, the concern over border control and the tightly related assumption that the island position affords ways of enforcing border controls not available to continental Europe is not entirely erroneous, coupled with peculiar migration channels resulting from postcolonial ties, enhanced by the hegemonic position of the English language. Second, subsequent British governments have not opposed multilateral policy coordination with their European counterparts, but have been simply wary to cede autonomy in this domain.

Italy

Italy has a rapidly growing immigrant population, but this development and its political regulation are of extremely recent provenance. Traditionally a country of emigration, Italian lawmakers have in the space of

Legacies of the Past and Currents of Change

20 years created the often somewhat internally contradictory contours of a migration regime that initially was inspired by French approaches. A major milestone was the initial 1986 Law 943. Italian migration legislation has become increasingly concerned with three priorities: first, implementing restrictive border control policy, despite obvious limitations due to the geographic position, implying very selective enforcement and, second, the integration of existing migrant communities, a goal partially pursued through legalization programs primarily by the political left. Third, the attempt has been made to manage labor migration by creating migration quotas, based on both functional and sectoral perceived needs and countries of origin (Basso and Perocco 2000). The latter have been used to "reward" and "punish" third countries for their efforts in joint migration control, border enforcement, and deportation. Asylum was historically largely embryonic and tightly confined to cover refugees from eastern Europe only.

The relatively recent nature of migration regulation is obviously conditioned by a history of generating emigration, rather than attracting immigration. Major emigration streams led from Italy to the United States, Canada, Australia, France, and Germany until the 1960s. The first foreign migrants to arrive came from former Italian colonies Somalia and Ethiopia in the 1980s. They were followed by arrivals from Albania and Yugoslavia. Only over the past few years has Italy become both transit country and destination for newcomers from the Middle East and East Asia (China, Sri Lanka), the Indian subcontinent, the Maghreb, and sub-Saharan Africa, as well as Latin America (Peru, Brazil, Dominican Republic).[18]

The skeletal migration regime was ill-prepared and the original 1986 legislation quickly amended by the 1990 *legge Martelli*, the 1995 decree no. 489, and the 1998 Law on the Regulation of Immigration and the Living Conditions of Foreigners. Though these legislative acts suggest a comparatively liberal basis of the asylum and migration regulation regime (Contel and De Biase 1999), more recent policy is much more restrictive, rendering any attempt to sketch a coherent legacy in Italian migration policymaking extremely difficult. Restrictive legislative packages are commonly combined with legalization programs for undocumented migrants. Though broadly in line with the pan-European trend to distinguish between useful labor migrants and burdensome others, no real clearly distinguishable unique legacy emerges.

Commencing with the 1998 Consolidation Act, and more recently with the passing of the Bossi-Fini Law of July 20, 2002 (legge no. 189), this much more restrictive stance is evident. Asylum recognition rates are extremely low, Italian authorities have often sought to prod and cajole refugees and asylum seekers to move across the northern borders. Local authorities, particularly in the south, are often poorly prepared to offer even basic services to arriving refugees.

In Italy itself, most foreign population is concentrated in the north and the center, especially the Lombardy, Veneto, Tuscany, and Lazio regions (MinofInt 2000). There is a close correlation between low unemployment and relatively high rates of foreign population, suggesting strong economic pull factors and labor market shortages. Foreigners are disproportionately employed in construction, agriculture, and the service sector in general (Andall and King 1999; Chiuri and Ferri 2001; MinofInt 2001).

Italian citizenship criteria are a mixture of elements of *ius sanguinis* and *ius solis*. Italian-born residents that can prove consistent residency in Italy can choose Italian citizenship on their 18th birthday, while ethnic Italians receive citizenship automatically. Descendants of Italian ancestors can claim citizenship, but only in combination with residency in Italy prior to the 18th birthday. There is little tradition of either integrating or assimilating substantial foreign populations (Andall 2002). The radical policy of Italianization employed by Mussolini towards the German-speaking minority in the northern region of South Tyrol has caused a significant backlash, and is thus unlikely to be repeated. Strong regional identities and the historical absence of a significant foreign population will undoubtedly influence any future attempt to define Italian identity and citizenship.

Given the historic absence of immigration and an absence of a clear legacy, the Italian regulation pattern has most recently been broadly in line with developments elsewhere in Europe, with noteworthy attempts to create national migration quotas with third countries in exchange for cooperation in immigration flow detainment and deportation efforts within the framework of bilateral treaties. In terms of the relationship with EU level regulation, a historically important emphasis was placed on securing intra-EU freedom of labor mobility, which was of particular interest to Italians during the postwar decades.

Ireland

Though legislation on the regulation of migration has existed since 1935 (Aliens Act) and 1946 (Aliens Order) respectively, only in 1999 was a comprehensive Immigration Act passed. This reflects the extremely recent nature of immigration as a statistically significant phenomenon in Ireland. Historically, the country has traditionally been a sending country of migrants to Australia, Britain, Canada, and the United States and has only experienced significant immigration since the mid-1990s, concurrent with the remarkable economic boom of that decade, often referred to as the "Celtic Tiger" phenomenon.

Ireland has had a Common Travel Area with the UK, permitting easy and uncontrolled travel and full rights for residency and work for citizens of the respective country, a regulation dating back to administrative agreements in 1922 and 1952 (Ryan 2001). This agreement is cited as one of the factors leading Ireland to reject entry into the Schengen regime (Fletcher 2003).

While Ireland had accepted a small annual quota of refugees from the UNHCR, asylum did not emerge as a significant category until the mid-1990s either. In 1993, there were 91 applications, in 1994, there were 362. This figure rose to 1,179 in 1996 and 3,883 in 1997 and had reached 10,938 by 2000 (Hughes and Quinn 2004). The Immigration Act of 1999 introduced a number of new restrictive measures in that area, including the payment of a minimal subsidence allowance, rather than standard welfare and a work permit for asylum seekers whose claims were being processed. In addition, police powers to stop and search and even "temporary arrests" of up to eight weeks have been introduced. The government further sought to "disperse" migrants throughout the country and thus alleviate the housing shortage in Dublin, without, however, making appropriate grants to local communities.

Irish citizenship regulation traditionally presented a generous mixture of *ius sanguinis* and *ius solis*, but its contours have recently been rendered more restrictive. Under the terms of the new Irish Nationality and Citizenship Act 2001, citizenship is acquired by birth and/or descent from at least one Irish parent. A more restrictive policy is applied to individuals acquiring citizenship through naturalization or marriage. Traditionally, the country has had a very ethnically defined self-concept and no experience with a significant foreign population. It is therefore difficult to predict how a movement towards a more encompassing concept will progress.

A significant exception to the generally restrictive migration policy is labor migration. The Irish government has actively solicited and encouraged significant labor immigration, both by highly skilled and by low-skilled migrants, focusing primarily on the tertiary sector, but with significant allowances for the still significant primary sector as well, regulated in a somewhat more state-led fashion by the 2003 Employment Permits Act. Work permits are available for IT and computing professionals and technicians, construction professionals (architects, engineers, building surveyors), and nurses. Individuals with these skills are granted work permits for up to two years, reflective of labor market shortages in these sectors. In addition, no limits on labor mobility from the EU-10 translate into employees from these countries serving as a labor pool (Ruhs 2005). Even before EU enlargement, significant numbers of Polish and Baltic workers were employed in Ireland, creating ethnic and professional networks that continue to transmit workers (Barrett et al. 2006).

Irish migration regulation is therefore broadly in line with the combination of restrictive asylum regulations and recent overtures towards labor migrants found elsewhere. In light of a booming economy, continuing labor market shortages in the primary and tertiary sectors and skill shortages in some sectors, it appears likely that these priorities will continue to be pursued. Though somewhat less isolationist than the UK, there are signs of British inspiration discernible in Irish migration policy. Also, due to the importance attached to the Common Travel Area, it would appear more likely that Ireland continues a policy of selective "opt-ins" into AMP, rather than jeopardize the existence of this zone by joining Schengen as a fully-fledged member. While it is therefore difficult to identify a distinct Irish legacy, current patterns in migration regulation display striking similarities with developments elsewhere in Europe.

Poland

Poland is also traditionally associated with emigration. Indeed, emigration continues, especially and worryingly so among the highly skilled, in fields such as medicine, banking, finance, and engineering. However, since the late 1990s, Poland has for the first time in decades attracted significant numbers of immigrations. It attracts both transit migration and labor migration (Okólski 1994*a*; Stola 2001). The former category sometimes involuntarily remains detained indefinitely; Poland is considered a "safe third country" by German authorities since 1993, meaning that transit migrants aiming to reach Germany via Polish territory can immediately be turned away and deported to Poland (Okólski 2006). Due to the implications of the Dublin II Treaty, asylum seekers, many interested in West European target destinations are also compelled to apply for asylum in the first EU country of entry and thus are received in Poland. Low-skill labor migration, primarily of importance in the primary sector, largely stems from Ukraine and much less so Russia and other successor republics to the USSR. Most of it is seasonal in nature or indeed of the regular transnational "commuting" (*pendel*) variety, for example small-scale trans-border commerce. There is also very limited high-skill labor migration from Western Europe and North America, especially aimed at managerial positions (Kicinger 2005; Okólski 2006).

It is often argued that Polish migration and asylum policy are largely products of top-down Europeanization (Geddes 2003), since implementing the EU *acquis* and conditionality placed the country in a weak negotiation position (Kicinger 2005; Kicinger et al. 2007). In addition, Polish regulation was archaic, outdated, and, in fields such as asylum, largely embryonic. Its largely ethnically based concept of citizenship was deliberately formulated to permit the repatriation of ethnic Poles, especially from areas claimed by the Soviet Union under the terms of the 1945 Potsdam Treaty, an issue still of relevance even today, but also from the classic countries of emigration, including notably the United States (Lodziński 2001). In that sense, one might expect the country to be largely a policy "taker." However, there are a number of other relevant factors bearing upon Polish migration policymaking, including significant unilateral pressure from the German government, sweetened by significant grants for the training and development of border enforcement. Also, Poland's close relationship with Ukraine has meant some reluctance to alienate both the government in Kiev and its own eastern population that enjoys close cultural, ethnic, economic, and political ties with Ukraine. Simply implementing EU policy was facilitated by a climate in which migration was neither particularly politicized nor empirically strongly visible (Kicinger et al. 2007). Though the latter has not changed much since, the former certainly has. There are no major initiatives to manage labor migration in the short-term, given high and persistent structural unemployment and an oversupply of unemployed manufacturing and agricultural workers.

In light of a somewhat atypical labor market situation, extremely recent and largely externally shaped migration policy and delegitimization affecting previous regulatory policy, it would appear unlikely that Poland will emerge as a major actor in bottom-up Europeanization. Its regulatory legacy cannot quite be described as *tabula rasa*; however, it is ultimately too recent and too strongly influenced by the EU *acquis* to be particularly potent in its own right.

Conclusion

This chapter has introduced the concept of the competition state as an invaluable heuristic device in charting the newly emergent neoliberalized European state, which is embracing new forms of migration management. Along with the tertiarization of the European economy and the transnationalization of the production process and structure, these changes combine to help account for new forms of migration management that unite restrictive policy towards unsolicited categories of migrants with carefully designated selection mechanisms for labor migrants corresponding to distinct national production systems, labor market regulation, and skill shortages. Different institutional systems of political economy will solicit different skill profiles of migrants.

The concept of securitization needs to be amended to reflect rhetoric recourses to economic competitiveness and its dependence on smooth transmission channels for human resources. It would be misleading to posit a mere link between repressive efforts to control external and internal borders or the often constructed relation between migration and politically, ethnically, and religiously motivated violence. Securitization ought to be conceptualized in broader terms, permitting economic considerations to be incorporated that are floated by organized business and commonly accepted and internalized by governments.

However, migration policymaking does not unfold on an empty canvas past regulatory legacies, concepts, ideas, norms, and values continue to shape contemporary regulatory efforts both at the EU and at the national level. At the European level, early efforts to coordinate migration policymaking have treated the policy portfolio from early on along issues such as transnational crime and terrorism. At the national level, distinct regulatory patterns exist in the more established countries of immigration, while in the newly emerging countries of immigration it is often very difficult to distill clear contours of any national legacies due to powerful external influences, muddled and unclear broad lines, and a related lack of continuity. While past historical patterns continue to shape contemporary policymaking attempts, European migration policy is marked by a punctured equilibrium and a paradigmatic change. The new forms of managed migration hinge on differences in the system of political economy. However, policymaking also unfolds over several venues, arenas, and layers and proceeds both in a top-down and bottom-up fashion, a process which shall be examined in more detail in the following chapter.

Notes

1. Note the appeal by two migration scholars not usually associated with political economy questions seriously to consider developments in the European labor market seriously (Favell and Hansen 2002).
2. It is notable that the very concept of competitiveness is not uncontested when applied to nations in a vulgar neo-mercantilist fashion, as Krugman (1994, 1996) demonstrated in a lucid critique of some of the US literature that helped shape policy in the 1980s and 1990s (Porter 1990; Thurow 1999).
3. It is no coincidence that the UK, as the most archetypical European representative of the competition state, was the first European country to implement a points system.
4. By 1970, when the temporary ban on labor mobility ended, Italy, the only country potentially interested in taking advantage of it, had already concluded bilateral labor treaties with France and Germany and some of the first generation of migrants were already returning. Similarly, Irish emigration to the UK, another major incident of intra-EU migration, already benefited from a common travel area long before both countries joined the EU in 1973. Linguistic and cultural barriers stood in the way of massive intra-EU migration, as did the absence of major wage and income gaps in the early years, with the possible exception of Italy and Ireland. Newcomers Greece, Spain, and Portugal were all subject to a seven-year temporary ban on labor mobility. Small numbers of highly skilled professionals, students, pensioners, and the adventurously inclined apart (Favell 2004, forthcoming), intra-EU migration continues to be low today, notwithstanding the divergent economic performance and unemployment figures among EU levels.
5. The Council of Europe had advocated the implementation of a common EU asylum policy as early as 1971, while the Commission proposed common measures against illegal immigration (Geddes 2000*b*: 55). The German government suggested common migration measures in January 1973. But in the wake of the economic slowdown of the early 1970s, other national governments were unwilling to Europeanize this domain and preferred taking a national and restrictive approach.
6. See also Koslowski (1998) and Huysmans (1998).
7. By 1985, West Germany was attracting 73,832 and thus nearly half of the EU15's 159,176 asylum seekers, rising to 193,063 out of 403,496 respectively for 1990 (Eurostat 1996, cited in Levy 1999: 16). Asylum applications had been already inching towards the mark of 200,000 per annum by the late 1980s. They had increased tenfold between 1983 and 1990. By 1991, 256,110 applications were lodged, with an all time high of 438,840 in 1992 (Marshall 2000). The Kohl government was particularly keen on stepping up communal efforts at policing and securing external borders, exchanging information transnationally, and, where possible, dispensing refugees and asylum seekers

across Europe so as to avoid the sort of concentration in one country experienced by West Germany in the 1980s.
8. Since 2004, qualified majority voting is exercised in application to asylum, but not to issues of labor migration.
9. "...any future cooperation, association or equivalent agreement which the European Union...concludes with any country should include a clause on joint management of migration flows and on compulsory readmission in the event of illegal immigration." (Art. 33). Consider also the openly menacing rhetoric of Art. 35: "{It is}...necessary to carry out a systematic assessment of relations with third countries which do not cooperate in combating illegal immigration. That assessment will be taken into account in relations between the European Union and its member states and the countries concerned, in all relevant areas. Inadequate cooperation by a country could hamper the establishment of closer relations between that country and the Union."
10. In 2001, the Commission had (unsuccessfully) proposed a council directive on economic migration (COM 2001, 386 final, July 11, 2001), entitled "Council Directive on the conditions of entry and residence of third-country nationals for the purpose of paid employment and self-employed economic activities." In 2005, the Commission produced a Green paper on managing legal economic migration (COM 2004, 811 final, January 11).
11. Decision No. 572/2007/EC of the European Parliament and of the Council of May 23, 2007 establishing the European Return Fund for the period 2008–13 (OJ L 144 of June 6, 2007, p. 45)
12. See for example the Regulation (EC) No. 1905/2006 of the European Parliament and of the Council of December 18, 2006 establishing a financing instrument for development cooperation (OJ L 378 of December 27, 2006) and the earlier Regulation (EC) No. 491/2004 of the European Parliament and of the Council of March 10, 2004 establishing a program for financial and technical assistance to third countries in the areas of migration and asylum (AENEAS) (OJL 80 of March 18, 2004, p. 1).
13. It should be noted, however, that the Schengen agreement can in theory be temporarily suspended by any signatory state to reintroduce identity document controls at the border and prevent political dissidents from entering in the run-up to major demonstrations.
14. The official name is European Agency for the Management of Operational Cooperation at the External Borders of the Member States of the European Union (Council Regulation (EC) 2007/2004 (October 26, 2004; OJ L 349/November 5, 2004), amended by Regulation (EC) 863/2007 of the European Parliament and of the Council of July 11, 2007 establishing a mechanism for the creation of Rapid Border Intervention Teams.
15. Prussia had adopted an ethnical citizenship concept as early as 1805 related both to exclusionary motives—seeking to obstruct access to citizenship for

ethnic Poles—and to the ambition to include ethnic Germans outside of the actual Prussian territory.
16. Grundgesetz für die Bundesrepublik Deutschland, Bundesgesetzblatt I (1949), Arts. 16, 116.
17. In fact, one could argue that most of the internationally successful exponents of (West) German culture, whether in social science (Frankfurt School), literature (Boell, Grass), art (Wenders, Fassbinder), or popular music (Kraftwerk), have defined themselves in political opposition to the Bonn republic.
18. Major source countries of immigration include Albania (142,066), China (60,075), the Philippines (65,353), Egypt (32,841), Yugoslavia (36,823), Morocco (159,599), Tunisia (45,680), and Romania (68,929) out of a total foreign population of 1,388,153 million, including some 151,798 EU citizens (absolute figures as of December 31, 2000, collected by the Ministry of the Interior).

3

National Actors and European Solutions: The Contours of Conflict

AMP policymaking is a politically embattled process, unfolding over several institutional arenas and bridging European, national, and, in some instances, even regional levels. Not only does it touch upon some of the most central preoccupations of public authority, but it is also a policy domain where decision-making processes are commonly shrouded in secrecy. In fact, the decision to negotiate at the European level and thus "venue shop" (Guiraudon 2000*a*) can itself in some instances be seen as an attempt to avoid the more intense scrutiny of the media and nongovernmental actors in national capitals as well as a legal authority of courts. EU member state governments prefer the discretion and relative insulation that decision-making in the Council of Ministers and even more so the European Council affords, where like-minded homologues and a congenial atmosphere of *esprit du corps* are formatted. Documentation on the position of member states routinely anonymizes contributions. Until most recently the role of the European Parliament was limited to a consultative role and unanimous decision-making in the Council engendered a culture of consensus-oriented decision-making processes, a legacy which continues to influence decision-makers.

This chapter examines the insights offered by the Europeanization approach to the study of migration policy. It proceeds to develop this study's key contention in more detail, analyzing how nongovernmental actors seek to influence the respective governmental positions both as an end in itself and in anticipation of these positions setting the agenda for EU AMP. Finally, it applies these conceptual tools to the long-winded genesis of three key AMP directives, focusing on family reunion, asylum reception, and labor migration.

Europeanization proceeds in both a top-down and a bottom-up fashion. Both existing categories can be refined, while important amendments are proposed regarding bottom-up or "uploading" processes, particularly through agenda-setting (Héritier 1996), and the minimization of transaction costs through the promotion of national initiatives.

Labor market interest associations are interested in feeding migration into certain economic sectors or indeed segments of the labor market, but their ability to do so hinges on organizational characteristics and often underdeveloped access channels to the relevant ministry of interior affairs. Their interests derive from the systems of political economy and the labor market structure they are embedded in. Humanitarian NGOs, by contrast, are generally less concerned with labor migration policy design and focus their efforts on the reconfiguration of political asylum regulation. Interest group literature applied to migration (Freeman 1986, 2001, 2006; more general: Olson 1971; Richardson 1993) has generally argued that advocates of migration tend to dominate the political debate owing to their superior organization of characteristics in comparison to the often diffuse and poorly organized opponents. This is an insight that requires some refinement and additional development. In addition, the institutional structure of actors mediates the influence they can hope to command. In a number of European countries, trade unions have lost members and institutional power, severely jeopardizing their ability to influence government policy and to resist employer initiatives. As critics of the concept of civil society (Brand 2000) remind us, NGOs can also become co-opted and hijacked by governments, seriously compromising their agenda.

Decision-Making in a Multilevel System of Governance: Conceptualizing the Politics of Europeanized AMP

The top-down effects of European Union (EU) membership on state–society relations, domestic policies, and institutions have recently attracted significant scholarly attention from both sides of the Atlantic (Bache 2008; Börzel 2002; Héritier et al. 2001; Radaelli 2000, 2003; Schmidt 1996). This strand focuses more on everyday politics, rather than the grand contours of European integration, thus clarifying the nature, circumstances, and degree of the "central penetration of national systems of governance" (Olsen, 2002). Though liberal intergovernmentalists argued that European integration *strengthens* national governments, as it helped them negotiate in Brussels insulated from the demands of competing national or subnational actors (Moravcsik 1998), the empirical findings of the Europeanization literature cast some doubt over this claim. Europeanization therefore proceeds in a top-down fashion, but it may be amended to include bottom-up processes of agenda-setting and the provision of blueprints or national models. While governments have sought to escape to Brussels in creating AMP to avoid the unwelcome influence of national actors, especially courts, such insulation will not and cannot be complete and national positions will be influenced by nongovernmental actors at the national level. EU level NGOs are not central to this inquiry and indeed past scholarly efforts have revealed that these actors tend to be fairly weak and ineffective (Favell 1998; Geddes 2000*a*).

Europeanization is generally conceived as the internalization of Europe, thus not only incorporating the "emergence and development at the European level of distinct structures of governance, that is, of political, legal, and social institutions associated with political problem-solving that formalizes interactions among the actors, and of policy networks specializing in the creation of authoritative European rules" (Cowles et al. 2001: 2) or through straightforward top-down implementation and adaptation processes that derive "from European decisions and impacting member states' policies and political and administrative structures" (Héritier et al. 2001: 3), but also through ways in which the institutional rules of the game are affected at the national level (Cowles, Caporaso, and Risse 2001; Jordan and Liefferink 2004; Knill 2001; Knill and Lehmkuhl 1999) or even the matter in which the identity of national actors becomes affected (Jordan 2002). Radaelli's (2003, 30) highly encompassing and top-down oriented definition includes "processes of a) construction b) diffusion, and c) institutionalization of formal and informal rules, procedures, policy paradigms, styles, 'ways of doing things', and shared beliefs and norms which are first defined and consolidated in the making of EU public policy and politics and then incorporated in the logic of domestic discourses, identities, political structures, and public policies."

Knill and Lehmkuhl (1999) suggest adding a third category to Scharpf's (1996) "negative" and "positive" modes of integration, namely, a framing mode, which does not propose a direct EU model, but that indirectly affects the national level by opening up room for entrepreneurial domestic actors who can support their activity and discourse by invoking future EU activity or can legitimize their course of action with reference to the EU, attracting associated sympathy or indeed antipathy. In that sense, the EU serves as a reference point (Hanf and Soetendorp 1998). Börzel and Risse (2003, 63ff) propose focusing on squaring two separate logics of action, drawing on earlier institutional work by March and Olsen (1998). They posit that Europeanization needs to be understood as a synthesis of a logic of consequentialism on the one hand that creates new venues for political battles and changes the incentive structure and rules of the game, and a logic of appropriateness on the other, which affects the socialization and learning processes of actors and may include "norm internalization" and the "development of new identities." The latter is akin to Bourdieu's concept (1990) of "habitus."

Radaelli (2000, 2003) is somewhat critical of Börzel and Risse's definition and especially the strong focus on "goodness of fit" as a measure of whether Europeanization will cause domestic change. Summarizing earlier research, he proposes four initial categories to measure the impact of top-down Europeanization: inertia, absorption, transformation, and retrenchment. He usefully suggests a number of intervening variables, notably veto players and technocratic capture potential, and suggests stronger focus in future research on the role of advocacy coalitions.

Table 3.1 summarizes the key strides in top-down Europeanization literature and indicates the amendments to it this book suggests at the theoretical level and illustrates by example.

One commonly neglected insight is the realization that Europeanization constitutes a "shaped process, not a passively encountered process"

Table 3.1. Conceptualizing top-down Europeanization (cf. Börzel and Risse 2003; Knill and Lehmkuhl 1999; Menz 2005*a*; Radaelli 2003; Scharpf 1996)

Top-down Europeanization
"Positive": presents pan-European solution (e.g. directive); mandatory implementation → Leads to: inertia, absorption, transformation, retrenchment → Outcome depends on: "goodness of fit" and role of intervening variables, notably veto players, technocratic capture potential, and role of advocacy coalitions → Suggested amendments to the literature: posit that bottom-up Europeanization and "framing the agenda" is important; suggest ways of assessing organizational power of interest groups, which conditions impact; pre-existing policy legacies need to be accounted for, interaction effects with existing regulation can be considerable and are underspecified
"Negative": impact of economic liberalization, presents no single model for adoption → Leads to: regulatory competition → Outcome: cannot be readily predicted, but reconfigures domestic opportunity structures → Suggested amendments to the literature: outcome can be predicted through assessment of power of relevant policy actors
"Framing": no clear or very vague (possible future) EU activity underway in a given policy → Leads to: offers room for maneuver for policy entrepreneurship by domestic actors' coalitions

(Wallace, 2000: 370) and that it is "circular, rather than unidirectional, and cyclical rather than one off" (Goetz 2002: 4). Rather than simply conceptualizing Europeanization as a process of imposed implementation or "learning to cope with Europe," it is more appropriate to conceive of it as a two-way process entailing both top-down *and* bottom-up processes, unleashing potential for new and dynamic games played out in several arenas, often concurrently (Putnam 1988; earlier: Snyder 1977). Europeanization involves "new opportunities to exit from domestic constraints, either to promote certain policies, or to veto others, or to secure information advantages" Goetz and Hix (2001, 10). Börzel and Risse (2000) suggested the concepts of upload and download; while these terms are heuristically useful, they rather infelicitously imply a degree of automaticity that is rarely present and denies the reality of protracted political battles. I argue that Europeanization urgently needs to be (re)considered as an often heavily embattled two-way process, spawning several institutional arenas and involving a multitude of governmental and nongovernmental actors. Notwithstanding efforts to engage in venue shopping and "hide" in Brussels, governmental actors are engaged in two types of games: on one level, they negotiate the elaboration of new EU regulation with other governmental actors in EU venues, while on a second level, they face domestic nongovernmental actors in the creation of domestic policy. One crucial weakness in current Europeanization debates concerns temporality and, relatedly, ontology: it is commonly assumed that the second process follows the first in direct sequence. Yet logically there may be temporal overlap or even synchronicity. More importantly, however, the second process may indeed *precede* the first in bottom-up Europeanization, where national actors attempt to shape the agenda employing their own national regulatory model as a template for future European regulation.

If we take the suggestion seriously that Europeanization is a two-way process, we need to consider the ontologically—and usually temporary—preceding process of bottom-up Europeanization seriously, as it may help set the broad parameters of the debate at the EU and "frames the agenda." In other words, rather than the EU shaping national processes, policies, and identities, close analytical attention needs to focus on the logically prior process involving the opposite causal flow. This is, of course, especially true with respect to a "new" European policy field such as migration and asylum, which has only recently attracted scholarly attention influenced by considerations of Europeanization (Faist and Ette 2007; Graziano and Vink 2007; Vink 2005). Therefore, the analytical focus needs to be recast so as to embrace the national negotiation positions that inform member state representatives at the EU level. In doing so, the organizational power of interest groups which influences governmental positions needs to receive the scholarly attention it merits, as earlier work on the domestic–international divide suggested. In that vein, Helen Milner (1992: 494) argued that the "national interest will be the sum of the preferences of different interest groups as weighted by their access to policy-making institutions." Another important amendment that bottom-up Europeanization can contribute is an incorporation of pre-existing policy legacies that continue to shape national regulatory patterns as well as governmental negotiation positions. Such path-dependent effects need to be better accounted for than is currently the case in the Europeanization literature. These pre-existing legacies in migration and asylum regulation, sketched in Chapter 2, strongly shape governmental preferences. While the existing literature recognizes that top-down Europeanization may lead to subtle "absorption", radical paradigmatic "transformation", or even "retrenchment", exceptionally directed in the opposite direction, it is important to recognize that such preexisting paradigms will have an important bottom-up effect. We will also note that the interactive effects of new EU rules with existing regulation ("absorption") can be considerable and are somewhat underspecified. The pressing need for greater theoretical sophistication in charting these interactive effects becomes evident given the frequency of this pattern in empirical terms outside of policy domains where clear prescriptive models are designed, such as environmental policy, a common empirical application of scholarly efforts in this vein (Börzel 2002; Jordan and Liefferink 2004; Knill 2001; Knill and Lenschow 1998). But even in this policy domain (Jordan 2002), and much more so in most others, including labor and social policy (Falkner et al. 2005; Menz 2005a), these interactive processes are crucial, warranting close examination of interest groups.

Nongovernmental actors will play an active and pivotal role in affecting "what determines the responses, adaptability and robustness of domestic institutions, including their ability to ignore, buffer, redefine or exploit external European-level pressures" (Olsen 2002: 933). Knill and Lehmkuhl (2002: 260ff.) emphasize in subsequent work that changes in the national regulatory environment due to Europeanization are most likely to occur if there is no dominant domestic actor coalition. By contrast, change will occur if such a dominant actor coalition embraces the EU impetus. But this ignores the possibility that interest organizations may both be present and very potent, but simply not interested or even adamantly opposed to a European regulation. Certain employer organizations may well prefer national migration schemes to European plans they cannot as easily influence. Similarly, humanitarian NGOs may consider the national regulatory arena preferable to the more opaque and impermeable European level. Interestingly, actors may anticipate battles at the EU level they would prefer to avoid and thus battle for maintaining control over the *arena* as much as over the *content* of regulation. It becomes crucial how EU impact affects "the changing distribution of resources (and ultimately power) between domestic actors" (Radaelli, 2000), including state–society relations. In examining the politics of the domestic level game, it is helpful to conceptualize "advocacy coalitions composed of people of various organizations who share a set of normative and causal beliefs and who often act in concert" (Sabatier 1988: 133). Sabatier's emphasis on belief systems that such coalitions will attempt to translate into governmental policy is useful also because it allows a focus on the ideational glue underpinning such coalitions, whereby ideational chance will disrupt or even dismantle the core of the coalition. Advocacy coalitions help frame debates ideologically, thematically, and rhetorically, aiming to "adopt a strategy(s) envisaging one or more institutional innovations which it feels will further its objectives" (Sabatier 1988: 133). Framing the debate and helping shape the vocabulary, notably in the form of intertwining economic migration with notions of competitiveness, are key avenues for influencing public debates and public policy. Even in the absence of a clear EU model to emulate, it is useful to refer to EU debates or suggest ideational similarities of one's own agenda with future or proposed EU initiatives so as to garner additional "EU legitimacy," in line with Knill and Lehmkuhl's third category (2002). But such constructed affinity with European plans is not always strictly necessary and the existence of a punctured equilibrium permits a policy window for new policy proposals to move onto the agenda, especially regarding labor migration, where new perceived problems such as demographic shortcomings, skill shortages, structural transformations of production processes, and the ideological shift towards the competition state congregate to create amiable conditions for certain perceptions of the problem, a proposal for solutions and political receptivity (cf. Kingdon 1984). It is much more difficult to construct similar claims regarding asylum regulation, rendering the advocacy of more liberal policy equally more challenging.

Bottom-up Europeanization is a promising line of scholarly inquiry. Taking Europeanization seriously as a research agenda for the next era in European studies rather than a mere fad, the scope of analytical inquiry needs to be broadened to cover the entire genesis of European policy, which inevitably involves "messy" interactive processes, spilling over and being played out in several arenas, often simultaneously, rarely in synchronicity in the Jungian sense. Public policy in particular—but other aspects of Europeanization as well—does not simply emerge out of thin air at the EU level, but is generally the mutated offspring of national initiatives, heritage, patterns of regulation and governance. In the migration policy domain, the Committee on Immigration and Asylum is an important consultation forum where Commission officials and member state representatives liaise to exchange positions, ideas, and interests, thus assuring that Commission draft policy is well informed of potential veto positions and veto players (interview EUR-COM-1). There is no automatism in the increase in EU competence; the European arena relies on the interaction of actors who possess a strong interest in molding policymaking according to their preferences. Properly understood, we need to distinguish between two separate modes of bottom-up Europeanization. First, EU member states may respond at the national level to top-down Europeanization by implementing national reregulation, which may not, of course, directly contravene EU policy, but may significantly modify, alter, or even distort the original EU impetus. This is a process not captured by the top-down Europeanization and consists of the formulation of what I have elsewhere referred to as national response strategies (Menz 2005*a*) to European top-down deregulatory efforts or negative integration in Scharpf's sense (1996). The second major avenue of bottom-up Europeanization consists of actively shaping deliberations at the EU level to influence the eventual outcome according to national preferences. This aspect of Europeanization remains somewhat bereft of scholarly attention. Modifying Radaelli's definition (2003: 30) of top-down Europeanization, and building on Börzel's concepts (2002: 194) of pace-setting, foot-dragging, and fence-sitting, this second avenue can thus be defined as *processes at the EU level that (a) aim to influence other governmental actors, (b) diffuse one's own agenda and preferences to other actors, (c) color, shape, modify, influence, or even dominate to varying degrees emerging EU formal and informal rules, procedures, policy paradigms, styles, and shared beliefs and norms by making use of formal and informal EU venues, themselves influenced by national patterns and traditions of regulation in the relevant policy domains and the interaction of national governmental actors and nongovernmental actors.*

While it may be promising to consider top-down Europeanization as an instance of Gourevitchian (1978) second image reversed processes, as

Radaelli suggests (2003, 34), it would appear just as fruitful to borrow from the international relations literature in exploring the politics of bottom-up Europeanization. Exposing the notion of national interest to careful scrutiny and disaggregating it, the role of domestic nongovernmental actors engaged in various forms of advocacy coalitions as domestic sources of governmental preferences emerges as a clear and central theme from studies in this vein (Fioretos 2001; Gourevitch 1996; Keohane and Milner 1996; Milner 1997; Rogowski 1989).

It is recognized that member states can enjoy significant advantages in setting the agenda or "pace setting" (Börzel 2002; Héritier 1996), as they minimize their own transaction and adaptation costs that arise in the process of implementation of EU directives. The "first mover advantage" may thus motivate governmental actors to take adequate steps to ensure that their own propositions provide the basis for future EU regulation. However, such process needs to involve coalition-building, given the requirement to secure a minimum of a qualified majority (or indeed unanimity) in the Council of Ministers. Here, the role of domestic actors needs to be taken into consideration again: where such actors sense an opportunity to shape not only the position of the corresponding national governmental actors but indeed the very future of EU regulation in a given issue-area *via* "their" respective national governments, their advocacy efforts will be more pronounced.

As Börzel and Risse mention (2003, 62), it is very unlikely and indeed extremely difficult for any one actor or even coalition to be successful all the time in agenda-setting. Indeed, with the requirement to secure a compromise solution, there is a trend towards non-intrusive lowest common denominator solutions. In some policy fields, there is a pronounced likelihood of the Commission pursuing lowest common denominator policy design in a form of anticipatory obedience, as common informal consultations with member states, such as in the framework of the CIA, are aimed at anticipating member state reactions, but may also impede ambition. The Commission can also resort to various tactical maneuvers to soften resistance and garner support, permitting, for example, "grandfather" clauses, implying no change to existing national regulatory deviations that are "grandfathered in," "moonshine" clauses that permit generous adjustment periods during which national regulations may continue to be applied before they fade out, and numerous other forms of abrogation and exception. It is obvious that proposed regulations need to appeal as widely as possible even outside the coalition of national actors within which they originate.[1]

National Actors and European Solutions

In pleading for the importance of the national arena and emphasizing the crucial role of national-level interest groups, I move beyond the recently formulated insight that the impact of top-down Europeanization is conditioned by the changes of the strategic position of domestic actors (Dimitrova and Steunenberg 2000; Knill 2001), as I argue that the organizational power, including government access, of domestic interest groups *combined with these actors' preferences* critically shape the overall policy outcome. Domestic level interest groups will attempt to shape national strategies. But, challenging previous work in this vein (Radaelli 2003: 40–2), it is maintained that these preferences are not necessarily shaped by "regulatory competition" nor is the outcome of the changing equilibrium decisively shaped by Europeanization. However, in considering bottom-up Europeanization this organizational power needs to be taken into consideration as a crucial variable as well, with access to government playing an important role *ex ante*. Table 3.2 below summarizes the discussion about bottom-up Europeanization.

The Europeanization literature deals primarily with the EU-15 and commonly neglects the twelve newcomers. Grabbe (2003) posits that because of the added coercive element arising from conditionality, an extensive definition of the *acquis*, the condensed time frame, and the challenges arising from the repercussions of an economic and political transition process executed at breakneck speed, the Central and Eastern European countries are not in a strong position to resist top-down Europeanization. However, she cautions against confusing the EU's effects with unrelated transition processes and assuming a regulatory *tabula rasa*. Other

Table 3.2. Conceptualizing bottom-up Europeanization (cf. Börzel and Risse 2003; Héritier 1996; Knill and Lehmkuhl 1999; Menz 2005*a*; Radaelli 2003)

Bottom-up Europeanization
Member states compete in process of "uploading" their own regulations to save transaction costs and avoid compliance problems → Leads to: coalition building, "first mover advantages," offers room for maneuver for enterprising domestic actors coalitions → Outcome: regulatory patchwork of EU rules and regulations depending on who moves first and is most successful in agenda-setting; coalition-building important; same actor(s) unlikely to be successful all the time, hence "patchwork" style of regulations → Suggested amendments to the literature: underspecified area, in instances of QMV proposals need to be presented in a fashion that appeals to all members, for example through use of presentation as "best practice"; OMC permits "testing the water" Currently, role of national (and subnational) actors is somewhat underspecified in influencing government negotiation position *ex ante*, such influence, it is argued, depends on institutional power and access to governmental actors

scholars take issue or at least emphasize auxiliary variables in shaping conditionality (Jacoby 2004; Schimmelfennig et al. 2003; Schimmelfennig and Sedelmaier 2005). Top-down Europeanization is extremely influential in migration policy because pre-existing AMP is part of the *acquis* and because migration has been of particular concern to the EU-15 since the early 1990s with early attempts made to externalize own border controls (Grabbe 2001; Lavenex 2001). Migration policy was seriously underdeveloped—though not nonexistent—throughout the EU-12 for obvious historical reasons, making this policy domain particularly susceptible to wholesale policy transfer from Brussels. Due to these particular circumstances, top-down Europeanization effects of AMP in migration policy will be profound in the EU-12. At the EU level, governmental actors have only acted as equals since accession in 2004, but the power dissymmetry that arose out of the mandatory requirement to implement the *acquis* wholesale may have created a legacy that impedes agenda-setting and coalition-building by newcomer governmental actors who are not perceived as equals: "the overall reward of membership still outweighs the costs of adopting suboptimal rules on movement of workers and border protection" (Grabbe 2005: 128). In addition, given the relatively modest scope of their own regulation in migration policy—often antiquated, rudimentary, or indeed simply the product of implementing the EU *acquis* over the course of the 1990s in preparation for accession (Grabbe 2005)—their potential for successfully brokering agenda-setting drawing on their own national traditions and regulations is obviously seriously compromised.

Other factors peculiar to Central and Eastern Europe include the infancy of the humanitarian NGO sector, while labor market interest associations play important roles, despite uneven retrenchment by trade unions as a result of economic liberalization. Civil society is thus characterized by relatively weak homegrown actors and by transplanted representatives of internationally active NGOs and intergovernmental organizations (IGOs). In such an environment, successful advocacy coalitions are highly unlikely to emerge. Governmental actors will be less constrained by non-governmental actors at the national level, but they will be in a relatively weak negotiation position at the European level.

Europeanization must not be confused with policy transfer or policy learning. To claim that horizontal policy transfer can be subsumed under the Europeanization label is to engage in fallacious concept stretching. As will be analyzed in Chapters 4 and 5, recent immigration countries have sometimes adopted aspects of their migration regulation from other countries that were perceived to share cultural, geographic, economic, or political similarities, including similar structures of the political economy and the welfare state. While it might be crude to posit the existence of a distinct Mediterranean model of migration management, Italian policymakers have been influenced by French initiatives. Likewise, though mainly for historical reasons and aided by the existence of a Common Travel Area, Irish immigration legislation has been heavily influenced by developments in the UK, a pattern that continues to this very day (interview IRL-GOV-1). Irish policymakers examined UK recruitment programs for professionals in health while devising their own; a similar logic applies to the liberal interpretation of labor mobility from the EU-12. The contention made is that such policy transfer is strongly facilitated—though not caused—through similarities in the structure of the political economy; thus, latecomers to immigration look to structurally similar examples for inspiration in their own migration policy design.

Finally, top-down Europeanization in migration may also proceed *negatively* in Scharpf's sense (1996), involving principally the liberalization of labor mobility and transnational service provision in the European Union as part of the Single Market program. Implemented on January 1, 1970 following a transition period and rediscovered as two of the so-called four freedoms of the Maastricht Treaty, a series of events and key ECJ decisions coincided to revive it only in the early 1990s. As I have explored in great detail elsewhere (Menz 2005*a*), on March 27, 1990 the ECJ "Rush Portuguesa" ruling[2] rendered null and void the decision of the French immigration office OMI to impose work visa requirements on Portuguese workers posted to a construction site near Paris as subcontractors to French conglomerate Bouygues.

The implications of the LSP for countries with high wage levels are manifold. Companies from low-wage countries gain access to markets in the service industries of high-wage countries, and do so with a considerable competitive advantage. National regulatory mechanisms, which in the past had been used to control access to the labor market, market entry, and thus foreign competition more generally, and immigration, were overridden and rendered obsolete by the LSP. At the same time, the Court made clear that

... communal law does not forbid that the member states apply their legislation or their collectively agreed wage regulations to all persons performing a paid activity upon their territory ... (author's translation from the French)

This ruling thus opened room for national response strategies to negative top-down Europeanization.

Migration touches upon the perceived core competencies of the nation-state, such as the regulation of territorial access, the composition of its constituents, and mechanisms of internal and external inclusion and exclusion. This perception along with the related legacy of securitization have meant that governmental actors have been extremely reluctant to permit nongovernmental actors substantial input, even in countries with legacies of neocorporatist patterns of governance in other policy sectors. However, both in top-down and bottom-up Europeanization processes, governments cannot insulate themselves entirely from the influence of nongovernmental actors, though they may attempt to do so. The analytical framework for conceptualizing two-way Europeanization processes is thus applied to a particularly challenging empirical case study, satisfying the conditions of a "critical case" (Eckstein 1975).

Lobbying at Home and in Brussels

In their attempts to shape government policy, nongovernmental actors enjoy different degrees of access and potential influence, depending on two main factors: the *institutional framework* of the state–society nexus and actors' *internal organizational characteristics*. The first factor relates to institutionalized forms of dialogue between governmental and nongovernmental actors situated along the pluralism-neocorporatism continuum. Such dialogue may even extend to the granting of considerable autonomy and self-governance, as in the case of neocorporatist self-administration of policy domains, notably in labor and social policy affairs. Some governments may be inclined to consult nongovernmental actors active in migration policy in more or less formalized consultation fora. Elsewhere, authorities may be cooperating with nongovernmental charitable actors in the distribution and provision of services to new migrants. However, fashionable rhetorical invoking of civil society engagement and the privatization of migration flow management notwithstanding, competence over migration and asylum policy is so jealously guarded by governments that nongovernmental actors may engage in lobbying, but they are not offered comanagement. However, neocorporatist traditions in labor and social market policy become relevant where and if migration management affects this domain. *Ceteris paribus*, we would thus expect trade unions and employers to be more likely to be both consulted and involved in migration policymaking in such instances in those European countries with neocorporatist patterns and institutions of interest intermediation. Among our cases this includes Germany and more recently Ireland and Italy, but not Britain, France, and Poland (Ferner and Hyman 1997; Hardiman 2002; Lehmbruch and Schmitter 1981; Penninx and Roosblad 2000; Regini 2000; Schmitter 1979; Siaroff 1999; Stark and Bruszt 1998).

Internal organizational characteristics of interest associations are themselves a function of three key components: first, *degree of centralization* and hierarchy, which can be measured by the number of actors. A large number of actors representing one camp or cause shall be considered an indicator of a low degree of centralization. Second, *internal cohesion* matters, based on the nature of internal command structures: can the core control its sectoral members? Do the sectoral members have input into decision-making? How is the flow between umbrella organization and components constituted? Third, *representation among clientele* is pivotal, measured in terms of the percentage of total potential constituents that are members of the interest associations.

It follows that highly centralized and internally coherent interest groups with a strong base among their clientele can be expected to be more successful in influencing governmental actors. With regard to labor market interest associations, scores on all three indicators can be extrapolated from the industrial relations literature (Bohle and Greskovits 2004; Crowley 2004; Ebbinghaus and Visser 2000; Hyman and Ferner 1997; Streeck and Hassel 2004; Traxler et al. 2001). None of the actors receive high scores. German unions and employers are characterized by a "medium" level of organizational strength, as are employers in the UK, France, Italy, and Ireland. However, unions in these four countries receive only low scores, as do both employers and unions in Poland. Table 3.3 displays the scores.

Table 3.3. Organizational power of labor market interest associations

	Unions	Employers	Neocorporatist legacy
UK	Low	Medium	No
France	Low	Medium	No
Germany	Medium	Medium	Yes
Italy	Low	Medium	Yes, recently
Poland	Low	Low	No
Ireland	Low	Medium	Yes, recently

For humanitarian NGOs, representation among clientele is somewhat less important; many groups represent migrants only indirectly and their activists and supporter base do not predominantly consist of migrants. However, *internal cohesion* and *degree of centralization* remain important variables with which to assess organizational power. Commonly relative low scores on both impair the impact and lobbying capacity in institutional terms. Hence, well-organized highly professionalized humanitarian NGOs can be expected to exert more vociferous and influential lobbying efforts. Prominent examples include Amnesty International (Favell 1998) and national refugee organizations cooperating with the European Council of Refugees and Exiles (ECRE) (Geddes 2000*a*). Obviously, groups with anarchist roots are unlikely to cooperate with the very state apparatus whose authority they question and oppose. Indeed, in cooperating with government authorities in the administration and provision of housing, education, training, and social services, there lies a certain danger of being co-opted. The political independence and legitimacy of groups such as ECRE who are cofinanced by the European Commission may also be questioned (Table 3.4).

In the literature on interest group representation and collective action (Olson 1971; Ostrom 1990), it has been argued that organized interest groups with sometimes very particular interests will shape a public policy agenda more successfully—or, by extension, be better apt at resisting governmental policy they oppose (cf. Pierson 1994) than scantly organized diffuse groups of individuals. Freeman (1986) has extended this argument to explain why in the US-organized interest groups with particular interests—especially employers striving to liberalize US immigration policy, permitting a wider pool of labor supply and presumably a downward pressure on wages, and also ethnic lobby groups—manage to affect

Table 3.4. The role of nonstate actors in shaping migration policy

- Labor market interest associations will be consulted where their core policy domains are affected, especially so in countries with a neocorporatist tradition.
- The power of interest groups depends on their internal organizational characteristics. Among our case studies, only German labor market interest associations and British, French, Italian, and Irish employers command significant organizational power; unions in these four countries receive low scores. In Poland, unions and employers receive equally very low scores.
- In countries with a neocorporatist tradition, labor market interest associations will be more likely to be consulted on issues pertaining to the migration–labor market nexus.
- Labor market interest associations are generally much better institutionally positioned than humanitarian NGOs to influence government policy.
- Very few NGOs possess powerful organizational characteristics, many may be wary of cooperating or being co-opted by the state apparatus.

policies that may prove costly or otherwise detrimental for society as a whole. The costs migration imposes are diffuse, often widely spread and its opponents generally poorly organized.

There are important caveats to consider, however, before considering the application of Freeman's concept to Europe (Freeman 2006; Statham and Geddes 2006). The strong support by employers and the vociferous opposition by unions in the United States are a historical particularity (Haus 2002); in a number of European countries, trade unions either at least initially welcomed immigrants (Britain), reached out to organize them (Italy), were involved in the comanagement of migration flows (Germany, the Netherlands, Sweden) or at least accepted immigration (France) (Penninx and Roosblad 2000; Watts 2002). Postwar immigration was generally channeled into the regular labor market, carefully monitored and commonly approved by trade unions, though this did not prevent abusive substandard working conditions or exploitative pay levels altogether, of course. West European unions changed course from the mid-1970s onwards, supporting equal rights, anti-discrimination, and integration, and also endorsing the recruitment stop of new labor migrants (Penninx and Roosblad 2000). Also, anti-immigration sentiments have spawned remarkably successful xenophobic parties from Denmark to Portugal, casting some doubt on the extent to which opponents of immigration indeed remain reticent (Minkenberg 2000; Schain et al. 2002). Blue collar "globalization losers" fearing competition over jobs and wages from immigrants feature prominently among Austria's Far Right Freedomites (Heinisch 2003). In public opinion surveys, anti-immigration advocates are commonly in the absolute majority throughout Europe (Lahav 2004).

With a larger supporter base in particular and superior organizational characteristics in general, labor market interest associations stand in a much more privileged position to shape immigration policy than humanitarian NGOs. Among the latter, certain more "professionalized" groups are more influential than others, as scholarly work on interest groups would suggest (Grant 1999; Imig and Tarrow 2001).

Interest groups enjoy a plethora of possibilities for seeking to secure government access. They can organize conferences and workshops, be invited to parliamentary or ministry of the interior hearings and expert committees, seek to produce publications with a view to influencing media and public opinion, and lobby the legislative and executive branch either directly and formally or informally. In countries with neocorporatist institutions, labor market interest associations will commonly be represented in tripartite fora that may be asked to comment on migration policy development, such as the Irish social partnership agreements (Hardiman 2002). Such neocorporatist legacy will induce governmental actors to consider the opinions of labor market interest associations regarding the migration–labor market nexus. Informal ad hoc hearings can and will be organized by legislative and executive branches of government even in the absence of any neocorporatist tradition, of course. However, during interviews with representatives of the national ministries of interior it emerged that in Germany, Italy, and Ireland such informal hearings were both more common and more frequent than in either France, Poland, or Britain (interviews DE-GOV-1, FR-GOV-1, FR-GOV-2, ITA-GOV-1, IRL-GOV-1, UK-GOV-1, DE-UNI-1, DE-UNI-2, DE-EMP-1, DE-EMP-2, IRL-EMP-1, PL-EMP-1, UK-EMP-1). Representatives of NGOs confirmed this pattern (interviews DE-NGO-1, FR-NGO-1, IRL-NGO-1, UK-NGO-1, FR-NGO-2, PL-NGO-1).

Having examined the institutional mechanisms through which non-governmental actors can hope to influence policy, it becomes important to explore the interest positions of these actors. It seems imprudent to assume a simple dichotomy between labor and capital in the stance towards immigration. The influence of different systems of political economy on labor market interest group positions will be examined in the next section. Generally speaking, managed labor migration is thus not contentious.[3] Meanwhile, humanitarian NGOs focus their efforts on policy towards asylum seekers and refugees. They insist on an appropriate application of the obligations arising out of the Geneva Convention and are concerned about the tendency to violate the commitment to this treaty both at the national and European level.

The Disintegration of Labor Markets: Multiple Tiers, Multiple Working Conditions

Before turning to a detailed examination of employer and union preferences, it is important to consider background conditions including fairly high unemployment across Europe and a diversification and segmentation of the labor market structure, especially in LMEs. No employer organization can politically afford openly to advocate undocumented migration. Where interests between unions and employers diverge is with respect to the secondary tier of the labor market, where low pay and precarious and dangerous work conditions prevail (Berger and Piore 1980;

Piore 1979). This secondary tier of the labor market, now predominantly, but not exclusively to be found in the service sector, with niches also in low-skill agricultural jobs and manufacturing, has been enhanced over the past 30 years by corporate restructuring strategies entailing outsourcing and subcontracting, including the elaboration of subcontractor chains. In this segment of the labor market, union influence is limited and regulations governing pay, working hours and conditions, and health and safety are being routinely ignored. Obviously, conditions are aggravated in undocumented or illegal situations, including "black in black" work by undocumented migrants in irregular sectors of the labor market, present in France and Italy. LME employers may welcome migration to help perpetuate a highly (Ireland) or extremely (UK) diversified labor market with stark differences in working conditions, employment rights, and remuneration. Alternatively, some employers may welcome migration in a quest to establish deregulated precarious secondary tiers within otherwise relatively highly regulated labor markets, as the support of German employer association BDA for the epidemic use of Portuguese subcontractor companies in the German construction sector since the early 1990s suggests or the use of Baltic subcontractors by Irish ferry companies and Swedish construction companies. Destroying a unified labor market structure may appear advantageous to advocates of a third truly minimal tier of the labor market (Lillie and Greer 2007; Menz 2001). While some economic liberals rather misguidedly call for lower regular wages to decrease undocumented employment (*inter alia* Boswell and Straubhaar 2004), similarly spirited advocacy of Dickensian working conditions and Victorian era wages is limited within employer associations (UK-EMP-1, DE-EMP-1, DE-EMP-1, PL-EMP-1). Such rhetorical reticence regarding neoliberally tinted wage policy needs to be considered behind the backdrop of an already quite sizable secondary labor market. Employers much prefer eager and compliant migrant workers to welfare recipients forced into low-paid employment as a condition for further transfer payment receipt. Much to the chagrin of US-inspired workfare advocates (Peck 2001), architects of Germany's egregious Hartz IV reforms are faced with complaints from farmers voicing their preference for Polish and Ukrainian farmhands over forced German social assistance recipients (*Der Spiegel* April 25, 2005) whose physical incapacity for taxing manual labor—usually the reason for their original eligibility for social assistance—renders them significantly less productive. Even at punitive hourly wages of €1, this form of forced labor is not an immediately attractive prospect for employers.

Employer and Union Interest Positions

Different national production strategies associated with different systems of political economy, recently identified in the comparative political economy literature (Amable 2003; Hall and Soskice 2001; Hollingsworth et al. 1994; Schmidt 2002; earlier: Shonfield 1965; Katzenstein 1978; Zysman 1983), influence national migration management, though it is only relatively recently that such strategies have diverged sufficiently to produce substantially different policy outcomes.[4]

Hall and Soskice define coordinated market economies as environments where "firms depend more heavily on nonmarket relationships to coordinate their endeavors with other actors and to construct their core competencies...based on...more reliance on collaborative...relationships...[and] strategic interaction" to set them apart from the more "competitive market arrangements" in liberal market economies (2001: 8). Though this dichotomy has invited several avenues of criticism (Blyth 2003; Coates 2005; Hay 2005; Pontusson 2005; Watson 2003), not least focusing on the core concept of mutually reinforcing institutional complementarities, it rejects simplistic notions of convergence on one single best model. The neoliberalization of Europe's coordinated market economies and the embrace of competition state policy must not be conflated with such convergence. Institutional differences persist, though these institutions may serve different policy outcomes (cf. Menz 2005). The typological attempt to map Europe's different models of capitalism helps focus attention on persistent differences along a number of dimensions, most crucially including labor market structure and organization (Regini 2003; Thelen 2001), corporate strategies (Hall and Soskice 2001; Vitols 2001), educational and training systems (Culpepper 2001, 2003; Thelen 2003), and the contributory role of the state (Hancké, Rhodes, and Thatcher 2007). Recent contributions (Hancké, Rhodes, and Thatcher 2007) argue that many southern European countries constitute amalgamated mixed market economies (MMEs) with a coordinating and enabling rather than dominating an *étatiste* role for the state (Amable 2003; Schmidt 2002) and that in Eastern Europe an even more transitory emerging market economy (EMEs) category has appeared (Lane 2005; Mykhnenko 2005; Stark and Bruszt 2001).

Applying these insights to labor migration policy, it is argued that employer associations will seek to attract and recruit economic migrants that complement existing corporate strategies (gradual innovation and concentration on high value added production in CMEs, radical innovation in LMEs), labor market regulation, and industrial relations, encouraging codetermination, sectoral wage bargaining, sectoral wage parity, greater job security, and longer tenure in CMEs, despite serious erosion syndromes (Hassel 1999, 2007; Streeck and Hassel 2004); significantly more pronounced wage and working condition differentiation, more macrolevel abjurations from wage settlements, deregulation and legally constrained trade unions, shorter tenure and higher turnover in LMEs, training and education systems (sectorally portable skill sets, high skill and specialization training strategies to sustain high value added export strategies in CMEs, individualized company-specific skills and "on the job training," low general skill and education levels with important sectoral exceptions in advertising, corporate finance and consulting. Following the varieties of capitalism argument further, the state will regard such endeavors favorably (cf. Soskice 2007).

This allows us to formulate the following hypothesis regarding employer preference:

H1 (VoC hypothesis): The system of political economy with its numerous complementarities will condition employer preferences and demands for labor migration. LME employers will ask for migrants with general and transferable skills that can be easily accommodated into flexible corporate strategies. They will also be interested in migrants that feed directly into high value high-skill "islands." CME employers will be more interested in migrants with specific skill sets. MME and EME employers' preferences will be the result of employer attempts to emulate either LME or CME strategies. MME and EME employers will be more internally divided, reflecting the transitory state of these categories, and their preferences will ultimately reflect the model they are approaching.

Relatedly, employers will also seek to reinforce existing sectoral subdivisions by pressing for legislation that ensures appropriate economic migration reflective of concentrations on the secondary or tertiary sector respectively. Thus, in a CME such as Germany, we would expect to see an employer preference for highly skilled top-tier labor migration, complementing the pattern of "diversified quality production" (Streeck 1992) and feeding into the secondary sector in particular. There is no appetite for low-skill migration. "In contrast, in the UK, 'deregulated' labour markets and the absence of labour as a countervailing force make a lower-cost, lower-price strategy, underpinning service-sector expansion more realistic than in the high-value high-skill approach of the CMEs that continues to serve their manufacturing companies well [...], while service-sector development (both high- and low-value added) in the CMEs is more restricted" (Hancké, Rhodes, and Thatcher 2007: 32–3). Thus, in an LME, employers are likely to advocate recruitment of highly skilled labor *both* for select niches with labor shortages and for poorly paid sectors of the labor market that experience recruitment problems and high staff turnover due to low wages, poor morale and prestige, and unappealing working conditions. The service sector employs a higher percentage of the workforce, but this does not reflect a higher contribution to overall GDP, suggesting a sizable low-wage low-skill sector. In LMEs, there is generally less staff loyalty to their employers, higher turnover, less job security, and less labor market regulation. There is also more employer-specific and on-the-job training (cf. Culpepper and Finegold 2001; Thelen 2004). All of these factors further promote a widening of the pool of available human resources.

Despite their heterogeneity, MMEs such as France and Italy have often sizable high-skill high-wage clusters in the secondary sector. EMEs such as Poland would appear to be slowly constructing these, but, setting themselves apart from either southern or northern Europe, also still command sizable primary sectors.

H2 (sectoral hypothesis): Employers will take into account the relative size of component sectors of the economy (primary/secondary/tertiary sector). We expect the relative size of the component sectors to influence the profile of economic migrants deemed desirable by employer associations.

Trade unions do not block employer initiatives favoring liberal immigration policy, in fact, they support them. This is partly due to unions sharing the notion of maintaining and increasing "competitiveness." In that sense, the description of unions as pragmatic liberalizing "modernization brokers" (Heinisch 1999) may be highly accurate in ideological terms. But this attitude is in part also born out of making virtue out of a necessity; where structural transformations of the production process, decline in membership numbers, privatization of public sector enterprises, labor market segmentation and disintegration even in highly organized systems such as the German one (Hassel 2007; Silvia 1999) conspire to undermine union power, outright rejection to economic migration *tout court* or at least strong skepticism, as had been expressed by some European unions in earlier decades, for example in Austria and France (Penninx and Roosblad 2000), is difficult to maintain. In that sense, Penninx and Roosblad's first dilemma that unions face in confronting labor migration, whether to support it or not, has almost dissipated because attempts to be regarded as reliable comanagers of migration flows or aspirations to become involved in such role are further reinforced by a ideological pragmatic shift towards embracing migration as an inevitability. Haus (2002) is correct when she ascribes great importance to globalization pressures, which have led to a very different stance in France, where unions resign themselves to accepting economic migration on the condition that such flows feed into the primary layer of the labor market. Trade unions are generally adamant about avoiding migrants from being used to undercut current wages and working conditions. As a result, they prefer managed migration to a policy of zero migration that would indirectly promote irregular flows and subsequently irregular forms of employment, engendering downward pressures on wages and working conditions in all segments of the labor market. In that sense, unions are much more concerned with equal pay, working conditions, employment rights, and anti-discrimination and have resolved Penninx and Roosblad's (2000) second major conundrum by affirmatively attempting to secure equal working conditions for migrants.

Government Interest Positions

The national interest positions which national government representatives take up at the European level are thus conditioned by the influence exercised by domestic nongovernmental actors. This influence itself is affected by different degrees of organizational power in institutional terms these actors can marshal and the impact of different systems of political economy in ideational and interest terms. Despite these divergences, there are also a couple of pertinent commonalities, as we have examined previously. European governmental actors operate behind the backdrop of a highly securitized agenda that frames migration questions as an issue menacing—or at least challenging—the integrity of the state. They have also internalized a competition state agenda that compels them to secure the necessary framework conditions for an amiable business and investment climate.

The Contours of Conflict in Brussels

The 1999 Tampere Council raised high hopes for swift and decisive action in creating an AMP framework. In the final communiqué, Article 20 sets out the need for approximation of national legislations on the conditions for admission and residence of third-country nationals, based on a shared assessment of the economic and demographic developments within the Union, as well as the situation in the countries of origin. It requests to this end rapid decisions by the Council, on the basis of proposals by the Commission. These decisions should take into account not only the reception capacity of each member state, but also their historical and cultural links with the country of origin.

Despite the determined-sounding rhetoric and sustained Commission activity over the course of the following years, responses from member state representatives in the Council were very mixed, including apathy, antipathy, and even significant open resistance. At the same time, bottom-up Europeanization played a role, especially in the protracted negotiations surrounding the regulation of economic migration. This section analyzes the genesis of three key AMP directives, exploring the politics of the creation of the family reunion directive, the asylum "qualification" directive, and the ultimately frustrated attempt to create a labor migration directive.

The Politics of AMP-making

The ambitious, far-reaching, and comprehensive roadmap provided by the Tampere Council very quickly ceded to more sober considerations of national sovereignty, security, reluctance and foot-dragging, and dedication to the national traditions of migration regulation. The language of the Seville Council of 2002 was notably more restrictive and seems to have been strongly influenced by the experience of the September 11, 2001 incidents in the United States (Levy 2005). Some member states were highly concerned about an overtly interventionist, stringent EU directive that would require significant adaptation costs and exert top-down Europeanization pressures; others questioned the very legitimacy of Commission authority in this domain. While AMP-making efforts were unfolding in earnest, sometimes vociferous and heated national debates on migration were accompanying reforms to national regulation in a number of national arenas. Such interactive effects of bottom-up Europeanization were particularly pronounced with respect to the major overhaul of German immigration policy. Though member states and the Commission jointly shared the right to propose directives until 2004, even during that period the vast majority of proposals originated with the latter, with only a few exceptions, such as member state initiatives on joint deportation measures, eventually to include the mutual recognition of deportation decisions. Shortly after the end of this transition period, the Council decided on December 22, 2004 (2004/927/EC) to act by qualified majority voting, as opposed to the previous mode of unanimous decision-making, on initiatives either covered by Arts. 62.1.2.a and 3 or Arts. 63.2.b. and 3.b of the EC Treaty. Fundamentally, the former covers internal border controls and the intra-EU freedom of mobility for third-country nationals, while the latter concerns reciprocal arrangements with respect to asylum seekers and undocumented migrants, along with the presence and deportation of undocumented residents. However, very significantly, unanimous decision-making was maintained in other areas of Title IV, most importantly regarding the contentious issue of labor migration. The 2004 deadline for establishing a basic policy framework set forth in Tampere proved invaluable in generating practical results, spawning a veritable flurry of legislative activity immediately prior to it.

It proved difficult at first to build real momentum, as much of the Commission's initiative encountered often serious resistance from the member states, with a notable gap in ambition between the often fairly sweeping scope of the Commission's proposals and the more hesitant reaction on the part of the Council of Ministers. The result is not only a general pattern of dilution between the original proposals and the final result but also multiple occasions of abrogation and nonintrusive "umbrella-style" regulations that create an overarching, if at times somewhat porous, framework pattern. The larger member states with more established regimes of migration regulation, particularly Germany and to some extent France, proved particularly reluctant to accept the significant adaptation cost that top-down Europeanization imposes. However, for the 2004 and 2007 newcomers and the Mediterranean countries which commonly possessed relatively little regulation, particularly regarding asylum, top-down Europeanization was extremely significant, strongly shaping and at times virtually rewriting national legislation. For these countries, *any* EU directive had significant consequences.

Interestingly, some provisions entailed in the relevant directives are explicitly designed to create a lowest common denominator-style bottom tier which does not preclude more favorable national regulations, though few governments are likely to choose such a path, given the difficulty in justifying politically exceeding the low standards set by the EU directive. In normative and ideational terms, the tendency towards dilution means that much of the policy output lacks true ambition and inspiration and is often not particularly innovative or progressive, either.

The Family Reunification Directive

The long-drawn-out negotiations over family reunion demonstrated that an initially relatively liberal and progressive piece of proposed legislation encountered fierce resistance from the member states, leading eventually to a considerably diluted compromise solution that was much less intrusive, but also largely surrendered its progressive edge in the process.

The Commission first took action immediately after Tampere, producing a draft directive on the issue as early as December 1, 1999 (COM 1999, 638). This draft never made its way into any actual legislation. Since this initiative is based on Arts. 6.3.3 and 4, it did not pertain to the UK, Denmark, and Ireland. It was considered by the European Parliament (EP) first, which may provide input under the consultation procedure. The EP committee issued its report in July 2000 ("Watson Report" A5–201/2000 of July 17, 2000). On September 6, 2000, the EP passed a vote on the directive, suggesting some very minor liberal modifications, but supporting the main provisions. Surprisingly, the Commission accepted the suggestion to exclude persons with subsidiary protection from the coverage of the directive.

However, the reception in the Council was very cool indeed. Having initially discussed the issue on December 2, 1999 and then again in May 2000, it had become obvious from early on that significant opposition to some of the key provisions of this directive existed.

In light of these reservations, the Council Strategic Committee decided that it would be best to move ahead with a directive covering only individuals with residence permits extending to periods of more than one year. But subsequent discussions in the Council on May 28–29, 2001 and September 27–28, 2001 did not induce any compromise, either. On November 16, the directive was scheduled to be under discussion again, but was moved off the agenda. The four council meetings witnessed considerable disagreement with the Commission's initiatives, but simultaneously no consensus on alternative proposals emerged.

In the meantime, the Commission had produced a modified directive on October 10, 2000 (see COM 2000, 624 final), incorporating EP suggestions. Despite this disagreement, member states realized the importance of the issue, lodging a request to the Commission during the Laeken Council meeting of December 14 and 15, 2001 to relaunch deliberations on a revised directive reflective of the opinions expressed previously by April 30, 2002 (Groenendijk 2004*a*; Schibel 2004).

Discussions resumed in the context of the working party on migration and expulsion on July 8 and 26, hurried along by the June 2002 Seville European Council decision to agree on a directive by June 2003. These discussions proceeded on the basis of a third version of the directive, amended on May 3, 2002 (COM 2002, 225 final).

On February 27, 2003, an agreement on this version was reached in the Council. On September 22, the Council formally adopted the directive 2003/86/EC. However, in the meantime, the Commission had committed what some might consider a procedural faux pas. Thus, on December 22, 2003, the EP brought an action for annulment before the ECJ, protesting that in violation of Art. 67 of the EC Treaty the EP had not been properly consulted (ECJ case C-540/03, O.J. 2004/C47/35). The amended proposal had been transmitted to the EP on May 2, 2002 and the latter had approved it with significant amendments on April 9, 2003, highlighting its skeptical stance towards the tangible "toughening up" of regulations. But in the meantime the Council had already discussed and approved the draft, completely ignoring the skeptical stance the EP adopted. The EP Legal Affairs Committee and the Committee on Citizen's Freedoms and Rights, Justice and Home Affairs felt that the Commission had rushed matters and EP President Pat Cox concurred. But more importantly, the EP was critical of the abrogation of the issue of the age of children, permitting member states to end family reunion rights to children above 15 years of age and restrict them to children above 12 years of age, thus allegedly violating the European Charter of Human Rights, especially Article 8 guaranteeing the right to private and family rights.

This criticism was shared by a number of national humanitarian NGOs. Under the able stewardship of French group GISTI (Groupe d'information et de soutien des immigrés), combining resources with the pan-European umbrella association COORDEUROP (European Coordination for Foreigners' Right to Family Life), sympathetic MEPs were identified, contacted, and lobbied in favor of submitting a formal complaint (COORDEUROP October 6, 2003; November 10, 2003). This proved successful and on December 22, 2003, the EP used the new procedure introduced in the Nice Treaty (Art. 230 para 2) to lodge a complaint based on an alleged violation of the right to family life and the principle of nondiscrimination (Art. 6 para 2) (OJ2004/C47/35 of February 21, 2004). However, the ECJ rejected the complaint (ECJ C540/03).[5]

Open resistance to the Commission's position came principally from three member states, namely Germany, Austria, and the Netherlands. All three governments sought to safeguard existing national arrangements, avoiding administratively and politically costly adaptation costs. In so doing, the three representatives in the Council of Ministers were free from the pressure of labor market interest associations, which generally did not become active on this issue (interviews DE-UNI-1, DE-BUS-1, FR-UNI-1, FR-UNI-2). By contrast, humanitarian NGOs at the national level were following the elaboration of the directive very closely and, in the German case, communicated their grievances to the ministry of interior affairs (interviews DE-NGO-1, DE-NGO-2, FR-NGO-1, FR-NGO-2, FR-NGO-3; ProAsyl 2004; Amnesty International 2007). However, these lobbying efforts were largely unsuccessful initially. The age of children covered by family reunion rights was emerging as an unlikely yet significant point of contention during the concurrent domestic discussions of the new German immigration law (*Berliner Zeitung* February 1, 2002; February 10, 2003; FAZ February 7, 2002), with German humanitarian NGOs (interviews NGO-DE-1, interview NGO-DE-2) seeking allies also among the Green Party, part of the coalition government. But the German ministry of the interior, though receiving a wide array of NGOs for informal consultations (interviews GOV-DE-1, NGO-DE-1) did not budge on this question. The NGO camp was largely united on the question in principle, but no real concerted coordinated effort was made and some organizations, notably Amnesty International (interview NGO-DE-1), were very active, while others remained reticent, thus undermining the overall effectiveness of the lobbying efforts. With the German NGO camp relatively weakened on this issue, the German ministry of interior affairs sought to achieve a relatively restrictive EU regulation so as to have more room for maneuver regarding the national regulation, either leaving it at 16 or possibly reducing it to as low as 12 (interview GOV-DE-1, *Berliner Zeitung* February 10, 2003). In using the EU as a political scapegoat to justify a more restrictive domestic position, the ministry also very skillfully maneuvered a two-level arena (Groenendijk 2004*b*). It received assistance from its Austrian homologue (OJ 120222/01 of September 24, 2001). The Austrian government was keen to preserve the stringent national legal status quo, including quotas, limiting annual family reunion flows to 5,490, annually set by the Ministry of Interior Affairs in consultation with the *Länder* governments. In addition, under Austrian law, residents applying for family reunion rights had to prove convincingly that their income, living situation, and health insurance provided adequate coverage to guarantee local customary (*ortsüblich*) living standards (*Der Standard* December 18, 2003; Evrensel and Höbart 2004). Despite ongoing debates about possible reforms, eventually spawning minor modifications (*Fremdengesetznovelle*) in 2002 and especially a legal challenge by the Austrian Constitutional Court, the Austrian ministry of interior affairs sought both to maintain the national regulation and safeguard it against European impetus for change. The court had ruled only the fairly restrictive administrative procedures of this quota unconstitutional as well as subsuming family reunion privileges granted for humanitarian reasons under this annual quota (VFGH G119/03 ua 17013 of October 8, 2003; *Der Standard* October 9, 2003). In addition to quotas and restrictive administrative procedures, the maximum age for children joining family members already resident in Austria was limited to 15 for migrants having entered Austria prior to January 1, 1998, a regulation eventually changed to contain the peculiar regulation that family reunion could now cover children up to the age of 18, but only if an application for their entry was made before they had reached the age of 15 due to yet another legal challenge from the Constitutional Court (Evrensel and Höbart 2004: 85, Biffl 2005). These changes were eventually to lead to the much revised July 7, 2005 Residency Law (*Niederlassungs- und Aufenthaltsrecht* 2005). The Austrian government warded off protest both from the NGO camp and from the two political opposition parties SPÖ and Greens. It was adamant in watering down the original Commission proposal to insert the possibility of two- to three-year waiting periods for applicants for family reunion, thus permitting the de facto and *de jure* safeguarding of the national quota system in principle.

But a coalition of member states managed to influence the European level also regarding two other points: first, a Dutch–German–Austrian alliance successfully attained national room for maneuver to impose the requirement on new migrants to attend integration and language classes (OJ 14727/02), including as a set condition even prior to arrival. Second, the German and Dutch ministers jointly secured the possibility to impose minimum ages for spouses benefiting from family reunion during the Council meeting on February 27, 2003, ostensibly to reduce forced marriages. The Dutch minister was particularly active, as such EU regulation permitted honoring the coalition agreement with the far-right xenophobe Pim Fortuyn movement to impose age limits (Groenendijk 2004*b*: 127) and take highly visible action in "cracking down." The Germans were supportive of such stance as it extended the national room for maneuver in the ongoing reform of national migration law, permitted highly visible political action sure to placate the political Right and, once again, might have proven useful in blaming the EU for restrictive national legislation. Despite some lobbying activity, the German NGO camp was not united on this point and failed to influence the government's position (interviews NGO-DE-1, NGO-DE-2, ProAsyl 2004; Amnesty International et al. 2007).

The need to accommodate the apparent resistance to some of the Commission's ideas pervades the revised 2002 (225) version. This is acknowledged as leaving "room for manoeuvre in national legislation" and "limited cases of exceptions" (para 2.1). More specifically, the Commission now permitted room for national abrogation concerning the contested issue of the age of children, of particular interest to the Austrian and German delegations who threatened to block any further progress if no such concession was made. Though the final version of the directive imposed the respective national legal age of maturity as the maximum age for family reunion rights for children along with the requirement for children to be unmarried, it permitted member states to examine children above the age of 12 in more detail, with respect to them having to fulfill national integration criteria, such as language examinations.

In a similar vein, the directive only makes mandatory provisions for the spouse and minor children, while the regulation of the status of other relatives in the ascending line, children over whom custody is shared, dependent adult children, and unmarried (including same sex) partners is left up to the member states if they so wish (Franz 2006: 50). Reservations about unmarried partners came from Spain, Greece, and Portugal. Member states may, but do not have to, impose age limits on spouses to prevent forced marriages. They may continue previous practices of examining applicants still located outside of the country, as the directive applies regardless of physical location of the applicant.

In addition, room was being opened for more favorable national regulations (Art. 3.5), though unlikely to find much use in practice.

Another heavily contested issue concerned the requirements for lodging an application. There was some debate as to whether substantive requirements should be made in addition to proving a certain level of income. The Austrian delegation demanded health exams, language requirements, and also queried how this threshold should be determined and whether it should be re-examined after a certain amount of time, this time even moving beyond safeguarding existing national legislation, but actively suggesting restrictive European policy in bottom-up fashion. However, the Austrians failed to find support for their position, which was considered of no interest by the German delegation (interview DE-GOV-1) or any other (interview FR-GOV-1). The compromise line adopted by the Commission rendered the requirement of adequate housing and health insurance optional and found a threshold income level as the lowest common denominator position just above the minimum level of social assistance. With this regulation, found in Art. 7 of the directive, the Austrian status quo was safeguarded, but was not successfully imposed as the basis for a new European regulation due to the failed attempt at coalition-building.

The next contested point concerned the amount of time an immigrant has to spend in a member state before becoming eligible for family reunion, increased from one to two years between the first draft directive and the final version. Further, member states were granted the right to impose waiting periods of up to three years, in line with the Austrian demands, where existing legislation accounted for the receiving state's "absorption capacity."

The modified directive also contained significantly fewer progressive clauses regarding immigrants' rights. In the initial 1999 draft, the Commission sought to align the rights of immigrants covered by this directive to those of EU citizens with respect to access to the labor market and education. This suggestion came under fierce criticism, especially from Austria, Germany, and the Netherlands (Hauschild 2003). Subsequently, it was only proposed to align the rights of the applicant's family with those enjoyed by the third country nationals.

Decoupling the rights of the family with those of the applicant proved similarly thorny. The Commission eventually addressed this point by setting a relatively high minimum residence requirement of five years before "sponsored" family members obtain independent residency permits (Art. 15).

Due to the major resistance encountered, the difference between the first 1999 draft and the final result, which had to be adopted into national law by October 3, 2005, is stark. Revealingly, the directive no longer contains any right to family reunion as such, but instead merely seeks to "determine the conditions in which the right to family reunion may [sic] be exercised" (Art. 1). Whereas the first draft was aimed at all categories of immigrants, including Geneva Convention refugees and asylum seekers, refugees with subsidiary status of protection, long-term third-country nationals and non-EU citizens that were family members of EU citizens, the final directive *does not* cover the latter three categories nor those third-country nationals who do not fall under the separate EU directive (2003/109/EC). Similarly, while the first draft was based on a very inclusive definition of family, including in cases of economic hardship also relatives in the ascending line (Art. 1d of original 1999 version), the final version excludes nonmarried partners and applies a very restrictive definition of family, while leaving room for more liberal national interpretations of the latter two points.

Resistance from member states has led to a significantly less ambitious and progressive output than the original proposal would have constituted. The Commission defended the final result, in particular the so-called standstill principle, which establishes the directive's provisions as the lowest possible standard of regulation and does not permit downward abrogation. Thus the new and arguably somewhat less rigorous rules on family reunification implemented in Italy, Belgium, and Denmark in 2002 could not be modified retroactively to offer an inferior level of protection. However, the concurrence between policymaking at the national level and the EU level, with developments underway in Portugal, Austria, and Germany prove important, especially as the latter two countries pushed for relatively restrictive rules that would prevent any "softening" of their own policies. Substantial skepticism also came from the Dutch who often supported the German and Austrian delegation. As a southern European new immigration country, Greece, and less so Spain, attempted to slow down or stop ambitious developments that would have generated substantial adaptation pressures on their relatively underdeveloped migration regulation system. On this issue, the national delegations in the Council of Ministers could proceed without significant input by labor market interest associations who considered this issue immaterial to their interests (interview EU-UNI-1, EU-BUS-1). By contrast, national humanitarian NGOs did attempt to exercise influence, using both traditional forms of lobbying, especially in the particularly restrictively minded case of Germany, and assisting and supporting a legal challenge lodged by the EP. Ultimately, however, due to internal ideational divergences and lack of successful attempts to construct access channels to governments, these lobbying efforts were relatively limited in their impact. Mounting the legal challenge through the COORDEUROP umbrella association proved possible because there was both a general disquiet shared by NGOs over the ever more restrictive contours of the directive and the symbolically important rallying point of the age for children benefiting from family reunion.

The Asylum Qualification Directive

Tampere and even more so The Hague signified the commencement of considerable activity in the field of asylum. The 2005 Hague Program explicitly proclaimed the goal of creating a Common European Asylum System by 2010, while Council and Commission agreed on an action plan in June 2005 specifying concrete measures (C 198 of August 12, 2005), with the Commission presenting a first array of measures on September 1, 2005. Prior to The Hague, the Commission shied away from harmonization attempts, settling instead on the much less exacting aim of specifying common minimum standards, thus laying the foundation for more ambitious endeavors. As we have seen previously, the implications of Dublin II proved profound, leading to significantly higher asylum case figures in countries along the external geographical frontiers, while the common databank EURODAC also deserves mention, as it stores fingerprints and other personal information about asylum seekers in all EU member states, thus constituting a valuable tool in the arsenal of the state apparatus to control, survey, and monitor migrant movements. The justification employed to encounter concerns about such intrusion on civil rights was to refer to the possibility of reducing the number of dual applications.

Creating the basis of a European asylum system consisted of proposing directives regulating both the procedures and the content of the protection afforded. The first issue was addressed in the form of the so-called procedure directive (2005/85/EC). The qualification directive's first incarnation came in the form of the Commission's September 12, 2001 draft (2001/510 final) under the title "minimum standards for the qualification of third-country national and stateless persons as refugees or as persons who otherwise need international protection and the content of the protection granted." It was then forwarded to the EP, again under the consultation procedure. The EP approved the draft in a single reading on October 22, 2002, suggesting a number of amendments that were all subsequently completely ignored, including extending coverage to anyone, notably covering citizens of EU countries, removing a clause that permitted "stable quasi-state authorities" as guarantors of protection, and providing equal conditions for refugees and beneficiaries of subsidiary protection, especially with regard to labor market access rights.

The Council again assumed a reserved stance towards this draft proposal. Negotiations extended over nearly 18 months, with meetings on October 15 and November 28, 2002, February 27, 2003, May 8, 2003, and

February 19, 2004. Political agreement was finally reached on March 30 and the directive was formally adopted on April 29, 2004. The UK and Ireland had agreed to "opt in," while Denmark stayed out. There were at least three major lines of conflict. First, the issue of exclusion and revocation of refugee status incited considerable controversy. Art. 12 specifies the grounds for exclusion, broadly in line with the Geneva Convention: Thus, individuals that have committed war crimes or acts "contrary to the purposes and principles of the United Nations" can be excluded. But securitization is tangible in Art. 14.4.a. that permits revoking or ending refugee status for individuals that can be regarded as a "danger to the security of the Member State," without this term being clearly defined. Similarly, the original provision for cessation of refugee status placed the burden of proof with the member state, a provision that was subsequently deleted in the final version of the directive. Second, there were differences about the question of rights awarded to beneficiaries of subsidiary protection. This relatively new category had been used consistently by a number of European authorities in practice, but it lacked a clear basis in international law and was seen by critics as a conscious attempt to avoid the bestowal of refugee status under the terms of the Geneva Convention or fully-fledged recognition of asylum rights. Not all member states were prepared to concede formal rights (or at least not particularly expansive rights) and associated pecuniary benefits to this category. This conflict reflects national practices to use the absolute level and even the form (vouchers, etc.) of social assistance payments as a mechanism to "deter" applicants by reducing payment and introducing complicated and difficult to negotiate payment in kind schemes, as is the case in Germany and the UK. Other member states had no or only rudimentary previous regulation governing eligibility for social assistance payments by refugees and asylum seekers (e.g. Poland, Italy, Ireland). The difficulty of attaining consensus on this point is reflected in para. 34 of the preamble, which defines "core benefits" as constituting "minimum income support, assistance in the case of illness, pregnancy and parental assistance," but immediately modifies them by making them dependent on the extent to which they "are granted to nationals according to...legislation." Beyond this core, the "modalities and detail of the provision of core benefits...should be determined by national law." Indeed, Art. 28 explicitly permits member states to limit the provision of benefits to beneficiaries of this subsidiary protection to this minimal core. Another concession to the more critical stance of some member states lies in the differentiation between Geneva Convention refugees and individuals afforded subsidiary protection, with the latter group enjoying notably fewer extensive rights, not only in terms of access to benefits but also regarding the issuance of documents valid for international travel, the right to family reunion, and, of course, the duration of the residency permit, valid only for a minimum of one year, as opposed to a minimum of three for refugees. Third, substantial national opposition came yet again from Germany. The German delegation was particularly concerned about two issues, namely, labor market access rights for beneficiaries of subsidiary protection and recognition of persecution by nonstate actors as a legitimate legal basis for asylum. While a consensus on the general thrust of the directive was established by June 2003, the German government refused to give in on these two issues until the labor market access question was resolved in its favor and the recognition of persecution by nonstate actors had been accepted as a novelty into the reformed domestic law as part of the domestic bargaining process.

Though touching upon the labor market, German unions and employers ultimately focused their lobbying efforts on individuals specifically recruited for economic purposes, while the question of labor market access rights for asylum seekers or refugees was considered somewhat more peripheral. The employer association BDA was also much more interested in highly skilled economic migrants, rather than what it perceived to be largely low-skill political refugees (interviews DE-UNI-1, DE-BUS-1). The humanitarian NGO camp focused its lobbying efforts not on this issue either (interviews DE-NGO-1, NGO-2). The German representative in the Council was ultimately successful in obtaining a dilution regarding individuals with subsidiary protection that permits taking into account "the situation of the labour market" when granting work permits and to do so for an undefined "limited period of time...in accordance with national law" (Art. 26). With limited enthusiasm over the German approach elsewhere in the Council, the German delegation was content with securing a European regulation that permitted the safeguarding of the national status quo.

Prior to the major 2004 reforms of German immigration legislation, persecution by nonstate actors was not recognized as grounds for political asylum. On this issue, the German position was somewhat of an anomaly by international comparison (Duchrow 2004). France did not share this same commitment to stall negotiations over this point, as both regulation of asylum and refugee status and practice accepted persecution by nonstate actors as legitimate grounds for application in principle, despite a highly restrictive application in practice, notoriously arbitrary in regard to persecution by Algerian so-called militia groups.

Labor market interest associations unsurprisingly did not become active on this point, but German NGOs had been lobbying the government for quite a while to modify national legislation in this respect as part of the major immigration legislation reform (Amnesty 2002; UNHCR 2002; Durchow 2004, interviews NGO-DE-1). This was a position shared within the NGO community, which facilitated maintaining a common position vis-à-vis the ministry of the interior during hearings and informal rounds of consultation. In addition, the NGOs successfully created an advocacy coalition with members of the Green Party taking an active interest in this issue. Though seemingly a minor detail, it emerged as one of the points of contention in the domestic arena, where the conservative CDU/CSU parties rallied against what they considered to be an excessively liberal immigration reform (*Berliner Zeitung* February 1, 2002). Referring to the allegedly undue influence of the Green Party on the draft legislation, Bavarian Minister of the Interior Beckstein demanded that "much Green [influence] needs to go out and much more Black [conservative influence] needs to go in" (*Berliner Zeitung* February 10, 2003). But the internal consistency and united stance of the NGOs on this issue, its cohesion and successful advocacy coalition construction permitted ultimately successful lobbying that changed the position of the initially highly skeptical ministry of the interior (interview GOV-DE-1, Green 2004). The comparatively well-organized and funded NGO Amnesty International took a particular interest in this issue and was particularly active in its lobbying and networking efforts, serving to create the foundation for coalition-building which other NGOs then joined (Amnesty 2002, interviews NGO-DE-1, GOV-DE-1).

The German government once again successfully playing a multilevel game that delayed stringent European regulation until a domestic compromise had been found that precipitated EU-induced change. These delays were all the more remarkable as the particularity of the German stance on this point meant that no allies could be found in the Council, as other member states displayed little appetite for permitting the uploading of the German regulation to the European level, which would have implied significant adaptation costs for them.

The final result of the deliberations (2004/83/EC), which needed to be implemented by October 10, 2006, sets forth minimum standards for the qualification of either non-EU citizens or stateless persons as refugees or beneficiaries of subsidiary protection and defines the minimum levels of rights and benefits associated with both categories. Its content is somewhat mixed in nature: in most sections, it does not venture much beyond the status quo in established countries of immigration. However, there are a few positive and several negative surprises. Most of these innovative passages are, however, couched in such vague terms that this choice of wording appears deliberate. Thus, while the term "refugee" is defined as an individual "fearing to be persecuted for reasons of race, religion, nationality, political opinion" or, interestingly, "membership of a particular social group" (Art. 2.c.), this latter, relatively innovative, point is later undermined when applied to persecution for gender-specific reasons, as "gender related aspects might be considered, without by themselves alone creating a presumption for the applicability of this Article" (Art. 10.1.d). Similarly, though recognition of persecution by nonstate actors is now recognized (Arts. 6.b. and c.), this is then counteracted by defining nonstate authorities such as UN peacekeeping forces as "actors of protection," despite the obvious failure of this concept in practice, for example in the enclave of Srebrenica. In fact, the presence of "internal protection" may be grounds for rejection, even "notwithstanding technical obstacles to return to the country of origin" (Art. 8). Interestingly, spouses and minor children are also covered (Art. 2.h). Once again, provisions are made to permit member states to maintain higher standards (para. 8 of preamble and Art. 3) and grant discretionary protection "on compassionate or humanitarian grounds" (para. 9 of preamble). A positive and potentially innovative element is the obligation to grant subsidiary protection in general (Art. 18) and the detailed provisions specifying the details that need to be taken into account for the individual assessment of each application (Art. 4). Strikingly, there is explicit exclusion of individuals deemed a "threat to public security."

The final directive generally represents a much more restrictive document than the initial draft. A few examples may suffice to illustrate this point. In the original draft, using the availability of internal protection as grounds to refuse recognition was much more tightly limited, namely, to instances in which authorities "have established that the fear of being persecuted or of otherwise suffering serious and unjustified harm is well-founded."

A similar retreat can be observed regarding the issue of military service, which can only be considered legitimate grounds for refugee status if such service would entail the obligation to partake in war crimes (Art. 9.2.e), but no longer if the individual objects to military service for religious, moral, or political reasons.

As we have seen, resistance to this directive was quite enduring and substantial, featuring the German government in a prominent role. The

Germans did not want to be obliged to be liable for benefit payments and grant labor market access to refugees and especially beneficiaries of subsidiary protection, a position which, though particular, elicited enough passive sympathy from other delegations to ensure that an abrogation was created to ensure the safeguarding of the German status quo. Here, as with respect to the notion of persecution by nonstate actors, the German delegation could not secure bottom-up Europeanization in the form of proposing the national regulation pattern as a blueprint. However, on the latter issue unfolding events in the national arena led the German delegation to change its stance as change to national German legislation appeared inevitable due to NGO pressure. But even on this point, the Germans successfully managed to slow down European negotiations to ensure that top-down Europeanization would be delayed and muted in its impact.

The Labor Migration Directive

If the battles over family reunion and asylum had been prolonged and extensive, with a common pattern of national concerns in the Council resulting either in abrogations to secure the national legislative status quo or successful uploading of national and commonly more restrictive regulation, the Commission's initiative to create the contours of actively managed labor migration regulation encountered even fiercer resistance from the member states. Motivated and newly empowered by Tampere, and further endorsed by The Hague, the Commission endeavored as early as 2000 to create common criteria for admitting third-country nationals, both self-employed and regular employees, based on the "beneficial effects" for the economy in the case of the former and on "economic needs," for example labor market shortages, for the latter. More radical, perhaps, was the principle of creating one single common application procedure that would permit applicants to obtain a combined title, encompassing both residence and work permit, thus bypassing the often highly complex and divergent existing national procedures. It was hoped that this superimposed EU pathway might in the long term supersede or at least streamline national procedures. The radical nature of this approach arises from the absence of an automatic link between work and residency permit in some national legislation. As a concession and preempting obvious concerns, member states were to be permitted to limit admission temporarily or permanently (Art. 26 of the 2001 draft directive) or even operate sector-specific national recruitment schemes; however, they are obliged to justify such schemes through the demonstration of exceptional circumstances (Art. 6). Finally, the Commission suggested an "open coordination mechanism" in its 2000 communication on a Community Immigration Policy (COM 2000, 757), accepted by the Council on November 22, which would entail regular exchanges of national "best practices" and presumably eventual harmonization (cf. Caviedes 2004).

A draft directive on "the conditions of entry and residence of third-country nationals for the purpose of paid employment and self-employed activities" was issued on July 11, 2001 and transmitted to the Council on September 5 as well as to the EP for consultation. It contained relatively detailed procedures for labor migrant recruitment, based on an individual examination of each application by member state authorities, taking into account the state of the labor market and the sensitivity of this issue by including the requirement for employers to demonstrate the failed attempt to recruit domestically and EU-wide and imposing the requirement to grant preference both to legal residents, whether EU citizen or not, and to citizens of 2004 newcomer states (Art. 5 + 6). The permit was to be sector-specific (Art. 8) and could be revoked if the holder was out of work for more than three months during the first year of residence (Art. 9). Member states could also set income limits (Art. 6), thus protecting low-wage jobs from immigration, or impose charges on employers for these permits, based on the understanding, however, that such monies would be used for the administrative costs incurred, plus, where applicable, for vocational training. The initial permit was to be issued for a period to be determined by the member states, but up to a maximum of three years, with the possibility of an extension by another three years.

The EP issued its opinion on February 12, 2003. But the Council was much less favorably inclined. The most vocal opponents to this directive were Germany and Austria; both were highly concerned about any EU initiative that would jeopardize member state monopoly over regulating labor market access. Both governments openly questioned the Commission's competence in this area, arguing that Art. 63.3. of the Amsterdam Treaty which called for common regulations on "conditions of entry and residence" did not actually cover this sensitive point.[6] But the more substantial concern arose out of a potential impact on the design of the German national high-skill migration scheme in the making in mid-2002 and later watered down considerably. Though the identity of national delegations making comments during deliberations is deliberately obscured in the Council documents (Council doc. 9862/02 of July 8, 2002 and 7557/02 of June 10, 2002), the German hostility becomes obvious in repeated references to "the new immigration law" being potentially affected.

The opposition to such EU activity was partly fuelled by German employer resistance to regulating labor migration at the EU level. The BDA was extremely skeptical of seeing regulatory power over such sensitive policy domain escaping the national arena, with its own influence being potentially deleteriously affected. Internally united on the issue, it very clearly communicated its preference to the German ministry of the interior (interviews DE-GOV-1, DE-EMP-1). A particular worry was the creation of overly broad European "one size fits all" policy that would not have permitted the national fine-tuning of desired skill profiles. In a later policy paper, the BDA reiterated this position, very strongly defending "national room for maneuver" both in quantitative and qualitative terms, and seriously questioning the value of any pan-European initiative (BDA 2005).

The French government was also strongly skeptical of Commission activity in this field, based on concerns that the principle of subsidiarity was being violated (Sénat 2005). Given the somewhat indecisive internal position of the French employer association MEDEF in combination with some inferior institutional characteristics, it did not manage to undertake a lobbying campaign on this point (interview FR-GOV-1). However, a position paper by European employer association UNICE (2005) indicates that both MEDEF and BDA do not see any "substantial visible added value in a common EU framework" (UNICE 2005). While other national business associations are less critical, the summary of national preferences clearly reveals a general antipathy towards Commission interference into quantitative aspects of migration regulation; but even any "fast track" or "green card" procedure is being rejected. What UNICE supports is a limited "horizontal framework covering all categories of economic migrants with more favorable provisions for trainees, intra-corporate transferees, contract service, suppliers, business visitors, seasonal workers" (2005: 2). Perhaps not coincidentally, this is precisely the direction into which the Commission's anticipated future activity is headed. A 2006 position paper (UNICE 2006) restates the original position, but welcomes the Commission's policy plan and its planned four sectoral directives on labor migration. However, "European employers are opposed to a general framework directive dealing with the rights of third-country national workers." Instead, EU directives should lead to "unbureaucratic, rapid, and transparent procedures" at the national level (UNICE 2006: 1).

With German employers remaining deeply skeptical of European regulation that might have impaired national regulation favoring highly skilled migration, the prospects of successfully engineering an EU-level labor migration directive appeared dire. The draft directive received formal reading during repeated meetings of the Council throughout the first half of 2002, but it had become obvious early on that neither the Germans nor the Austrians were prepared to retreat, while the other delegates displayed no great enthusiasm, either, despite the remarkable decision of Ireland (but not the UK) to "opt in." By summer 2002, it was clear that no agreement was forthcoming. In light of the sustained resistance, the Commission officially withdrew the proposal on March 17, 2003.

This was not quite the end of this proposal, however. In a remarkable incident of bottom-up Europeanization, the Italian presidency revived negotiations by suggesting a common EU labor migration approach, using the Italian model of labor migration quotas as a blueprint (interview ITA-GOV-1). The adaptation would have not only minimized transaction costs, but it would have also seemingly addressed increasing commitment to create partnerships and cooperation agreements with the sending countries, albeit in the slightly cynical Italian fashion of employing such quotas as bargaining chips for concessions in deportation and migration flow detainment efforts. The Italian delegate submitted this proposal during the informal gathering of the ministers of internal affairs in Rome on September 12 and 13, 2003 (interview ITA-GOV-1), suggesting the use of these quotas as a tool in negotiations, while assuaging the concerns over subsidiarity by leaving the determination of the exact national quota to the authority of member states (*Bulletin Quotidien Europe* 8539 September 11, 2003; 8541 September 13, 2003). The Commission and the Spanish and Austrian governments welcomed this initiative. But once again, the Germans were not convinced. During the Rome meeting, Minister of the Interior Schily rejected this proposal, emphasizing that "every member state has to be able to determine the necessary level of immigration depending on the situation of the labor market" (*FAZ* September 13, 2003). The French government shared the German position. During the Thessaloniki Council meeting on June 19–20, 2003, President Chirac emphasized that "the position of France, Germany, and a certain number of other countries is, a priori, hostile towards the very system of quotas" (Sénat 2005: 34).

Not easily frustrated, the Commission issued a new communication on June 3, 2003 (COM 2003, 336 final), in which it strongly emphasized the economic and demographic importance of immigration,[7] two themes that would come to predominate in future communication from the Commission, even more so after Franco Frattini became the new Commissioner in 2004. Indeed, the Barroso Commission proved even more dedicated to the task of engineering a labor migration directive. Meanwhile, during the Thessaloniki meeting, the national governments had paid lip service to the issue, declaring a "need to explore legal means for third-country nationals to migrate to the Union, taking into account the reception capacities of the member states." In the December 2004 Hague program, outlining a coherent AMP policy program by 2010, additional reference was made to "a policy plan on legal migration, including admission procedures capable of responding promptly to fluctuating demands for migrant labour in the labour market." Reflecting the competition state obsession with attracting economically useful migrants, it is noted that for a "knowledge-based economy in Europe, in advancing economic development, and thus contributing to the implementation of the Lisbon strategy" labor migration is crucial. But crucially German reservations entered the document, reflected in the commitment to ensure that "the determination of volumes of admission of labour migrants is a competence of the Member States." In conclusion, the somewhat muddled invitation is issued to the Commission "to present a policy plan on legal migration including admission procedures capable of responding promptly to fluctuating demands for migrant labour in the labour market before the end of 2005" (Conseil européen 2005). But reservations over EU regulation affecting national labor market access regulation were not to cede quickly. During the elaboration of the directive on students and interns, on which political agreement was reached in March and which was adopted on December 13, 2004 (COM 2002, 548), member states had once again limited remunerated employment by students and interns to periods outside term time and subject to the state of the labor market in the host country (Monar 2005, 135).

On January 11, 2005, the Commission presented its Green Paper "on an EU Approach to Managing Economic Migration" (COM 2004, 811 final). In its introduction, the same arguments are being rehearsed as in previous Commission documents; economic migrants are required in light of demographic developments and also "in light of the implications...on competitiveness" [sic]. Conceding defeat, the right to set quantitative targets is clearly allotted to the member states, as "the Commission has taken into account the reservations and concerns expressed by the Member States during the discussion of the 2001 proposal." The Green Paper sets out three options for future discussion: first, to introduce a "horizontal approach" on the conditions of entry and residence or, second, and less ambitiously, to introduce a series of sectoral regulations, similar to the ones on students (COM 2002, 548 and researchers (COM 2004, 178), focusing, for example, on seasonal workers and intracompany transferees. Third, a form of EU Green Card is proposed, through the establishment of a common fast-track procedure for specific labor and skills shortages. This green paper solicited more than 160 responses from NGOs, trade unions, employer and business associations, governments, academics, and other individuals, culminating in a public hearing on June 14, 2005. On June 2, ministers debated the green paper, demonstrating a willingness to work towards a common framework, but simultaneously finding no consensus as to whether communautarization was necessary on minimum admission standards and "fast track" admission and whether admission should be linked to specific labor market shortages. Opinions on the former point remained divided. As Frattini was to summarize during a speech delivered to the Dublin Institute of European Affairs on June 20 (Speech 05/364), some voices during the public hearing called for a common framework of rights for immigrants, while a job seeker permit was also advocated.

The responses from the national governments suggest that the old concerns resurfaced. Thus the German government's response highlighted severe reservations over EU regulation of labor market access *tout court*, rejected any "fast track" procedure or an EU Green Card and advocated a very limited "horizontal" framework. The document reveals limited support mainly in areas such as information exchange or border control, but displays generally pronounced skepticism, repeatedly arguing that in the absence of a truly European labor market the benefits of developing a pan-European labor migration policy remain obscure (Bundesregierung 2005). Despite its opt-out, the British government's reaction paper is even more skeptical, questioning the value of AMP extension with the exception of information exchange. The emphasis on border control is palpable and any measure seen as interfering with member state capacity to regulate labor market access is regarded with pronounced skepticism, bordering on animosity (UK Government 2005). Though perhaps of less immediate political consequence due to the opt-out, the British stance added weight to the skeptical camp in symbolical terms. The reservation was shared by the British employer association CBI, though while it communicated its position to the Home Office, it did not feel the need for sustained lobbying given the obvious British exemption from EU regulation in this domain (interview UK-BUS-1).

Official French responses similarly reiterate reservations towards undifferentiated "catch-all" policy. A report by the French Senate (Sénat 2005)[8] is remarkably frank in its criticism of the very rationale behind the Green Paper, demonstrating that the demographic argument is poorly presented, since immigration obviously cannot serve as a panacea to redress the shifting age pyramid. It is also underlined that demographic trends differ widely among the EU-25, as does the state and the regulation of the labor market. An argument about inherent difficulties in accurately predicting long-term labor market developments is used to cast further doubt on the desirability of Europeanized labor migration policy. The main areas in which EU activity is being welcomed are in the exchange of information, in the fight against undocumented migration and in closer cooperation with countries of origin. The 2004 newcomers, especially the Polish government, expressed surprise and anxiety over encouraging immigration from third countries while restrictions regarding intra-EU labor mobility and service provision were still in place (interview PL-GOV-1).

The Commission presented the promised policy plan on legal migration on December 21, 2005 (Memo 05/494). Given vociferous opposition at first and continued skepticism notwithstanding some rhetorical overtures, it focused on measures unlikely to encounter much resistance. Thus the second option proposed in the Green Book is pursued by promising to elaborate four specific directives on the following categories: *highly skilled and seasonal workers, intra-corporate transferees and remunerated interns and trainees*. This appears to constitute terrain where common ground can be found. By contrast, the outlined "horizontal" framework looks somewhat less substantive; it will include a list of basic rights of all migrant workers. The evidently more thorny and ambitious path of elaborating general regulation concerning the procedures and conditions for admission of immigrants has been abandoned in light of the sustained resistance experienced.

The policy plan also covers other future endeavors, notably the creation of a website providing information on vacancies and job seekers, entitled European Job Mobility Portal (EURES) and exchanging information on national practices regarding integration (COM 2005, 606).

More interesting perhaps, is the commitment to more cooperation with sending countries, including the elaboration of "instruments to encourage return and circular migration" and vocational and language training courses offered in the countries of origin, similar to the pilot projects the Italian government is conducting in North Africa.

Conclusion

In its May 1, 2004 Assessment of the Tampere Program (COM 2004: 4002; Juss 2005), the Commission claimed "undeniable and tangible" progress, yet had to admit that

> Member States are sometimes reluctant to cooperate within this new European framework when their interests are at stake. Moreover, the right of initiative shared with the Member States sometimes had the effect that national concerns were given priority over Tampere priorities. [...] The original ambition was limited by institutional constraints, and sometimes also by a lack of sufficient political consensus.

This probably constitutes a fair summary of the first phase of AMP-making. O'Keeffe (1999) argues that the Amsterdam provisions "fail to establish a complete European immigration policy and the provisions on asylum are largely concerned with the setting of minimum standards or are procedural rather than focussed on high-level common substantive standards."

This judgment, though harsh, alludes to the severe problems and tangible resistance encountered by the Commission. It therefore permitted room for national fine-tuning. The top-down impact is more significant in countries with very fragile or non-existing systems of asylum in particular, notably in Southern and Eastern Europe. However, for the more established countries of immigration, notably France and Germany, the top-down impact remains relatively limited. Despite Germany's relatively proactive role in advocating the communautarization of migration policy, major resistance from the German delegation can be expected whenever top-down Europeanization threatens to lead to serious adjustment costs. The German position is influenced by the fact that some of the German Länder are highly skeptical of AMP, fearing the loss of their own power if decision-making authority is shifted from Berlin to Brussels. Thus the German government skillfully played a two-level game, blocking the family reunion directive until a concession had been secured that permitted maintaining maximum room for maneuver regarding the maximum age of children. Similarly, Berlin blocked the asylum qualification directive until a much watered down version no longer automatically granted labor market access to beneficiaries of subsidiary protection. Meanwhile, the question of recognition of persecution by nonstate actors was delayed until a modification in national law had been made, following a domestic political negotiation process. Finally, labor migration policy has been similarly delayed and eventually obstructed. The Austrian government supported the German position on several occasions. Vienna was particularly keen to avoid any "liberal" coloring of its rather restrictive immigration policy through top-down Europeanization processes.

Having failed to implement a universal labor migration directive, the European Commission is now taking a sectoral, qualification-specific piecemeal approach (interview EU-COM-1, Guild 2007; EurAsylum 2007). On asylum matters, the Commission is moving towards greater harmonization. In both policy domains, very serious member state resistance to top-down Europeanization appears likely to persist and unanimous decision-making in the Council will help perpetuate a pattern of significant concessions and room for national maneuver. An element of uncertainty is introduced through the implications of the EU eastward enlargement. Eastern member states do not perceive the same need for sectoral labor migration and will likely question preference to third-country nationals for labor market access in the EU-15 as long as their own nationals are still subject to restricted labor mobility and service provision.

Though rhetorically committed to encouraging circle migration and avoiding brain drain, the Commission's approach vis-à-vis sending countries (Memo 07/197 Circular Migration and Mobility Partnerships between the European Union and Third Countries, May 16, 2007), especially African countries under the auspices of Art. 13 of the Cotonou Agreement, can be criticized for taking up some of the ideas indirectly first flouted by the unsuccessful Italian bottom-up Europeanization attempt. The creation of the European Employment Agency in Mali is seen as a pilot study for managing mainly low-skilled economic migration in the source countries, to be rolled out to Senegal, Gambia, and Mauritania. As the Director-General for Justice, Freedom and Security admitted openly in an interview "mobility partnerships... help third countries secure better access to the EU for their nationals—and in particular for the purposes of economic migration—provided that they commit themselves to fighting illegal migration more actively" (EurAsylum 2007). Other Commission officials

National Actors and European Solutions

likewise refer to it as a "carrot-and-stick deal" (interview EU-COM-1). Though largely congruent with the ideological *zeitgeist* of the Sevilla Council conclusions, the original Italian proposal raised so much concern among the member states that it could not hope to achieve adoption. Much of the opposition was linked to the issue of quotas, strongly opposed at the time by the German delegation.

The creation of pilot "regional protection programs" in Tanzania and plans to launch a similar program in the Western Independent States, for example in Moldova (EurAsylum 2007), could be similarly interpreted as a Commission attempt to revive the earlier British bottom-up initiative to create regional asylum seeker detention and processing zones outside of EU territory. Commission officials confirm that the British initiative "inspired" them (interview EU-COM-1).

The inter-governmental tradition, represented through the legacy of the TREVI group, the originally extra-communautarian Schengen, Dublin, and, most recently Prün agreements, and institutionally embedded until late 2004 in the principle of unanimity on all areas of AMP—restricted since to border control, visa, and migration policy—is alive and well. EU policymaking continues to proceed relatively slowly and in small steps. With its directive on long-term residents (2003/109/EC), permitting legal residents of more than five years to move relatively freely to another EU member state, the Commission could be applauded—or criticized— for promoting "negative integration" or integration by stealth, as the ramifications of this measure may well lead to secondary migration movements, thus undercutting the regulatory capacity of the individual state. Interestingly, the second member state may also limit this sort of influx, if such legislative limitation instruments were already on the books prior to the passage of this directive, a "grandfather clause" once again benefiting the skeptic Germanophone countries.

AMP can be criticized for simply distilling the pan-European trend to distinguish between burdensome unsolicited undesirables and the highly sought after labor migrants that Europe attempts to poach from the more established countries of emigration in North America and Oceania. While the former are deterred through a concentric circle of deterrence zones, in the form of carrier sanctions for transportation companies, deportation agreements with third countries, "safe third countries" and "safe countries of origin" regulations, along with the increasing militarization of the EU's external geographic borders, the latter remain actively sought after. In its persistent evocation of the neoliberal Lisbon Agenda, emphasizing "competitiveness" ahead of other world regions, the Commission's documents demonstrate clearly how important the logic of the competition state has become for migration policy.

Notes

1. This necessity spawns the myriad of games over a variety of institutional arenas actors are involved in, including the Council of Ministers, the European Council, the Committee of Permanent Representatives (Corefer), and a variety of specific committees.

   One key avenue of influencing the regulatory outcome is the successful presentation of proposals as representing "best practice," a delusive fashion of seemingly depoliticizing policy proposals, by employing the technocratic purportedly neutral and objective language of EU policymakers themselves, claiming to suggest simply "what works best." Obviously, such "best practice" proposals do need to appeal to common ground among governmental representatives and cannot simply masquerade as such. An innovative way of identifying such common ground is the employment of the "open method of coordination." Though its application in migration policymaking is still somewhat rare (Caviedes 2003), it adds an additional venue for strategies of persuasion and agenda-setting, albeit indirectly. The open method of coordination was introduced as a soft law mechanism, encouraging the coordination and eventual convergence of national policymaking in policy areas in which one single, common EU model was unlikely to emerge either as—often structurally embedded—national diversity presents an insuperable hurdle or some other fundamental practical impediment. Using this venue, governmental actors can place their own national regulatory model on display and monitor the showcasing of other models, copying, and emulating aspects. This "sounding board" thus presents an additional arena for disseminating aspects of one's own model outside of the formal framework of EU institutions. However, it can also be used not only to shop for ideas but also to "test the water" and take the temperature among other governmental decision-makers in terms of approval for new policy initiatives.
2. Act C-113/89 Rush Portuguesa Lda against Office national d'immigration. The Court's "Seco and Desquenne" decision (February 3, 1982) Act 62–63/81, collection 1982 p. 223 had already opened up room for national response strategies, but this decision had largely been ignored by actors throughout Europe.
3. A sentiment especially expressed during interviews with DE-UNI-1, DE-BUS-1, FR-UNI-1, FR-UNI-2, IRL-UNI-1, IRL-BUS-1.
4. During the *trente glorieuses*, labor shortages existed across all economic sectors, hence skill levels of potential migrants did not concern policymakers. However,

in the wake of the decline of the primary and secondary sectors in favor of the tertiary sector of the economy and the concomitant pursuit of divergent production strategies in coordinated versus liberal market economies, national labor recruitment strategies do diverge to a much greater degree. Of course, given the pan-European character of the structural metamorphosis of the economy, all national policymakers can be expected to solicit labor migrants for vacancies in the service sector, but to different degrees. However, in high-wage high-skill countries associated with coordinated market economies, particular emphasis is placed on highly skilled labor migrants, while liberal market economies attract migrants at both ends of the skill curve. They commonly possess significantly sized low-wage low-skill sectors, which require labor demand, and will shape overall migration management accordingly.

5. The German government even supported the Council of Ministers in the ECJ case, as did the Commission. In the final plea by state attorney Kokott of September 8, 2005, the case was seen as unfounded even though the attorney general agreed that the EP's consultation rights had been formally violated. However, it was argued that individual cases cannot be brought because of disagreements with components of directives, which was the case here: the EP justified its disagreement on account of the modified Art. 4 para 6 of the directive concerning the age of children.

The Court did not consider the critical question of age to constitute undue discrimination and found the limited room for maneuver for member states to choose their own age to be in line with European law and nondiscriminatory. In substantial terms, the Court seemed to consider the choice of the age of 12 years quite appropriate, arguing that: "In diesem Zusammenhang stellt die Wahl des Alters von 12 Jahren kein Kriterium dar, mit dem gegen das Verbot der Diskrimierung weges des Alters verstoßen würde, da dieses Kriterium auf eine Phase im Leben des minderjährigen Kindes abstellt, in der es bereits über einen verhältnismäßig langen Zeitraum ohne seine Familienmitglieder in einem Drittstaat gelebt hat, so dass eine Integration in ein anderes Umfeld zu mehr Schwierigkeiten führen kann." [In this context the choice of an age of 12 years does not constitute a discriminatory criterion based on age because this criterion is aimed at an age at which the minor will have already lived in a third country for a relatively long period of time without any of its family members, therefore, integration into a new environment might cause more difficulties.] (ECJ C540/03, 74, cited in Franz 2006: 52).

6. Indeed, the Germans managed to maintain the principle of unanimity regarding the issue of labor market access in the European Constitutional Treaty, as modified Art. III-168 (para. 5) indicates: "This article does not affect the right of the member states to regulate how many third-country nationals from third countries may enter the national territory to search for employment either in a self-employed capacity or as an employee."

7. Thus it is somewhat simplistically argued that "immigration should be recognised...[for] contributing to entrepreneurship, diversity and innovation, its economic impact on employment and growth is also significant as it increases labour supply and helps cope with bottlenecks. In addition, immigration tends to have an overall positive effect on product demand and therefore on labour demand" (2.2.) and the trend towards a shrinking working age population in Europe in combination with various push factors in the developing countries is likely to generate a sustained flow of immigrants over the next decades. Immigration can help in filling current and future needs of the EU labour markets. In addition, it can contribute to spreading the effects of the demographic transition.... It will therefore be important to find ways of managing these migratory pressures through adequate policies of entry and settlement. (2.5)
8. A report by the French parliament contains similar conclusions (Assemblée Nationale 2005).

4

Political Battles at Home and in Brussels: Labor Migration and Asylum Policy in Established Countries of Immigration: France, the United Kingdom, and Germany

Migration policymaking unfolds both at the European and at the national level. While national ministers of interior affairs engage with often like-minded homologues in the Council of Ministers in a somewhat more sheltered policy environment, at the national level they encounter a wide array of actors in a setting which witnesses much more contestation and at times open conflict. Three principal tasks are being carried out in this chapter: first, major migration regulation patterns are being chartered based on an analysis of key national legislative initiatives since 1989; second, the framework of analysis developed earlier is being applied, and the role of interest groups in migration policy is being analyzed; and third, the dynamics of Europeanization are being explored in more depth. Empirically, the chapter focuses on France, the United Kingdom, and Germany. Labor migration policies are influenced by labor market interest associations seeking to imprint their preferences on regulatory policies. Therefore, the sectoral composition of the economy is an important factor in shaping considerations concerning labor recruitment strategies. Table 4.1 illustrates the composition of the three economies in terms of contribution to both gross national product and employment levels.

Table 4.1. Sectoral composition and distribution of workforce in the UK, France, and Germany (OECD country reports, various years)

	Percent of the GDP	Percent of the labor force
UK agriculture	1.1	1.5
French agriculture	2.5	4.1
German agriculture	1.1	2.8
UK industry	26.1	19.1
French industry	21.4	24.4
German industry	28.6	33.4
UK services	72.9	79.5
French services	76.1	71.5
German services	70.3	63.8

France: The Slow Rediscovery of "Selected" Immigration

A traditional country of immigration, labor migration played an important role both throughout late nineteenth-century industrialization and during the postwar economic boom. However, since the mid-1970s, the willingness to accept humanitarian forms of migration has waned significantly. French immigration policy can be said to display four pattern-forming traits. Tables 4.2, 4.3, and 4.4 summarize developments in French immigration policy since the early 1980s.

First, immigration is a strongly divisive partisan issue; accompanied by clamorous rhetoric, political reforms regularly overhaul and revise past strides by precedent governments. Yet on close inspection, much of this reformatory impetus affects regulatory details rather than the grand contours that have proven more stable and enduring. For the Left, the priorities have been to foster societal integration and pursue a pragmatic approach to the administration of immigration both at the national level and at the local level, including occasional regularization initiatives and a somewhat liberal administration of political asylum, but without surrendering a fairly restrictive framework of border control. By contrast, for the Right it has been imperative to implement restrictive measures on undocumented migration that then permit highly visible and ostentatious measures such as public arrests and deportations, and also more generally to broaden legislative authorization of police powers, to impede access to residency permits and citizenship, and to grant wider discretionary powers to local authorities in the administration of vital components of visa applications.

Table 4.2. French immigration policy in the 1980s

January 10, 1980 "Bonnet Law"—legal entry and work permission is made dependent on proof of job offer; limits for number of foreign employees in certain economic sectors; easier deportation of foreigners, especially if unemployed or convicted of legal infractions, more restrictive border controls.

October 27, 1981 Major legislative modification of the Bonnet Law, reinstating the right to appeal, limit of deportations to foreigners condemned to one year in prison or more or individuals deemed a national security threat.

1981–82 Regularization program, offering one-year residency and work permits to 105,000 individuals.

July 17, 1984 Law 84–622 creates a combined residency and work permit, again modifying the Bonnet Law, the new *titre de séjour et de travail* is valid for 10 years.

September 9, 1986 Law 86–1025 "regarding the entry and residency of foreigners in France" ("Pasqua Law I," *relative aux conditions d'entrée et de séjour des étrangers en France*); facilitates deportations by permitting regional head of government to decree such measures, legally significantly modifies the liberal October 29, 1981 "Questiaux Law," limits criteria for eligibility for work and residency permit, facilitates refusal of visa, introduces new identity spot checks.

June 22, 1987 Marceau Long, Vice-President of the Council of the State is charged by Prime Minister Jacques Chirac with preparing reform measures to the citizenship law within the framework of the *Commission du code de la nationalité*; vivid national debate about citizenship in the media, political parties, and among public intellectuals, Commission presents its final report entitled "Being French today and in the future" (*Etre Français aujourd'hui et demain*) on January 7, 1988, recommending facilitation of the acquisition of French citizenship by young French-born descendants of foreigners between the ages of 16 and 21 that have been resident in France for at least five years.

August 8, 1989 Socialist Minister of the Interior Pierre Joxe announces modifications of the rightist Pasqua law; the "Joxe Law" (89–548) protects individuals with relatives in France against deportation, introduces tighter administrative limits on regional governments' deportation decisions, reintroduces legal avenues for challenging deportation decisions.

January 7, 1990 Prime Minister Michel Rocard (in)famously declares: "We cannot accommodate all the misery of the world" (*Nous ne pouvons pas accueillir toute la misère du monde*), while addressing Socialist MPs of Maghrebian origin; President François Mitterrand opined on December 10, 1989 in a radio interview with Antenne 2 and Europe 1 that the upper limits of tolerance have been reached in the 1970s.

January 10, 1990 Law 90-34 abolishes the legal recourse against deportation decisions.

Table 4.3. French immigration policy in the 1990s

August 31, 1991 Decree 91–829 imposes the requirement on visa applicants to provide proof of invitation or accommodation in France and authorizes local government to verify the authenticity of this accommodation before issuing this certificate.

January 1, 1992 Law 91–1383 against illegal employment and against undocumented entry and residency in France.

February 29, 1992 Law 92–190 confirms the legality of declaring select zones in airports and maritime ports to constitute "transit zones" in which undocumented migrants can be held for up to 30 days, without acquiring rights arising out of access to French territory; this law also introduces carrier sanctions for airlines, shipping, and trucking companies.

July 2, 1992 "Quilés" Law 92–625 permits the detention of foreigners arriving at airport or maritime ports in these waiting zones for up to four days, during this period the ministry of the interior can decide whether it deems applications for asylum "manifestly unfounded." This law legalized a common practice already applied without any legal basis, including the detention of asylum seekers in sealed hotel rooms. This practice had been declared illegal by a court in November 1990, while the Constitutional Court ruled the practice of using "extraterritorial zones" unconstitutional in February 1992. In the same decision, the Court found carrier sanctions to be legal.

July 22, 1993 Méhaignerie Law 93–933 reforms the citizenship code. Following another prolonged public debate about the contours of citizenship in France and informed by the earlier commission work, French-born descendants of foreign legal residents may acquire citizenship, but must formally express their interest to do so, spouses of French citizens can acquire citizenship only after a one-year waiting period, children of individuals born in Algeria prior to independence automatically receive French citizenship.

August 10 and **August 24 1993** "Pasqua Laws II" (93–1027) facilitate identity spot checks and extend grounds for refusal of residency permits, while permitting the withdrawal of residency permits for certain refugees, motivated by Charles Pasqua's defined policy goal of "zero immigration." The Constitutional Court declares several of the clauses unconstitutional, including the detention of foreigners with no valid identity documents for up to three months, the ban on students to take family members to France, and the one year entry ban for deportees. A very slightly modified version of the law is passed on December 30, 1993 (93–1416), purporting to address the court's concerns. The revised law, however, further facilitates spot checks of identification documents.

December 28, 1994 Law 94–1136 modifies some of the 1945 legislation in light of the Schengen Agreement; creates legal penalties for "facilitating illicit entry." The accusation of undocumented residency in France can also be based on previous or current presumably undocumented residency in the Schengenzone. "Transit zones" are created at train stations; transferring detainees between such zones is rendered legal where it aids in deportation efforts—this is one way to circumvent the Court's earlier decision on such zones.

Summer of 1996 Demonstrations of undocumented migrants and their supporters in Paris for a regularization of the "*sans-papiers*." On June 25 a delegation occupies the town hall of the 18th arrondissement in northern Paris, home to a high number of residents of foreign origin, another delegation occupies the Church Saint-Bernard de la Chapelle in the same part of town, some of the squatters start a hunger strike; on August 23 police raid the Church and arrest 228 mainly African squatters, the majority of whom are sent to a deportation camp in suburban Vincennes.

April 24, 1997 Debré Law 97–396 contains provisions to facilitate the deportation of destitute foreigners, increases the leeway of local governments in issuing certificates of acceptable accommodation necessary for securing a visa, and increase the powers of the border police; the Constitutional Court earlier struck down some of the planned provisions regarding routine criminal background checks on asylum seekers and the abolition of the right to a renewal of the residency permit after 10 years. This law proves heavily contested: NGO Ligue des droits de l'homme presented a petition to parliament against this law signed by 150 prominent personalities; 59 film directors launch an appeal for "civil disobedience" and several center-left mayors of Parisian arrondissements and suburban townships bestow citizenship on individual sans-papiers. Minister of Local Government and Integration Eric Raoult responds by challenging the film directors to live on a tough public housing project in the notorious suburban district of Seine-Saint-Denis for one month to "see for themselves that integration is nothing to do with the movies."

June 10, 1997 Office of Prime Minster Lionel Jospin announces a partial regularization of some of the sans-papiers. NGOs welcome this measure. Jospin announces a major re-examination of French immigration policy, commissioning a major report by political scientist Patrick Weil.

Table 4.4. French immigration policy since 2000

July 31, 1997 Weil submits two reports on immigration and citizenship, containing a number of recommendations that present a major departure: strengthening the right to asylum, more accommodating regulations regarding the right to family life and hence family reunion, facilitating the formalities for entry, improving the accommodation of foreign students, introducing more efficient measures in reducing illicit forms of employment, and strengthening the *ius solis* aspect of citizenship status, thus abolishing the requirement to express serious commitment to French citizenship for French-born descendants of foreigners as an application requirement.

December 1997 Samir Naïr, counselor on integration and developmental affairs in the ministry of the interior submits a commission report to Jospin suggesting closer economic cooperation with major source countries of immigration.

March 16, 1998 Law 98–170 modifies the regulation of citizenship, following the Weil Commission's recommendations the *ius solis* principle is being extended, thus abolishing any "declaration" requirement for French-born individuals in order to obtain citizenship and permitting applications for citizenship at age 13 with parental authorization or 16 without; grants residency cards to all French-born individuals with the future option of citizenship, thus eliminating the loophole of stateless descendants of (especially Maghrebian) non-French citizens created (deliberately?) by the Pasqua Laws.

May 11, 1998 "Chèvenement" Law 98–349 (*relative à l'entrée et au séjour des étrangers en France et au droit d'asile*) is passed, following a favorable ruling by the Constitutional Court with one minor exception; the procedures regarding the contested accommodation certificate are streamlined and liberalized, and family reunion provisions are extended; one-year residency permits are granted to individuals married to French citizens, parents of French citizens, or individuals who can prove residency in France for 15 years; special consideration is given to highly skilled individuals (e.g. scientists) who intend to migrate to France; a new secondary tier of protection inferior to ordinary asylum known as "territorial asylum" (*asile territorial*) is being created that permits a significant degree of administrative discretion and is temporary in nature.

March 26, 2003 New Minister of the Interior Nicholas Sarkozy announces in a press conference that the government wants to fill one charter plane full of deportees every week; in September he reinforces this message by encouraging local prefects to double the numbers of deportees and to disregard the protests of nongovernmental groups which supposedly only "speak for themselves."

October 29, 2003 The French and Belgian governments agree on a scheme to operate joint deportation charter flights that will collect deportees both in Paris and in Brussels.

December 10, 2003 "Sarkozy and Villepin Law" 2003-1119 (*relative à la maîtrise de l'immigration et au séjour des étrangers en France*) contains the following provisions: foreigners can be detained for longer periods at the borders, a centralized digitalized record of asylum seekers is being created, the accommodation certificates are subjected to tougher controls, marriages can be examined if there is suspicion of fraud in the interest of obtaining citizenship, more exacting conditions for obtaining a residency permit are being introduced, the so-called double sentence (*double peine*) for foreign delinquents is being abolished, that is, first imprisoning and then deporting an individual—the latter has been a long-standing demand of NGOs.

September 15, 2004 In cabinet the Minister of Employment, Labor and Social Cohesion proposes creating a single authority responsible for the administration of migration, thus merging the Office of International Migration (*Office de migrations internationales* OMI) and the Social Services for the Aid of Emigrants (*Service Social d'aide aux émigrants*). In addition, plans are circulated to create a legal basis for the new "reception and integration contracts" (CAI = *contrat d'accueil et d'intégration*) that new immigrants have to agree to.

2006 Sarkozy Law ends the automatic legalization of undocumented migrants after 10 years of residence in France; raises the period for family reunion applications to up to 18 months; creates a new category for labor migrants (*competences et talents*), prolongs the residence period required of non-French spouses of French citizens to qualify for an independent residency permit and citizenship; formalizes the obligation to sign a CAI, entailing the obligation to partake in language classes.

November 20, 2007 "Hortefeux" Law 2007-1631 makes language and "values" exam mandatory for beneficiaries of family reunion even before entering French territory, specifies minimum income and renders possible DNA exams for beneficiaries of family reunion, limits appeals against asylum decisions, and enables asylum cases to be dealt with in waiting zones in airports and seaports; creates "development savings account."

It is at the microlevel where the ideological difference most tangibly translates into different policy outputs. Detailed provisions of migration control, regarding for example the detention of newcomers, deportation measures, the regulation of family reunion, or the administrative procedures regarding visas, are constantly tinkered with. Such activism, though admittedly of significant consequence at the microlevel, may obscure the perception of continuity dominating the grand contours of French migration policy. Active labor recruitment ceased in 1974 with the exception of seasonal labor migration programs especially for the agricultural sector attracting around 100,000 employees annually up until the early 1990s, though since reduced to around 10,000 annually (Currle 2004, 111). An initially relatively liberal constitutionally guaranteed asylum policy has been rendered more restrictive through endless tampering that has over time and through numerous changes impaired territorial access, facilitated detention and deportation, and granted significant administrative discretion. Immigration reform is often accompanied by regularization programs for undocumented migrants.

Second, in immigration policy as indeed in other areas, the French state attempts to insulate decision-making from demands by social actors and societal pressure. Hall's (1986, 164 ff.) characterization of *l'état actif* possessing both the "capacity to implement policy, if necessary over the objections of key social groups," and a "monopoly on political virtue" remains of analytical value. Nongovernmental organizations struggle to influence new legislation, yet do succeed, though generally based on the fortuitous congruence of several underpinning factors, including favorable public opinion and the ability to launch highly visible campaigns based on straightforward demands. Such campaigns resonate well with public opinion, can connect to somewhat mythical republican values of a sheltering asylum for dissidents, and spawn regularization programs, stop individual deportations, or attack the *double peine* ("double penalty") imposed on convicted perpetrators first obliged to serve a jail sentence, only to be deported afterwards. Following a highly influential NGO campaign led by CIMADE in the fall of 2001 that quickly garnered overwhelming public opinion support, the right-wing Chirac/Raffarin government modified its stance on this issue, applying the standard conventions on deportation to individuals convicted of legal infractions, thus no longer automatically deporting anyone having served a prison sentence of at least five years (Titre 1, Art. 22.6 of the Law 2003–1119). Very importantly, individuals born in France and resident there before the age of 13 can no longer be deported to their countries of citizenship under any circumstances. However, as developed in more detail below, NGOs struggle to influence the coloring of asylum policy, largely due to organizational deficiencies.

The commissioning of expert reports suggesting broad contours of future policy development is a noteworthy recent development, though their importance must not be overestimated. These expert panels, composed predominantly of academics, wield considerable power in setting the agenda for subsequent policy reform measures but obviously do not determine the implementation and ultimately do not undermine the relative insulation from pressure groups the government seeks to assure.

Third, much of the public debate on immigration has in fact focused on integration, more often than not *via* citizenship. The establishment and broad acceptance of this link in the public debate marks a success for the Right and the Far Right. Much of the public debate in the 1980s and 1990s revolved around this issue, couched in the terminology developed by the electorally increasingly influential Far Right *Front National* on the one hand and the new vocabulary emerging from a rapidly politicized second generation of *beurs* on the other, vocal in their demands for access to housing, education, and the labor market. The pervasive discrimination against descendants of non-European immigrants—often compounded by geographical isolation in economically deprived and socially excluded suburban postwar public housing developments (*cités*)—obviously raised vexing questions regarding the ideal of a color-blind republican identity (cf. Favell 2001). The problem of racism in everyday life, especially relevant with regard to access to the labor market, raised by migrant associations such as *SOS Racisme*, remains virulent. The debates surrounding citizenship focused particularly on the application, modification, or even abolition of *ius solis*, especially in regard to pre-independence Algeria. By the late 1990s, it appeared that the potential emerged for a clash between the cultural and especially religious norms that some newcomers and, more remarkably, their descendants were unwilling to relinquish or newly embraced and the often flouted unifying universal and all-accommodating republican ideals.

It is no exaggeration to attribute the electoral rise of the far right *Front Nationale* to the skillful exploitation of concerns over immigration and especially citizenship. Though its electoral fortunes have waned over time (Perrineau 1997), its regional base was particularly strong: successful in the southern and eastern regions, negating any obvious correlation between the physical concentration of immigrants and their descendants and electoral successes, with the exception of parts of the South, for example the region of Provence-Alpes-Cote d'Azur. The Ile-de-France region, by contrast, has proven remarkably resilient to the lure of the far right despite or possibly because of the highest proportion of residents of foreign origin in France. On its own terms, the far right has been successful in at least three ways. It has raised the profile of migration, successfully engendering the mutation of a policy domain otherwise influenced either by progressive considerations of human rights or by the technocratic lingo of administration, steering, and management into a subject of highly politicized, emotional, and fiery debate. Second, the very specter of the Front ensures that immigration remains at the forefront of the political agenda. Third, and perhaps more worryingly, the Front has succeeded in coloring the rhetoric, ideas, norms, and public intellectual debate. The accusation of the *lepenisation* wielded against current president Nicholas Sarkozy is only one example, but even more moderate politicians such as Jacques Chirac can be fairly accused of pandering to Le Pen's rhetoric—and presumably his electorate—with his infamous sympathy for the imaginary ordinary citizen's concerns over foreign *odeurs et bruits* (smells and noises), emitting from the public housing dwellings of polygamous welfare cheats of African origin.[1] The Front's highly publicized division following internal battles between Bruno Megret and Jean-Marie Le Pen is less significant than its slight shift in rhetoric over the years from an unashamedly and bluntly racist discourse to a slightly more sophisticated advocacy of "national preference" and "tough" law enforcement, not entailing any ideological modification, however. Following the 2002 presidential elections, the Front has successfully discovered and exploited a second pillar skillfully rhetorically linked to immigration, creating a concern over insecurity and crime that triggers and connects with xenophobe sentiments without resorting to the blatantly racist past rhetoric. On its own terms, the Front can boast remarkable achievements, witnessing mainstream political parties and their representatives borrow its rhetoric and sometimes concepts, impregnating public debates, and rendering restrictionist, xenophobe, and ultimately racist positions if not quite *salonfähig* than at least no longer unacceptable.

Fourth, as argued by other scholars, there has been considerable juridical activity by the constitutional court (*conseil constitutionnel*) that has in a number of instances reigned in the excessively stringent

Political Battles at Home and in Brussels

legislative initiatives of right-wing governments, concerning, for example, the maintenance of nonterritorial detention and exclusion zones, and infringements on the civil liberties of noncitizens. This increase in scope and quantity of rulings on migration issues by the court, established in the 1958 constitution of the Fifth Republic (Title VII, Art. 56–63), needs to be considered behind the backdrop of a significant increase in the number of rulings,[2] but analysts stress its significance in French migration policymaking (Hollifield 2000), and cite it as one factor further encouraging governments to choose the European level (Guiraudon 2000a). One might be tempted to dismiss the council's involvement as a mere tool that isolated parliamentarians employ as a desperate recourse, but it is probably more accurate to consider its emergence as the permanent consolidation of a serious new actor governments need to take into account.

System of Political Economy: Poststatism

The French system of political economy has generally been described as being strongly shaped by a pervasive and persistent statist legacy that presumably influences all aspects of macroeconomic policymaking. However, developments including major economic liberalization and privatization initiatives since the 1980s, the legacy of Mitterrand's abandonment of neo-Keynesianism, the dramatic decline of the union movement's membership numbers and political power, and the gradual abandonment of state-led economic development and politico-economic management all render the neat categorization of the French model extremely challenging. Variously described as a mixed market economy (Hancké, Rhodes, and Thatcher 2007), a liberalized statist model (Schmidt 1996, 2002) constituting a bastardized hybrid (Clift 2007) or indeed a separate Mediterranean model (Amable 2003; Levy 1999), the close nexus between government and organized business remains a constant feature, but the power dynamics have changed radically with the employers commanding significantly more influence (cf. Hancké 2002; Levy 2005). The consensus in the comparative political economy literature is to set France apart from the Germanic Rhineland (Boyer 1997), "continental European" (Amable 2003) or coordinated market economy (Hall and Soskice 2001) model due to the absence of a Germanic system of industrial relations (Lallement 1999). Trade unions are disproportionately well represented institutionally in tripartite structures such as the *Conseil économique et sociale* and in informal consultation rounds with the government, yet unionization rates are low, particularly outside the public sector, leading to a feeble position at the grassroots level.[3] Corporate structures (Hancké 2002) exacerbate this union weakness, as the plethora of small companies active as subcontractors involved at the bottom end of the production process often operates in the virtual absence of union presence.

French Employers and Migration Regulation

The major internationally active corporations, often benefiting from oligopolistic market structures, are particularly influential within the employer association MEDEF, which does, however, also represent small- and medium-sized enterprises, claiming that 70 percent of its membership base has less than 50 employees, thus rivaling with the CGPME, though generally the MEDEF is considered to be by far the most influential voice of organized business (Woll 2006, 496). Until most recently, there has been no consensus among French business regarding strategies for labor recruitment. The major internationally active companies have not been adverse to recruiting highly skilled migrants, but until most recently were content with the provisions of the 1998 Chèvenement Law which permits the fast-track processing of residency and work permit applications by "desirable" labor migrants. Persistent high unemployment and high politicization created a political climate highly unsuitable for lobbying efforts, but the regulatory status quo seemed to fulfill French business interest until recently anyway. De-industrialization and competition from low-cost high-quality production sites in manufacturing not only from East Asia but also from Central Europe, and from Francophone North Africa for low-cost service provision such as telemarketing and telephone customer service centers mean that certain sectors are unlikely to expand or in some cases even sustain production sites in France. Furthermore, low unionization rates permit an often fairly cavalier attitude towards wage agreements and statutory working conditions. De facto secondary tiers of the labor market already exist in France and many, though not all, of these "three D" jobs (dirty, dull, dangerous) are filled by foreigners. This is particularly true in economic sectors such as gastronomy, construction, seasonal agricultural work, and textile (Marie 1999). Remarkably, the most common infraction found by French labor inspectors is *not* the employment of individuals not entitled to work on French territory, but rather illicit forms of employment that contravene existing labor laws, for example regarding working hours, remuneration, or health and safety (Ministère de la Justice 1999). French business disposes of a ready pool of domestically available labor, employable at often substandard conditions, and is much less dependent on new and undocumented immigrants now than was the case as recently as in the 1990s, as Samers (2003) argues. This does not, however, mean that immigrants are not welcomed at all, not least in such substandard tiers of the labor market, but such practices are not openly acknowledged, much less endorsed. Terray (1999) analyzes employer lobbying activity against the March 1997 Barrot Law that would have shifted the burden of proof on the employers in cases of infractions against employment laws, thus forcing employers to prove credibly that they were not aware of labor law violations, including in instances further down the subcontracting chain. These efforts were largely successful (Rapport Annuel 1999).[4]

Historically, French business, especially farms in the first part of the twentieth century and major manufacturing companies in sectors including construction, automobile assembly, metallurgy, and iron and steel during the postwar boom, were highly interested in labor recruitment, assisting and even surpassing the efforts and indeed the importance of the governmental labor recruitment office ONI and its pre-World War I predecessor SGI (Weil 1991). The ONI—and before it the SGI and the bilateral treaties it helped administer—focused exclusively on European migrants, somewhat unduly so given the rapid quantitative rise in non-European labor migrants in addition to the largely clandestine nature of emigration from the authoritarian regimes of the Iberian peninsula. Employers heavily influenced the broad contours of labor migration policy almost designed and operated themselves, or at least both. They were actively involved in facilitating administration at the microlevel (Weil 1991). Renault representatives recruiting workers in Algerian villages outright and de facto post hoc legalization of new arrivals who could demonstrate work contracts underline the pre-eminent role played by business in labor recruitment in France prior to the recruitment stop in 1974. By 1968, such post hoc *régularisations* represented more than 80 percent of all entries (*Dictionnaire* 2004). In this sense, the recruitment stop can be interpreted as a restatement of statist authority. However, seasonal labor migration continued and remained significant for agriculture in particular (Hollifield 2000, 121). Nevertheless, the MEDEF only recently rediscovered an interest in labor migration. While migration debates at its 2000 summer school focused more on avoiding brain drain of highly skilled French professionals to the United States and the UK, by 2006 Sarkozy's speech, peppered with references to "chosen immigration" for "those for whom we have work" rather than the "tolerated" flows arriving through family reunion, was indicative of the new stance embraced (MEDEF 2000, 2006).

This changing attitude is also reflected in publications produced by business think tank Institut Montaigne, headed by outspoken member of the supervisory board of insurance giant AXA Claude Bébéar, vociferously advocating the introduction of migration quotas and the active recruitment of highly skilled migrants (*Le Point* May 7, 2002; *Le Figaro* February 15, 2006). The institute maintains links with and receives funding from nearly all major French CAC40-listed corporations, including Total, LVMH, Bouygues, BNP Paribas, Carrefour, Capgemini, Sodexho, Vivendi, and Suez. Its publications make the link between competitiveness and selective immigration very explicit, criticizing that human right considerations have taken precedence over economic concerns in past French migration policy (Institut Montaigne 2003, 192).

The 2001 governmental initiative to grant working and residency permits to a total of 4,000 information technology specialists, first suggested in a July 16, 1998 letter to the regional governments, constitutes a first step in the direction of managed labor recruitment, a path since continued by the 2006 Sarkozy Law, as will be argued below. French employers are very reluctant to be seen as lobbying publicly for more liberal economic migration policy, yet senior department of the interior officials confirm "significant pressure," "sustained interest," and a "pivotal role" of employers in the creation of new channels of labor migration policy (interview FR-GOV-2).

For the trade unions, the situation presents itself differently. French unions remained historically skeptical towards immigration (Haus 2002), influenced by anxieties over downward wage pressures and a feeling of exclusion from policymaking (Lloyd 2000), though this position has evolved since. The French unions have been very active in battling discrimination and racism in the workplace (Lloyd 2000; interviews FR-UNI-1, FR-UNI-2). The politically centrist CFDT is more welcoming towards new economic migration, provided this feeds into the primary tier of the labor market (interview FR-UNI-1). But among the left-wing CGT and FO considerable skepticism prevails towards turning workers into objects and linking residence rights even more closely with employment (Force Ouvrière 2006, 2007). Active trade union lobbying efforts appear to be quite limited, but there is absolutely no interest in actively endorsing large-scale labor migration (interviews FR-UNI-1, FR-UNI-2).

Structure of Interest Intermediation

The presence of consultative body Economic and Social Council (*Conseil Economique et Sociale*) cannot be interpreted to indicate a neocorporatist structure in France. A traditionally well-insulated state has sought to minimize interest group influence, which means that access channels are informal, highly contingent, and fragile. Similar socialization and education patterns among the administrative and the business elite (*"énarquie"*) (Culpepper 2006; Hall 1986) enable representatives of employers to operate within a network of acquaintances with shared norms, perceptions, and ideas, leaving trade union and most NGO representatives at a distinct comparable disadvantage. This means that actors are reliant on amiable relations with public policymakers to be invited to parliamentary hearings, informal and often ad hoc hearings within the ministry, and possess a fair chance to have lobbying efforts received (interview FR-GOV-1, FR-GOV-2). The MEDEF enjoys relatively high degrees of centralization, internal cohesion, and representation among its clientele, which strengthens its position organizationally, while the unions are organizationally much more divided and also do not share a common position regarding the desirability of managed economic migration. Both in institutional and ideational terms the employers thus enjoy a considerable advantage, further enhanced by superior informal access channels to government ministries.

French humanitarian NGOs are handicapped by limited resources, internal dissent, organizational weaknesses, and serious difficulties in establishing informal links to relevant government ministries (interviews FR-GOV-1, FR-NGO-1, FR-NGO-2). Many therefore opt for more short-term high-impact high-visibility campaigns targeted at the mobilization of public opinion and the support of prominent personalities so as to influence public policy indirectly. Indeed, two reasons recommend this path: first, government administrators are in general very reluctant to respond favorably to direct NGO lobbying efforts (interview FR-NGO-1, FR-NGO-2, FR-GOV-1), so NGOs may not consider this path even worth their efforts, or reject such a strategy due to ideological affinities for anarchy; second, NGOs in the migration sector commonly do not have the financial, logistical, and personnel resources to see through persistent long-term lobbying efforts.

Development of Immigration Policy Since 1990

While French immigration policy has oscillated throughout the 1980s between a hard restrictionist line of the Right and the more pragmatic liberal stance of the Left, in the 1990s the policy space for new developments decreased. More pronounced and effective "tampering" with details of immigration policy administration emerged, especially regarding family reunion, asylum, and citizenship. By the late 1980s, the Socialists seemed to tire of attempts at revising the archetypical right-wing 1986 Pasqua Laws and Pierre Joxe's 1989 legislation remained below expectations, while the humanitarian NGOs consulted criticized it for being impregnated by the spirit of the Pasqua laws. Prime Minister Michel Rocard declared in a meeting with MPs of Maghrebian origin on January 7, 1990 that "we cannot accommodate all the misery of the world," while Mitterrand had earlier stated in a radio interview on December 10, 1989 that the tolerance capacity level for new immigration had already been reached in the 1970s. The stage was thus set for a shift towards the Right. The major immigration laws of the 2000s, the 2003 Sarkozy and Villepin Law, the 2006 Sarkozy Law, and the 2007 Hortefeux are restrictive right-wing initiatives that render asylum and family reunion regulations more stringent, while the latter two open channels for economic migration.

The first significant legislative initiatives of the 1990s were the August 1993 Pasqua Laws (August 10, 1993 for identity checks and 93–1027 of August 24, 1993). They were shaped by earlier debates about citizenship—which had spawned the July 1993 Méhaignerie Law (93–933), significantly limiting access particularly for foreign spouses and introducing the formal requirement for French-born descendants of immigrants to affirm their willingness to become French citizens—but also the increasing *lepenisation* of the issue, resulting in the Interior Minister's infamous declaration to endeavor for zero migration, later revised to zero *illegal* migration. As minister of the interior in the mid-1980s, avowedly right-wing Charles Pasqua had ushered in 1986 legislation that facilitated the refusal of visa and residency permits, placing a higher burden of proof on applicants, while stepping up identification checks by law enforcement agencies inside French territory. By the early 1990s, Prime Minister

Balladur endeavored to make a bid for the presidency; pandering to a right-wing electorate and especially those in the Front National was part of this strategy. In this spirit, the first law widened police powers to carry out controls of residency permits, while the second impeded applications for residency permits, permitting the refusal and even the retroactive withdrawal of the permit for individuals found to be living in polygamy, a practice ostensibly geared at West African immigrants. Revoking refugee status which had now become possible was an unprecedented measure in French law. New impediments were created regarding family reunion and border controls.

On August 13, 1993, the *conseil* ruled several of the provisions of the Pasqua Law unconstitutional, in particular the detention of noncitizens not in possession of valid identity documents for up to three months, a one year entry ban for individuals previously deported, an end to family reunion for students, and the newly introduced right for the attorney-general to authorize local mayors to disregard marriages for the purpose of establishing eligibility for residency, especially if fraud was suspected. It also criticized some provisions regarding asylum and the facilitation of residency permit controls by law enforcement officials.

Pasqua responded swiftly and presented a revised version of the bill to the Council of Ministers on September 22, leading to the successful implementation of a slightly modified version.

Before moving to an examination of labor migration policy and the role of unions and employers, the role of humanitarian NGOs will be explored by focusing on two major contested issues, namely deportation and the detention of newcomers in "deterritorialized zones."

Previously, important partisan cleavages existed regarding deportation: the Left sought to maintain or expand juridical avenues for contesting decisions on either asylum and/or residency permits, including the creation of a special commission (*commission de séjour*) that had the authority to conduct hearings and receive appeals, while the Right reduced such possibilities, including side-stepping and castrating this commission. This latter goal was pursued in the 1993 Pasqua Laws, while the precedent Socialist Rocard government had assured the competency of this commission to examine refusals of residency permits and reopened juridical contestation of deportation decisions in the August 1989 Joxe Law (89-548), reinforced in the January 10, 1990 Law (90-34) that further clarified conditions under which an appeal (*recours*) against deportation decisions can be lodged. The issue attained national prominence and led to a heated political conflict in 1996, by which time undocumented immigrants had successfully managed to organize themselves into a movement that attracted significant sympathy from left-wing local and regional governments and the nonparliamentary Left. The degree of support for the *sans-papiers* was also conditioned by other factors, including declining public support for Le Pen-esque immigration policies and the collapsing approval ratings of the Chirac/Juppé government due to the odious privatization initiatives and social security cuts that spawned the major 1995 *refus* strikes. The *sans-papiers* movement was successful in influencing the political agenda and contributing to the Left rediscovering the issue, though in the short term the occupation of the Saint-Ambroise, and then Saint-Bernard de la Chapelle church in the impoverished Parisian 18th and 11th arrondissements and later the district town hall in June 1996, itself the heart of African immigrant communities, elicited a hard-line response from the state. Prime Minister Alain Juppé declared that this "painful hunger strike...makes no more sense" on August 22 (Siméant 1998). The next day, riot police descended on the church, the squatters were arrested and most of them deported. Though lip service was subsequently being paid to eradicating excessively long administrative delays, the new immigration legislation presented by minister of the interior Jean-Louis Debré to the council of ministers on November 6 continued the restrictive line. Deportation and detention of undocumented migrants were further facilitated, external border controls stepped up, and the rights of undocumented migrants that could not be deported for legal reasons (e.g. the Geneva Convention ban on *refoulement*) further curtailed. However, NGO Human Rights League (*Ligue des droits de l'homme* = *LDH*) successfully submitted a petition against this law to parliament on February 3, 1997, signed by 150 persons of public life, demanding a moratorium on all deportations, the *régularisation* of all undocumented migrants, and the abandonment of the Debré law. Several leftist local arrondissement mayors in Paris and the Ile-de-France region publicly organized citizenship ceremonies for *sans-papiers,* while 59 film directors called for civil disobedience regarding the new law. Once again, the *conseil* intervened, declaring some of its provisions unconstitutional. However, the law was implemented on April 24, 1997 (97–396).

But in the long-term, the *sans-papiers* movement, supported by humanitarian NGOs sympathetic to their cause, incited the Socialists to shift back to the left. Under the Socialist Jospin government, 15,700 *régularisations* were carried out during the first year in power and 80,000 by 1999; financial incentives and psychological counseling were offered to those willing to return home. LDH, SOS-Racisme and the Movement against Racism and for the Friendship among Peoples (*Mouvement contre le racisme et pour l'amitié entre les peuples* = *MRAP*) were content. The Left's reawakened interest in migration generated two 1998 legislative acts on citizenship and migration (Law 98-170 and 98-349), partly inspired by an expert commission headed by political scientist Patrick Weil. While not abolishing previous conservative legislation, and lacking ambition in the eyes of critics, including the National Commission on Human Rights, this legislation placed a clear time limit of 14 days on detention periods and strengthened the *ius solis* by abolishing the requirement to declare formally intent to assume citizenship. The June 23, 1998 Decree 98-502 abolished the much contested accommodation certificate for visa applicants, originally constructed by the Right as a stumbling block.

After the May 2002 election had brought the rightist Chirac/Raffarin government to power, another church occupation in northern Paris in August 2002 met a clear refusal by minister of the interior Nicholas Sarkozy to consider mass regularizations. This time the *sans-papiers* were not able to secure the same level of public support. The NGOs did not manage to launch a support campaign. The government made deportation of failed asylum seekers a core component of its asylum reform laws first proposed in September 2002, eventually informing the 2003 Sarkozy and Villepin Laws (2003-1119) that re-established the previous pattern of French migration policymaking by revising several of the predecessor government's measures, including extending the detention periods, introducing tougher scrutiny of the accommodation certificates and marriages, and encumbering the path to residency permits. In October 2003, France and Belgium reached an agreement to organize joint deportation charter flights.[5] The European Commission's offer to support such joint efforts with a grant of €30 million over two years, announced at the Council meeting in Dublin in February 2004, further consolidated these efforts and helped create a "burden-sharing" scheme to this end.

Another contested issue that NGOs focused on is the existence, the affirmation and later the extension of detention zones, first at airports and seaports, eventually also at train stations, in which undocumented migrants could be forcefully detained. This practice was established at Roissy airport in the late 1980s and included the use of hotel suites that were declared extraterritorial and thus could not be used to establish claims for asylum requests, political refugee status, or indeed any other migration rights. This constituted a legally highly questionable interpretation of Art. 35 of the November 2, 1945 decree that permits detaining asylum seekers during the time it takes to determine whether an asylum request is "manifestly unfounded" or for undocumented migrants to be deported, all for a maximum of 20 days. Oddly, while asylum claims could not be lodged within this "international transit zone," declarations on "manifestly unfounded" applications without any in-depth examination were permitted. Deportations could be easily pursued with minimal transparency and no accountability whatsoever. In a January 25, 1990 administrative order by the minister of the interior to the departmental administrations precise instructions were given for dealing with potential deportees in the respective department first, before the transfer to deportation facilities in other departments could occur. While a November 1990 court decision highlighted procedural mistakes and declared that the resorting to such zones could constitute a serious infringement of an individual's liberty (Julien-Laferrière 1996a), the immediate response with Law 92–190 of February 26, 1992 officially sanctioned the use of "detention zones" and extended the period of detention to up to 30 days. It also placed carrier sanctions against airlines and other transportation companies on a firmer legal basis.[6] However, a February 25, 1992 *conseil* decision (nr. 92-307 DC, http://www.conseil-constitutionnel.fr/decision/1992/92307dc.htm) accepted the carrier sanctions, but ruled the detention zones unconstitutional because decisions about access to the French territory had to be made "in pursuit of and with respect to the international treaties signed and the constitutional values." A second attempt was thus made in the form of the July 2, 1992 Quilès Law (92–625),[7] this time modifying the 1945 decree, so as to permit the detention of foreigners for up to 48 hours at the border, which could be prolonged to up to 20 days, in order to verify their identity or the validity of their request for asylum. Having thus placed such detention zones on a firm legal basis, they were extended two years later to train stations in the law 94–1136 of December 27, 1994.[8] Art. 2 of this law also permitted the internal transfer within France into such zones, thus permitting the Roissy airport zone to be used as a centralized facility for deportations.

These extra-territorial zones served as a rallying point for humanitarian NGOs, who perceived them, not without justification, as a sly means to circumvent the obligations of the Geneva Convention and the indirect implications of the asylum right guaranteed in the preamble to the 1946 constitution that was added to the 1958 constitution of the Fifth Republic, by introducing a questionable "buffer zone" that permitted rapid deportations and cursory reviews of asylum requests. In January 2001, minister of the interior Daniel Vaillant commented after visiting the newly expanded transit zone at Roissy Airport ZAPI 3 that permitted less reliance on the long-standing practice of renting entire floors in the nearby Ibis hotel that this zone constituted a "site of an equilibrium where the two demands of controlling the borders and accommodating refugees play out every day" and emphasized "our ambition to look at the individual circumstances of the nonadmitted individuals and examine these cases with all the guarantees and rights offered by the law and in consideration of the respect for the human being that a democratic country like France owes" (ANAFE 2001). Representatives of NGOs that visited these sites were more candid and shocked at the appalling hygienic conditions and the often abusive conduct by the guards. Representatives of ANAFE, an NGO defending foreigners' rights, supported by Amnesty International, LDH and CIMADE among others, found substantial evidence for police conduct involving the refusal to accept asylum claims or, more disturbingly, even registering the very arrival of newcomers, thus permitting indefinite detention (ANAFE 2001). Several of the legal provisions were simply ignored, including the obligation of juridical authorization for detentions after 48 hours, and the mandatory delay of at least one calendar day between arrival and forced deportation. According to ANAFE, though the number of detainees has decreased, which has resulted in somewhat improved living conditions, frequent abuses still occur, and, more than ever, asylum applications are declared manifestly unfounded after a highly superficial review by the authorities. According to its data, whereas 60 percent of detainees were eventually granted access to French territory in 1995, this figure had declined to a minuscule 3.2 percent by 2003 (ANAFE 2004, 2005).

However, the NGO lobbying campaign was not particularly successful. In 2003, the center-right government sought to eradicate the administrative authorizations required for detentions of more than 48 hours and to expand the period of detention overall as part of its encompassing Sarkozy–de Villepin Law package, eventually passed on November 26 (Law 2003-1119). In the final version, the government refrained from significantly modifying the administrative requirements pertaining to the length of the stay as the relevant modification of Art. 35 quarter of the 1945 ordonnance indicates. However, the "detention zone" is now extended to cover the detainee *legally* during his entire stay in France, unless a decision to the contrary is made, regardless of the actual *geographic* location of the individual, including, for example, away from the airport and in a court building—thus creating *moving islands of deterritorialized law*. Simultaneously, the government agreed to negotiations with NGOs that would permit a more permanent representation in the detention zones rather than heavily regulated occasional visits. An agreement between ANAFE and the minister of interior affairs Sarkozy was reached in March 2004, permitting ANAFE more regular and less regulated visits, but only to ZAPI 3 at Roissy airport. However, a permanent presence of up to 15 "mediators" was only afforded to the apolitical Red Cross, itself not a member of ANAFE, and indeed this presence was financed by the ministry of interior affairs. Indeed, the contact between the association and the ministry since this agreement, which took more than two years to negotiate, is limited to two annual meetings. The stance seemed to confirm the impression that the government's approach towards humanitarian NGOs was quite utilitarian, while it sought to limit tangible policy impact. ANAFE associates report that confused border police officers assumed that ANAFE was an association facilitating and aiding in the deportation process and commonly refer detainees to ANAFE representatives with requests the police is legally responsible for (ANAFE 2004).

If the NGO influence remained limited to certain instances, French employers and, less so, unions shed earlier reservations about active labor migration recruitment. In 1998, an internal administrative circular had advised provincial governments to "fast-track" (or at least consider with leniency) residency permit applications from information technology experts.[9] The dogma of zero immigration was slowly being abandoned,[10] even among the Right.[11] French business cautiously embraced this shift concurrently, though the unfolding liberalization of the labor market (Samers 2003) and the rapid decline in low-skill primary and secondary sector jobs (Hancké 2002), affecting resident ethnic minorities particularly strongly, with unemployment reaching more than 25 percent among French residents of North or sub-Saharan African descent (INSEE 2003; Richard 2004), led to an early and clear concentration on skilled migration. Calls for unskilled migration would have been politically extremely difficult to sustain and appeared simply unnecessary. The attempted shift to more concentration on high value-added production patterns (Culpepper 2006; Hancké 2002) further reinforced this focus. French employers sought to broaden the talent pool for highly skilled migrants in the secondary and tertiary sectors, including finance, information technology, management, and research and development (MEDEF 2000). A study by think tank Institut Montaigne (2003, 41, 177) argues: "But a doubling of the migration flow, accompanied by a selection of the candidates could add another 50,000 employees per year to the French workforce" to address "already apparent shortages" of skilled labor. Medef was slowly embracing the notion of actively recruited skilled migration. In 2003, the Economic and Social Council, jointly staffed by union and employer representatives, issued a lengthy report on migration, examining and advocating the creation of enhanced and more encompassing labor migration quotas, due to predicted labor shortages arising from demographic trends and the retirement of the baby boomer generation from the workforce. Such quotas could be based on the fast track procedures in place for highly skilled IT professionals, but would need to be better managed and much more broadly conceived (*Conseil économique et sociale* 2003, 209 ff.). The very consideration of quotas is nothing short of iconoclastic in the French context, where active labor recruitment is condemned by the Left for engendering economistic "disposable migration."

That same year, the National Agency for the Reception of Foreigners and Migrations [sic] (Agence Nationale de l'Accueil des Etrangers et des Migrations = ANAEM) was established, responsible for administering the "reception and integration contracts" (CAI) rolled out first as pilot projects and then nationwide in 2005 (enshrined in Law 2005–32 of January 18, 2005),[12] which oblige new migrants to partake in cultural and linguistic training programs and to accept the legal and cultural "republican" national values. The motivation for this new law was partly a more punitive approach taken by minister of the interior Sarkozy seeking to impose integration.[13] However, it also set out the institutional framework for more actively managed migration. The rhetorical justification for managed migration arises out of the distinction between "chosen" (*choisie*) rather than "imposed" (*subie*) migration. The need for "chosen" economic migration is claimed to constitute an inevitable economic necessity as, according to Sarkozy, "France is the only developed country which robs itself of the possibility to invite on its territory migrants that it needs to contribute to growth and prosperity" (*Le Monde* April 15, 2006). In the course of a 2004 press conference, the minister stated that "The question of quotas, in other words, 'immigration by choice' as opposed to 'immigration by submission', must be the subject of true debate without taboos or exclusions. [We must] not be content with the failure which, after ten years of illegal immigration, leads all governments to debate wide-ranging integration" (Kretzschmar 2005, 15).

Actively managed migration, including the concept of quotas and "quantitative objectives," features in Sarkozy's book "Libre" (Sarkozy 2003; also *Le Monde* April 15, 2006; interview GOV-FR-2). "Mastering" (*maitriser*) immigration spawned the 2006 Sarkozy II Law, "regarding immigration and integration" (*loi relatif à l'immigration et à l'intégration*) (interviews FR-GOV-1, FR-GOV-2). It combines a more restrictive approach towards family reunion in particular, motivated by concerns over rising numbers in this category as well as asylum seekers (interview FR-GOV-2), with new work permits aimed at highly qualified migrants who "constitute an asset for the development and influence of France." The legislation also establishes the requirement for the government to submit an annual report to parliament about the "direction" of immigration policy, including "annual quantitative objectives" regarding residency permits and visas. In line with the intention to reduce "endured" flows of migration, the previous practice first established in 1984 of automatic legalization of residency for individuals able to prove 10 years of residence in France was abolished and hurdles for family reunion raised considerably. Family reunion rights accrue only after longer waiting periods and require proof of economic self-sufficiency. Similarly, foreign spouses of French citizens have to wait for three years as opposed to two before being granted an independent residency permit and need to prove four years of marriage, rather than two, before being able to apply for citizenship. Finally, the CAI now becomes mandatory (*Le Monde* April 15, 2006, June 18, 2006). Most innovative, however, is the introduction of the *carte compétences et talents* for skilled migrants, motivated by the intention to raise significantly quantitative levels of labor migration, also evident in the abandonment of previously pursued general labor market reviews as a precondition for approving new work permits. The creation of a separate ministry for immigration, integration, national identity, and codevelopment in June 2007 marked another symbolic break with the past.

The law marks a paradigmatic shift in the rediscovery of economic migration. For the first time since the end to active labor recruitment in 1975, actively solicited and chosen economic migration is being welcomed again and even the preconditions for the hitherto nearly taboo topic of quantitative targets are being created. Though annual labor contingents had existed previously, principally in agriculture, horticulture, and viticulture, by 1999 the total annual quota had declined to a mere 7,600 from 58,200 at the beginning of the decade (*Conseil économique et sociale* 2003, 90). Technological progress led to significant decline in labor demand, while economic progress on the Iberian peninsula had affected push factors, only partly alleviated by fresh demand from Morocco.

Employer association MEDEF was being informally consulted throughout the gestation process and played an essential role in shaping governmental thinking about the need for more flexible, nonbureaucratic, and accommodating labor recruitment policies, especially regarding highly skilled professionals in information technology, management, and research (interview FR-GOV-2). The larger multinational corporations within MEDEF were most proactive, but there was a more general concern over current and future staff shortages and a consensus on the need for more accommodating policy. Internal ideational cohesion, organizational coherence, a strong degree of linkage with the membership base and on this occasion formidable informal access channels to government all strengthened the employer position and facilitated lobbying. Most provisions concerning labor migration were hatched out within the ministry based on informal consultation with the employers and to a much lesser extent the unions. The ministry encountered strong enthusiasm from MEDEF and felt content to design legislation "almost in partnership" (interview FR-GOV-2).

The unions found it much more difficult effectively to influence the legislative process because their informal input was much less pronounced and the ministry did not consider their position as vital. Internal organizational problems, including low membership levels, ideological divisions, and uneven internal governance structures, that perennially bedevil the French unions surfaced again and there was no ideational consensus. The more left-wing unions, especially the CGT and to a lesser extent the FO (interview FR-UNI-2, Force Ouvrière 2006), assumed a very critical stance, embracing criticism from the NGO camp about "throwaway immigration" (*immigration jetable*) and co-organizing demonstrations with the NGOs against it. The more centrist CFDT remained relatively reticent. With the unions being internally divided, only sporadically informally consulted and no coherent counterproposal being developed, the ministry of the interior found it possible to proceed without much input from the employee camp.

The role of the humanitarian NGOs was minimal, as these groups were not being consulted and their critical stance was being virtually ignored (interview FR-NGO-1). Attempting to choose the more direct route of staging public protests and demonstrations did not succeed in markedly altering the public opinion or marshalling extra-parliamentary support. The law was approved in both houses of parliament, though some of the provisions concerning foreign spouses of French citizens were liberalized somewhat (*Le Monde* June 18, 2006). The highly visible restrictive application and *implementation* of deportation orders under Sarkozy caused some controversy, including the arrest of schoolchildren during school hours, an eerie sight bearing an uncanny resemblance to Vichy era deportations.

Conflicts over impending deportation once again spawned the occupation of a public building, this time a school in Poitiers (*Le Monde* June 22, 2006), but this did not resonate with the wider public in the way the *sans papiers* movement had.

The November 20, 2007 "Hortefeux Law" (2007-1631) continued the impeding of family reunion, including the contentious introduction of DNA testing to establish family links, and asylum, notably the creation of "fast track" processing of asylum claims in detention facilities and the limitation of appeals. There were no additional amendments made regarding economic migration. In the elaboration process, humanitarian NGOs were not being consulted and their input was ignored.

The Impact of Europeanization

The French government remained actively committed to the general goal of creating an AMP (interviews FR-GOV-1, FR-GOV-2), but it remained a much less energetic actor than the German delegation. However, as noted before, the French were deeply skeptical about EU level policy that would have set labor migration quotas, partly due to the domestic political sensitivity of the concept and indeed the very term, and also related to embedded concerns over subsidiarity. The passivity in policy design initiatives in other AMP areas can be accounted for by three factors: first, an ideational congruence by the French Right and the perceived more restrictive turn of EU level policy after 2001 coupled with competition state notions of carefully selected economic migrants to assuage demographic shortcomings and enhance national competitiveness.[14] With the EU creating the foundation for more restrictive external border policing on one level, it appeared that there were ideological commonalities also regarding the regulation of other areas of migration control. Second, both regarding family reunion and asylum policy in particular, there was a perceived need for reformatory action, but a distinct lack of ideational impulses. Europe served as a databank for such inspiration, spawning top-down "anticipatory obedience," that is, tempting policymakers to foreshadow anticipated AMP measures by implementing generally restrictive measures, or indeed mere top-down implementation. The perceived need for re-regulation of asylum was linked to slowly rising quantitative levels throughout the 1980s to an all-time high of 61,000 in 1989 and a second upward trajectory from 22,400 in 1998 to 47,300 in 2001 (*Conseil économique et sociale* 2003, 92). Third, there was no perception of a French model or approach that could have been transported upwards to Europe. With policy developments proceeding slowly and lacking inspiration, the national delegation was particularly poorly positioned to act as a vibrant agent of bottom-up Europeanization. However, the relatively feeble position of humanitarian nonstate actors and the only belated activity on the part of the employers in France also meant that activities in the national arena of the two-level game were easily contained and constituted only a very limited factor in the aggregation of the national interest position.

Rather than the French delegation in the Council acting as a proactive driver of policy development, proposing blueprints, and engaging in agenda-setting, its stance was that of a policytaker. Therefore, most Europeanization took the form of top-down processes. This is particularly true of asylum policy. The major December 10, 2003 asylum reform law (2003-1176) is "largely inspired by EU law currently being developed or already applicable," as the council of ministers' comments aptly describe it (*compte rendu de conseil des ministres*). Indeed, the first presentation of the bill by minister of foreign affairs Dominique de Villepin on September 25, 2002 took place a mere three months after the Seville Council meeting and followed the more restrictive tone adopted in the final communiqué that emphasized the battle against undocumented migration. Ministry of the interior officials confirmed that EU developments "influenced" the elaboration of this bill (interview FR-GOV-1).

Its main points are as follows: first, to streamline procedures, speeding up the decision-making process; second, to reform the bureaucratic machinery, extending the remit of the French Office for the Protection of Refugees and Stateless OFPRA (*Office Français pour la Protection des Réfugiés et Apatrides*), itself reporting to the minister of foreign affairs (Arts. 1 and 2); and third, to implement several substantial procedural reforms that are clearly inspired by CAMP development, especially the recognition of persecution by nonstate actors and the incorporation of safe third country lists into French laws, previously used, but only exceptionally awarded in relation to Algeria in particular. Fourth, the legislation further clarified the status of territorial asylum. Observers of French asylum policy have noted that the recognition rate has dropped steadily over the past two decades, from roughly 45 percent in the mid-1980s to approximately 15 percent currently. However, this rate masks the significant variations among different nationalities, which are even more pronounced for territorial asylum: while Francophone Southeast Asian nations and the Maghreb feature prominently, both asylum seekers and refugees from Turkey, former

Yugoslavia, and China are rarely awarded recognition (Freedland 2004; Currle 2004, 81–113).

This passive stance is also evident during the elaboration of the EU Family Reunion directive. On this issue, too, the French acted as passive policytakers, content with top-down flow of policy. The more stringent hurdles on this issue, especially regarding linguistic and "value" tests for beneficiaries of family reunions are restrictive interpretations of guidelines that permit but do not oblige member states to implement such measures. There may have been some inspiration from the particularly restrictive Dutch approach, as a senior representative of the Ministry of the Interior claimed (interview FR-GOV-2), but this new requirement fell on fertile soil and dovetailed well with the Right's proclaimed desire to reduce unsolicited and presumably undesired migration access channels.

United Kingdom: From Unwilling Country of Immigration to Europe's Premier Competition State?

By the 1990s, four notable factors had crystallized that are crucial towards understanding British migration policy. First, the original extremely broadly conceived citizenship concept, perhaps aptly described as *ius civitatis*, was used as the primary tool to manipulate migration flows during the postwar decades and well into the 1980s. This encompassing character was linked to the construction of Empire, covering both descendants of British colonial settlers, and in this sense functionally similar to Germany's ethnic citizenship concept, and imperial subjects of the Crown. Attracting return migration remained important as emigration flows exceeded immigration well into the 1980s. Manipulating citizenship eligibility criteria with a view to arresting immigration flows from the New Commonwealth in the course of subsequent reforms (1962, 1968, 1971, 1981) perhaps inevitably invited charges of racism, as the *ius sanguinis* element was strengthened. Yet one advantageous legacy of an imperial citizenship concept was precisely its nonethnic design *ab initio*. In practice, however, British identity was severely shaken and the nonethnic character of citizenship (cf. Favell 1998) sat uneasily with an often xenophobic and often openly racist backlash immigrants encountered.[15] Immigration policy was very much an elite project, hatched out first by the Foreign and Commonwealth Office and only later by the Home Office (Hansen 2000). There was historically never any appetite to become a destination country of immigration, neither at the elite level nor among the general populace, though recent policy design suggests new approaches. This stance accounts for the extremely restrictive stance regarding family reunion and asylum (Joppke 1999, 114ff.), immigration categories deemed even less desirable. The acceptance of immigration historically hinged on economistic calculations, a thread of continuing importance.

Second, unlike elsewhere in Europe, the role of courts and, more remarkably, parliament is not as pronounced, affording the executive significant political power in shaping policy. Some observers have commented on the increasing presidential element in British politics since Thatcher (Foley 1993; Thomas 2000), further contributing to this concentration of unchecked political power. Within the civil service, there had been a slight division between a more restrictive Labor Department and a more paternalistic liberal-minded Colonial Office (cf. Hansen 2000), but the rising prominence of the Home Office to the detriment of these two has been marked by a securitized restrictive approach. Given the weakness of veto players (Hansen 2000, 237ff., cf. Joppke 1999), stringent policy becomes easier to implement. Also noteworthy is the degree of continuity since the mid-1970s between the Left and the Right in pursuing an ever more restrictive stance. But even earlier, contention focused on integration and race relations, while liberal immigration policy attracted scant support.

Third, there is an almost slightly obsessive focus on border control informing migration policy design and discourses, with the geographic peculiarity of an island nation nourishing the illusion of feasible control. However, this preoccupation with access control clashes with the "pull factor" of a post-Thatcherite deregulated labor market with feeble trade unions and lax labor regulation enforcement. A highly stratified deregulated labor market has created manifold precarious short-term low-skill low-pay jobs. Combined with the relative dynamism of the British economy since the late 1990s, both Eastern Europeans and non-Europeans have been attracted to such positions (cf. Recchi et al. 2003), escaping unemployment in their home countries, begetting a remarkable cultural Europeanization of the capital city of one of Europe's most staunchly Euro-skeptical countries (Favell, forthcoming). This difference in economic vitality between London and the rest of the country partly accounts for demographic trends that have led to more than two-thirds of all ethnic minorities and a substantial proportion of new immigrants making their home in the greater London region. The post-Thatcherite labor market rather than the mythical "soft touch" regulations acts as a migration magnet,[16] as it encourages labor market segmentation and the permanent institutionalization of substandard employment. London, often characterized to be a paradigmatic Sassenian "global city" (Favell 2004; Sassen 2001), along with Southeastern England, has also attracted significant numbers of highly skilled professionals, especially in fields in which the region has assumed European or even global predominance, including finance, advertising, insurance, and fashion. In fact, "each year since 1978, around 60 percent of immigrants and emigrants in employment were professional or managerial workers" (Salt 1992, 488; cited in Recchi et al. 2003, 34). As argued in more detail below, the decision not to impose mobility bans on CEE citizens in 2004 can be understood as part of a deliberate strategy of attracting migrants to segments of the labor market that current residents either cannot fill due to a skills mismatch or are not prepared to due to the working conditions and wage levels. The pragmatic stance towards economic migration must not be equated with permissiveness. We will also note that such a laissez faire approach creates considerable public policy problems regarding housing, transportation, and urban and regional planning, perhaps partially contributing to the continuing high rate of emigration.

The much-cherished attachment to border control informs British reserve towards AMP formation, not mere Euro-skepticism. The British government prefers "cherry picking", selecting pan-European control instruments over communautarization. The "opt-out" of Schengen ensured the continued viability of an ostensible display of state power at the external borders. Control devices signalling human presence have replaced the unprepossessing specter of immigration officers crawls beneath arriving motor vehicles at the channel ports. European policy elements do inform British policymakers, but openly acknowledging top-down Europeanization remains politically risky.

Fourth, the rhetorical and policy conflation of regulatory categories and moral judgment regarding newcomers thus confined is highly developed in the UK, spawning belligerent discourse juxtaposing "deserving" "good" (labor) immigrants and "scrounging" "bad" refugees and asylum seekers. Rising application figures encountering ever more restrictive regulation, processing, and recognition rates is, of course, hardly a peculiarly British tale.

For decades, the numbers of asylum applications were minimal and only between 1988 and 1991 did a sharp upward turn occur, from roughly 4,000 to 44,840; but this mirrors developments elsewhere in Europe. During the second half of the 1990s, the UK received the highest number of asylum seekers in absolute figures, hovering first around the

Table 4.5. British immigration policy since the 1980s

1981 British Nationality Act legally defines British citizenship, introduces two new inferior categories for British Dependent Territories (BDTC) and British Overseas Citizenship (BOC); final end to "colonial" citizenship law embodied in the 1948 British Nationality Act, culmination of decade-long efforts to keep family reunion claims low, especially from the Indian subcontinent.

Throughout the 1980s, no major change in policy; at the end of the decade, numbers of asylum seekers begin to rise from the extraordinarily low annual average of 5,000.

1993 Asylum and Immigrations Appeals Act (Chapter 23), amends the 1971 Immigration Act and introduces "fast track" procedure, category of "manifestly unfounded" claims, routinely registers personal data including fingerprints of all asylum seekers, limits scope of individuals eligible to appeal against asylum decisions, implements sanctions against traffickers.

1996 Asylum and Immigration Act (Chapter 49) further amends asylum regulations by introducing "safe country of origin" and "safe third country" concept, abolishes income support, child benefit, and housing benefits for asylum seekers.

1999 Immigration and Asylum Bill ("Fairer, Faster, Firmer—A Modern Approach to Immigration and Asylum," Chapter 33) implements carrier sanctions, control of "suspicious marriages," steps up border controls, including the use of UK immigration officials overseas, outlines deportation procedures, removes all benefits from asylum seekers except for small payments in voucher form, disperses asylum seekers geographically throughout the UK to avoid concentration in London and the southeastern county of Kent, permits detention of asylum seekers, extends police powers ("stop and search," arrest) to immigration officers, goal of deciding most asylum cases within six months.

2002 Nationality, Immigration and Asylum Act (based on the White paper *Safe Haven, Secure Borders: Integration with Diversity in Modern Britain*), further modified on January 8, 2003, introduces "Application Registration Card," implements measures against "traffickers," abolishes eligibility for benefits of any nature—including basic accommodation—for asylum seekers deemed not to have filed their application immediately upon arrival or who have submitted incomplete or incorrect information, reintroduces "safe country of origin" (successfully challenged in court earlier), abolishes right to work for asylum seekers, further steps up police powers in the execution of deportations.

Introduction of the Highly Skilled Migrant Program (HSMP) for "entrepreneurs" and individuals with desirable skills, especially in medicine, IT, finance, and engineering, introduction of the sectors-based scheme (SBS) for low-skill migration (Immigration rules HC 395, paras 135I–135K).

Introduces language and cultural skills test for applicants for citizenship who need to pledge allegiance to the Crown and the country.

2005 White Paper *Controlling our Borders: Making Migration Work for Britain*, sets out four new points-based categories of labor migration, thus abolishing all other labor recruitment schemes, all are "employer-led," based on perceived economic necessity, sectoral skills shortages, and applicant's profile; limits rights of short-term labor migrants in regard to remaining in the UK longer, family reunion and change of migration status, introduces English language test for all newcomers, introduces mandatory fingerprinting for all visa applicants and electronic background checks on all air passengers to and from the UK, introduces mandatory identification card for all foreign residents in the UK, including personal data and fingerprints, aims to detain all failed asylum seekers, deploying more UK immigration officers at overseas airports.

2008 Modification to labor migration policy; roll out of points-based system.

30,000 mark and reaching 80,000 by the end of the decade (Currle 2004, 131ff.), exceeding Germany for the first time in 1995, though certainly not in terms of asylum seekers received per capita. Legislative initiatives in 1993, 1996, 1999, and 2002 further impeded access and spawned lower recognition rates, implementing carrier sanctions and safe third country provisions, as well as in-kind provisions of benefits and regional dispersion. While the treatment and accommodation of asylum seekers has thus become increasingly punitive, the opposite applies regarding the approach towards labor migration, heavily colored, however, by competition state prerogatives of securing national competitiveness.[17] (Table 4.5).

System of Political Economy: Thatcherite Shocks and the Embrace of a Liberal Market Economy

The British system of political economy has commonly been subsumed under the category of liberal market economy (Hall and Soskice 2001, 8), sharing traits with other Anglo-American economies, though this is technically only accurate since Thatcherism radically recast the role of the state, the size and function of the public sector, industrial relations, and to a lesser extent welfare state provisions, since "only in 1979, under the ideological onslaught of Thatcher, did the UK become anything like a pure case of LME" (Goodin 2003, 207). The temporal dimension is important (Blyth 2003), highlighting the pivotal impact of Thatcherism on the British political economy, itself partially a result of the widely held conviction that more actively managed continental European style macroeconomic policy, relying on neocorporatist mechanisms to set wage and price policy, could not be successfully implemented in Britain due to institutional deficiencies and an antagonistic culture in industrial relations (Rhodes 2000). Such a system is generally characterized by the absence of coordinated wage bargaining arrangements and few institutions providing public goods or aimed at overcoming distributional conflicts: "firms coordinate their activities primarily via hierarchies and competitive market arrangements" (Hall and Soskice 2001, 8). The power of trade unions has been severely reduced through Thatcherite legislation in the 1980s. This means not only greater wage dispersion but also incentives for companies to delay the introduction of new technology in favor of relying on low-wage labor. The decline of apprenticeship and common training schemes further encourages labor "poaching," which in turn can appear preferable to costly in-house training. Such incentive structure has important implications for human resource strategies, including a willingness to rely on "imported" immigrant skilled labor. 1995 OECD data similarly demonstrates the concentration of individuals born outside of the UK and/or not in possession of UK citizenship in the services sector (657,000), as opposed to manufacturing (178,000).

One of the results of the monetarist shock therapy of the early 1980s has been the rapid and at least partially deliberately caused decline—if not to say destruction—of manufacturing and the concurrent encouragement of the growth of financial and business supply services. As Table 4.1 indicates, the tertiary sector employs nearly 80 percent of the total labor force and accounts for almost three quarters of the GDP. By contrast, the percentage of employees in industry (19.1) is significantly lower than in all other countries included in this study. The slight discrepancy between the percentage of the workforce and the actual contribution to the GDP in services suggests relatively low productivity, affordable and tolerable for employers due to widely dispersed wage structures.

The openness to the import of labor extends to the public sector. For the recruitment of healthcare professionals bilateral treaties were signed with the governments of India, the Philippines, South Africa, and Indonesia, including a legally nonbinding commitment to refrain from potentially damaging "poaching" practices, which in practice do occur. Indeed, between one third and one half of staff positions in the NHS are filled with foreign nationals (Kelly, Morrell and Sriskandarajah 2005). Similarly, in the education sector, labor recruitment from abroad assumes an important dimension, both at the secondary level where recruitment from Australia and New Zealand plays an important role (BBC News 2000) and at the tertiary level.

A widely cited study by London think tank IPPR (Gott and Johnston 2002) suggests that migrants are slightly overrepresented both among top income earners and among (means-tested) recipients of transfer payments. Indeed active recruitment proceeds aimed at both extremes of the skill distribution curve, broadly supportive of Sassen's (2001) global city argument that highlights the bifurcation of the labor market in centers of the global service sector such as London. Recent legislative activity suggests a preference for increasing the share of the highly skilled or individuals with skills in short supply to the detriment of low or unskilled categories.

The flexibility, additional skill base, often superior training and educational standards and soft factors such as higher motivation associated with economic migrants are factors leading British employers to embrace managed migration and strongly lobby in its favor. In that sense, the statement by a Confederation of British Industry (CBI) representative that the association had "no aversion" to economic migration must be regarded as a case of classic British understatement (interview UK-BUS-1). In 2005, the CBI president at the time, Digby Jones, stressed the advantage Britain enjoyed thanks to its flexible labor markets and pragmatic labor migration schemes, having earlier proclaimed that "capital can't afford to be racist for lots of reasons" (CRE 2003).[18] This public intervention came in response to the Conservative Party's plan to introduce tightly capped migration quotas. The employer position has been warmly received by the government. Then Prime Minister Tony Blair argued in an April 2004 speech at the CBI that "recognition of the benefits that controlled migration brings not just to the economy but to delivering the public and private services on which we rely" was needed, along with "being clear that all those who come here to work and study must be able to support themselves. There can be no access to state support or housing for the economically inactive" (cited in Geddes 2005). Revealingly, asylum is only mentioned in the context of "abuses" and "clamp[ing] down." British employers assume an active stance in advocating immigrants considered of economic utility, both in very highly skilled service sector jobs, especially in finance, law, health, in natural science research, and in low-skill jobs in food processing, agriculture, gastronomy, and construction. By contrast, there is no real interest in asylum matters (interview UK-BUS-1). The CBI conducted a detailed survey among its members to produce a detailed response to the White Paper "Secure Borders, Safe Haven" in 2002. Along with the union and certain NGOs, its representatives are invited to the biannual "user panel" planning sessions of the Immigration and Nationality Directorate in the Home Office. The CBI is also part of the employer taskforce group, which is responsible for providing policy suggestions to the Home Office's Border and Immigration Agency. Recommendations from this group have fed into the establishment of an Australian-style high-skill migration program in February 2008 and the illegal working stakeholder group (interview UK-BUS-1). Within this taskforce group, along with a trade union delegate, major internationally oriented businesses such as Shell, Ernst & Young, Tesco, Citigroup, and Goldman Sachs are represented as well as sectoral employer associations in engineering, hospitality, and employment services, alongside, perhaps more controversially, NASSCOM, the Indian IT sector chamber of commerce. Both formal responses to government initiatives and informal approaches to the Home Office are fairly well received (interview

UK-GOV-1) and the CBI has positioned itself well to influence governmental deliberations. An added strength of the CBI is its internal ideational consensus on the desirability in principle of economic migration and its vast benefits, shared by all members, including small- and medium-sized enterprises (interview UK-BUS-1). Internal cohesion is strong and the degree of centralization is high given the successful monopolization of business representation the CBI enjoys despite comparatively low representation among its core clientele, encompassing only about 13 percent of all companies in the private sector (Rhodes 2000).

The British unions have historically maintained a fairly reserved stance towards immigration, perceiving it as a potential threat to wage levels and working conditions (Hansen 2000), or at the very least socially problematic (Wrench 2000). However, this position began to change in the 1970s, when the unions became active in fighting discrimination and racism at the workplace level. In assessing the stance of the unions and its capacity to shape policy, the fiercely anti-union political climate created by Thatcherite legislation and the slightly obsessive attempts by the Blair and Brown governments to establish to the labor movement's need to be taken into consideration. The Trades Union Congress (TUC) is much more critical of managed migration as a paradigmatic concept, criticizes seemingly epidemic abuse and exploitation of migrant workers, and is somewhat more wary of the de facto use of migrants as a flexible labor tool in lieu of training and education of the domestic workforce (interview UK-UNI-1). There are also serious doubts over the amount of political influence it can exercise, due to relatively low representation among clientele, some internal dissent over positioning itself towards the question of new migration with some members questioning the need for new migration management and limited access channels to government. A TUC representative claimed "very little influence at all" was exercised and "marginal change at best" could be expected due to the tendency to be presented with faits accomplis by government departments that leave little room for meaningful contribution. For example, concerns over the limited family reunion rights for temporary economic migrants seemed to be both ignored and met with a complete lack of understanding on the part of the government. Likewise, the stakeholder interviews appear often quite farcical with the union representatives occasionally being "accidentally" not invited (interview UK-UNI-1). Organizational shortcomings thus limit the amount of influence wielded. There is a general willingness to support continuing economic migration, provided, however, that this entails strict adherence to standard wages and working conditions. The observation that managed migration is accompanied by restrictive asylum policy and reintroduces guest worker notions is cause for some concern (interview UK-UNI-1). Despite persistent lobbying activity in the field, the trade union's ability to influence migration policy design in Britain therefore appears to be quite limited.

Structure of Interest Intermediation

Prima facie lobbying groups in the UK face a fairly hostile environment, given the absence of corporatist structures of interest intermediation, strong executive control of the agenda, a tightly closed, highly loyal, efficient, and generally secretive civil service, and pronounced party discipline. Regular consultation exercises, invitations to ministerial working groups and "stakeholder interviews," along with the government's declaration of intent in 2005 to work proactively with both employers and unions notwithstanding (Home Office 2005b), the Home Office remains keen on standing insulated from societal pressure (interview UK-GOV-1). Interest groups are not in an enviable position (Grant 1999). Trade unions, employers, and NGOs can and do release press releases, call press conferences, contribute to parliamentary hearings, and organize conferences on migration themes. The TUC has issued a number of reports highlighting abusive treatment of migrant workers (TUC 2003, 2005, 2006). It has also been successful on the issue of regulation of so-called gangmasters in agriculture. The social partners are certainly interested in responding to and even shaping governmental policy, but the employers are both institutionally in a stronger position and ideationally more committed to pressing for liberalized migration policy. The influence of the Foreign and Commonwealth Office on migration policy, traditionally displaying a paternalistic liberal stance, has waned, though arguably the Department of International Development can play a progressive role, for example, in regard to "brain drain" issues (cf. Ensor and Shah 2005, 18).

Notwithstanding the tendencies towards presidentialism and the reliance on unelected advisors, evident since the 1980s, certain sectors of the ministerial bureaucracy have rhetorically committed themselves to semiformalized "dialogue" with civil society actors. Thus, the Home Office's Immigration and Nationality Directorate (IND) has instituted a number of so-called stakeholder groups, membership of which it determines itself, based on the allotted "influence" and considerations of "balance." These groups, including the "NGO quarterly" group, are then to be consulted at least once and given at least 12 weeks before any draft bills are submitted to parliament, according to a legally nonbinding "Code of Practice on Consultation" (Ensor and Shah 2005, 26). In practice, NGOs report that their concerns might be received, but rarely appreciated, much less integrated into policy (interview UK—NGO1).[19] Indeed, Ensor and Shah (2005) demonstrate how lip service might be paid to the letter of the consultation procedure, and in some cases not even that, but that input is sometimes simply being outright ignored, concluding that "it seems unrealistic...to expect voluntary...organisations to expend time and resources to a process that demonstrates itself to be meaningless."

Development of Immigration Policy Since 1990

If a generally restrictive line characterized British migration policy throughout the 1990s, it is important to distinguish between ever more fierce and aggressive attempts to reduce the number of asylum claims on the one hand and an increasingly pragmatic, if staunchly "economistic" approach towards labor migration on the other. Very little discernible partisan cleavage exists—the distinction between "bad" asylum seekers and "good" economic migrants evident in New Labour's approach was ultimately shared even by the architects of the openly xenophobic 2005 Conservative electoral campaign.

Convinced of the necessity to impede access to asylum, the conservative Major government abolished income supplement and housing benefit payments to asylum seekers in 1996, a direction continued by Labour in the form of the 1999 Immigration and Asylum Bill that not only replaced all cash payment of benefits with vouchers but also introduced an ill-fated dispersal scheme to avoid the concentration of asylum seekers in Greater London and southeastern England (Geddes 2000b). The grand contours of this new approach to asylum policy were fleshed out in the 1993 Asylum and Immigration Act. Faced with a significant rise in the number of applicants from the mid-1990s onwards, the Major government responded by introducing the category of "manifestly unfounded" claims, taking fingerprints of all applicants for storage in a central register, and introducing carrier sanctions. The 1996 Asylum and Immigration Act implemented the safe third country concept and widened the remit of the "fast track" procedure to asylum claims, thus continuing an identical policy line. The continuity of policy under Labour auspices is striking: the

2002 Nationality, Immigration and Asylum Act cuts all forms of assistance to asylum seekers deemed to make inaccurate statements and denies assistance to those not lodging an application immediately upon entry to the UK, introduces an "application registration card" and steps up the fight against "traffickers." The 2004 Asylum and Immigration (Treatment of Claimants) Act implemented minor modifications, including punishing individuals not in possession of valid travel documents. There are plans to end the practice of granting recognized refugees permanent residency and work permits along with family reunion rights and replace them with temporarily limited schemes, entailing an examination of the sending country's political situation after five years (Home Office 2005a, 24; quoted in Ensor and Shah 2005).

Labor migration has undergone considerable changes in recent years. After repeated legislative measures had limited the legal access to the labor market considerably, three key entry avenues remained for non-EU citizens, all of them tightly regulated: the Working Holidaymakers Scheme, principally geared at short-term working experiences by Commonwealth citizens, an annual quota of 10,000 temporary work placements for Central and Eastern Europeans, principally in agriculture, and case-by-case work permits granted to highly skilled individuals whose employers filed applications for them in select economic sectors experiencing labor shortfalls. The 2002 Act itself changed little, as it was principally geared at limiting territorial access by asylum seekers and undocumented migrants—thus rendering British migration policy indeed "firmer," though not necessarily "fairer and faster" as the 1999 Green Book had promised. However, since then, there has been considerable activism in this domain. Remarkably, initiatives have principally been inspired by advocacy by employers and activism on the part of the Home Office, while Europeanization has played only a minor role (interview UK-GOV-1). The main thrust of the reforms is to restructure and ultimately limit the schemes pertaining to low-skill migration, based on the strategy to permit EU-10 citizens free access to the labor market after 2004, though not generally extended to citizens of Romania and Bulgaria in 2007, while streamlining procedures for high-skill migrants into a "points" system, reflecting qualifications and labor market needs. Thus, the Working Holidaymakers Scheme was first broadened in scope in 2003 to make greater allowances for New Commonwealth countries, only to be quantitatively limited again in February 2005. Meanwhile, the Seasonal Agricultural Workers Scheme (SAWS) has similarly been reduced in size in 2004 and since 2007 been open only to Bulgarian and Romanian citizens. At the same time, an explicit quota "sector-based" scheme was introduced for low-skill short-term labor migration in select sectors,[20] especially gastronomy and food processing (Matthews and Ruhs 2007), since 2007 also only open to Romanians and Bulgarians with exceptions for already resident migrants within this category.[21]

With low-skill migration thus relegated to certain sectors and a clear bias in favor of European migrants over non-EU citizens, the attempt was made to design new categories for highly skilled migration. The first attempt came in the form of the 2001 Highly Skilled Migrants Program (HSMP) that introduced an explicit points system, taking into consideration formal level of education, work experience, salary level, overall qualifications, and qualifications of the spouse. Additional points were added for applicants in sectors with shortages—especially medicine—and, unlike the previous procedure, applicants themselves filed the application rather than their employer. Such a points system is also used to evaluate applications by "entrepreneurs" who plan to establish businesses. The HSMP was replaced in 2008 by a new points-based system with two tiers for "highly skilled" and "skilled" migrants respectively, also taking into account available funds and past UK residence or educational experience, ostensibly modeled on Australia (*The Guardian* October 30, 2007).

The current regulatory approach, its pervasive competition state logic already apparent in its subtitle "Making Migration Work for Britain," to be driven by a "flexible, employer-led" logic (Home Office 2005*a*, 9), therefore replaces little by little past schemes with a single, points-based labor migration system. Comprising four tiers, the top tier is reserved for highly skilled professionals in fields such as IT, finance, medicine, and engineering, as well as "entrepreneurs." Applicants in these groups receive permission to enter the UK to assist them in their job search. The second category is geared towards applicants in sectors experiencing shortages that cannot be filled domestically or within the EU, especially in nursing and teaching. The third tier consists of short-term, tightly quantitatively limited quota schemes that can be opened—and presumably closed—on short notice, eventually to replace the agricultural and sector-based schemes. Finally, the fourth tier encompasses the working holiday schemes and short-term schemes for students. Both of these bottom two tiers will only be open to nationals of countries which have concluded repatriation agreements with the UK.

It is no coincidence that the document reiterates on twelve occasions that employers will be consulted or that the scheme is employer-led.

Some independent advisory body on skills will also be consulted. The UK points scheme as proposed is a paradigmatic example of business-driven labor recruitment schemes, emblematic of European migration schemes of the twenty-first century: it distinguishes between "good" labor migrants and "bad" asylum seekers, whose figures need to be reduced (Home Office 2005a, 19 ff.), it is based on competition state logic and rhetoric ("Managed migration is not just good for our country. It is essential for our continued prosperity."; Home Office 2005a, 7) and it entails a carrot-and-stick approach towards third countries to coax them into cooperating in deportation.

Recent economic migration policy is influenced by competition state rhetoric and ideology and strongly shaped by employer concerns and interests. Embracing these positions, labor migration policy has been rediscovered and liberal provisions for employees perceived as adding to existing sectoral strengths especially in information technology, health, finance, natural science research, and to some extent engineering. Simultaneously, recruitment channels for low-skill migration have been created in sectors such as food processing, hospitality, and agriculture with recent policy changes aimed at channeling Romanians and Bulgarians into these two sectors rather than non-Europeans.

The Impact of Europeanization

As a result of "opting out" of AMP, the British government is not in a strong strategic position to affect bottom-up Europeanization and has proven very resistant to accept top-down processes. With the exception of asylum, the British government has refused to adopt EU directives and persisted with pursuing a separate path, insisting on a particular definition of third-country nationals, that is, granting limited priority status to Commonwealth citizens, not least with respect to the Working Holiday Scheme for citizens of Old Commonwealth countries, and remaining wedded to separate border controls justified by geographic peculiarities. The fear of European migration policy implying a liberal deregulatory bias, however irrational, is evident in the refusal to accept the family reunion directive, with past patterns being marked by relatively restrictive and de facto quantitatively limited approaches, especially vis-à-vis South Asia. Finally, the capability to design independent labor migration policy is dearly cherished.[22] Though the assertion of an independent national path may be somewhat bewildering given the similar nature of challenges experienced in other European countries, the policy content does strikingly resemble similarly restrictive approaches elsewhere in Europe. There are clear parallels with European developments in labor migration and asylum policy, but the former follows an approach colored by a liberal market economy model that values labor market flexibility, generalist training and education approaches that often spawn serious skill deficits and a wide labor pool. Competition state logic prominently flavors British migration policy. This economistic approach can backfire as it potentially nourishes populist media attacks on humanitarian forms of migration as such newcomers are facilely depicted as exploiting and draining. It has also informed a willingness to permit EU-10 citizens to access the UK labor market after EU eastward enlargement in 2004 behind the backdrop of a favorable economic climate. But while British migration policymakers may have traditionally labored under the misapprehension that a "soft" AMP would undermine the tough national regime (cf. Joppke 1999), the circulation of ideas about control and management in the multilateral frameworks established in Europe would seem to influence official thinking. In adopting measures such as carrier sanctions and the safe country of origin and safe third country concepts simultaneously with other European countries, the British government is certainly not averse to policy learning and transfer, if mostly of repressive instruments. Indeed, in hosting the November 1992 meeting that facilitated the policy diffusion of these new instruments in asylum and created the concept of "manifestly unfounded" asylum application, the British government demonstrated its willingness to partake in multilateral initiatives, provided they do not result in mandatory communautarization. One might be tempted to describe this approach as cherry-picking, especially of the more restrictive elements.

The UK government has generally chosen to align its asylum policy to European trends, commencing with the signature of both Dublin Conventions and continuing with all EU asylum directives. Such top-down Europeanization was relatively easy to accept, given that the transaction cost in implementation was minimal and the role of humanitarian NGOs at the national level extremely limited. In this policy field, the game at the national level does entail consultation of NGO "stakeholders," but their impact is tightly constrained. While the UK subsequently reintroduced working permits for asylum seekers awaiting a decision for more than twelve months and those granted asylum (a revision of the general ban on working permits as part of the deterrence measures introduced in 2002; cf. Ensor and Shah 2005) inspired by Art. 26 of the asylum "definition" directive, this amounts to a minor adjustment, since the processing of most asylum cases would not exceed this threshold. It could also be argued that the adjustment dovetailed with the realization that asylum seekers and refugees constituted a valuable hitherto untapped labor resource and would only contribute further to economic impetus[23] (Bloch 2002, 2008). The unconvincing claim that granting work permits to asylum seekers would somehow act as a pull factor, employed to justify the 2002 amendment, was never underpinned by actual evidence and rather embarrassingly had been refuted in a Home Office-commissioned research project (Robinson and Segrott 2002).

British NGOs, including the Refugee Council (2003), have long criticized the government for seeking to suggest more restrictive aspects of UK asylum regulation as the basis for AMP. One such unsuccessful attempt to engage in bottom-up Europeanization was the 2003 proposal to "achieve better management of the asylum process globally through improved regional management and transit processing centres" (March 10, 2003 Letter to the Greek Prime Minister Costas Simitis by British Prime Minister Tony Blair), effectively outsourcing initial responsibility to comanaged detention camps in the unstable periphery, including countries with questionable human rights records such as Libya, Morocco, Ukraine, and Belarus. The initial policy draft, emerging in February 2003 in a Cabinet and Home Office policy paper by the name of "A New Vision for Refugees" still employed the term "safe havens," later modified in light of the unfortunate resemblance with the desperate failures of Srebrenica, had been leaked to the daily *The Guardian* and unsurprisingly incited a storm of protest among domestic NGOs (interview UK-NGO-1; *The Guardian* February 10, 2003, ECRE Press Release March 17, 2003). It was warmly welcomed by the far right Danish People's Party and possibly inspired by the Australian "Pacific solution" of forcing arriving refugee boats into the territorial waters of Nauru and Papua New Guinea (Hathaway 2004). Despite considerable sympathy in Dutch and eventually Spanish and Italian government circles, the vast majority of representatives united at the June 5–6, 2003 Thessaloniki Justice and Home Affairs Council, including notably the German delegation, viewed this proposal with considerable skepticism (Debendetti 2006). Blair had proposed to alter the relevant Art. 11 of the draft Constitutional Treaty and received support from the Danish Ministry of Refugee, Immigration and Integration Affairs which had prepared a memorandum in April in which the applicability of jurisdiction of destination countries was explicitly ruled out. The questionable legal basis, including an implicit violation of the non-refoulement principle of the Geneva Convention, combined with unclear financial and political implications arising out of comanagement of such centers with third countries, impaired chances for successful coalition-building. National NGOs across Europe very firmly expressed their opposition to this proposal, fearing a de facto abolition of the Geneva Convention (interviews DE-NGO-1, UK-NGO-1, FR-NGO-1, FR-NGO-2; Amnesty International 2003; Deutsches Rotes Kreuz 2003; Human Rights Watch 2003). Curiously, despite initial misgivings, shared to some extent by the European Commission (2003) a joint German–Italian initiative by Ministers of the Interior Schily and Pisanu relaunched this idea following the June 2004 Cap Anamur incident, when a German NGO boat rescued 37 undocumented migrants attempting to cross the Mediterranean between Libya and Italy. Diplomatic wrangling over the responsibility for these migrants, also involving the Maltese government, was accompanied by heavy media coverage, and eventually lead to the internment in closed detention centers and eventual deportation of all but one of the migrants (Debendetti 2006). However, yet once again there was no majority for this proposal, with the French government being particularly skeptical and even the British displaying less interest (interview FR-GOV-2, UK-GOV-1). With coalition-building being unsuccessful, bottom-up Europeanization failed.

Germany: The Long-Winded Road Towards Acknowledging Immigration

Since the mid-1980s, migration policy has first featured prominently and later almost dominated public policy debates in (West) Germany. This partly reflected the significant rise in immigration figures, entering largely through the fairly generous asylum procedure, constitutionally enshrined in Art. 16 of the Basic Law and matched by initially relatively high recognition rates. With the exception of tightly curtailed temporary seasonal labor programs with a number of Eastern and Southeastern European countries (Menz 2001), labor migration was no longer actively recruited after 1973. The disintegration of Yugoslavia and the Soviet Union were of particular pertinence due to geographic proximity, existing ethnic networks, and the initially exclusively ethnic base of citizenship (Bade 1992; Green 2004; Marshall 2000; Thraenhardt and Wolken 1988). Notwithstanding the de facto increases, neither of the major two political parties accepted acknowledging that Germany was well on its way to becoming a country of immigration.²⁴ Both the citizenship concept and the refusal to accept officially the status of net immigration country are often somewhat misunderstood in the English-language literature (a notable exception is Green 2004). The ethnic nature of the citizenship concept needs to be appreciated against the backdrop of the ideological refusal to recognize separate East German citizenship; hence the often rehearsed claim about the power of its nineteenth century ideological roots (Brubaker 1992) is not unproblematic. Similarly, the official denial of immigration was obviously not meant as an empirical description, but rather as a stance spawning closed borders, while promoting simultaneously the slightly contradictory goals of repatriation *and* integration.

German migration policy can be characterized by the following six developments.

First, while policy continuity existed between the restrictive Social Democratic approach of the 1970s and the Christian Democratic stance after 1982, by the late 1980s, consensus had evaporated. During its long spell in opposition, the Left went through a significant metamorphosis, adopting a much more pragmatic and centrist stance, with the Greens abandoning their more innovative proposals of the early 1980s. No shared left-wing consensus emerged, however. The role of the churches, center-left charities, NGOs, and trade unions in influencing the stance of the SPD is considerable. By 1998, when Gerhard Schröder's Red–Green government assumed office, it promised paradigmatic changes regarding nationality, migration, and asylum regulations. Though many of the original propositions never came to fruition, not least due to the conspicuous ideological differences between the hard-line Minister of the Interior Schily and the Greens, the Left did implement reforms in all three areas. From the mid-1980s onwards, a growing schism among the Right emerged too. West Germany's Far Right only ever boasted limited national electoral successes in the early 1950s and the late 1960s. Since then, parties such as the *Republikaner*, the *Deutsche Volksunion,* or most recently the Hamburg-based *Partei für Ordnung und Rechtsstaatlichkeit* (Party for Order and *Rechtsstaat*) only recorded temporarily limited and regionally based representation in parliament. The Christian Democrats and even more so the Bavarian CSU attempted to curtail the electoral rise of the Far Right by assuming a tough restrictive line and occasionally pandering to populist xenophobia, as it had done throughout the 1980s. This explains the genesis of the excessively restrictionist first draft of the foreigner law of 1990 that led to the demission of the right-wing minister of the interior Eduard Zimmermann in 1989 (Green 2004, 50 ff.). In the run-up to the

1999 regional elections in Hesse, the CDU candidate Koch launched a petition against dual citizenship, floated by the federal Ministry of the Interior, deliberately playing on xenophobe sentiments. Similarly, CDU candidate for the 2002 national elections Stoiber had gone on record warning against the dangers of a "racially mixed and soiled" (*durchrasste*) society. But such populist posturing is by no means accepted among all sections of the Right. The churches and the ever dwindling CDA employee wing of the party assumed a much more centrist stance. In addition, the employer organization was beginning to rediscover labor migration in the late 1990s.

Second, official dogma notwithstanding, by the late 1980s, temporary labor migration schemes had been re-established, albeit on a very limited scale. It is worth noting that the so-called Green Card scheme for highly skilled labor migrants particularly with skills in IT, established in 2000 and closed in January 2005, does not mark as radical a shift as is sometimes implied, since throughout the 1980s and 1990s (West) Germany employed temporary contract workers from a range of Central and Eastern European countries, though exclusively in low-skill sectors such as agriculture and construction (Menz 2001).[25] Indeed, along with plans to recruit computer engineers, temporary labor recruitment schemes for personal care in private homes were rolled out in 2002 and the bilateral labor agreements were expanded in numbers and sectoral scope in the late 1990s.[26] Strikingly, the 2001 proposal for a new migration law from an expert committee headed by former president Süßmuth (Unabhängige Kommission 2001, esp. p. 87) proposed a Canadian-style points system for labor migrants and an annual quota, a proposal reiterated in the report of the 2004 expert commission (Sachverständigenrat 2004, esp. pp. 170 ff.). This suggestion was not incorporated into the actual law, mainly because of intense resistance from the Christian Democrats who correctly calculated that there was little appetite among the general population for such measures, given mass unemployment, economic malaise, and xenophobia. Much to the dismay of organized business (interview DE-GOV-1, DE-BUS-1), labor migration remains a tightly regulated exception, rather than a key pillar of Germany's most recent migration legislation.

Third, the somewhat peculiar nature of German migration regulation combined with political unrest both in Europe's periphery and in traditional sending countries with large resident communities in Germany rendered asylum an important legal entry gate. The dramatic 1993 restrictions to hitherto very generous asylum guidelines have not been significantly revised since. Since Kohl first became chancellor, Germany has been among the most vocal and influential advocates of a common EU approach to border control, asylum policy, and in particular schemes to share the costs for the accommodation of asylum seekers and refugees or to disseminate the individuals themselves across Europe, the latter often referred to with the hideous technocratic term "burden-sharing." German asylum policy has become more restrictive since, acceptance rates have plummeted, and special "contingent" refugee categories have been created, for example for the refugees from the civil war-torn Balkans, which permit considerable administrative leeway and do not afford the same temporarily unlimited status as regular political asylum. There is no reason to assume more progressive change in the future (cf. interview DE-GOV-1).

Fourth, after decades of complete neglect of family policy, resignation to remarkably low female labor market participation rates, and often insufficient child support facilities, contemporary Germany is experiencing one of Europe's lowest birth rates. The demographic pyramid has turned already, with birth rates declining rapidly since the early 1970s. While labor market policy is currently concerned with enticing or even forcing welfare recipients back into employment, the end of mass unemployment will arrive very soon for simple demographic reasons. Indeed, labor market *shortages*, particularly in highly skilled niches or unattractive low-pay sectors already surface. More so than elsewhere in Europe, migration is considered a serious option to redress the impending problems for the pensions and welfare system.[27]

Fifth, with considerable delay compared to other European countries and often in connection with the issue of citizenship, debates over assimilation, integration, and national security have taken place since the early 2000s. The coming-of-age of the third generation of immigrants, or, more accurately, young Germans of migrant origin, combined with the acknowledgment of their existence implied in the abandonment of the doctrine of *kein Einwanderungsland* ("no country of immigration") imposes a number of challenging questions about integration and assimilation.[28] Part of the rationale behind the ethnically based character of German citizenship lay in the purportedly provisional character of West Germany that portrayed itself both a legal successor to the Third Reich, legitimating claims to citizenship by individuals resident in the borders of pre-World War II Germany, and a systemic alternative to state socialism, thus maintaining open borders to refugees from East Germany and ethnic Germans from elsewhere in Eastern Europe. These theoretical

Table 4.6. German immigration policy in the 1980s and 1990s

1981 Asylum seeker entitlement to social benefits is being reduced and voucher payments are experimented with in some *Länder*, consequently the "deterrence" approach spawns detention centers for rejected applicants and communal accommodation with mobility bans for all asylum seekers, from 1987 onwards, asylum seekers are banned from working (ban abolished in 1991, reintroduced in 1997).

1990 Foreign Resident Act (*Ausländergesetz*) approved (April 26, by the Bundestag, May 11, by the Bundesrat), modifying the earlier 1965 Law, after failed attempt by right-wing minister of the interior Zimmermann to implement highly restrictive bill in 1988, which met sustained resistance by the unions, churches, charities, the opposition parties, and some segments of the government coalition itself. Codification of conditions for family reunion, reducing notably the discretion allotted to regional governments in "interpreting" the rules, clarification and legal codification of different categories of residence and working permits, facilitates acquisition of citizenship for long-term legal residents and young foreigners—bill receives mixed to hostile reception from unions and NGOs, but is pushed through parliament successfully by the center-right government.

1993 (January 23) Following a compromise between the opposition Social Democrats and the center-right government, Art. 16II of the Basic Law, guaranteeing the right to asylum in Germany, is modified substantially, introducing the safe third country concept and a "fast track procedure" for "manifestly unfounded" claims to be administered at airports and seaports, leading to the July 1 Asylum Procedure and Aliens and Nationality Provisions (*Gesetz zur Änderung asylverfahrens-, ausländer- und staatsangehörigkeitsrechtlicher Vorschriften* (BGBl I, 1062) and the April 1 Law on the New Format of the Asylum Procedures (*Gesetz zur Neuregelung des Asylverfahrens*).

Simultaneously, an informal quota of 100,000 annual temporary labor contract workers is set for Central and Southeastern European countries, most of which were now considered "safe third countries," this reduces the contingent from up to 210,000 in 1992, though in practice figures remain well above 100,000.

1993 Act on Asylum Seeker Benefits (*Asylbewerberleistungsgesetz*) comes into effect on November 1, reduces benefits for asylum seekers during first year of residence; revision in 1997 introduces further cuts in benefits for all asylum seekers and refugees, more *Länder* reduce cash payment and introduce voucher schemes.

1999 (January 13) New Bill to Facilitate the Acquisition of German Citizenship (*Gesetz zur Erleichterung des Erwerbs der deutschen Staatsangehörigkeit*) introduced by the new Red-Green coalition: Major modification of the 1914 Law modifies the hitherto predominant *ius sanguinis* principle. German-born descendants of German-born residents or long-term residents can acquire citizenship, long-term legal residents acquire a legal claim to citizenship (with exceptions). In light of pronounced criticism from the opposition Christian Democrats and their populist opposition to dual citizenship, permitting them to win the Land elections in Hesse, the final bill, introduced on March 16 and in force since January 1, 2000 (Law on the Reform of the Citizenship Law, *Gesetz zur Reform des Staatsangehörigkeitsrechts*) limits dual citizenship to German-born descendants of foreigners who need to choose one citizenship over the second upon reaching the age of 23.

Table 4.7. German immigration policy since 2000

2000 (February 23) Chancellor Schröder announces the introduction of a five year labor migration scheme for highly skilled IT personnel ("Green Card" initiative), leading to the August 1 "Regulation on Residency Permits for highly qualified foreign employees in information and communication technology" (*Verordnung über Aufenthaltserlaubnisse für hochqualifizierte ausländische Fachkräfte der Informations- und Kommunikationstechnologie*), opposition enters Land elections in North Rhine Westphalia with the slogan "Children, not Indians" (*Kinder statt Inder*), insinuating that family policy is preferable to (Indian) high-skill migration, Social Democrats carry the elections.

In June, minister of the interior Otto Schily forms bipartisan independent commission on migration headed by former president Süßmuth, opposition forms a rival commission the same month.

October 2001 Minister of the Interior manages to find a compromise agreement between the opposition proposals, the position of the Greens, particularly concerned with the recognition of asylum seekers fleeing for gender-specific reasons of persecution, and select elements of the final report of the independent commission, though notably no formalized system for labor recruitment is being created. Immigration remains the tightly constrained exception, rather than the rule.

2002 An odd political battle over the largely symbolic age of children permitted to enter as part of family reunion ensues, the eventual compromise age being 12. Despite having colored the bill substantially and pressure from the employers to accept the government's version, the Christian Democrats attempt to block the bill at the last minute. During the voting process in the Bundesrat, the verdict of the Land of Brandenburg is considered ambiguous, reflecting the somewhat divided opinions within the grand coalition government there. In the end, the Land's vote is taken to be in the affirmative, thus permitting the passing of the bill. The Constitutional Court declares the acceptance by the Bundesrat unconstitutional in December 2002 due to these procedural problems.

2003 The bill is reintroduced by the government coalition, but the opposition now commands a majority in the Bundesrat and can block it.

2004 (July 1 and July 9) *Bundestag* and *Bundesrat* accept the "Law on the management and limitation of inward migration and the regulation of the residence and integration of EU citizens and foreigners (*Gesetz zur Steuerung und Begrenzung der Zuwanderung und zur Regelung des Aufenthalts und der Integration von Unionsbürgern und Ausländern*), which comes into effect as of January 1, 2005 (BGBl Part I, No. 41, 1950 of August 5, 2004). Reduces the previous five categories of residency permit to two (unlimited and limited), creates a new coordinating agency for migration and refugees, reporting to the ministry of the interior and assuming the duties of the central unit for asylum claims, designs highly constrained labor migration channels for entrepreneurs investing at least €1 million and creating at least 10 new jobs and carefully delineated categories of highly skilled migrants, including teachers, scientists, and skilled managers earning in excess of €100,000 (all defined in Art. 19), permitting foreign graduates of German universities to remain in the country for one additional year to search for employment, a minor improvement for the "tolerated" refugees who are granted residency permits if no deportation can be implemented within 18 months, and eligibility for language and civic culture courses for newcomers, with this right becoming an obligation for specified resident migrants. Language skills are now a mandatory requirement for both ethnic Germans and Jewish migrants from the successor states to the Soviet Union.

2007 (June 14) Law on the Implementation of EU Directives on Residence and Asylum (*Gesetz zur Umsetzung aufenthalts- und asylrechtlicher Richtlinien der Europäischen Union*) passed by the *Bundestag*, implements EU directives on family reunion, deportation, trafficking, third-country national rights, asylum minimum standards and procedures, students and interns, and researchers; obligation for beneficiaries of family reunion to demonstrate German language skills; foreign graduates of German universities receive one-year work and residency permit contingent on employment offer; sanctions for "refusal" of integration offers, notably attendance in language classes.

rights turned into the real claims by the *Aussiedler* from Romania, Poland, Russia, and other Soviet successor republics in large numbers from the 1980s onwards and the *Übersiedler* from eastern Germany. The resultant policy response has been a tightening of eligibility for the ethnic German *Aussiedler* and a revision of the exclusive *ius sanguinis* principle of citizenship. Green (2004) correctly asserts that debates surrounding the citizenship law reform and not least the ultimately successful petition campaign against dual nationality in Hesse in 1999 reflected the deep unease in significant parts of the population about liberalizing access to citizenship. The 1999–2000 debate about a dominant culture (*Leitkultur*), instigated by the Christian Democrats, unfortunately proved not very insightful, perhaps not surprising in light of the political motives informing those initiating it. But the questions about the nature of mainstream identity and culture that newcomers are expected to become part of remain pressing. The discussions about the legitimacy of displaying Christian symbols in Bavarian classrooms and banning a young teacher of Afghan origin from wearing a headscarf as a secondary school teacher in Baden-Württemberg are intimately related to national self-identity and the role of religion therein. While the domestic secret police (*Verfassungsschutz*) have always kept an eye on the activities of migrant organizations, particularly those deemed extremist and targeting the large-scale Turkish and Kurdish resident communities, carefully orchestrated paranoia in the aftermath of the 2001 terrorist attacks has been exploited to legitimize considerable infringements on civil liberties for all residents, but especially migrant communities. The discovery of the Hamburg base of the September 11 pilots revealed not lunatic maniacs, but ostensibly well-adjusted, well-educated, polite young multilingual university graduates of a profile corresponding closely to the "desirables" targeted by labor recruitment schemes such as the Green Card program.

Sixth, it would be misleading to exaggerate the role of independent expert committees. In fact, Green (2004, 121 ff.) highlights the strategic interest of minister of the interior Otto Schily in using the formation and existence of the 2001 Süßmuth "Independent Commission" in sidelining the Greens and placating the Right. Citing Angenendt (2002, 42), he stresses that the ministry's own 2001 draft bill differed considerably from the commission's report and may have been prepared both completely independently and temporarily concomitantly with the commission report! The ministry draft combined elements of the commission's report with more restrictive suggestions made by a Christian Democratic commission (Green 2004, 123), though some of the recommendations of the final document were included, but notably not in labor migration. The expert commission, whose permanent institutionalization was suggested in this 2001 report, suggested detailed and wide-ranging policy options in subsequent annual reports. But immediately following its 2004 annual report (Sachverständigenrat 2004) funding was cut and it was dissolved at the end of 2004 (Cyrus and Vogel 2005, 26 ff.). These two commissions should be perceived as expressions of lingering neocorporatism; they included representatives of the religious apparatus, the union, employer association, welfare organizations, academics and the major political parties as well as one Turkish-born businessman. Re-establishing a bipartisan consensus was no small feat, which the 2001 commission succeeded in doing, having organized more than 100 hearings, including on the need for actively managed immigration (Tables 4.6 and 4.7 above).

System of Political Economy: The Slowly Mutating Coordinated Market Economy

The German political economy served as the paradigmatic model for Hall and Soskice's (2001) category of coordinated market economies (CMEs). Its traits are said to encompass a mutually re-enforcing network of highly organized industrial relations, tight networks between banks and private sector companies, and para-public institutions providing public goods, notably high and specialized educational standards. One of the most vivid debates in the comparative political economy literature focuses on the question to what extent this German model may be in decline, disintegration, or metamorphosis. A number of empirical studies underline the radically changing nature of its institutions (Dyson and Padgett 2005; Harding and Paterson 2000; Streeck 1997; Streeck and Höpner 2003) and policy output (Menz 2005*b*, 2005*c*). "Convergence within diversity" (Lütz 2004) appears more likely than full convergence on the Anglo-American liberal model. Germany continues to rely on high-wage high value-added high-quality production. Employers are interested in maintaining and enhancing institutions that provide public goods, including education, but recently they have been considerably less committed to traditional neocorporatist institutions of industrial relations. Traditionally highly regulated labor markets have become considerably less so due to the decline of union density, more aggressive employers, questionable strategies to "exit" from the general wage brackets by businesses leaving their employer organizations or pursuing corporate restructuring with an eye on escaping the confines of these organizations and hence the obligation to pay standard wages (Menz 2005*b*; Streeck and Hassel 2004). In the West (East), a striking 32 (48) percent of employees were not covered by standard wage agreements in 2004, a further 7 (12) percent were subject to an in-house company level contract. In the service sector, particularly in low-skill professions, this shift away from regulated industrial relations has probably proceeded furthest, although secondary substandard tiers of the labor market existed previously, as the influential journalistic exposé *Ganz Unten* reveals (Walraff 1988). The absence of a national minimum wage can become problematic, given the absence of sectoral minimum wages in certain areas.[29] This became evident in the large-scale posting of employees from low-wage EU member states to Germany in the framework of the EU-induced liberalization of service provision, which affected especially the construction sector (Menz 2005*a*). Portuguese subcontractors could thus offer their services based on Portuguese wages. But marked differences in preferred corporate strategies surfaced in the elaboration of the German legislative re-regulation of the EU liberalization of service provision: SMEs perceive subcontractors employing posted workers or undocumented employees as a menace, larger companies welcome these "exit" opportunities. The problem inherent in a nonexistent national minimum wage has resurfaced following EU eastward enlargement. While bans apply both to labor mobility and to service provision from CEE, "independent entrepreneurs" are not covered and receive central European wages while employed by German meat-processing plants (Czommer and Worthmann 2005).

The employers maintained an interest in the guest worker system even after the end to active recruitment, but were isolated in their advocacy. Joppke (1999, 70) among others suggests the increasing "securitization" of the migration issue from the 1970s onwards, including concerns over "ghettoization" and xenophobic sentiments, which meant that economic prerogatives faded in importance, while Green (2004) points to the much better links the labor market interest associations maintained with the ministry of labor and social affairs rather than the ministry of the interior, which became predominant in designing migration policy. The employers remained relatively taciturn on this issue until the mid-1990s, having witnessed the failure of their earlier campaign for a continuation of the guest worker system. Advocating new labor migration was an ungrateful task, given internal divisions even among the center-right Christian Democrats and slow but steadily rising unemployment throughout the Kohl years, and did not prove economically necessary. Labor supply was unproblematic and already existent cracks in the regulated labor market did permit some substandard employment practices in such sectors. A more structural explanation is the delayed change towards the tertiary sector covering only 55 percent of all employees as recently as the late 1980s. By the early 1980s, employer organization BDA had not only abandoned earlier lobbying efforts, but it also supported the end to active labor market recruitment (Marshall 2000, 155), along with restrictive border controls, repatriation measures and efforts to boost the educational levels of the then second generation, as a position paper reveals. However, though it still considered unnecessary, a specific immigration law containing quotas for the highly skilled, it no longer rejected the rediscovery of a limited guest worker scheme (BDA 1983). Its dominant constituent sectoral member, the metal processing association *Gesamtmetall*, did not face significant skill shortages. The impetus for change originated within the association representing larger companies BDI and its outspoken mid-1990s president Hans-Olaf Henkel. Henkel's radical rejection of traditional tenets of the German model and his tiresome advocacy of neoliberal restructuring very much incorporated legal labor migration. The BDA slowly embraced this attitude.[30] Henkel partook in both expert commissions and harshly criticized the Christian Democratic reticence towards labor migration quotas. BDA head Dieter Hundt rejected any quantitative limits to quotas or setting them at 300,000 annually—a tenfold increase over the quota proposed by the 2001 commission (*Süddeutsche Zeitung* June 11, 2001). The BDA enthusiastically welcomed the "new paradigmatic change" inherent in the hotly contested 2002 draft immigration bill. The association claimed to have demanded such change "for a long time" (BDA 2002). Convinced of the necessity to "compete for the best brains" and "internationally mobile high flyers" to address "labor market shortages" and ensure the continued "competitiveness of Germany as place to do business," regulation concerning economic migration needs to be liberalized, permitting both temporary and long-term migration flows, with minimal discretion for local and regional administrative interventions, while more stringent procedures and increased deportations should render asylum less attractive (BDA 2002, undated); with this more stringent stance presumably rendering a more liberal stance on labor migration more palatable to the electorate. The BDA very strongly lobbied the ministry of the interior and was invited to formal hearings and informal meetings (interviews DE-GOV-1, DE-BUS-1); ideational unity and internal organizational coherence enhanced the business lobby's influence. BDA and BDI were only interested in minimum EU level regulations that would leave maximum room for maneuver at the national level, ostensibly over concerns of subsidiarity and Commission regulation of qualitative standards (BDA 2001*a*, 2001*b*, interview DE-BUS-1), but in reality anxious about exercising maximum influence on the establishment of national level quotas and qualitative targets without EU interference.

In 2000, *Gesamtmetall* launched a vociferous, if ill-informed, PR campaign entitled New Social Market Economy (*Neue Soziale Marktwirtschaft*), aimed at influencing public opinion and media reports in favor of neoliberal restructuring, including orchestrating support for the substantial cuts to welfare provision and labor market stability enacted by the Social Democrats (Leif 2004).[31] Immigration of "highly qualified foreigners" featured prominently among the proposals (Stiftung Marktwirtschaft 2002, 8). Indeed, labor migration is generally seen as only one component of measures advocated to liberalize and "break up rigid structures" of the labor market and introduce more punitive measures for social transfer income recipients (BDA undated).

The trade union stance towards migration has not changed as strongly over the years. The DGB's main concern traditionally has been the integration of immigrants into the primary labor market and the avoidance of any bifurcation. It has traditionally utilized its contacts among the Social Democrats to lobby in favor of respect for the rights of resident migrant populations. At all levels of the organization, the official stance has been one of favoring nondiscrimination and antiracism (Kühne 2000; interview DE-UNI-1). Naturally, the slow disintegration of the labor market in some parts of the service sector through the strategic use of immigrants is a development that has caused some concern within the union. Thus, the union was open to suggestions for long-term labor migration, but remained highly skeptical of short-term labor migration, including the Green Card program and the bilateral labor treaties. Its concern was that labor migration would be pursued in place of (re)training measures for resident migrants and the resident unemployed (DGB 2002). It therefore supported sector-specific labor migration, but tightly regulated, defined by annual quotas as well as a point system assessing the qualification level, and dependent on the sectoral labor market situation (interview DE-UNI-1, DGB 2001*a*, 2001*b*). The DGB published a joint position paper with the employers in which the desirability of long-term permanent migration, accompanied by greatly enhanced integration measures, including language classes, was strongly emphasized (DGB and BDA 2004). Represented in the expert committees, the unions generally supported the draft migration bill of 2002, continuing the pragmatic stance of preferring managed and tightly controlled labor migration to undocumented entries, but remained wary that excessively permissive labor migration regulation would contribute to the disintegration of the labor market, while no attention was paid in government circles to long-term residents with no legal access to the labor market at all, especially the "tolerated" refugees (DGB 2001c, 2003). The strongest sectoral union *IG Metall* strongly supported this position (IG Metall 2002). The unions were not unhappy about responsibility for the actual examination of the labor market situation—carried out to determine the labor market access of individual newcomers—remaining under the auspices of local employment administrations, where a somewhat restrictive legacy exists (Cyrus and Vogel 2005, 26ff.). The trade union was not as active as the employers, but general ideational consensus and strong internal organizational coherence aided in lobbying efforts targeted at the ministry of the interior.

Structure of Interest Intermediation

The German political system is shaped by a neocorporatist legacy and a complex system of institutionalized checks and balances replete with "veto points" (Immergut 1992), creating "semi-sovereignty" to limit excessive concentration of political power (Katzenstein 1987). This potentially permits more access by interest groups, especially where established neocorporatist networks between labor market interest associations and ministries can be utilized. Green (2004) accurately points out that the shift of authority in migration policymaking from the ministry of labor and social affairs to that for the interior impeded the influence of unions and employers. Obviously, informal lobbying is open to all actors. Unions and employers have managed to establish connections to the ministry of the interior since this shift over the course of the past twenty years, but these are not nearly as tight or formalized (interview DE-GOV-1, DE-BUS-1, DE-UNI-1). Both actors were represented in the two expert committees on migration. By contrast, humanitarian NGOs face a much more difficult task. Not only do they encounter governmental actors somewhat suspicious of their aims, but they also do command formalized lobbying channels. In fact, prior to the 1998 arrival in power of the Red-Green coalition, the government refused even to receive delegations from

NGOs (interview DE-NGO-1). Limited personnel and financial capacity further impede access to parliamentary hearings or lobbying efforts targeting MPs who display relatively high party discipline in Germany. The nongovernmental actors thus face a structurally and fundamentally unfortunate position and struggle to make their position heard, much less convey it in a meaningful way. In addition to organizational faults and shortcomings, ideological divisions undermine the NGO camp, given the more confrontational tactics and methods favored by grassroots groups with anarchist leanings and the more bourgeois camp aiming at affecting change through lobbying or even cooperation with the state apparatus (interviews DE-NGO-1, DE-NGO-2). Some ideological positions are shared by the political Left, especially the Green party. This proximity permitted the inclusion of new asylum categories in the initial legislative draft on migration, especially the recognition of persecution by nonstate actors and for gender-specific reasons. While the NGO camp thus contributed to inserting important new categories that the employers strongly opposed (BDA 2002, undated; interview DE-NGO-1), this concession to the Greens was made only after the party had threatened to quit the government coalition. Even then, the treatment of "tolerated" (*geduldet*) individuals—political refugees who did not qualify for either asylum or official refugee status and relied on reluctantly extended "tolerated" status that did not permit legal labor market access—did not improve tremendously and "tolerated" status was abolished altogether in 2004, despite concern over this status being shared by the union. With some internal divisions apparent, poor organizational capacity, and limited channels for informal lobbying activity, the NGO sector is hard pressed to affect regulatory change. Participation in public and expert hearings and the frequent publication of statements and studies constitute the principal feeble tools in the arsenal.

Development of Immigration Policy Since 1990

The 1980s center-right Kohl governments sought to encourage return emigration by offering resettlement payments. Despite newly imposed visa requirements on key sending countries, political asylum applications increased from around 5,000 per annum in 1973 to hover above the mark of 100,000 per annum throughout the 1980s. The decade was marked by an uneasy melange of restrictive measures, in particular regarding the treatment of asylum seekers, and remarkable, if largely rhetorical, commitment to the integration of existing migrant communities. Both the federal and the conservative *Land* governments took measures to discourage asylum applications, offering poor accommodation and only in kind benefits, cutting resources for language training and allowances, limiting access to the labor market, imposing carrier sanctions on airlines in 1987 and brokering a deal with the East German authorities to prevent entry into the enclave of West Berlin, whose borders formally remained under the control of the Western Allies. The center-right government was neither willing to modify citizenship regulations to facilitate access by German-born descendants of migrants nor willing to limit such access by ethnic Germans from Eastern Europe. Many earlier *Aussiedler*, especially those settled in Southern Germany, were strong supporters and dedicated voters of the Christian Democrats. Three events coincided in the early 1990s spurring quantitative migration peaks: the fall of the Berlin Wall and unification caused massive intra-German migration, the removal of the intimidating road block that the Iron Curtain had constituted facilitated new East–West flows and the violent disintegration of Yugoslavia unleashed refugee flows. Asylum applications were already inching towards the annual mark of 200,000 by the late 1980s, and by 1991, 256,110 applications were lodged, with an historic record of 438,840 being reached in 1992. This coincided with an annual inflow of up to 400,000 ethnic Germans. Another cohort of migrants were Russian Jews, for whom an annual quota of 20,000 was established in 1991 by the last East German government and then continued by Kohl. In addition, 350,000 refugees from the former Yugoslavia were accommodated in 1996 and 70,000 in 1999 (Rühl and Currle 2004, 38ff.). The EU-induced liberalization of service provision also enabled the mass transnational posting of EU workers, particularly in the construction sector, peaking at about 100,000 per annum in 1994 (Menz 2005*a*). In the early 1990s, estimates about stock levels of undocumented migrants ranged between 100,000 and 500,000.

After years of scheming, interrupted by long spells of dithering, four major measures were undertaken in the 1990s. Access to political asylum was drastically curtailed, while access to citizenship by long-term non-German residents was rendered less arduous and bureaucratic, new annual quotas for ethnic Germans were imposed, and bilateral labor recruitment programs with Eastern Europe sought both to regulate existing migration patterns and limit new flows. Substantial qualifications to the previously unqualified right to asylum laid out in Article 16.II of the Basic

Law, rendered possible through a compromise with the Social Democratic opposition, were accompanied by the November 1993 Asylum Seekers Benefit Law (*Asylbewerberleistungsgesetz*), severely limiting benefits. Changes to the Foreigners Act in 1993 introduced the "safe third countries" clause, enhanced by readmission agreements with Romania and Bulgaria. The so-called airport Asylum Procedures Act permitted immediate deportation in some cases and generally accelerated processing of the asylum applications, especially for "manifestly unfounded" applications.

On citizenship, the April 1990 revision of the 1965 Foreigners Act enabled easier access to German citizenship and more rights for long-term foreign residents and German-born residents. Naturalization was greatly facilitated for legal residents of 15 years, reducing the unlimited amount of discretion local and regional authorities had previously enjoyed. German-born residents no longer faced restrictions in returning to Germany after a lengthy stay in their "home countries," and individuals that had originally benefited from family reunion now benefited from legal residency independently of the head of family.

The Ethnic German Reception Law of July 1990 significantly raised the burden of proof for applicants. In 1993, an annual quota of 200,000 newcomers was established.

Simultaneously, a number of bilateral labor treaties with eastern and southeastern European countries permitted temporary labor migration (*Werkvertragsarbeitnehmerabkommen*) into sectors experiencing labor shortages, including construction, agriculture, and tourism. Commencing in 1988 and initially focused on Czechoslovakia, Hungary, Poland, Yugoslavia, and Austria, numbers rose from a total of 14,593 in 1988 to an all time high of 94,902 in 1992.[32]

The more restrictive asylum policy was implemented against a chorus of disapproval from the humanitarian NGOs. Unions and employers remained reticent regarding labor migration until the mid-1990s. Even then, the response to the temporary labor contracts with Eastern Europe and the massive posting of EU employees from low-cost southern European to German construction sites revealed internal divisions between the more protectionist minded SMEs and sectoral employers and the increasingly more economically liberal umbrella association BDA. Similarly, DGB was still more committed to the integration of existing migrants, while viewing the new forms of labor migration as largely exploitative strategies to undercut standard wage levels (Menz 2001, 2005*a*).

The path to more radical reform proved quite thorny. The Social Democrats prepared a draft immigration act in 1996 while in opposition.

The Red–Green government program of 1998 is notably less liberal than earlier positions among the Greens and the Social Democrats might have suggested. The acrimonious 1999 *Land* elections in Hesse and the remarkably popular CDU campaign against dual citizenship signalled considerable hesitancy among the populace to endorse more liberal policy, much less annual migration quotas. The government commenced reforms with a more pragmatic modification to the original 1913 citizenship law in 1999 (Morris 2002). First, citizenship applications became possible after eight, rather than fifteen years of documented residency and application fees were lowered somewhat. Second, German-born noncitizens with at least one parent legally resident in Germany for a minimum of five years could register as dual citizens, with the obligation to choose between the two nationalities by the age of 23, including concessions for nationals of countries whose citizenship is legally impossible to shed.

The changing stance of the employers and concerns over recruitment difficulties in the booming IT sector combined with Schröder's consistent pandering to business interest spawned the 2000 IT sector labor migration recruitment program for a total of 20,000 highly skilled professionals, somewhat misleadingly christened "Green Card" initiative and launched with great fanfare (Menz 2002). But the opposition Christian Democrats maintained a skeptical and increasingly xenophobic stance, responding to the government's initiative with the hideous slogan *Kinder statt Inder* (Children instead of Indians), insisting on superior training rather than immigration. On this issue, the party remained substantially unaligned with the employers (BDA undated; interview DE-BUS-1).

The government continued its strive for reform. In 2001, Minister of the Interior Schily charged a commission composed of academics, legal experts, the social partners, and politicians from all parties, and headed by moderate Christian Democrat Süssmuth with formulating independent expert advice. Of symbolical significance is the report's first sentence "*Deutschland ist ein Einwanderungsland*" (Unabhängige Kommission 2001), directly negating the well-rehearsed traditional claim. Key recommendations include improved integration, doubling expenditures on language classes and both incentives and sanctions to ensure enrolment by foreign residents. It is debatable how much attention Schily was willing to dedicate to the conclusions (Green 2004) and whether the concession to the Greens to consider traditional NGO demands regarding the introduction of persecution on gender-related issues and by nonstate actors as legitimate grounds for political asylum was not merely strategic. Both BDA representatives within the Commission and outside strongly lobbied in favor of more "demand oriented managed migration" and less bureaucratic leeway for regional labor market administrations in the context of more "competition for the best brains," coupled with faster asylum decisions and more rigorously enforced deportations to "avoid any signal that could be understood in countries of origin that immigration for non-labor market related reasons will be expanded" (BDA 2002). Employers were particularly interested in highly skilled migrants, not least due to the positive experiences with the IT sector program, and contributed to the demand for an annual migration quota, based on a points system (interview DE-BUS-1). The unions supported such a quota based on points, but unlike the employers rejected any reinvention of guest worker-style temporary migration schemes (DGB 2001a, 2002). They supported the extension of grounds for asylum claims that the NGOs cherished, but generally focused on "advocating loudly a pragmatic and managed migration policy" (interview DE-UNI-1). The ministry of the interior proved unwilling to heed the call for annual migration quotas, however (interview DE-GOV-1). Part of this hesitancy might have arisen from the sustained opposition from the Christian Democrats who were commanding a narrow majority in the *Bundesrat*. But consistent lobbying efforts by the labor market interest associations did lead to the creation of migration channels for highly skilled high-wage professionals in the new immigration bill. Procedural mistakes made by the SPD in the *Bundesrat* delayed the approval of the draft bill. The Constitutional Court thus declared the new law void in 2002, requiring a lengthy renegotiation with more overtures to the Right, focusing bizarrely on the fairly trivial question of the maximum age for children benefitting from family reunion provisions. The Right was unwilling to budge on labor migration (*Frankfurter Rundschau* January 17, 20 and 30, 2004; *FAZ* January 20, 2004). Final acceptance was only ensured on July 1, 2004 by the *Bundestag* and on July 9, 2004 by the *Bundesrat*. The revealingly entitled "Law on the management and limitation of inward migration and the regulation of the residence and integration of EU citizens and foreigners" (*Gesetz zur Steuerung und Begrenzung der Zuwanderung und zur Regelung des Aufenthalts und der Integration von Unionsbürgern und Ausländern*), came into effect on January 1, 2005 (BGBl Part I, No. 41, 1950 of August 5, 2004). Its main provisions include the following: the previous bewildering array of five categories of residency permits (Morris 2002, esp. 47 ff.) was reduced to two (unlimited and limited); a new coordinating Agency for Migration and Refugees was established, reporting to the Ministry of the Interior and assuming the duties of the central unit for asylum claims; labor migration channels were created for entrepreneurs investing at least €1 million, creating at least ten new jobs; carefully delineated categories of highly skilled migrants were permitted access, including teachers, scientists, and skilled managers earning in excess of €100,000 (all defined in Art. 19); foreign graduates of German universities were permitted to remain in the country for one additional year to search for employment; a minor improvement was granted to "tolerated" refugees who are granted residency permits if no deportation can be implemented within 18 months; and eligibility for language and civic culture courses for newcomers was affirmed, with this right becoming an obligation for specified resident migrants. Language skills are now a mandatory requirement for both ethnic Germans and Jewish migrants from the successor states to the Soviet Union. With regard to labor migration, Art. 18 is of particular importance, given that it specifies that in processing an application for a work permit (henceforth linked to a residency permit), consideration should be given to the labor market situation, the fight against unemployment, and the exigencies of securing national competitiveness.

Meanwhile, deliberations for AMP were gathering pace. On June 14, 2007 and with considerable delay, the new EU directives on family reunion, deportation, trafficking, third-country national rights, asylum minimum standards and procedures, students and interns, and researchers were implemented in the 2007 Law on Implementation of EU Directives on Residence and Asylum (*Gesetz zur Umsetzung aufenthalts- und asylrechtlicher Richtlinien der Europäischen Union*). There were a number of more punitive provisions regarding language skills of future beneficiaries of family reunion, further obligations for resident migrants to partake in language training and only marginal improvements for foreign graduates of German universities. Generally, nonstate actors were disappointed (DGB 2007; *Die Welt* July 7, 2007). The NGOs were skeptical regarding the more stringent requirements imposed on beneficiaries of family reunion, though they had not become particularly active on this issue, while employers and unions once again had their hopes crushed that continued advocacy would lead to a points-based system of labor migration (*Berliner Zeitung* August 23 and 25, 2007). However, following an August 2007 cabinet meeting in Merseburg, business-friendly concessions were made effective as of November 2007, including facilitated access for EU-10 engineers, three-year work permits for foreign graduates of German universities and the creation of a working group within the Ministry of Labor and Education charged with developing "a labor market-oriented management of migration," including the examination of a points-based system measuring qualification levels, age, and language skills (*Berliner Zeitung* August 6 and 25, 2007). Vice Chancellor and Minister of Labor Müntefering announced specifically that there was no need for low-skill labor migration. The employers enthusiastically welcomed the liberalization of access, emphasizing labor shortages not only in engineering but also in banking and business services (BDA 2007a), and continued their advocacy of the "long overdue introduction" of such a points-based system (BDA 2007b), pointing to Britain as a possible model (BDA 2007c, 2007d).

The Impact of Europeanization

The initially multilateral and extracommunal Schengen Treaty was the product of Franco-German collaboration. But the Kohl government—and indeed the Chancellor himself—was extremely keen to develop tangible pan-European regulation of asylum and migration. This ambition was not only fuelled by Kohl's relentless Euroenthusiasm but also was heavily influenced by between 50 and up to 90 percent of all asylum seekers and refugees in the EU being accommodated by Germany by the end of the 1980s. Both the Schengen Treaty and the 1990 Dublin Convention were the fruits of German initiative and Kohl's personal involvement. However, other EU member states did not share this enthusiasm: aside from British (and to some extent Irish) reluctance to "communautarize" AMP,[33] German activism aimed at creating pan-European "burden sharing" or asylum seeker reallocation plans encountered skepticism or even resistance from the French and Spanish governments. National egoisms and the not unfounded empirical observation that Germany seemed to encounter a disproportionate number of asylum seekers may have helped consolidate the impression that there was a particular "German problem" and other European governments were hardly enthusiastic about importing it. Ironically, some compromise on burden-sharing might have been found at negotiations in the run-up to the 1997 Amsterdam Treaty; however, the German *Länder* turned this issue into a protracted conflict over the right of the federal government to negotiate on their behalf (Boesche 2003).

German attempts to create bottom-up Europeanization of asylum reallocation failed. The Kohl government shifted gear and engaged in skillful two-level bargaining. The Dublin Convention had proven influential for German domestic asylum law, as it helped design the concepts "safe third country" and "safe country of origin."[34] These concepts already contradicted or at least undermined the constitutional right to political asylum. In practical terms, they quickly spawned a number of bilateral deportation agreements, notably with Poland on May 1, 1991, and followed by other CEE states. Having helped negotiate and initiate Schengen and Dublin, the Kohl government cunningly claimed in public pronouncements and in negotiations with the Social Democrats that Art. 16 of the Basic Law needed to be amended, claiming that Germany risked being excluded from the Schengen area (*Süddeutsche Zeitung* February 13, 1992) and was therefore forced to harmonize and "Europeanize" its asylum system (*Süddeutsche Zeitung* September 5, 1991). Given that the decision-making modus for these (as yet) extra-communautarian treaties had been unanimous, it seems difficult to fathom that the other EU member states imposed such change on an unwilling German government, official pronouncements to the contrary notwithstanding.[35] This Machiavellian employment of two-level strategic game-playing, inspired by the insight that no Europe-wide "fair" distribution of asylum seekers would be forthcoming, helped affect German public opinion and crucially secure the two-thirds majority in the Bundestag required for implementing such a wide-ranging modification of the constitution.[36] The Social Democratic opposition accepted this line of argument (*Frankfurter Rundschau* March 17, 1992, *FAZ* March 7, 1992). The clever maneuvering permitted this change to be portrayed and marketed as an instance of imposed top-down Europeanization, undermined domestic opposition, and aided in circumventing the potential veto point of the Bundestag.

The German government under Kohl was equally outspoken about integrating large parts of Schengen and Dublin into the communautarian framework, thus post hoc legitimizing and institutionalizing the changes to the German asylum legislation. The creation of the third pillar for justice and home affairs under the terms of the Maastricht Treaty and its consolidation in the Amsterdam Treaty was once again strongly pushed forward by the Germans, though this time without any explicit strategic considerations in mind. Efforts to continue to set the agenda or at the very least influence it, continued unabashedly. The Red-Green government generally supported European initiatives in asylum and refugee policy, but continued the skillful employment of two-level strategies by blocking (labor) immigration proposals and refusing to surrender regulatory peculiarities that were useful as bargaining chips in national negotiations with the opposition and nonstate actors. Along with the Austrians, the German government was a driving force behind torpedoing the Commission proposal on labor migration by TCNs, submitted to the Council in

November 2001; negotiations were abandoned in the fall of 2002. While it became clear that no consensus emerged rapidly, the Austro-German initiative successfully challenged the role of the commission, pointing out that according to Art. 4 of the EC Treaty, the commission has no authority over the regulation of labor market access by TCNs. Politically, the Commission initiative could not have come at a more unwelcome time for the Schröder government, seeing that it found itself in the midst of the prolonged battle surrounding its own national *Zuwanderungsgesetz*.[37] Blocking the Commission's proposals helped broaden national room for maneuver, including reserving the right seriously to entertain the consistent proposals made by unions and employers to implement actively managed labor migration policy, possibly including quotas and a points-based system. Any such national proposal could have then been used as a blueprint for Europe, but accepting top-down Europeanization was unacceptable to the government and the clear rejection thereof by BDA (2001*a*, 2001*b*) aided in this decision.

The Germans were successful in negotiations leading to the "procedures directive," as the safe third country provision was incorporated into it. Similarly, the asylum "reception" directive governing minimal conditions for asylum seekers (2003/9/EC) was colored by successful bottom-up maneuvers engendering the import of German provisions limiting the geographic mobility of asylum seekers to certain districts and guarding national autonomy in determining labor market access eligibility (Art. 4). Support for these provisions was relatively easy to garner, as a generally restrictive mood seemed to prevail in the Council negotiations. With the directive on temporary protection (2001/55/EC), the first post-Amsterdam directive, some harmonization attempts regarding subsidiary protection schemes were made. However, this directive, first presented in May 2000 and accepted by the Council in July 2001, is not very intrusive and leaves a lot of room for member state arrangements. In the German case, the most significant implied change was the obligation to permit labor market access. This concession was easy to make, as the ministry of the interior accepted a major reshuffling of the previous category of "tolerated" refugees anyway in the context of concessions to NGOs in the protracted introduction of the *Zuwanderungsgesetz*.

During the discussion of the qualification directive (2004/83/EC), the German government assumed an obstinate position at first. This directive attempted to define the refugee and asylum seeker status based on the Geneva Convention. It did permit member states some status quo practices, including the refusal of subsidiary protection if certain geographic

187

regions of the sending country in question could be considered safe. Responding to the September 2001 Commission proposal (2001/510/EC), the German delegation was hesitant to endorse the acceptance of persecution for gender reasons and by nonstate actors as grounds for asylum claims. Other member states were already accepting these reasons, though the Commission initiative was not modelled on a national bottom-up proposal, but seemed to constitute genuine top-down progressive policy change. In French law, these reasons could be accepted, though interpretation by courts differed by country of origin, but the French government had little interest in uploading its own practice as the basis for Europeanized regulation (interview FR-GOV-1). At the national level, the *Unabhängige Kommission*, trade unions and NGOs demanded the incorporation of these two new categories, but the employers, the CDU, and indeed the ministry of the interior were initially opposed. As Green (2004, 123) argues, these two points were offered to the Green Party as a last minute concession to secure their acceptance to the compromise draft bill engineered by the ministry of the interior. However, since the CDU subsequently derailed the immigration bill over the course of 2002, the government was cautious not to accept regulations at the EU level that might still be useful bargaining tools at the national level. It thus delayed negotiations on this directive until early 2004, agreeing to a proposal on March 30. By then, political agreement had been secured domestically anyway and the provisions (Art. 60.1) had been incorporated into national law. Under these circumstances, it was easy for the German delegation to accept "conceding" to this clause being part of the EU directive.

Conclusion: Rediscovering Labor Immigration at Last

In Europe's three largest economies and most heavily populated countries, similar trends were observed towards more restrictive external border control measures and internal reception and processing mechanisms for deterring unsolicited and undesired forms of migration, principally aimed at asylum seekers and refugees coupled with liberalized labor migration policies. This empirical chapter highlights how politics can and do matter. Nonstate actors seek to influence governmental policy and their attempts to do so hinge on strong organizational characteristics. Nongovernmental organizations have been able to publicize and very occasionally affect the plight of those on the receiving end of restrictive control policies. Spectacular direct action campaigns in France occasionally forced governmental actors to back down and reconsider more punitive measures; more traditional forms of lobbying delivered slightly toned down and inclusive government proposals in Germany, while NGOs in the United Kingdom had extremely limited success in lobbying despite recent rhetorical commitment towards the inclusion of stakeholders.

Trade unions have been relatively successful in advocating a policy of managed labor migration, which represents a departure from a traditionally much more skeptical stance towards labor migration. The de facto fragmentation of the labor market, most pronounced in the UK in consequence of Thatcher's antiunion and deregulatory measures of the 1980s, has been a particular concern. In all three countries, unions have become active in fighting racism and discrimination in the workplace. German and to a lesser extent French unions have also attempted to lobby for enhanced and improved integration measures.

Across Europe, business lobbies in advocacy of more liberal labor migration policies. The precise quantitative and qualitative profile of the desired economic migrants is influenced by the respective production strategy and the particular characteristics of the system of political economy. Thus the import of labor with sector-specific skills is of significant interest in CMEs, while LME employees are keen both on highly skilled labor pools contributing to sectoral strengths and on labor with generalist skills feeding into a low-wage service sector. The advocacy of economic migration is no simple enterprise in a context of high unemployment, extending to the UK where an extraordinarily high incarceration rate and the use of incapacity benefits in areas with pronounced structural unemployment distort statistics on joblessness. Clothed in the rhetorical terms of the competition state, evident in all three countries, such appeals by business or employer-sponsored think tanks such as the Institut Montaigne and *Stiftung Neue Soziale Marktwirtschaft* to enhance national competitiveness by ensuring ready labor supply through liberal economic migration policy have borne fruit. With the exception of Britain, where labor migration of all skill levels is welcomed by employers, low-skill recruitment programs have been of less interest. This is a result of the structural dependence on specific skill sets in France and Germany, but, of course, low-skill immigration is both particularly difficult to advocate in light of high unemployment and unnecessary. Aside from radical neoliberals, few are prepared to advocate substituting low-skill migrants with welfare recipients forced into the labor market in the context of "workfare" programs. Employers are hesitant to do so both because of the unpalatable nature of such demand and the low motivation and productivity of such forced labor. Most welfare recipients are not part of the labor market for serious reasons, hence misguided active labor market policies in the UK and Germany have had such mixed results. Migration can sometimes be used for problematic purposes, for example to sustain artificially low remuneration patterns in the UK education and health sectors or to maintain downward pressure on low-skill service sector wages, a strategy euphemistically described as "avoiding wage inflation."

British employers have become actively concerned with labor migration policy in the wake of the highly advanced tertiarization of the economy and clearly apparent skill and labor shortages, especially in engineering, IT, and finance. French employers have rediscovered the benefits of labor migration much more recently, as similar skill shortages existed neither quantitatively nor qualitatively. Competition state rhetoric is informing pronouncements by the employer-financed Institut Montaigne. In Germany, advocacy of labor migration by the employers, especially the federation of larger industry BDI, first surfaced in conjunction with a more aggressive and openly neoliberal stance since the mid-1990s. But BDA has embraced such advocacy of skilled migration since, based on concerns among its members regarding skill shortages both in the service and in the manufacturing sectors. As elsewhere, political demands for more liberalized migration provisions are couched in terms of ensuring "national competitiveness."

Notes

1. Note also Socialist Prime Minister Laurent Fabius's assertion in a 1985 interview that Le Pen provides the "wrong answers" to the "right questions" (*Le Monde* October 29, 1985).
2. Thus, between January to March 1994, "the Constitutional Court delivered as many decisions on the constitutional verification of rules as in the 25 years from 1958 to 1974" (www.conseil-constitutionnel.fr), largely due to legislative changes permitting minority factions in parliament to submit draft bills to the council for scrutiny.
3. While the national minimum wage SMIC and statutory working conditions as part of the *Code du Travail* do, of course, apply, as do sectoral wage contracts extended by the ministry of labor, there is a significant potential gray area of the labor market.
4. This would not surprise Terray who argues that "legislation [...] keeps foreigners without any legal status in a state of vulnerability which makes them exploitable, but at the same time permits them to remain in France in

sufficient numbers [...] to give those employers practising 'localized outsourcing' the effectives that they require. [...] Prosecutions are rare, convictions exceptional, and they practically never catch the real employers" (Terray 1999, 22).

5. On July 26, 2004, a new modification of the original 1945 legislation further broadened the array of infractions considered legitimate grounds for deportation, including "provocative acts explicitly and deliberatively aimed at inciting discrimination, hatred and violence." By then, top-down Europeanization of the issue was starting to become tangible, in this instance strengthening the position of the government. In 2001, a directive had been passed ensuring the mutual recognition of deportation decisions (EC 2001/40). Following bilateral talks between the French and the German and the British governments, an Italian initiative was launched that led the JHA Council to adopt an initiative to organize joint charter flights among EU member states for deportation on November 6, 2003. This initiative can be reviewed online at www.statewatch.org/news/2003/nov/14025-03.pdf—see also Council 2003 and witness the Commission proposal on an EU deportation policy (Commission 2002). This included a proposed handbook with guidelines for deportation and a scheme that organized the financial contribution of member states.

6. In September 1991, the French border police had signed an agreement with airlines Air France and UTA (the latter focusing on routes in Francophone Africa, later absorbed by Air France), which permitted passport controls during the flight, especially from countries considered a particular "risk," such as Ghana or Zaire. For a detailed account on the development of carrier sanctions and the "outsourcing of control," see Guiraudon (2002).

7. Officially known as the "loi no 92–625 du 6 juillet 1992 sur la zone d'attente des ports et des aéroports et portant modification de l'ordonnance no 45–2658 du novembre 2, 1945 relative aux conditions d'entrée et de séjour des étrangers en France," this law once again modified the relevant 1945 decree; it was accompanied by a clarifying administrative circulaire on July 17 ("relative au maintien des étrangers en zone d'attente des ports et aéroports").

8. Officially known as the law "portant modification de l'ordonnance no 45–2658 du novembre 2, 1945 relative aux conditions d'entrée et de séjour des étrangers en France," see also Julien-Laferrière (1996*b*).

9. Circulaire DPM/dm2–3/98/767 du 28 décembre, 1998, see also Morice (2000).

10. This was stated explicitly in the joint Franco-British-German proposal tabled at the Council of Ministers meeting in Luxembourg on October 4, 1999, in preparation of the Tampere summit. Note, however, that this call for an AMP carried also strong language about the danger of illegal migration and crime, often confounding the two (Joint Note by France and Germany concerning asylum/migration for the European Council in Tampere, October 15/16, 1999, dated August 17, 1999 and UK, France, Germany Note, October 4, 1999).

11. In a much noted August 3, 2000 article in the influential center-right daily *Le Figaro*, the authors argued that "the call for foreign labor does not only target 'brains', [...] but also low-skill or unskilled workers, seasonal and not."
12. The notion of such contracts was first suggested in the final report of a new council on integration (*Haut Conseil a l'intégration*) created by the Raffarin government in 2002 and headed by philosophy professor Blandine Kriegel.
13. In a press conference in 2004, Sarkozy argued that "We are now in a situation where immigration is uncontrollable because we refuse to demand an immigration we choose and for which we are responsible. Our integration system has broken down." (cited in Kretzschmar 2005, 15).
14. As early as 1999, Alain Juppé surprised some of his party friends by arguing that in light of changing mentalities and demographics, "Europe will need the inflow of foreign labor" in a October 1, 1999 *Le Monde Diplomatique* article (Morice 2000).
15. Notwithstanding the slightly embarrassing attempts by the Blair governments in the 1990s to exploit the presence of the descendants of non-European migrants as part of a publicity campaign stressing Britain's modernity and "coolness" ("Cool Britannia"). Thus while the Notting Hill carnival is now seen as contributing to what could be considered a corporate image of being multicultural rather than being perceived as a political threat, and while chicken massala is being reclassified as English pub food, there is a profound sense of unease and uncertainty over a distinctly British culture in light of the pervasive North American cultural influence.
16. Such claims must be contrasted with empirical evidence emphasizing the lack of knowledge among asylum seekers and refugees in particular about their country of destination's politics, culture, and even language. Indeed, immigrants cooperating with traffickers often have very little say in determining the country of destination (*inter alia* Koser and Pinkerton 2002). Freedman (2004, 66) cites the results of a questionnaire conducted with potential asylum seekers at the Sangatte camp near the French port of Calais, according to which only 7.4 percent of those interviewed cited unemployment as the reason to leave their home countries, as opposed to 39.4 percent citing war, and 34.2 percent citing political persecution. "Soft touch" regulations were not responsible for attracting the mainly Iraqi and Afghan refugees to the UK.
17. Thus, a press release from the UK Home Office ("Removal Figures continue to rise for failed asylum seekers, November 22, 2005") expresses this dichotomy between deserving and undeserving migrants very crisply:

We are continuing to work towards our target of removing more failed asylum seekers on a monthly basis than there are unfounded claims. We recognize this is a tough target and more still needs to be done, but we will continue to work towards this goal and expect to meet it in February 2006. [...] Accession nationals are continuing to come to the UK to work and are contributing to the success of the UK economy, paying tax and national insurance and filling key jobs in areas where there are gaps, such as in education and health. At the same time they are making few demands on our welfare system or public services, and are likely to come to the UK for limited periods of time in the same way UK citizens take advantage of work, trade and travel in the enlarged EU.

18. In a January 5, 2006 policy statement (CBI 2006), the CBI reaffirmed this position, announcing that: "The CBI believes that migration is beneficial to the UK. Migrants have made an important contribution to the UK economy—bringing valuable and scarce skills that have benefited UK business and helped contribute to economic growth. Migrant workers are an integral part of the UK workforce and the CBI shares the Government's belief that a carefully managed migration policy can bring further benefits to the UK. Although a well-targeted migration policy can alleviate current skill and labor shortages, raising the skills of the domestic workforce and improving labor market participation rates must be the priority. The CBI supports the Government's plans, outlined in the five-year strategy, to introduce a points test for skilled migration and rely on EU migration for lower-skilled workers, with a reduced role for schemes such as the SBS and SAWS. It is important that the Government maintains a range of routes into the country in order to react to labor market needs. The CBI has written to the Home Office opposing the imposition of employer bonds for migrant workers and the use of on-the-spot fines for illegal working."
19. In the course of an academic conference on migration issues at Oxford University in June 2006, a representative of the Home Office pre-empted his remarks by pointing out that the Home Office was interested in consulting with third parties, including academics and NGOs, listening to their contributions and then would proceed to ignore them completely. Perhaps intended as a joke, the remark elicited sober recognition rather than smiles among the representatives of NGOs in attendance.
20. The so-called sectors-based scheme is contained in Immigration Rules HC 395, paras. 135I–135K (Ensor and Shah 2005).
21. Further details on these categories are available from the Home Office's Border and Immigration Agency (www.bia.homeoffice.gov.uk).
22. Reflective of its stance towards labor migration is the response by the Home Office minister to the Commission's Green paper on labor migration that what is most welcomed is the "Commission's recognition that it is for individual member states to determine the number of economic migrants that are granted access to their territory" (UK Parliament 2005).
23. See for example recent initiatives aimed at recognizing skills among refugees and the promotion of their rapid integration into the labor market (www.employabilityforum.co.uk).

24. Thus the federal government issued a statement in 1982, affirming that "the Federal Republic...is not a country of immigration and...it should not become one. The cabinet agrees that a further influx of foreigners from outside the European Community should be prevented by all legal means" (quoted in Marshall 2000, 13). Accordingly, the Social Democrats ignored the more liberal recommendations made by the government's office known as the Ombudsman for the Promotion of the Integration of Foreign Employees and their Relatives, established in 1978, its title quite revealing of the predominant conception of the role and position of foreign residents. The only suggestion endorsed was the right for second-generation immigrants to apply for citizenship, a proposal abandoned by the Kohl center-right government.
25. Bommes and Kolb (2005, 15) make the interesting argument that the Green Card scheme should be considered an aid primarily for SMEs, given that larger and especially multinational corporations availed themselves of fast-track labor market clearance schemes for intracompany mobility. However, their claim that the relative failure of the Green Card scheme not being indicative of this being a botched tool in competing for human capital cannot be sustained. The underlying assumption that temporarily limited working permits would be attractive to highly skilled engineers was deeply problematic, to say nothing of obvious cultural and linguistic problems in attracting migrants from southeastern Asia at whom the scheme was ostensibly targeted. Note that there were also extremely limited exceptions to the general ban on recruitment prior to the major legislative overhaul of 2004–05. Employers can hire non-EU citizens, but have to prove the "public interest" (Art. 5, Section 2 of the Regulation concerning exceptions to the recruitment ban or *Anwerbestoppausnahmeverordnung*) and employees need to pass a stringent locally administered labor market test, proving that they do not crowd out domestic or EU applicants.
26. Thus additional sectors covered now include fairground and festival attendants, wood processing plants, and the hotel and catering industry. Given the fact that these treaties often simply legitimized pre-existing semi-legal or illegal migration chains and labor markets, Cyrus and Vogel (2005) make the interesting argument that these treaties can be considered a subterfuge form of German-style regularization.
27. Indeed, there is arguably a slight contradiction in barring nationals of the 2004 newcomer states from access to the German labor market for a transitory period of seven years, despite the near future or even current labor market shortages. In seven years time, emigration pressure in Central and Eastern Europe may indeed have succumbed, as happened during the two Mediterranean rounds of enlargement during the 1980s, but by then labor market shortages in Germany might have become even more pressing and a

whole generation of would-be migrants from Eastern Europe already absorbed by more welcoming alternative countries of emigration, such as Canada and Australia.

However, immigration cannot serve as a panacea for demographic pressures or indeed labor market shortages. Two obvious caveats limit the extent to which migration can provide a panacea for the demographic challenge to the welfare state. First, migrants adopt the fertility rates of their host societies within one generation and will inevitably age themselves. Second, since any long-term change to the demographic profile of a given society takes a whole generation or about 20–25 years to have any effect, replacing the "missing generation" would necessitate an amount of inward migration that would fundamentally reshape the demographic makeup of European societies and therefore meet considerable political resistance. According to an influential UN study entitled "Replacement Migration: Is it a Solution to Declining and Aging Populations?," maintaining a three-to-one ratio between pensioners and active members of the labor force would require an average annual EU wide intake of 3.07 million migrants between now and 2050, simply maintaining the 1995 ratio would call for 13.48 million new migrants per year, and even simply seeking to maintain a constant population of working age (defined as between 15 and 64 years of age) still necessitates an annual intake of 1.58 million migrants, of which Germany alone would require 487,000 (cited in Grimblat 2003). Even those two latter figures are quite remarkable, when we consider that total net immigration during the peak years after the fall of the Berlin wall 1990–95 saw 2.6 million new migrants in Germany and thus an annual average of 500,000. The EU as a whole received 5.23 million new migrants (UN Population Division, cited in Grimblat 2003). If we break this figure down to an annual average of 1 million new migrants for simplicity's sake, it follows that this figure is still far below the 1.5 million new arrivals required to guarantee a constant size of the labor force and almost on a par with the figure required (949,000) to maintain a constant total EU population!

28. In this context, it might be interesting to observe the still pervasive use of the term foreigner (*Ausländer*) and the various clumsy linguistic constructs used to describe residents who are not German citizens, themselves perhaps a reflection of the often confused approach to regulating migration: "foreign fellow citizens," "humans with a migration background," "non-Germans" (*ausländische Mitbürger, Menschen mit Migrationshintergrund, Nichtdeutsche*).

29. But even where they exist, some sectoral minima are really truly minimal, as research by the union think tank Boeckler Foundation highlights. Not only do only 6 out of 40 economic sectors have nationwide wage agreements but some sectoral minimum wages in low-skill manufacturing, gardening, security, and security services hover around €5 per hour (WSI 2005, quoted in Czommer and Worthmann 2005).

30. Thus the BDA's attitude regarding the issue of posted workers, employed at a fraction of standard German wages predominantly in the construction sector, is highly significant in this regard. In 1994, the association still pondered whether a temporary re-regulation of these wages could be acceptable. One year later, driven by *Gesamtmetall*, it categorically rejected any concessions on this issue, openly demanding downward flexibility of wages, enhanced through the use of foreign workers (for details, see Menz 2005a).
31. By then, labor market shortages were becoming much more apparent. In the fall of 2004, Kannegiesser, president of *Gesamtmetall*, declared that not only were there 150,000 open positions in his sector, but this figure had also increased by 40,000 since the beginning of the year.
32. Typically, bilateral labor contracts are concluded with countries that already serve as pools of illegal labor migration. Thus, illegal migration is channelled, controlled, and presumably curtailed, with beneficial effects for all involved: higher wages and greater security for workers and protection from law enforcement "crackdowns" for employers. However, abusive pay and work conditions often persist and these legal channels are commonly used to transmit illegal workers as well (Menz 2001).
33. The British government was not, however, opposed to creating an extra-communitarian border control policy. Hence, while the British delegation (along with the Irish and Danes) rejected a council decision to facilitate cross-border traffic by EU citizens (Official Journal 1985, No. C 47, 19/02/1985 p. 5), the UK government did initiate the Ad Hoc group of Immigration Ministers in 1986.
34. These were then further detailed and more clearly defined at the November 30, 1992 Minister of the Interior meeting in London (UK Parliament 1992), during which a "resolution on a harmonized approach to questions concerning host third countries" ("safe third countries"), a "resolution on manifestly unfounded applications for asylum" and "Conclusions on countries in which there is generally no serious risk of persecution." During this meeting, ministers of the interior agreed "to seek to ensure that their national laws are adapted, if need be, and to incorporate the principles of this resolution as soon as possible."
35. Unlikely as this version may appear, this is what the German Ministry of the Interior claims on its website: "Germany implemented the above resolutions when it amended the asylum law as of July 1, 1993, and introduced the principles of the "safe third state" and of the "safe country of origin." (Bundesinnenministerium 2006). Bendix and Steiner (1998) also doubt that the government deliberately used the EU level to create domestic pressure, but see Thielemann (forthcoming).
36. Bendix and Steiner (1998, 43 f., quoted in Boesche 2003) argue that an argument about a consistent pro-European foreign policy was also put forward to

garner support for the change in asylum law: "Only in the 1993 debate did supporters of tighter asylum laws argue that such laws would promote foreign policy goals, and then only to argue that, because promoting European unity was a central foreign policy goal of Germany, tightening asylum would bring the country in line with the Dublin and Schengen agreements that had tried to harmonize European migration policies."

37. Meanwhile, the Black–Blue coalition in Austria had promised—and was implementing—restrictive immigration law at the national level and was keen to avoid seeing these initiatives being "watered down."

5

Contested Areas of Sovereignty: Labor Migration and Asylum Policy in New Countries of Immigration: Ireland, Italy, and Poland

Since the late 1990s, immigration has come to dominate public policy debates in nontraditional destinations in southern, northwestern, and eastern European countries as well. Though regulation is of much more recent provenance than in the more established locales, labor market shortages, large informal sectors, adverse demographic trends, and geographic position have combined to generate migration inflows that are generally warmly welcomed by employer associations. Humanitarian migration is an even more recent phenomenon in these countries, which is reflected in the genesis of asylum policy, and has also opened avenues for policy learning and transfer from more established neighboring immigration locales that are geographically and culturally close. Thus British regulatory patterns influence Irish policymakers, Italian policy design draws on French experiences and Poland has copied many notions from Germany, aided by bilateral aid and border police training, although top-down Europeanization plays a particularly pivotal role there. Despite immigration being such a recent phenomenon, Irish and Italian employers vociferously advocate liberalized labor migration, while given economic adversities and a continuing net flow of emigration, Polish business is only slowly though steadily developing an appetite.

Ireland: Labor Migration to Feed the Celtic Tiger

Only as recently as 1995 did Ireland turn into a country of net immigration after generating considerable emigration throughout the nineteenth and twentieth centuries. The extremely recent nature of this phenomenon is reflected in most regulatory policy being designed over the course of the past 10 years, especially regarding refugees and asylum. However, a general legislative framework was already created by the 1935 Aliens Act and the 1946 Aliens Order, providing the executive with considerable power in regulating the accommodation, reception, deportation, and living and working conditions of non-nationals, including considerable police authority. Notably, the burden of proof of innocence rests firmly with the non-national and there is no legal avenue for appeal. Though severely modified, this framework has not been abolished and remains the keystone of Irish migration legislation. By contrast, the definition of citizenship, laid out in the 1956 Irish Nationality and Citizenship Act, has been historically very generous and inclusive, in reflection of the widely disseminated Irish diaspora, thus combining *ius solis* with *ius sanguinis*. An ancestral link consisting of one Irish grandfather sufficed for a successful citizenship claim prior to a 1986 modification, while in 2004 unrestricted *ius solis*—hitherto applied to the whole of the Irish island—was abolished and replaced with eligibility for a discretionary naturalization application. There are three major patterns in Irish migration policy warranting discussion.

First, it is important to note the sharp legal distinction drawn between citizens or ethnic descendants in the broadest sense and noncitizens. In 1991, two-thirds of all immigrants could in fact be classified as ethnically Irish return migrants, while in 1999 just over 50 percent of all newcomers were already in possession of an Irish passport. Only in recent years did this ratio change; by 2004 a mere quarter of all immigrants were returning Irish (Hughes and Quinn 2004). The reforms inherent in the 2004 Irish Nationality and Citizenship Act followed a June 2004 referendum that informed an abolition of automatic *ius solis*. The positive referendum hinged on a well-publicized case of a Chinese woman who had entered Northern Ireland and gave birth to what then became an Irish citizen, generating considerable excitement (High Court judgment Leontjava and Chang; interview IRL-GOV-1, IRL-NGO-1).

Second, the phenomenon of immigration correlates closely with recent economic fortunes. Immigration is widely perceived as contributing to this development and hence being welcomed. The sluggish economic performance of the 1980s still led to an average annual emigration rate of 20,606 throughout the decade (Hughes and Quinn 2004, 6). But by the early 1990s, decreasing unemployment and rising economic growth were beginning to affect migration patterns, promoted by a more cooperative social partnership-style approach to industrial relations and macroeconomic governance, the successful attraction of foreign direct investment, especially of North American provenance, and higher skill levels emerging due to the introduction of free secondary education in 1967.

Labor migrants are welcomed, especially to fill shortages and provide needed skills. Non-EEA labor migrants are required to apply for work permits for individual positions from abroad, initially for permits that are valid for one year (Ruhs 2003). However, little attention has been paid to integration and noneconomic immigration channels, notably asylum, are tightly restricted. The predominant focus on labor migration is perhaps influenced by an absence of the common European demographic quagmire, given both a young population and a relatively high birth rate (1.98 in 2003, as opposed to the EU-25 average of 1.48). During the 1990s, net outflow halved and return migration by overseas Irish expatriates increased by one half. Intra-EU migration emerged as a quantitatively significant phenomenon, most prominently from the UK, leading to 45 percent of the total foreign resident population in Ireland being British, while another 24 percent stem from the rest of the EU-27. Until 2004, employees of multinational corporations did not even require a working permit for secondments for up to four years. Liberal economic immigration policies were seen as vitally contributing to an economic boom that raised the total number of employees by almost one-third between 1996 and 2001. Labor migration was employer-driven, based on employer-specific working permits granted by the Department of Enterprise, Trade and Employment. In 1999, 6,250 such permits were issued; in 2003, 47,551. The number of permits quadrupled between 1999 and 2000 (4,328 and 15,434) and nearly doubled again in 2001 (29,594). Both Irish return migrants and the immigrants of the 1990s possessed on average higher levels of formal education than the resident population (cf. Hughes and Quinn 2004). Much of this cohort fed into employment in high-skill administration, engineering, and IT jobs. By 2000, the continuing Celtic Tiger phenomenon was generating jobs for which native residents were either not qualified, especially construction-related engineering jobs related to the booming construction industry, but also in nursing, or which they did not want to undertake, particularly in low-wage gastronomical and agricultural positions. The rapidly escalating cost of living, linked to the inflationary effects of the Euro introduction and exploding real estate prices especially in Greater Dublin, increased this unwillingness on the part of natives to fill low-wage positions. The government responded by raising the number of work permits. However, a new category of migrants was starting to arrive that received a much less hearty welcome. The annual number of asylum seekers rose from a paltry 39 in 1992 to 1,179 in 1995 and peaked at 11,634 in 2002, before declining partially due to the restrictive provisions of the 2003 Immigration Act. Ireland had previously also accepted a limited quota of refugees. The 2003 Act reflected many of the measures adopted elsewhere in Europe, notably the safe country of origin concept. It clarified the procedures of asylum application, including the creation of a new "fast track" category, but it did so in a very restrictive vein. There is no reason to presume a more liberal much less tolerant approach due to the legacy of Irish emigration. Economic prerogatives shape a liberal labor migration policy, but recent changes in citizenship and asylum policy clearly indicate that sentiments of solidarity informing more relaxed humanitarian migration policy are very limited.

Third, the geographic and cultural proximity and historical links to the United Kingdom generate patterns of policy transfer and learning. The 1951 reciprocal Common Travel Area (CTA) abolishing routine border controls and permitting mutual residency, work, and even voting rights (Ryan 2001), initially an Irish priority to facilitate easy emigration and its return, is a key factor behind the Irish opt-out of much of AMP (Department of Justice, Equality and Law Reform 2003). Euroskepticism is less pronounced, yet fully-fledged AMP participation would have jeopardized the CTA and raised the unpalatable specter of the Schengen zone border dividing the Republic from Ulster. Not unlike Britain, the geographic peculiarity informs a conviction that restrictive migration policy can be effectively administered. The careful monitoring of Whitehall's policy output extends to both labor migration and asylum (interview IRL-GOV-1). British newspapers, including the rabidly xenophobic tabloid press, sell widely in Ireland and help shape opinions and public policy debates, though the scale and nature of immigration is quite different. The laissez-faire approach assumed regarding labor migration from the 2004 newcomer states was informed by economic prerogatives consistent with a liberal market economy rather than policy learning. Some of these countries had already established emigration channels; Latvia, Lithuania, Poland, Romania, and the Philippines accounted for

43 percent of all permit holders in 2002, with the East European countries being well represented from the late 1990s onwards (Quinn and Hughes 2004, 14 ff.).

System of Political Economy: An Uneasy Fit into the Liberal Market Economy Category

Ireland is often neglected by scholars of comparative political economy and is commonly simply assumed to be subsumable under the liberal market economy heading, thus broadly comparable to the UK. Such categorization accurately reflects the dominant tradition of economic liberalism in macroeconomic policymaking, but fails to capture the dynamics entailed by the creation of an institutionalized social partnership since 1987, which has helped resolve collective action problems with regard to collective bargaining and noninflationary wage-setting by (re)creating national negotiation arenas (Aust 1999; Hardiman 2002) and enhancing coordination between governmental policy and union and employer preferences. The Irish social partnership represents a successful attempt to embrace "competitive corporatism" (Rhodes 1998) and escape the coordination problems and negative consequences of confrontational industrial relations that affect liberal systems. It largely confounds the implicit argument of a dual convergence found in Hall and Soskice's work (2001) and presents an interesting case of reinventing its own moribund neocorporatist institutions that had lain dormant from the mid-1970s onwards.

Since 1987, employers and trade unions have concluded a series of framework agreements at the national level, focusing primarily on pay, but encompassing a broader remit including issues of industrial, farming, forestry, education, social and labor market policy, and—albeit indirectly—monetary and fiscal policy (Program for National Recovery, 1987–90 and Program for Economic and Social Progress, 1990–93, followed by the Program for Competitiveness and Work, 1993–96, the Partnership 2000 for Inclusion, Employment, and Competitiveness from 1997 to 2000, the Program for Prosperity and Fairness, 2000–03, and Sustaining Progress, 2003–06).

The economic malaise of the 1980s proved a linch pin for the revival of tripartite dialogue. Lackluster economic growth and persistently high unemployment posed serious economic challenges. The governments of the 1980s responded by attracting foreign direct investment through cutting corporate taxation rates to the lowest levels in

Europe, while offering particularly US companies the advantages of a well-educated Anglophone work force within the Single Market. This strategy proved successful: by 1987, 42 percent of all employees in the manufacturing sector worked for foreign firms, which accounted for 65 percent of all output, but in sectors such as office and data processing (99.6), pharmaceuticals (97), and electrical engineering (90), the foreign share was even more pronounced (Hussey 1995, 275). Responding to an Allied Irish bank survey on motives to invest in Ireland, companies conceded frankly that tax considerations had played a predominant role, followed by the advantages afforded by a highly educated English-speaking workforce (*Sunday Tribune*, June 28, 1992). Between 1987 and 1992, annual economic growth was a steady 5 percent, inflation remained well below 5 percent since 1985, and Ireland boasted balance of payment surpluses and negligible government borrowing.

Despite decreasing industrial action throughout the 1980s, the government contemplated major legislative restrictions on union activity inspired by Thatcherism. It communicated its interest in reviving tripartite dialogue to unions and employers. The former feared Thatcherite industrial relations legislation and shared dissatisfaction with employers regarding the stagnating economic performance (interviews IRL-UNI-1, IRL-BUS-1). The Confederation of Irish Industry (CII), the Federated Union of Employers (FUE) (merging in 1992 to form the Irish Business and Employers Confederation) and the Construction Industry Federation, the Irish Congress of Trade Unions (ICTU) commenced negotiations. Ireland has a traditionally atomized and relatively militant trade union movement, making it challenging for the central association to control effectively the sectoral associations. In 1992, 11 out of a total of more than 50 unions accounted for 70 percent of all union members (Murphy and Roche 1997).

The role of the government was thus important "not only in initiating the 'social partnership' approach to pay bargaining in Ireland, but also in underpinning its stability and durability" and "a marked cross-party consensus on the desirability of this approach" (Hardiman 2002, 6) emerged. While not directly intervening into pay negotiations, successive governments provided fertile ground for wage moderation by offering tax cuts in the expectation of a quid pro quo bargain. Establishing numerous working groups, especially after inviting representatives of the voluntary and nongovernmental sectors in 2000, the government benefited from external expertise that informed its own legislative projects. Unions and employers entered proposals. However, the government remained

Table 5.1. Sectoral composition and distribution of workforce in Ireland, Poland, and Italy (source: OECD annual reports, various years)

	Percent of the GDP	Percent of the labor force
Irish agriculture	5	8
Polish agriculture	2.8	16.1
Italian agriculture	2.1	5
Irish industry	46	29
Polish industry	31.7	29
Italian industry	28.8	32
Irish services	49	64
Polish services	65.5	54.9
Italian services	69.1	63

in a dominant position and would override recommendations deemed unacceptable.

The social partnership agreements created an atmosphere of consensualism. Despite the steadily decreasing unionization rate, declining from a workforce density of 55.3 percent in 1980 to 38.5 percent in 1999, steady real wage increases were delivered throughout the 1990s, with the extraordinary "Celtic Tiger" economic boom of the late 1990s providing additional leeway for mesolevel "wildcat" agreements above the national framework. The implementation of a minimum wage in 2000 assured that low-paid workers would benefit, a pressing need given increasing income inequality.[1]

In addition to the presence of the social partnership, the structure of the Irish economy also differs in important ways from the British, as Table 5.1 indicates. The agricultural sector is still an important employer and contributor to GDP by West European standards. This also applies to the secondary sector, reflecting recent tertiarization and the historical role of hosting low value-added component production aimed at the UK market. The somewhat unfavorable ratio between employment and GDP contribution suggests a relatively sizable low-skill service sector.

The Irish economy is thus best characterized as an amalgam of residues of marginal component manufacturing and an actively marketed site of inward FDI flows feeding into cutting-edge technologies such as biotechnology and IT, and also low-skill "back office" service positions. Most accounts of the Celtic Tiger phenomenon highlight the role of the service sector in creating and sustaining remarkable economic growth patterns (Mac Sharry and White 2000; Nolan and O'Connell 2000). The service sector attracts most FDI and is the principal engine of new job creation, generating the need for "imported" labor. Data collected by Trinity College's Policy Institute (Ruhs 2003) indicates that in 2002, 77 percent of all non-EU citizen work permit holders worked in the tertiary sector, 15 percent in agriculture, and only 8 percent in manufacturing. While the number of permits increased almost fourfold between 1998 and 2002, the relative distribution and the concentration of labor migration feeding into the primary and tertiary sectors remained stable. The concentration of non-EU employees has become more pronounced in key areas: low-skill jobs in gastronomy, wholesale and retail, personal and protective services, unskilled occupations in plant and machine operations, professional categories that contain both high- and low-skill jobs in health, financial, and other business services, and highly skilled jobs in management and administration. There are also significant differences between working hours effected by residents and non-EU citizens, most pronounced in health (33.8 vs. 49.5 per week) and gastronomy (34.6 vs. 41.6). The distribution of non-EU migrants in two distinct clusters and the sampling points of 1998 and 2002, both well before EU enlargement in 2004,[2] permit the diagnosis of a socioeconomic bifurcation among migrant groups from outside the pre-2004 EU. Since 2000, there has been an increase in relatively low-skill immigration (Hughes and Quinn 2004). The number of EU-10 immigrants is remarkably high (85,115 between May 2004 and May 2005), compared to absolute figures in the UK (176,000) and Sweden (2,100 May to November 2004 only) (data from the national statistics offices, cited in Mac Éinrí 2005).

The employers generally strongly welcome labor migration. The IBEC regards economic migrants as a valuable addition, providing skills or simply manpower in the context of a rapidly growing economy. Flexibility, disposability, availability of an additional labor pool and minimum restrictions emerge as key demands from the employers. As the data indicate, there is a particular appetite for economic migrants in the primary and tertiary sectors with particular emphasis on low-skill migrants willing to display flexibility in accepting low wages, long working hours, and relatively precarious working conditions. However, highly skilled professionals contributing especially to the service sector are similarly attractive (interview IRL-BUS-1). They strongly supported the abolition of the work permit process for EU-10 citizens in 2004. Recently, the employers have been dissatisfied with both the pace and the lack of consultation that accompanied the introduction of more restrictive regulations pertaining to economic migrants. Though IBEC's membership base is ideationally united in favoring more liberal immigration policy and

205

adequate organizational dynamics to ensure satisfactory flow between member companies, constituent sectoral employer associations, and the umbrella association and while the degree of representation among companies is similarly unproblematic, access channels to government beyond the Social Partnership framework have been difficult to construct. The ministry responsible for the formulation of migration policy—the Department for Justice, Equality and Law Reform—attempts to limit its consultation exercises to humanitarian NGOs, while both formal and informal lobbying efforts by the employers are frustrated by the ministry's reticence to accommodate. IBEC also complains about an exaggerated preoccupation with security considerations in the traditional sense taking precedence over economic security and competitiveness at the heart of the ministry (interview IRL-BUS-1). Ministry officials acknowledge what they describe as a "balancing act" between security, societal, and economic interests and accept that scant formal attention is paid to incorporating employer demands for liberal economic policy (interview IRL-GOV-1; Department of Justice, Equality and Law Reform 2003). Employers are concerned that labor market access for non-EU citizens is not liberal enough. 2003 changes to the work permit scheme are criticized for allegedly rendering it more "cumbersome, expensive and inflexible" to hire "essential staff." The government pointedly refused to consult employers before abolishing the business-friendly intracompany transfer scheme in 2002 (IBEC 2003). In an internal policy strategy document, a "crude application of a slowdown strategy on visas" on the part of the government is criticized and attributed to a slight slowdown in economic growth (IBEC 2003). Asylum and other humanitarian channels of labor migration are of limited interest to employers. Labor migration is wholeheartedly welcome, but despite a relatively robust position in organizational terms, efforts to communicate preferences to the Department of Justice, Equality and Law Reform are not particularly successful. That said, the employers can and do shape debates in the Social Partnership agreements and the social partners are regularly formally consulted within this framework. The 2003–05 Social Partnership Agreement includes an acknowledgment of "the need for more systematic consultation at national level regarding economic immigration in the future, a review will be held [...] with a view to developing options with a particular focus on labour supply [...] as an input to Government economic immigration policy" (Part 2, Section 18). Local labor market conditions will be assessed by the Training and Labour Market Authority (FAS) to inform economic migration policy concerning non-EEA nationals and "local labour and business interests can contribute their perspective" (Part 2, Section 18.3). An overall liberal approach to economic migration is likely to shape policy in years to come (interview IRL-GOV-1), but this does not preclude some restrictive tampering, placating an increasingly protectionist public opinion.

The trade union ICTU is not quite as enthusiastic about labor migration, but is not opposed to it, as long as immigrants benefit from standard wages and the applicable labor legislation (interview IRL-UNI-1). This is not always assured, informing an acknowledgment in the 2003–05 Social Partnership Agreement that "increased immigration, which has benefited the economy significantly, can give rise to certain problems and pressures." Labor migrants are regarded as a welcome addition to the labor force, but the union has not actively lobbied any of the government ministries in favor of more liberal legislation and generally tends to be more reactive than proactive. Union presence especially in the private sector is fairly low at approximately 20 percent, organizational atomization and some indication of ideational differences over the immigration question further compound problems of effective interest communication. The difficulties in establishing lobbying channels to the Department of Justice, Equality and Law Reform are shared by the unions, leaving the Social Partnership framework as the principal vehicle to communicate preferences. The union movement is therefore generally not a particularly powerful actor in shaping immigration policy.

The use of immigrants as a tool to undermine wage levels is obviously of concern. A November 2005 headline case involved Irish Ferries resorting to a Cyprus-based subcontractor paying Latvian hourly wages of €0.71, dismissing Irish employees and claiming this practice to constitute a legitimate exploitation of the EU liberalization of service provision. The ICTU remained relatively passive at first, but the Services, Industrial, Professional and Technical Union (SIPTU) organized well-attended demonstrations throughout the country, eventually receiving the support of the ICTU. The resultant negative publicity has discouraged other companies from following suit, but the ultimate settlement, while imposing the obligation to pay the Irish minimum wage, still permitted the use of subcontractors and the application of Cypriot labor law (EIRO 2005). The show of force and sustained industrial action along with clearly communicating the willingness to suspend further Social Partnership talks bolstered the union movement's credibility, notwithstanding the generally low levels of unionization in the private sector.

Structure of Interest Intermediation

Unions and employers can convey their positions to governmental actors within the framework of the social partnership. Both social partners have repeatedly emphasized the need for a long-term oriented integration policy, with employers stressing the need for economic migration being rendered more attractive by generous provisions for accompanying family members. However, the executive enjoys skillfully asserted autonomy and seeks to defend maximum policy space. While opinions of the social partners—as well as NGOs—may well be solicited, this exercise is in no way binding (interview IRL-GOV-1, IRL-NGO-1). The June 2001 Public Consultation Procedure on Immigration Policies did solicit the input of NGOs, social partners, and indeed individuals, but the impact of this and the subsequent round of "stakeholder" consultations appears to be limited (interviews IRL-GOV-1, IRL-BUS-1, IRL-NGO-1). In the process of the hastily enacted citizenship reform, the government has not conducted any such consultation exercises.

In the social partnership agreements "Programme for Prosperity and Fairness" (2000–03), "Sustaining Progress" (2003–05), and "Towards 2016" (2006–08) NGOs active in antipoverty, equality, and unemployment issues are represented. Their position is apparent in the 2003 program, which emphasizes the strong role that immigrants have played in the Irish economic success story in their contribution to both the public and private sectors. They also call for a comprehensive policy for immigration from outside the EEA and the guarantee of standard wages and work conditions for non-EEA migrants (Mac Éinrí 2005, 17).

Formal consultation exercises apart, the relative autonomy of the executive branch of government, which is much cherished by the relevant Ministry of Justice, Equality and Law Reform, means that sporadic meetings with NGOs are entirely at the discretion of the ministry. While officials may be interested in ascertaining the positions of these groups, they are not necessarily favorably inclined towards them and they are sometimes openly opposed. Thus while over the course of the past five years the frequency of such meetings has increased, their actual effect on policy output has remained relatively limited (interviews IRL-NGO-1, GOV-1). Opinions on the asylum issue diverge very strongly.

The Department of Enterprise, Trade and Employment has become more centrally involved in migration management by administering the new "Green Card Permits," established through the 2003 and 2006 Employment Permits Acts to replace the Work Visa/Work Authorisation

Scheme. This scheme is aimed both at highly skilled labor migrants expecting to attract annual salaries above €60,000 and at those expecting to earn between €30,000 and €60,000 but seeking to fill shortages in an array of defined occupations, prominently in finance, IT, health, architecture, and natural science research. In the process, while administrative leeway still exists, employers face a more amiable governmental point of reference than the more restrictively oriented Department of Justice, Equality and Law Reform (Table 5.2).

Development of Immigration Policy Since 1990

Both the empirical phenomenon of immigration and the apposite regulatory legislation are of extremely recent provenance. The original legislative framework, consisting of the 1935 Aliens Act and the Aliens Order 1946, is extremely restrictive and granted complete control over migration regulation to the executive. Citizenship law was modified in 1986, but major legislative overhaul commenced in earnest in the late 1990s, with ongoing transformations on an annual basis. Thus, despite being a signatory country to the Geneva Convention and the New York Protocol, a comprehensive legislative framework based on a firm statutory footing for the accommodation and processing of refugees and asylum seekers was created only with considerable delay in the form of the 1996 Refugee Act (No. 17). It created an independent Refugee Appeals Tribunal and appointed a Refugee Application Commissioner. This office receives and administers asylum applications, while the former constitutes an appeals board, hitherto nonexistent. In line with developments elsewhere in Europe, more restrictive tools were created, Dublin I implemented, fines created for asylum seekers seen as interfering with the process, including the refusal to undergo mandatory fingerprinting, and legal avenues for detention designed, again mainly for noncompliant asylum seekers or those conceived as posing a threat to public safety. Subsequent amendments in the form of Section 11(1) of the 1999 Immigration Act and Section 9 of the Illegal Immigrants (Trafficking) Act 2000 further widened the list of offences and enhanced discretion over rejection, notably in "manifestly unfounded" cases. In April 2000, geographic dispersal of refugees and asylum seekers was introduced in line with British practice.

The 1999 Immigration Act (No. 22) reintroduced the legal framework for deportation after the Supreme Court had found the powers of the executive in this domain contained in the 1935 legislation excessively broad. Its main progressive innovation was the legal provision for a

Table 5.2. Irish immigration policy

Development of immigration policy since 1990

Year	Description
1935	Aliens Act provides the general framework for state power towards foreign citizens, extremely broad and sweeping powers regarding border control, detention for purposes of identification, requirements for residency permit, burden of proof rests with foreigner, no appeal possible.
1946	Aliens Order further elaborates regulations regarding noncitizens.
1996	Refugee Act creates legislative framework for refugees and asylum. Refugee Application Commissioner is responsible for receiving asylum requests, appeals against the decisions are possible and must be lodged with the Appeals Tribunals. This Act implements Dublin I. A number of restrictive tools are embedded, in particular detention.
	Responding to rapidly rising numbers of asylum seekers, subsequent amendments introduce considerable discretion regarding asylum cases, including the declaration of "manifestly unfounded" cases: the government commences the mandatory dispersal of asylum seekers following British practice.
1999	Immigration Act (No. 22) contains a number of amendments to the 1996 Act, creates a new Refugee Advisory Board issuing policy recommendation though this body is not truly nonpartisan.
2000	Illegal Immigrants (Trafficking) Act (No. 29) considerably enhances police powers, including stop and search and powers of seizure against individuals suspected of being involved in or victims of organized border trespassing.
2003	Immigration Act (No. 26) introduces carrier sanctions and the "safe country of origin" concept, facilitates deportation, further widens police powers in dealing with noncitizens.
2003	Employment Permits Act (No. 7) introduces employer sanctions in cases of employment of undocumented migrants, clarifies procedures for police raids on places of suspected undocumented employment. Subsequently, the Irish government announces that no labor mobility ban will be imposed on citizens of the EU-10; however, individuals from these countries must be able to prove "habitual residence" in Ireland and a minimum of two years of residency prior to being eligible for any welfare benefits following British approach.
2004	Immigration Act (No. 1) seeks largely to replace the 1946 Act: further widens police and border guard powers in dealing with foreigners, including detention and deportation, permits "fast track" decisions on asylum cases, introduces "monitoring" of citizenship claims arising out of residence (*ius solis*).
2004	Irish Nationality and Citizenship Act (no. 38 consolidates the largely vacuous 2001 Act and revises earlier 1956 legislation; ends once and for all generous *ius solis* application, citizenship claims arising out of *ius solis* will only be valid if one parent can claim legal long-term residency in the island of Ireland (thus including Northern Ireland); change in legislation arises out of slightly exaggerated concern over a case of a Chinese woman having given birth to her child in Ulster, thus claiming residency for herself and Irish citizenship for the child.
2006	Employment Permits Act: streamlines work permit procedures administered by Department of Enterprise, Trade and Employment; creates Green Card Scheme for highly skilled workers; total number of permits increases from 6,000 in 1999 to 34,000 in 2004.
2008	Immigration, Residence and Protection Bill seeks to replace 1935 Act entirely: creates robust institutional network for asylum, clarifies procedures for obtaining long-term residency permit, sets out procedures for deportation.

Refugee Advisory Board that could consult and advise government on policy, though given that its membership is composed of civil servants seconded by a number of relevant ministries its independence is obviously questionable.[3] In legal terms, it also rendered Irish immigration law acts of "primary legislation."

Meanwhile, the actual number of asylum applications rose sharply. In 1996, 1,179 applications were recorded, a figure that more than doubled annually until 1999 and reached 10,938 in 2000 (Hughes and Quinn 2004, 26). Subsequently, the Illegal Immigrants (Trafficking) Act 2000 (No. 29) presented further modifications by creating legal instruments to punish "a person who organizes or knowingly facilitates the entry into the State of a person whom he or she...has reasonable cause to believe to be an illegal immigrant or a person who intends to seek asylum" (Section 2.1) and the "trafficked" individual itself. It also permitted the confiscation of any vehicle used in this process and broadened police powers in "entry, search and seizure" (Section 7) in the framework of battling undocumented migration, while stepping up sanctions against individuals resisting police.

The number of asylum applications seemed to have peaked at 11,634 in 2002, but the trend towards more restriction continued with the Immigration Act 2003 (No. 26). It introduced carrier sanctions (Section 2), shrewdly justified rhetorically as an instance of mandatory top-down Europeanization that therefore could not be negotiated or modified,[4] facilitated deportation of individuals not permitted entry at the border (Section 5), introduced the "safe country of origin" concept (Section 7.12) and generally broadened police powers in regard to asylum seekers, including the introduction of "fast track procedures" (Section 7). It also permitted the exchange of information about asylum seekers among various ministries (Section 8).

The Irish NGO attempts at influencing legislation were largely frustrated. Weak organizational structures, limited resources, often very young and inexperienced organizations with equally junior staff (interview IRL-NGO-1, IRL-NGO-1) impeded effective lobbying and a ministry clearly motivated "to make sure that such a tide will not repeat itself in this country" (interview IRL-GOV-1) was unwilling to concede the establishment of more regularized access channels.

In 2003, only 7,900 asylum applications were lodged. Nevertheless, in April 2003, rent allowance payments for asylum seekers or individuals with unclear residency status were abolished. Given the ban on employment, this established complete reliance on the state for housing and living expenses. Meanwhile, recognition rates had reached an all-time low of 3.7 percent in 2003 and 17.9 upon appeal (ECRE 2003). Asylum was the main focus of legislative activity, but a few changes concerned other categories of migration as well. The number of work permits had risen meteorically from 6,250 in 1999 to 47,551 in 2003 and were handled in an employer-led highly liberalized fashion, much to the liking of business (interview IRL-GOV-1). With the Employment Permits Act 2003 (No. 7), a notably more restrictive stance was introduced even here: employer sanctions came about and clarified legal provisions for police raids on employers (Section 2), supplanting the hitherto exclusive focus on employee sanctions, and clarified the legal status of work permits. Employers protested and consultation was deliberately avoided (interview IRL-BUS-1). However, this tighter regulatory stance was sweetened considerably by forgoing any restriction on the freedom of mobility and service provision from CEE after enlargement (interview IRL-GOV-1). Perhaps not coincidentally, the act emanated from the more pragmatic Department of Enterprise, Trade and Employment, though it was nevertheless implemented without consulting unions and employers. The latter were not unexpectedly displeased (interviews IRL-BUS-1, IRL-UNI-1) that despite their ideological unity and at least satisfactory degrees of centralization, internal cohesion, and representation among the clientele for employers the employment permit administration seemed to become more restrictive. However, given the open doors to CEE, low-skill recruitment would in fact be facilitated, while the 2003 Act already contained the foundation, elaborated in a 2006 amendment, for a high-skill Green Card Scheme. On balance, despite the formal snub, business access to unskilled labor pools and increasingly also to limited categories of highly skilled migrants thus seemed assured. Not least to placate populist concerns over "welfare scrounging", a UK-style "habitual residency" requirement for the receipt of welfare transfer payments was implemented as a preparatory measure preceding enlargement.

The Immigration Act 2004 (No. 1) and ongoing discussions about a new Immigration and Residency in Ireland and Employment Permit Bill were influenced by the list of objectives set forth in the ministry's strategy statement for 2003–05 (Department of Justice, Equality and Law Reform 2003). This "wish list" ("High Level Goal 10") notably includes the following points: an asylum system that permits the processing of applicants within six months and a speedy resolution of pending cases, raising the number of deportations of unsuccessful applicants and addressing "abuse," developing a more comprehensive legislative package, monitoring and possibly reregulating residency claims arising out of parentage to Irish citizens, reducing undocumented migration and "trafficking" and "enhancing" relations with NGOs. However, continuing a trajectory of somewhat uneasy relations with the NGO sector, the Act was drafted at breakneck speed with no consultation of nonstate actors in direct response to the Leontjava and Chang High Court case (interviews IRL-GOV-1, IRL-NGO-1, IRL-BUS-1, IRL-UNI-1). The NGOs were disappointed that restrictive "securitarian" elements predominate; the main objectives appearing to be to enhance police powers and border control in general. Thus Section 3 specifies regulations pertaining both to the appointment of officers and to the routine control of arriving passengers, a theme elaborated in Section 4, which details conditions under which permission to land can be denied, including the fairly sweeping "reason to believe that the non-national intends to enter the State for purposes other than those expressed" (3.k.). In the same vein, Section 6 details "approved ports" outside of which entry is not permitted, while Section 7 grants extensive powers for officers in retaining non-Irish citizens before even entering national territory and Sections 13–14 further extend police powers. Section 9 creates a new obligation for foreigners to register with local authorities, while Section 17 creates the legislative possibility to implement visa requirements on select countries at short notice. In sum, this piece of legislation, meant to reform substantially the 1946 Act, continues its predecessor's repressive approach.

The insulated, yet highly publicized case of a Chinese woman who had given birth in Northern Ireland and was *quare* permitted to remain in Ireland as the parent of a new Irish citizen influenced not only immigration regulation but citizenship laws as well. In June 2004, a referendum was carried out regarding the hitherto unrestricted application of *ius solis*. The referendum supported a revision of citizenship regulation and the new Irish Nationality and Citizenship Act 2004 (No. 38), revising the largely unsubstantial 2001 Act as well as the more fundamental 1956 Act, which bestows claims to citizenship under *ius solis* only to newborns with at least one long-term legal resident parent on the Irish island, including Ulster.

The ministry's 2005 discussion paper "Immigration and Residence in Ireland" (Department of Justice, Equality and Law Reform 2005), eventually spawning the 2008 Immigration, Residence and Protection Bill, perpetuates the same dichotomy of restrictive policy towards unsolicited forms of migration and liberal provisions towards economic migrants. The paper set forth the task of creating a more comprehensive and detailed overarching migration policy, involving greater transparency in visa delivery, including in cases of refusal, the possible storage of biometric data of visa applicants, a review of border control measures including carrier sanctions, which may involve a legal and financial obligation for carriers to return refused entrants, coordinated legislation for labor migration, including more extensive employer sanctions, fast-track schemes for temporary skilled migrants, special provisions for researchers (p. 16), a general provision for family reunification for spouses of legal residents and children under 18, coupled with a registration requirement for foreign children (p. 17), the possible exclusion of "noneconomically active" migrants from entitlements to public services, a specification of the administration of residency permits, the creation of a somewhat unclear legal distinction between deportation and removal, a commitment to the maintenance of the common travel area (p. 24), and a promise to study other Anglophone regulatory approaches. Thus the authors affirm that new legislation shall be "in line with that of other common law countries of migration such as New Zealand, Canada, and Australia, all of whom have well-established migration systems in place... [these countries' legislation] set out policy objectives underlining those Acts (p. 30)."

The labor market associations were generally content with the approach taken to economic migration, characterized by feeding EU-10 immigration into low-skill sectors, especially in agricultural and low-wage service sector positions, while soliciting highly skilled migrants through the newly designed Green Card Permit (interviews IRL-UNI-1, IRL-BUS-1). Even the somewhat less pragmatic Department of Justice, Equality and Law Reform (2005*b*) recognized that "apart from immigration, other sources of additional labor supply are reducing. There will therefore be an ongoing requirement for significant immigration levels, particularly of people with higher level qualifications." This insight has informed the 2008 Act and is likely to shape future Irish economic migration policy. In a speech unveiling the 2008 legislation, the Minister for Justice, Equality and Law Reform stressed that "Ireland is in competition with other countries for people with sought-after skills and qualifications... [thus we need to] make Ireland an even more attractive destination for medium-term and long-term migration." It leaves the fairly liberal provisions of the 2006 Employment Permits Act in place and therefore meets the employers' approval (IBEC 2008), while part 7 implements the EU Asylum Procedures and Minimum Standards directives, while continuing to preserve substantial leeway for governmental authorities especially regarding family reunion, but even marriage, ostensibly to prevent forced marriages.

The NGO sector therefore criticized these elements (MRCI 2008). Reservations over method in 2004 notwithstanding, with an ostentatious "crackdown" in regulation perhaps necessary to placate increasingly xenophobic public opinion, the employers in particular are pleased with a fairly liberal regulatory approach regarding labor migration that is informed by their input, their concerns over sectoral labor shortages, their interest in simple, flexible, quick, and unbureaucratic access to low-skill migration, addressed through EU-10 migrants, and therefore fairly effective lobbying efforts, while the union supports regulated and well-managed labor migration.

The Impact of Europeanization

Deeply committed to maintaining the common travel area with the UK and sharing a somewhat illusionary concept of restrictive control presumably enabled by virtue of geographic isolation, the Irish government has opted out of many AMP measures, but top-down Europeanization is not absent. Not unlike its UK counterpart, the Irish government "cherry picks" areas it wishes to partake in, notably those focusing on a uniform visa and residency permit format, including biometric data, the retention and storage of passenger data, joint operations in patrolling borders, and the creation of an immigration liaison officer network (Department of Justice, Equality and Law Reform 2005*a*, 10). We have noted before the rhetorical justification of new asylum measures with reference to the allegedly mandatory character of top-down Europeanization. The Irish government is thus "opting in" selectively and even takes precautions to design policy in broad adherence to the evolving AMP (Department of Justice, Equality and Law Reform 2005*a*, 10, 2005*b*). Irish legislation is developed so as not to be incompatible with it and allow joining in the future. The Irish government is also highly active in AMP design discussions, even though it does not transpose all of these directives itself (interview IRL-GOV-1). Thus, during the Irish presidency of the EU during the first half of 2004, an active effort was being made to bring a number of AMP projects to fruition, notably regarding asylum. By contrast, bottom-up Europeanization has not been attempted, partially because the "opt out" status obviously impairs credibility, and also due to the extremely recent nature of national legislation, the highly fluent and in parts embryonic state effectively ruling out attempts to set agendas through the uploading of national models as blueprints. In fact, there is no evidence of bottom-up Europeanization based on Irish initiative.

Ireland therefore presents an interesting case where often somewhat delayed top-down Europeanization occurs, but based on selective "cherry picking," with alleged "European pressure" being rhetorically constructed to justify the implementation of certain new policy tools. Effective in insulating itself from demands by nonstate actors, especially humanitarian NGOs, the government can thus play a two-level game where national policy design includes European developments, while actively participating in such deliberations. However, at the European level, the Irish delegation is more of a policy taker when compared to the more established countries of immigration. There is no ideological divergence between Irish policymakers and AMP architects on the need to emphasize border control and to restrict entry pathways. Similarly, while the Irish government does not presently see much added value in AMP regarding labor migration, as its response to the Commission Green Paper clearly indicates, its national policy of work permits and recruitment programs for skilled employees is certainly closely aligned with EU-wide trends (interview IRL-GOV-1).

Poland: Being a Model European, Tolerating Ukrainians

Poland has only most recently attracted immigrants in any significant numbers; in the 2002 census (Korys and Weinar 2005, 5) only 0.1 percent of the total population was foreign. Historically, the country has been associated with short-term or permanent emigration to Austria and Germany as well as the more established Australasian and North American immigration countries. Since the fall of the Berlin Wall, Poland has turned into a transit country for migrants from the disintegrating USSR and later its successor republics as well as South Asia. In the aftermath of the imposition of martial law by General Jaruzelski in 1981, Polish emigration reached significant heights and did not subside until the mid-1990s.[5] Though emigration levels have remained at lower levels since, Poland remains a net emigration country. We can identify five pivotal patterns in Polish migration policy.

First, the top-down impact of the EU is extremely significant.[6] Polish policymakers were unable—and to some extent unwilling—to secure any significant concessions to secure EU membership in a timely fashion. Central elements of Poland's migration regime—and almost the entirety of regulations pertaining to asylum, refugees, visas, and border control—are instances of passive top-down Europeanization and follow the *acquis communautaire*. That said, the asylum and refugee regime was fairly rudimentary and thus particularly exposed to reform pressure. Given the long delay in formulating an EU labor migration policy, there has been more national autonomy in this domain. The Polish negotiation position was feeble and the unrepentant stance of the Commission and several member states (Grabbe 2005; Schimmelfennig and Sedelmaier 2005) led to a strong European coloring of Polish migration policy.[7]

Second, the painful economic transition following a rapidly implemented IMF-style shock therapy in the early 1990s has bequeathed Poland high unemployment, coupled with significant regional disparities between the relatively prosperous regions around Warsaw (Mazovia) and Krakow and Upper Silesia on the one hand and much poorer Lower Silesia, the East (Lubuskie) and Northeast (Warmia–Marzury) on the other. Labor market participation rates among the over-50s is low, as deindustrialization and the bankruptcy of large segments of the heavy industry as well as "de-agriculturalization" and the shutdown of the large state-owned farming collectives have affected this demographic cohort in particular. Henceforth, there is muted interest in large-scale (labor) migration programs, despite a particularly unfavorable demographic picture and very low birth rates. However, labor migrants do arrive in Poland, generally inhabiting either very highly skilled and well-remunerated managerial positions or poorly paid jobs in agriculture, horticulture, gastronomy, and construction. Many, though not all, of the migrants in the latter category work without a working permit in the undocumented sector of the economy, though they may well possess valid short-term visas. Surprisingly little public debate focuses on undocumented migration, though this may be related to the fact that most jobs taken by immigrants are "dirty, dangerous, difficult, and disdained" and not attractive to residents. Immigration is a quantitatively limited phenomenon limited to low-wage low-skill agricultural jobs, filled by Ukrainians. However, as emigration continues, "brain drain" assumes substantial proportions given the vast income gaps with Western Europe and North America in skilled professions, particularly in regard to medical professionals, but also in finance, IT, and the natural sciences.

Third, as elsewhere in Europe, particularly favorable treatment is reserved for ethnic descendants of emigrants, though attempts to "repatriate" such individuals from North America and Western Europe, especially Germany, have not been particularly successful. There has been somewhat more success in attracting ethnic Poles from Ukraine. Ethnic Poles completing their tertiary studies aided by special governmental scholarships tend to stay and assume Polish citizenship.

Fourth, asylum and refugee issues are the only migration themes that receive any public attention, though this must be seen as a result of relative, rather than absolute quantitative increases. According to the Office for Repatriation and Foreigners (2006), 8,079 applications for refugee status were received in 2004 of which only 305 were recognized under the terms of the Geneva Convention, while another 832 received tolerated status.[8] The implementation of Dublin I and II in Poland creates the odd obligation to process applications from refugees who never intended to remain in Poland, but simply entered EU territory there (interview PL-GOV1, PL-GOV2). Poland is thus accommodating Russian deserters from the Chechnyan war, Chechnyan refugees, and South Asian asylum seekers who sought to lodge claims further west. A financially hard-pressed government unwillingly accommodates unwilling refugees. Three state-operated and 11 privately owned refugee detention centers in Poland accommodate a total of 3,200 individuals, 3,000 of which are Russian citizens (interview PL-GOV-2). Located within a 200-km radius of Warsaw and mainly towards the East they accommodate destitute asylum seekers and refugees. The central center in Debak, 20 km south of Warsaw, serves as the initial point of accommodation from where individuals are then dispersed throughout the country.

Fifth, not unrelated to the close nexus between EU enlargement and imposed policy transfer, the relative autonomy of the government is striking. Civil society actors are underdeveloped, organizationally and financially feeble, and do not encounter an administrative apparatus supportive of their concerns. There are no formal arenas of interaction and no tradition thereof. Within the tripartite Committee for Social and Economic Affairs, migration affairs are not discussed (interview PL-UNI-1). Though the relative power of parliament vis-à-vis the executive has been noted (Zubek 2001), this does not apply to migration policy.

System of Political Economy: An Odd Amalgam

Central and Eastern European political economies defy easy categorization and confound much taxonomy. Much of the more recent comparative political economy literature neglects the region. Stark (1996, 995) finds "recombinant property" rights in Eastern Europe, consisting of partially privatized enterprises, forming a "new type of mixed economy...distinctively East European." However, the implementation of privatization, privileging insiders with party and state apparatus connections, led one observer to describe the process in Poland as "not a result of the expansion of the traditional private sector, but...a peculiar linkage of political power and capital" (Staniszkis 1991, 128). However, encompassing 1990s privatization programs have created a private sector accounting for 70 percent of the GDP in Poland and up to 80 percent elsewhere in CEE. Later studies argue that due to the hasty fashion in which privatization was implemented, the result has been self-ownership, cross-holdings *à la* Germany, and, in Poland less than elsewhere, foreign ownership, resulting in "capitalism without capitalists" (Eyal, Szeleny and Townsley 1998). The experience of economic transition, the modalities of privatization, and the "legacies" of state socialism vary significantly. Given the predominance of small companies in the economy, government steering and intervention in the economy, including protectionist barriers to investment, the decentralized industrial relations, feeble employee protection, a low degree of unionization, an underdeveloped stock market, but a relatively small private banking sector as well, a weak "Latin-style" welfare state and underdeveloped secondary educational institutions, one analyst of the Polish political economy (Mykhnenko 2005) finds it to constitute an odd blend, confounding both Amable's (2003) and Hall and Soskice's (2001) typologies, uniquely combining elements that seem to constitute oddities, rather than complementarities. Similarly, McMenamin (2004) finds that countries in this region either constitute a distinct group of their own, share most commonalities with marginal southern European countries, or indeed with continental Europe, depending on the number of clusters one wishes to sample for. The Polish political economy may be best conceived as a hybrid, containing elements from various types rather than a separate "emerging market economy" as argued elsewhere (Hancké, Rhodes, and Thatcher 2007).

The relative importance of the primary sector in terms of employment levels is striking, despite the privatization of the employment-intensive state-owned collective farms. Tertiarization has not progressed as quickly, a trend reflected in employment levels. High unemployment and a significant demographic cohort currently entering the labor market, coupled with limited welfare transfer payment mechanisms, mean that labor recruitment is largely domestically oriented, while labor immigration is a quantitatively limited phenomenon and limited to highly skilled service sector positions experiencing skill shortages or low-pay temporary flexible employees in agriculture under conditions that Polish employees are hesitant to accept.

The Polish union movement is not centrally concerned with immigration, but focuses much more on securing acceptable wages and working conditions for Polish *emigrants*. This became evident in the signing of a memorandum on common interests with the German union DGB (interview PL-UNI-1) or protests against the temporary bans on intra-EU labor mobility.[9] Joint consultation with employers has been held on labor mobility within the enlarged EU and the impact on emigration. The feeble unionization rate of 15 percent of the workforce in the private sector, an internal division of the trade union between the NSZZ Solidarność and the OPZZ,[10] in addition to "independent unions" and somewhat weak internal cohesion all undermine the negotiation position. Even in negotiations with employers, employer compliance with standard wage agreements is difficult to monitor. The unions show very little enthusiasm for labor migration, citing unemployment, already apparent abuses by employers of existent migrant workers and undercutting of wages, especially in the agricultural sector, combined with the more pressing concerns over brain drain and emigration (interview PL-UNI-1, PL-UNI-2). Similarly, there is of yet no interest or position regarding asylum and refugee issues. The internal divisions and organizational problems impede effective lobbying.

The employer camp is also organizationally divided and lacks organizational coherence, but shares an ideational lack of interest in new instruments in labor migration (interview PL-BUS-1). Documented labor immigration is largely of interest in highly skilled service sector positions and following an expression of interest by the employers, the 2004 legislation has created a labor permit scheme[11] permitting just such employment, following a relatively bureaucratic examination of the local labor market to ensure that new immigration does not bequeath replacement effects, while the job seeker is required to apply from abroad. Ministry of Economic Affairs and Labour data indicate that 46 percent of all migrants are employed as managers or consultants, mostly from EU countries, Oceania, and North America (Korys and Weinar 2005, 8). Most self-employed business owners, making up another 26 percent of the total, come from Asian countries, including prominently Vietnam and Turkey. Russia and other former Soviet republics are prominently represented among both legal and, according to more unreliable anecdotal evidence, illegal migrants. In 2004, 7,845 of the total 18,841 permanent residency holders in Poland stemmed from the EU-15, 2,750 from Ukraine, another 2,181 from successor republics to the USSR, and 3,563 from Asia. Though organizationally perhaps not best positioned to affect governmental policy, labor migration regulation already meets employer interests and, though restrictive, permits the limited recruitment of interest to employers in high-skill service sectors.

Structure of Interest Intermediation

Nonstate actors are relatively feeble in Poland in terms of their organizational structure and their effectiveness in influencing governmental policy. Their relationship to more formalized political actors, notably political parties, is not untroubled (Ekiert and Kubik 1997). Many humanitarian nongovernmental organizations are dependent on state funding or are simply local dependencies of IGOs, such as UNHCR or IOM, or indeed local representatives of relatively well-funded transnational NGOs, such as Amnesty International. Others, such as Caritas Polska, are charitable organizations working with refugees, without engaging in active lobbying. But even local independent actors, such as Polska Akcja Humanitarna, are financially dependent on local and regional government and EU funding in the assistance work they carry out (cf. Polska Akcja Humanitarna 2003). Relevant government ministries largely attempt to isolate themselves from nongovernmental actors and "it is frustrating" and "not always very effective" for NGOs to send petitions and statements and to request hearings and consultation sessions, as representatives of such transnational agencies are the only actors with which the government maintains regular dialogue, while other NGOs are either not consulted regularly or not even received (interviews PL-GOV-1, PL-NGO-1). Vocal efforts by some committed NGOs, such as Amnesty International, notwithstanding, the lobbying efforts are not particularly warmly welcomed and nonexisting informal channels to governmental actors impede effective access (interview PL-NGO-1, PL-GOV-1). Indeed, the government does not consult trade unions and employers on migration issues either (interview PL-GOV-1, PL-UNI-1, PL-UNI-2, PL-BUS-1). To the extent that there are corporatist-style institutions in Poland or that such consultation is being practiced, it concerns only labor and social policy initiatives in the narrowest sense (Leiber 2007; PL-UNI-2). The absence of much public debate and the hitherto dominant perception of having to implement policy passively as a precondition to membership may further enhance such relative state insulation. The comparable weakness of both NGOs and the trade union in financial, structural, and organizational terms further undermines their lobbying position (Table 5.3).

Table 5.3. Polish immigration policy

Development of immigration policy since 1990

March 29, 1991 Poland sign agreement on abolition of visa requirement for tourists with the Schengenzone countries; Poland signs Geneva Convention.

May 7, 1993 Poland and Germany sign bilateral agreement; Poland accepts status as "safe third country," implying obligation to accept asylum seekers who entered via Polish territory; similar agreements are signed with the Czech Republic, Slovakia, Romania, Bulgaria, and Ukraine.

December 14, 1994 Act on Employment and Combating Unemployment (revised in 2003 as J.L. of 2003, No. 58, item 514) creates employer-driven work permit schemes; applicant needs to apply from abroad and will only be granted permit if no domestic employee can be found.

November 24, 1995 First reading of the revision of the Act on Aliens during the 65th session of the Sejm's second term: first major revision of the original 1963 bill.

June 26, 1997 new Act on Aliens is passed by parliament, becomes effective as of December 27; act follows impetus of EU *acquis*, steps up border control, requires proof of economic self-sufficiency and accommodation for citizens of post-USSR republics, clarifies regulations for residency permits, stricter conditions for visa applications; introduction of carrier sanctions; facilitates deportations; UNHCR criticizes lack of specific categories for asylum seekers and refugees.

September 1, 1997 New Polish Constitution becomes effective, Chap. 2, Art. 56 incorporates the right to asylum: "1. Foreigners shall have a right of asylum in the Republic of Poland in accordance with principles specified by statute. 2. Foreigners who, in the Republic of Poland, seek protection from oppression, may be granted the status of a refugee in accordance with international agreements to which the Republic of Poland is a party."

September 9, 1997 Decree of the Ministry for Labor and Social Affairs regarding exceptions to the requirement of a work permit for foreign employees, finetunes work permit procedure.

November 9, 2000 Act on Repatriation (Journal of Laws 2000, No. 106, item 1118) modifies the original Law on Citizenship of February 15, 1962; clarifies procedures for returning ethnic Poles obtaining citizenship, addresses concerns by interest group Polish Community Association (Wspólnota Polska), law takes effect as of January 1, 2001.

2001 Act on Aliens is amended, a separate category for refugees not awarded Geneva Convention protection status is created that receive temporary protection and residence permits following UNHCR pressure, increases period of residency required to obtain permanent residency permit to five years; fast-track processing of "manifestly unfounded applications" becomes possible, "safe third country" and "safe third country of origin" concepts introduced; Office for Repatriation and Aliens (ORA) created; family reunion regulations modified with a view to adapting EU directive; crackdown on "marriages of convenience"; major overhaul of visa policy, hitherto containing visitor visa with or without work permit, transit visa, and repatriation visa for ethnic Poles, hitherto requirement to leave national territory for a minimum of 12 months after expiration of visitor visa with work permit—new regulation abolishes transit and visitor's visa with working permit categories, introduces one universal visa type, valid for three months only; political opposition (Democratic Left Alliance, SLD, and Polish Peasant Party PSL) criticizes lack of coherent legislative framework.

June 13, 2003 Act on Aliens (Journal of Laws 2003, No. 128, item 1175), permanent residency can be applied for after five, and in some cases three, years (Arts. 64–71), the conditions for application for a temporary residency permit are laid out, requiring financial self-sufficiency and being generally tied to work permits with certain humanitarian exceptions (Arts. 53–63), special consideration is given to individuals who are engaged in "an economic activity . . . beneficial to the national economy and in particular, contributes to the development of investments, transfer of technology, innovations or job creation. . . . "(Art. 53 1.2) border controls are regulated (esp. Art. 13 ff.), legal possibilities for expulsion and deportation increased (Art. 88 ff.), including for detention are outlined, the visa regulations are specified (Arts. 25–51), harsher measures on "bogus marriages" are introduced (Art. 57 1.4), introduction of a mandatory residence card for all foreign residents (Art. 72 ff.), introduction of a central database for all foreign residents (Art. 124 ff.), carrier liability is being stepped up (Art. 135 ff.); procedures for undocumented work, undocumented residency, lack of financial self-sufficiency, undocumented border crossing, being deemed a "threat to the state security" (Art. 88 5 ff.) and tax evasion (sic, Art. 88 8+9 ff.).

Helsinki Foundation unsuccessfully lobbies for separate provisions for foreign graduates of Polish universities.

Act on Granting Protection to Aliens within the Territory of the Republic of Poland (Journal of Laws 2003, No. 128, item 1176), refines concepts of "safe country of origin" and "safe third country," modifying the 2001 legislation, four forms of protection are specified: Geneva Convention refugee status, asylum, "tolerated stay" and temporary protection; applicants for refugee status need to apply at the border, outlines procedures for detaining applicants, especially if they have crossed the border illegally or have been arrested, creates a Refugee Board, members are appointed by the Prime Minister, analyzes, but does not determine bestowal and withdrawal of refugee status (Art. 81 ff.), outlines asylum procedures, including the withdrawal of status (Art. 90 ff.) and "tolerated stay" where danger to "right to life, freedom, safety" (Art. 97 ff.), temporary protection for victims of civil war, following a Council of Ministers decision (Art. 106 ff.).

September 4 to **December 31, 2003**, later extended until November 2004 Regularization offer (*abolicja*) for long-term undocumented residents of six years or more—offer entails a one year residency and work permit that then provides the basis for applications for long-term permits, provided proof of economic self-sufficiency and employment (or offer) can be provided, mainly taken up by Armenians and Vietnamese; outlined (Art. 101ff.).

October 1, 2003 introduction of visa requirements for citizens of Ukraine, Belarus, and Russia.

May 1, 2004 Act on Social Assistance (Journal of Laws 2004, No. 64, item 593) facilitates "individual integration" for refugees and their families, by granting need-dependent accommodation and language training assistance limited to one year.

June 1, 2004 Act on Promotion of Employment and Institutions of the Labor Market (Journal of Laws 2004, No. 99, item 1001) changes permit procedures for athletes and teachers, facilitates labor market access for certain categories of immigrants, notably refugees, temporary tolerated individuals and foreign spouses of Polish citizens.

April 22, 2005 New Amendment to the 2003 Aliens Act (Journal of Laws 2005, No. 94, item 788), covering registration of residents, education, social security, and employment, implements EU directives, *inter alia* the family reunion directive and the directive on TCN long-term residents, permitting application for unlimited residency after five years if proof of economic self-sufficiency, regular income, and health insurance can be provided.

July 14, 2006 Act on the entry into, residence in, and exit from the Republic of Poland of nationals of the European Union Member States and their family members (Journal of Laws, No. 144, item 1043).

Development of Immigration Policy Since 1990

Most immigration to Poland until the mid-1990s involved ethnic Poles arriving from the eastern sections claimed by the USSR after 1945. The 1962 Aliens Law[12] was largely a dead letter and the 1962 Citizenship Law much more pertinent. In addition to the approximately 2 million residents forcefully displaced to Poland, a second wave arrived in the 1950s, comprising approximately 225,000 individuals (Okólski 2000, 142). Commencing in the late 1950s ethnic German *Aussiedler* started leaving the country, followed by Jewish Poles, especially after the anti-Semitic government stance regarding the 1967 Five Day War, and ethnic Poles, adding up to a trickle of 20,000–35,000 emigrants per year. The imposition of martial war in 1981 instigated a major emigration wave in the 1980s comprising an estimated 1–1.3 million inhabitants, though only 271,000 were recorded, as most left clandestinely. The imposition of visa requirements for Polish citizens in 1981 by many Western countries, notably West Germany, though not in the enclave of West Berlin, impeded emigration only slightly. The 1990s also witnessed the emergence of temporary employment-related *pendel* migration, along with limited return migration by ethnic Poles from Ukraine and Western countries.

It is often assumed that Polish (and much of CEE) migration policy "has arisen almost entirely as a result of the requirements of EU accession and that EU policy models and ideas about borders, security and insecurity have been exported to CEE countries" (Geddes 2003, 173) and indeed this observation is largely accurate for asylum and refugee policy (Lavenex 2001; Kicinger 2005), but may obstruct the view on both limited domestic initiative, especially regarding visa policy, and the influence of policy transfer and political pressure from *individual* EU countries, most prominently Germany. As early as 1993, the German government had asked for the imposition of visa requirements for citizens of Poland's eastern neighbors (cf. Aniol 1996). The Polish government refused, but did accept declaring them "safe third countries" in the course of negotiations,[13] being handsomely rewarded in the form of a 120 million DM grant over the next three years to construct an administrative system for refugees and asylum seekers, including detention centers, and to invest in border control equipment for its border police force along the 737 miles of its eastern border. As a condition of this grant, a minimum of 50 percent of all technical equipment had to be purchased in Germany, ensuring compatibility in technical standards. Joint Polish–German border patrols commenced in 1998, a joint force was created, and a weekly binational coordination meeting initiated. That year, the German government offered another 9 million DM grant for new technical equipment for the border police *Straz Graniczna* and regular police units, permitting the establishment of short-circuit intracommunication, compatible with the German system and able to access international data storage systems (*FAZ*, August 28, 1998). Between 1999 and 2002, German border police BGS (since 2005: Bundespolizei) invested more than €5 million in ongoing cooperation with CEE border police forces, offering training, supplying vehicles, IT, and infrared detection equipment aimed at the "democratization and modernization of outdated border police forces" as far east as Georgia (Bundesgrenzschutz 2002, 25). BGS also provided training and technical expertise in the framework of the EU PHARE project for the training and equipment of EU-10 border guards,[14] including policy transfer through the so-called twinning process.[15]

An area in which Poland was able to maintain a degree of autonomy and fended off top-down Europeanization and unilateral German pressure concerned the visa policy towards its eastern neighbors. Given the close cultural and economic ties with Ukraine, especially the Western sections that had been Polish prior to the Potsdam Treaty, the government sought to avoid alienating its eastern neighbor and suppressing small-scale cross-border commerce. Such concerns proved well grounded, for the 1998 introduction of tougher requirements for crossing the border, including the "randomly" carried out economic self-sufficiency test, led to widespread public protests in the East, even including street blockades.

From the mid-1990s, the policy approach towards immigration became notably less liberal due to direct and indirect pressure to conform to Western expectations. The official application for EU membership was lodged in April 1994 and negotiations commenced in March 1998, with the Justice and Home Affairs chapter being negotiated from May 2000 onwards. Lavenex (1998, 223) points to the importance of the "Budapest Process" in shaping CEE policy, a forum that united European interior ministers and focused on preventing and reducing undocumented migration. Thus the 1997 Aliens Act was influenced by legislative approaches in Italy, Austria, and especially Germany, though not clearly by top-down Europeanization. It introduced genuinely new concepts into Polish law, notably the temporary residence permit and carrier sanctions (Art. 68). In asylum regulation, the impact of policy transfer was even more pronounced. Thus the concept of "manifestly unfounded application" was introduced; applications had to be submitted at the border[16] or within

14 days of entering national territory. Transit migrants thus were forced to apply for asylum in Poland or, failing to do so, could be deported. This horizontal policy transfer constituted a form of *pre-emptive obedience*.[17] The June 1996 Council of Ministers meeting in Warsaw was accompanied by an ostentatious and unprecedented series of police raids throughout the Warsaw region, leading to approximately 400 undocumented refugees being arrested and sent to the new detention camps (*Gazeta Wyborcza*, October 1, 1996). The hitherto laissez-faire stance towards immigrants turned back by the German border guards began to change. While previously administrative visas had been issued in such cases, entailing the requirement to leave Polish territory within a certain period of time and via a specified border crossing, in practice a thinly veiled invitation to attempt another Polish–German border crossing, immediate detention was now pursued. Though detention for up to 90 days for undocumented migrants had been introduced in 1995, only from 1996 did this practice become standard.

The feeble and juvenile NGO community was ill-prepared to counter an increasingly more restrictive stance towards unsolicited immigration (interview PL-NGO-1). The government justified this shift by claiming asylum was being "abused" and voicing nebulous security concerns (Kicinger 2005, 12). The number of asylum seekers had risen from 843 in 1995 to 3,212 in 1996 and 3,544 in 1997; new historical records for a country that only in 1997 constitutionally embedded the right to asylum. But the adoption of Western concepts in asylum demonstrated the willingness to incorporated transferred policy products, while the NGO sector was still underdeveloped and Western governments had to be convinced of one's bona fide credentials as a good future European citizen. Some measures were very unpopular, in particular the raising of entry requirements along the eastern border which spearheaded negative economic repercussions. Asylum figures began to rise, though primarily as implications of Dublin I and II, and the ongoing and escalating conflict in Chechnya. According to the Office for Repatriation and Aliens, figures hovered around 3,400 until 1999, increased to 4,662 in 2000, and have since reached 8,079 annually. In the parliamentary debates, the government resorted to employing rhetorically themes of security, highlighting the criminality of foreigners and concerns over the porosity of the border, and the importance of adhering to "modern" European norms. By the mid-1990s, the government stance towards asylum seekers had changed for good. In fact, the unclear distinction between general categories of foreigners and asylum seekers caused concern among several IGOs, including the UNHCR and the Helsinki Foundation, and it was mainly due to their intervention and lobbying that appropriate modifications were made. A mid-1998 police raid, entitled "project foreigners" (*akcja obcy*) and aimed at Romanian Sinti, seemed yet again destined to demonstrate "toughness" to the rest of the EU.[18]

NGOs were organizationally too weak to respond to the rapid onslaught of legislative restrictions. In the field of labor migration, the December 29, 1989 Act on Employment (Journal of Laws of 1989, No. 75, item 446) had already introduced the obligation to obtain agreement from the regional (*voivod*) labor office before work permits to foreigners could be issued, which was required to consider regional labor market trends before doing so. The December 14, 1994 Act on employment and combating unemployment (Journal of Laws of 1995, No. 1, item 1) reiterated this requirement, limited the initial duration of such work permits to one year and fixed the cost at the equivalent of one average monthly salary, thereby de facto reducing its scope to high-wage positions. The number of work permits issued annually throughout the early 1990s hovered around 11,000 according to the Ministry of the Interior, with employers exercising little lobbying activity and demonstrating very little interest in more liberalized provisions (interview PL-BUS-1). This began to change from the late 1990s onwards, as larger companies and Polish branches of MNCs began to attract more Western high skill migrants and communicated this development to the employer associations (interview PL-BUS-1). Partially in response, the September 9, 1997 Decree of the Ministry for Labor and Social Affairs specified exceptions to the work permit requirement for foreign employees and finetuned work permit procedures. In light of emerging short-term labor market shortages, the government looked favorably upon applications from its eastern neighbors, especially Ukraine, Russia, and Belarus. Partially as a result of the flexibilization, the number of work permits issued rose to 15,307 in 1997 and reached 21,487 in 2004; 74 percent of which applied to key staff in multinational corporations and only 339 to unskilled workers (Kicinger 2005, 20). Meanwhile, the absence of visa requirements for Ukraine in particular opened the path to flexible if undocumented economic migration into the agricultural, construction and personal care sectors. Local discontent notwithstanding (interview PL-UNI-2), the relevant 1997 Act on Aliens which rendered deportation of illegally employed foreigners possible was not applied rigorously, with labor inspections in 2003 unearthing only 2,700 cases of illegal employment of foreigners (Kicinger 2005), despite estimates of up to 500,000 undocumented employees. This undocumented pool of immigrants constitutes a flexible buffer that renders advocacy of regularized low-skill migration less pertinent, while relatively bureaucratic and costly procedures deter employers from work permit applications in such instances.

Another migration domain that escaped foreign adjustment pressure concerned ethnic Poles. The interest group Polish Community Association (Wspólnota Polska) was concerned over the relative neglect. Return migration was generally favorably regarded, especially if it involved highly skilled ethnic Poles from the West or Ukrainian-born ethnic Polish university graduates that graduated benefiting from special scholarships. But despite the small numbers involved, there was concern over abuse and lack of integration. Hence, the modification of the original Law on Citizenship of February 15, 1962, effected in the form of the November 9, 2000 Act on Repatriation (Journal of Laws 2000, No. 106, item 1118), clarified the procedures for returning ethnic Poles obtaining citizenship, but also limited such claims from eastern applicants to the regions politically part of Poland prior to 1945.

By the late 1990s, the unilateral German influence ceded in importance relative to full-scale top-down Europeanization. The 2001 Act consists almost without exception of simple transposition of AMP (Iglicka et al. 2003, 18; Kicinger 2005). This is perhaps unsurprising in light of the Polish government's positions vis-à-vis AMP. In the accession negotiations, the government described its stance, adopted on October 5, 1999, as follows: "Poland does not request transition periods or derogations in the area. [...] Poland declares its full readiness to commence the process of adherence to [all legally binding *acquis* provisions for full members] immediately after its accession to the EU" (www.negocjacje.gov.pl/neg/stne/pdf/stne24en.pdf). The Commission repeated in every annual report the necessity to step up border controls along the eastern frontiers (Iglicka et al. 2003, 18). The "wining and dining" culture that resulted from the PHARE agreements and the regular consultation between officials at the Polish Ministry of the Interior and the Commission created epistemic communities (interview PL-GOV-1) and aided in the diffusion of ideas and the acceptance of a common discourse, lingo, and ideology.

In some areas, the impact of EU regulations was immediate; in others policy design introduced ongoing EU-level negotiations in anticipatory obedience. Though the final EU family reunification directive was only accepted in September 2003, the Polish 2001 Act already introduces key new elements, entailing the right to family reunion encompassing the spouse and underage children after three years of legal residence. The creation of a separate category of temporary protection for (civil war) refugees not recognized under the Geneva Convention also constitutes direct top-down Europeanization, as this "download" in pre-emptive obedience anticipated the EU directive passed in July 2001 (2001/55/EC on minimum standards for giving temporary protection in the event of a mass influx of displaced persons) and was heavily influenced by EU-level discussions (interview PL-GOV-1). A third example includes a crackdown on "bogus" marriages, a legal provision seemingly inspired by Western models and not previously present in Polish law. The 2001 law continued the trend towards more restrictive policymaking: thus hitherto five, rather than three years of legal residence were required to apply for permanent residency, police powers were extended, new obligations were created to prove legal employment status, "safe third country" and "safe country of origin" concepts, already introduced in 1997, were finetuned, and fast-track processing of "manifestly unfounded applications" became possible. Visa policy was overhauled, creating one universal visa type and abolishing the previous distinction between visitor visa with or without work permit, transit visa, and repatriation visa for ethnic Poles. This revision also constituted a form of anticipatory obedience to European developments, abolishing visa types peculiar to Poland and nonexistent in the EU-15. Once again, security of the borders was a theme prominent in the parliamentary debates, but more dominant yet was the invoked need to accept top-down Europeanization. The political opposition criticized the somewhat piecemeal approach of the government. Following the recommendation of Commission advisers, the Act also created a specific administrative unit, the Office for Repatriation and Aliens within the Ministry of the Interior to coordinate policymaking in deportation, asylum and refugee status, residency, return migration, and citizenship. In sum, this act can be aptly described as fully-fledged top-down Europeanization with NGOs being effectively marginalized and unions and employers taking scant interest as labor migration was not affected.

 The pace of legislative change was relentless and the June 13, 2003 Act on Aliens continued the previous trend. It was accompanied, however, by a regularization of long-term undocumented residents (contained in Art. 154), permitting applications for a one year residency and work permit and eligibility for legalization thereafter, provided economic self-sufficiency and employment can be demonstrated. Without seeking to deny its partially humanitarian inspiration, this measure also helped "clear the decks" and justify an even more repressive stance towards those unwilling to avail themselves of the offer. Most beneficiaries were long-term Vietnamese (46%) and Armenian (38%) residents that survived economically by drawing on activities within tight ethnic networks, but had hitherto avoided contact with the authorities. Refusal was an initial concern; however, the approval rate reached 78 percent. As a condition of "going legal," personal data was now stored on the new general databank, in some instances even involving individuals refused legalization where "justified by the state security and defence as well as by the public security" (Art. 154.6; sic).

The ambition to be perceived as a reliable and acquiescent good European once again took precedence over genuinely domestic considerations. Impending EU enlargement neutralized all opposition. Discussions about migration policy became less inclusive and more dominated by technocratic advisors and debates about style, rather than substance. Even in instances in which no explicit EU directive existed, but only "soft law," loose templates, or indeed no immediate model, the internalization of the Fortress Europe ideology encapsulated in the process of perceiving oneself as part of EU-rope spawned restrictive policy across all sectors, but especially in border control and surveillance. But neither the relevant ministry nor parliament were subject to much lobbying by a largely underdeveloped NGO sector and the only very limited interest of unions and employers. The main intervention pertaining to the 2003 Act from the NGO sector, ultimately unsuccessful, came from the Helsinki Foundation and then only entailed an unambitious proposition of creating special favorable categories for foreign graduates of Polish universities. With feeble or even nonexistent lobbying, the government's competence monopoly went unchallenged.

The aim of the two key legislative acts of 2003 was twofold, first, to step up the repressive powers of the state apparatus and, second, to create a new category of temporarily tolerated (civil war) refugees, not eligible for full-scale Geneva Convention protection. In addition, relevant EU directives were implemented. More specifically, the June 13, 2003 Act on Aliens (Journal of Laws 2003, No. 128, item 1175) increased the duration of legal residency required for applicants for permanent residency to five years, stipulated the conditions to be met for temporary residency, containing the interesting stipulation that individuals engaged in "an economic activity ... beneficial to the national economy and in particular, contributes to the development of investments, transfer of technology, innovations or job creation..." (Art. 53 1.2) were to receive preferential treatment. For the first time, economistic competition state rhetoric found explicit mention in Polish legislation. The act also outlined police powers and increased the legal avenues for detention and deportation (Art. 88 ff.), especially in cases of undocumented work, residency, lack of sufficient financial funds to prove economic self-sufficiency, and, most strikingly, for being deemed a "threat to the state security" (Art. 88 5 ff.) and for tax evasion (sic, Art. 88 8+9 ff.). In line with the security theme, it created a mandatory identity card for foreign residents (Art. 72 ff.) and a central databank of foreign residents (Art. 124 ff.).

The second major legislation, the Act on Granting Protection to Aliens within the Territory of the Republic of Poland (Journal of Laws 200, No. 128, item 1176) followed EU notions by refining the "safe country of origin" and "safe third country" concept and notably creating the new category of tolerated refugee in instances in which the "right to life...freedom...safety" (Art. 97 ff.) was being threatened, following a decision by the Council of Ministers (Art. 106 ff.). In addition, the EU asylum "procedures" directive was being implemented, considering "particular vulnerabilities" and covering unaccompanied minors. The EU directive on temporary protection was interpreted in a way that permits applicants within the new temporary protection category to work and to exercise the right to family reunion, on both counts surprisingly moving above the more restrictive interpretation chosen by Germany. But this was a minor abrogation and the general past pattern of obedient top-down Europeanization with no effective interference by national veto players surfaced.

The final April 2005 amendment (Journal of Laws 2005, No. 94, item 788) did not imply major modifications, though it changed a few regulations pertaining *inter alia* to the registration of foreigners. Most importantly, it implemented another two EU directives on family reunion and long-term TCN respectively, allowing the latter an application for permanent residence after five years provided that economic self-sufficiency, a regular income, and health insurance can be proven. In substantive terms, this did not modify the existing legislative framework much, but simply codified the existing status quo. Once yet again, EU directives were merely interpreted in direct top-down fashion.

Minor autonomous initiatives prevailed regarding the imposition of visa requirements for Ukraine, Belarus, and Russia. This time there were no street blockades. The Polish government pre-empted such protests by refraining from imposing administrative fees on applications, thereby appeasing EU and German pressure, while ensuring that commercial trade links and undocumented short-term labor migration flows could continue. The measure continued the 1998 practice of demanding proof of self-sufficiency and a bona fide invitation from Polish residents.

Little legislative activity ensued regarding labor migration and labor market interest associations are content with the status quo (interviews PL-BUS-1, PL-UNI-1, PL-UNI-2). The official work permit procedure is lengthy and bureaucratic, although it permits for a few exceptions, especially foreign spouses of Polish citizens, foreign language teachers, athletes, pharmacists, and artists, following the legislative change in the form of the June 1, 2004 Act on Promotion of Employment and Institutions of the Labor Market. In general, the Polish government does not yet see the need for specific high-skill labor recruitment programs (interview PL-GOV-1, PL-GOV-2) unlike other Central European governments, notably the Czech Republic and Slovenia, and neither is there much appetite among employers (interview PL-BUS-1). Undocumented labor in low-skill sectors, especially agriculture, informal language tutoring, babysitting, care for the elderly, and gastronomy continues. It is not always clear whether the relatively lax enforcement at the local level is politically motivated or simply a function of administrative incapacity. Despite first skill shortages surfacing, emigration, and brain-drain problems, there are no current plans to liberalize labor migration policy or revive and remodel a briefly functional bilateral labor agreement with Ukraine, but this may well change in the medium term. In its reaction to the EU Green Paper on Labor Migration, the Polish government very clearly highlighted the problem of high structural unemployment and expressed skepticism towards the prospect of AMP extension in this field, demonstrating its willingness, however, to contemplate sector-specific flexible labor recruitment (Korys and Weinar 2005, 27) in line with the de facto policy today.

As in the Irish case, "uploading" policies and bottom-up Europeanization prove difficult if national level policy itself is still in flux and when reputational effects assume such priority. Thus there is no evidence of bottom-up Europeanization based on Polish initiative.

Italy: Invisible Walls for Extracomunitari and the Labor Needs of a Dual Economy

An emigration country for decades, Italy became a net country of immigration in 1973, though a substantial portion of the migrants of the 1970s were returning Italian emigrants from northern Europe. Internal

South–North migration assumed important dimensions from the 1950s onwards; between 1945 and 1975 close to 7 million Italians emigrated. Since the 1980s, immigration from outside the EU has increased. While any attempt at presenting reliable data is frustrated by diverging estimates, sloppy accounting, frequent double-counts, confusions of stocks and flows, and a sizable, though difficult to quantify, undocumented sector, available sources indicate a spectacular rise of absolute numbers of immigrants. Numbers rose from 263,731 (133,431 non-EU) residence permit holders in 1985 to 677,791 by 1995 (563,158 non-EU) and 2,193,999 (2,040,530 non-EU) in 2004, according to combined data from charity Caritas and the national statistic bureau Istat.[19] The vast majority of immigration is work-related (61% for 2000).[20] Migration policy in Italy is replete with paradoxes, reflected in five patterns.

First, until the mid-1980s, immigration has been neither actively solicited nor prevented. Instead, it has been tolerated, as long as figures were low and most migrants were either in transit northwards or entered the labor market. This may be somewhat surprising, given Italy's unfavorable demographic developments with a record low average birth rate of 1.3 births per woman. Calls for active labor migration management by business have spawned annual migration quotas since the passage of the 1990 Martelli law. Since 1986, physical border and labor market access control have become more pronounced as migration has become more politicized domestically and developments elsewhere in Europe have led to horizontal policy transfer. The far right has resurfaced as a formidable national actor and as elsewhere a link between certain migrants and security threats has been constructed. But the legacy of a minimal migration policy, selective application, and an unspoken reliance on migrants either to return eventually, move north, or integrate into the labor market continues to shape policy. Obviously, this stance is influenced by a geographic position that renders enforcement of physical border control impossible.

Second, "borders" in the Italian context are perhaps better conceived of in the internal exclusionary rather than the geographic sense. A rudimentary welfare state with emphasis on employment-related old age pension provision and a strong reliance on private charitable foundations and the family to offer services the state is unwilling to offer, migrants' access to welfare services is extremely limited. Migrants are routinely declared ineligible for public housing by local authorities. Though the 1998 Law 40 mandated the creation of "reception centers" for migrants, implementation at the local level has been often delayed, extremely limited, or is nonexistent. With the undocumented sector of the economy accounting for between 25 and 40 percent of GDP, employing an estimated 4 million, of which approximately 700,000 are immigrants, according to Caritas (2004), casual, highly precarious, poorly paid employment is available regardless of work permit status. Considerable bureaucratic burden, poor administration, and the logistical difficulties involved in applying for work permits, the "walls" surrounding access to regular employment and work permits are not negligible. Employers offering undocumented employment, including immigrant-owned businesses, obviously lack incentive to regularize employment status. "Borders" exist in other areas of migration regulation: six years of legal residency are required for applicants for permanent residency. Though the exact contours of these regulations have been the object of various partisan reforms during this period, foreign residents need to reapply consistently for extensions of their work permits and/or residency permits.

The Italian refugee and asylum system has been traditionally rudimentary. Top-down Europeanization has been of particular relevance. Though constitutionally guaranteed (Art. 10) very little legislation implemented and regulated asylum. Until 1990, the Geneva Convention was only applied to refugees from Eastern Europe. From 1990 until 2002, the Central Commission for the Recognition of Refugees (*Commissione centrale per il riconoscimento dello stato di rifugiato*) was charged with decisions on asylum and Geneva Convention refugee status, until the Bossi–Fini Law devolved decisions to local commissions. Recognition rates are extremely low, though not publicly available. Financial support for either category is strictly limited financially and temporally. Renewable one year permits are available to non-Geneva civil war refugees, but again based on administrative discretion. Asylum does figure in the migration mosaic, but it is tightly enclosed and conspicuously absent from public and media debates. Since 1998, the annual number of applicants has oscillated around 12,000 and only dipped significantly below that in 2002 to 7,200, according to UNHCR (Chaloff 2005*a*). Access to citizenship is even more tightly constrained. Generally based on *ius sanguinis*, minor exceptions are made for Italian-born residents that have continuously resided in the country until the age of 18. The Law 91 of February 1992 increased the period of legal residency required prior to lodging applications for citizenship to 10 years, though there is no legal entitlement. Administrative discretion is enormous and 90 percent of successful claims arise out of marriages to Italian citizens.

Third, much more so than in the other countries examined in this study, but much in line with developments elsewhere in southern Europe (Ribas-Mateos 2004), there is a considerable gap between legislation and actual implementation. Laws are implemented with delay or only partially. Regular legalization campaigns between 1986 and 2006 permitted undocumented migrants to regularize their status post hoc, thus highlighting the particular combination of lack of will and administrative enforcement capacity. Lackluster enforcement of labor law, wages, and residency regulations assumes such proportions that the political willingness to alienate employers seems unclear. Spectacular police crackdowns on highly visual undocumented migrants—notably foreign prostitutes—are mere windowdressing.

Fourth, not unlike France, the basic contours of migration policy have persisted despite considerable microlevel policy shifts depending on the political color of the government. These grand contours consist of more or less eagerly administered external border controls coupled with finetuning instruments of legal migration and, least vigorously pursued, the integration of existing migrant communities. The Left has generally adopted a pragmatic and at times liberal stance. Influences include the relatively recent experience of Italian emigration, a strong current of solidarity with the less developed world, represented not only by NGOs but also by the trade union movement, and a pragmatic approach to opening legal avenues for immigration and offering regularization to existing undocumented migrants to avoid social exclusion and the inferior, often exploitative working conditions associated with the shadow economy. The Right has pursued a much more restrictive approach, embodied prominently by the Bossi–Fini Law; yet it has not fundamentally altered the framework of Italian migration policy and has had to continue a pragmatic stance towards labor migrants on account of the economic interests of its business clientele. Even the far right *Lega Nord* and *Allianza Nazionale* proved remarkably acquiescent to pragmatic labor migration regulation given the importance foreign domestic aides played in the households of its northern bourgeois voters.

Fifth, Italian governments have applied a carrot-and-stick policy regarding source countries. The battle against undocumented immigration is linked with regulated economic migration; sending countries are immediately rewarded for cooperation with ongoing preferential quotas. This explicit link has been established in the 1998 Law 40 (also referred to as the Turco–Napolitano Law). While regulated labor migration channeled through work permit application processes was already part of the 1986 Law 943, subsequent legislative measures have further refined and elaborated the procedures for setting outright ceilings for annual labor migration. The 1998 law specified that consideration has to be given to the state of the labor market in setting these quotas, including unemployment among natives and resident non-EU citizens. The 2002 Bosso–Fini Law added a regional dimension, by permitting regions to formulate requests for specific contingents.

Countries that have been rewarded with preferential quotas include a number of Mediterranean neighbors, such as Albania, Morocco, Tunisia, and Egypt, and also Somalia, Nigeria, Moldova, Sri Lanka, Pakistan, and Bangladesh.

The quota system is not only a Machiavellian foreign policy tool, but it also serves the economic interests of Italian employers. These preferential quotas, amounting to a total of 22,000 slots for 2005, up from only 6,000 for 1998, are contained within more general quotas (99,500 for 2005, up from 58,000 in 1998), covering a high proportion of seasonal workers, especially in agriculture, temporally limited contract workers and a tightly limited number of self-employed. There was also a since suspended quota for highly skilled managers or executives and IT professionals, in addition to unlimited slots for nurses. Furthermore, special consideration is given to university professors and researchers, certified translators and interpreters, domestic aides and au pairs, trainees, language teachers, sailors, athletes, artists, temporarily posted workers, and accredited foreign journalists (Chaloff 2005a, 14).

In practice, the final decision on the quota size is made within the Ministry of Labor, permitting both unions and employers considerable influence in official and less visible forms of lobbying, consultation, and even codecision making.

System of Political Economy: High Tech Islands and Seas of Low-Skill Assembly

The Italian political economy is not well captured by Hall and Soskice's dichotomy; Hancké, Rhodes, and Thatcher (2007) consider it part of the French-style mixed market economy model, while Amable (2003, 102–14) associates it with "south European capitalism," which displays the following traits: a quantitatively and qualitatively pivotal position of small firms, product competition via the price rather than quality mechanism, strong employment protection among large firms, but more precarious employment relations in smaller firms and generally a tendency towards dualism in employment relations and the structure of the labor market, relatively high ownership concentration and bank-based financing with a relatively small role for equity markets, moderate levels of social protection with a high concentration on pension provision and low expenditures on education. Dualism is a striking feature of Italy's labor market, with the lower tier made up of short-term precarious contracts, which can be typically found in smaller firms and offered to new entrants to the labor market. The substantial undocumented labor market can obviously be subsumed in the second inferior category. Outsourcing has contributed to the growth of inferior forms of employment in this secondary sector (Guidi et al. 1974; Milanaccio and Ricolfi 1976). By contrast, the primary labor market used to be characterized by substantial employment stability in the legacy of the 1970 Workers' Rights (*Statuto dei Lavoratori*) and the subsequent 1975 wage-inflation link (*scala mobile*), though labor market deregulation under the Prodi and Berlusconi governments has undermined some of these earlier achievements and the *scala mobile* was abandoned in the early 1990s. Migrants sometimes, though not always, find themselves in this secondary tier of the labor market, regardless of the legal status of their employment and indeed residency. Employment in the lower tier is problematic, given the weak legal protection afforded, inferior wages, and absence of pension benefits. Some economists have claimed that more flexible and adaptable labor market structures have only been rendered possible through the use of immigrant labor (Macioti and Pugliese 1991).

The small specialized clusters of high value added production typical of north-central "Third Italy," often seen as the outgrowth of regionally specific competition strategies (cf. Bagnasco 1977; Storper 1997), one classical example involving textile and footwear production in the Emilia–Romagna region, have increasingly outsourced low value added basic components of their production chains to pseudo-independent subcontractor units either partly or entirely in the shadow economy, relying to a significant degree on foreign employees and sometimes even migrant-owned. Similar patterns of corporate restructuring can be observed in the construction industry. Thus two recent studies, undertaken by the regional Unioncamere Emilia–Romagna and the national organization respectively, highlight the concentration of migrant-owned enterprises in commerce, including the ubiquitous Internet and telephone cafés, and construction (Chaloff 2005*a*; Unioncamere 2006). The predominance of microcompanies, accounting for more than 50 percent of all Italian companies and their proliferation, is partly driven by attempts to circumvent taxation and labor law that only applies above certain employment level thresholds. Gastronomy, tourism more generally, health care, transportation, food processing, textiles, furniture, as well as agriculture are major employers of immigrants, defined as sectors in which one-third or more of all new hires in 2004 were immigrants according to Excelsior Unioncamere (Chaloff 2005a, 6), though independent of corporate restructuring. Just as the origin of immigrants is highly diverse,[21] so does labor market integration differ. Migrants are generally concentrated geographically in the north and center, extending beyond confines of the golden triangle between Bologna, Turin, and Venice, with high concentrations in Emilia–Romagna, Friuli–Venezia–Giulia, Marche, Umbria, Lombardy, Veneto, Piedmont, Tuscany, and Trentino–Alto Adige, as evidenced in new employment contracts starting in 2003 by non-EU citizens reaching between 20 percent (Tuscany) and 39 percent (Trentino–Alto Adige) of the total according to Inail (Chaloff 2005a, 5). In these regions, immigrants work in the primary and secondary sectors. The presence of foreign employees is much lower in the south and on the islands, where most find employment in the primary sector, often in an undocumented fashion. Strikingly, this means that there is a direct negative correlation between unemployment rates and the presence of foreign employees. Attempts to associate Italy with its Mediterranean neighbors are confounded by the stark regional division between north and south, which to some extent spillover into production strategies, product market competition tactics, production patterns, and employment patterns. The wealthy North, boasting near full employment, is driven by financial services, iron and steel, automobile production, high-end niche production in ceramics, footwear and textiles, and food processing centering largely around the triangle, but extending further north to the Swiss and Austrian borders and south as far as Umbria and Manche, and including the Third Italy, often localized somewhere between Tuscany and Frulia. In the much poorer southern *mezzogiorno* along with the islands of Sardinia and Sicily, agriculture, fishing, and not least tourism are pivotal sources of economic activity. Italy's economy is characterized by the dominant domestic market share and quantitative importance of often family-owned internally- or bank-credit financed SMEs on the one hand and a small number of internationally active companies on the other. Given the remarkable regional economic distinction, distinct regional labor recruitment preferences exist. Southern employers are less active and interested, with the exception of the agricultural sector, while northern employers are more active in calling for labor recruitment. Similarly, the employer associations representing SMEs (Confcommercio), artisans (Confartigianano), or both (Confesercenti) are somewhat more vocal than the representative of larger employers (Confindustria).

The relatively immigration-friendly stance assumed by the Italian union movement, composed principally of the left-wing CGIL (*Confederazione Generale Italiana di Lavoro*), the Catholic center-right CISL (*Confederazione Italiana dei Sindicati Lavoratori*), and the centrist UIL (*Unione Italiana dei Lavoro*), has surprised some foreign observers (Watts 2002). Not only have the unions consistently lobbied the government in favor of higher legal labor migration quotas, but they also generally assume a humanistic stance regarding other forms of migration and the regularization of undocumented migrants. Such a position is less perplexing if one recognizes that immigrants are very much perceived as part of the unions' core clientele. Unionization rates among immigrants have risen strongly in recent years; Mottura (2000) reports a 22 percent increase for the CGIL between 1998 and 2002. Given declining unionization rates and an ageing constituency, immigrants make a valuable contribution. The unions do not only want to improve the working conditions and wages for (documented) immigrants and improve their often precarious situation, but they also want to ensure that especially undocumented immigrants are not used by employers to apply downward pressure on wages and working conditions. The size of the shadow economy obviously is a concern (cf. Watts 2002, 73–9), as is the state's unwillingness, and in the South its inability, to take decisive action against it (Notizie Ansa 2002*b*). Henceforth, all trade unions have been involved in organizing immigrants as members and shop stewards, but also offering social and legal services. Watts (2002) chronicles how all three unions have established special immigrant liaison offices from 1982 onwards, with the CGIL even creating a special representative commissioner for immigrant concerns reporting to the national executive council until 1997. More strikingly still, in the late 1980s, UIL and CISL have created parallel union networks (the Unione Italiana Immigrati—UNITI—and Associazione Nazionale oltre le Frontiere—ANOLF—respectively) that reached out to *all* foreign employees, including undocumented migrants or legal immigrants in illegal employment. All three unions continue to maintain special departments and particular spokespeople for immigration matters. A recent statement of the UIL general secretary Guglielmo Loy encapsulates the prevailing sentiment very well: "[the problem is not] regulating or minimizing the flow, but how to reduce the lack of integration. [...] the next step is thus to empower local governments as actors and to allot them sufficient financial resources to create adequate social support" (press release UIL February 5, 2003). An official position paper of the CISL (2006) agrees in substance, highlighting the sectoral labor market needs, the worrying demographic development, and not least the moral responsibility of a wealthy country to accept immigrants. Criticism is reserved for "rigid and complex procedures linking the residency with the working permit, thus rendering the situation of immigrants confusing, contradictory and precarious." The CGIL concurs; its 2006 15th annual congress resolutions (CGIL 2006) call for a legalization of all undocumented migrants, implementation of a sophisticated asylum law, liberalization of citizenship, improvements in integration, devolution in administration of the residency permit, and an end to the general lack of congruence in Italian migration law.

The unions have thus been generally very concerned about immigrants' needs and wants and have supported both legal labor migration and the legalization of undocumented residents and hence their integration into the primary labor market. This stance might be influenced by the collaboration with the employers in helping coadminister labor migration quotas. In organizational terms, the degree of centralization and internal cohesion of the three main national unions are low (Ebbinghaus and Visser 2003), but the representation among clientele is a comparatively impressive 34 percent. In ideational terms, there is broad consensus regarding migration regulation and the unions have been both outspoken in their lobbying efforts and highly active in organizing immigrants as members.

The employer associations are generally supportive of actively managed labor migration. They take no official stance regarding undocumented (labor) migration, which contributes considerably to short-term precarious forms of employment, aided by the predominance of small companies in the Italian economy. Watts (2002, 98) reports that up until the 1990s, the associations representing predominantly SMEs and artisans, that is, Confartigianano, Confcommercio, and Confesercenti, were much more enthusiastic about labor migrants, as labor shortages in the North clearly surfaced and affected lobbying strategies regarding the 1998 law. But since then, Confindustria, where voting behavior is based on financial contributions, hence advantaging larger companies, has likewise discovered an interest in the issue (Codini 2001). All associations have specific spokespersons regarding immigration. Considerable lobbying activity is targeted at the Ministry of Labor, regarding the labor quotas in particular (interview ITA-GOV-1; ISMU-Cariplo 2001, 26), as will be discussed below. In March 2005, the highly active president of Confindustria's Young Entrepreneur Association Anna Maria Artoni organized a conference whose title reflects the new attitude among the clientele: "Immigration as a resource for Italy: Attracting Talent to win in the Global Competition." The main association's president Luca Cordero di Montezemolo agrees, as his speech to the 2005 assembly documents (Confindustria 2005).[22] The employers' main interests are threefold: first, a more comprehensive approach to immigration regulation, rather than the traditional somewhat ad hoc and piecemeal approach; second, improved integration of resident migrant communities, and third, active steering of labor recruitment, partly for economic, but also for demographic reasons (Confindustria 2001, 2002, 2005). In organizational terms, degree of centralization and internal cohesion is also relatively low (Ebbinghaus and Visser 2000), while approximately 51 percent of all Italian companies are organized. Good access channels exist to the Ministry of Labor, while lobbying avenues to the Ministry of Interior have only recently been constructed and are not as robust.

Structure of Interest Intermediation

Well-developed networks link the ministry of labor, unions, and employers. This has become relevant since the 1998 Law created an elaborate labor immigration quota system that was based on input provided both in qualitative terms and in quantitative requests from the social partners. Nonstate actors have been offered the opportunity to partake in the administration of immigration ever since and permitted sponsored immigration on a discretionary case-by-case basis, including sponsoring by unions, NGOs, or even individuals. The sponsoring system entailed 10,000 annual slots for one year residency permits and the permission actively to search for employment, while financial responsibility rested with their sponsors. New 2002 right-wing legislation abolished these slots, replacing them with the new one-stop shop *sportello unico*, jointly managed by the Ministry of the Interior and Ministry of Labor, which administers work visas based on a labor market examination to be conducted within 20 days. One condition is the guarantee of at least the minimum wage as well as the employer vouching for housing and deportation costs for the applicant, in case of unemployment or failure to apply for renewal. The non-EU Immigrant Service division within the Ministry of Labor determines the annual quota, at times very late in the year and lower than the employers in particular would want (interview ITA-GOV-1), but always following consultation with unions and employers and in consideration of estimates of labor market needs from regional labor offices. These regional offices also solicit input from the social partners, which highlights the two levels at which quantitative contours, sectoral distribution, and qualitative categories are influenced. These categories include preferential quotas for the "privileged countries" (*paesi privelegati*), *inter alia* Albania, Tunisia, Morocco, and Romania; executives or managers, seasonal workers, contract workers, self-employed, job seekers and IT specialists (both abolished in 2002), and nurses. Preferred treatment is allotted to countries with which readmission agreements exist.

Employers and unions are invited to comment on legislative drafts by the ministry and received periodically for consultation meetings. Their input is very seriously considered as they are perceived "as being on the frontline and having detailed expert knowledge which we here in the ministry in Rome cannot develop" (interview IT-GOV-1). Thus labor market interest associations not only effectively comanage labor migration administration, but they are also influential actors in shaping policy design and amendments.

NGOs are involved in the administration of migration through comanagement of local integration funds and projects. Catholic charity Caritas is particularly active in providing social services to migrants, but also in shaping public opinion and lobbying the political Right (Briguglio 1993). This includes support of the administration and provision of the very patchy accommodation services provided for immigrants. NGOs also actively lobby the Ministry of the Interior, generally requesting more liberal provisions regarding asylum seekers, refugees, and family reunion. NGOs also regularly submit petitions for legalization campaigns. However, there are no established regular meetings or consultations with NGOs on the part of the Ministry of the Interior and their input into policymaking remains extremely limited; they are perceived as "radical" and "out of line" with general strides in policy development (interview GOV-ITA-1). By contrast, the lobbying campaigns for legalization programs, supported by the CGIL, though not the CISL, have been ultimately successful and lobbying aimed at parliamentarians, for example in the early 1990s alliance Patto per un Parliamento Anti-Razzista have likewise successfully colored policy. But weak centralization and internal cohesion, limited financial and personnel resources undermine effective lobbying and the exertion of tangible influence on policy outcomes (Table 5.4).

Table 5.4. Developments in Italian migration policy

Development of immigration policy since 1931

June 26, 1931 Law No. 146 on Public Security (*Testo Unico delle Leggi di Pubblica Sicurezza*), revised in 1940; Title V addresses foreigners; obliges foreigners to register with local authorities, permits immediate expulsion of foreigners convicted of a crime which implies a permanent ban on re-entry.

Additional decrees modify this law during the postwar era: in December 1963, the Ministry of Labor issues a decree containing the following provisions: residency and working permits are always linked, restrictions on the geographical movement of migrants may be imposed, a working permit shall not be issued to individuals already resident in Italy, immigrants returning to their home country may only return after three years; in the 1980s, additional decrees limit legal immigration.

December 30, 1986 Law No. 943 "on work and treatment of non-EU migrant workers and against clandestine immigration," grants right of equal treatment and equal social rights to foreign workers (though often de facto ignored), stresses importance of integration, provides framework of first major regularization wave, covering approximately 188,000 individuals over the course of its application until 1988, consolidates previous decrees relating to restrictive border controls and the limitation of legal (labor) immigration; foreign employees need to apply for working and residency permit from outside Italy for specific jobs, supported by their potential employer, these applications are only granted if no qualified Italian (or EU) citizen can be found for the position.

Institutionalization of a national council responsible for monitoring the housing situation of immigrants.

February 28, 1990 Law 39 ("Martelli Law") creates the framework for integrative measures, especially regarding education and housing, includes financing of these projects, but also the creation of immigration reception and service facilities, which are *implemented and administered by the regions*, but underwritten by the central government and attract 30–40 billion lire annual funding.

Mandates the issuing of annual "integration action plans" that include the issuance of annual quotas for immigrants (Art. 2) each October based on a decree jointly issued by the Ministry of the Interior, Foreign Affairs, Budgeting and Economic Planning and Labor that will incorporate the following considerations: the state of the economy and the labor market and the capacity of social and educational facilities to cope with immigrants, employers, and labor unions shall be consulted, but de facto no quotas are issued until 1998.

Art. 11 includes the introduction of measures aimed at rendering immigration regulation more "transparent" in consultation with NGOs; stepping up border controls: in 1990 (1991) 61,813 (56,000) non-EU citizens are not admitted at the border; obliges undocumented foreign residents that have entered Italy prior to December 31, 1989 to legalize their stay: out of 240,087 applications 221,000 are accepted.

Worldwide extension of Geneva Convention, creation of a central commission for the granting of refugee status, also responsible for asylum (*Commissione centrale per il riconoscimento dello stato di rifugiato*).

February 12, 1991 decree permits legal resident automatically to extend their residence for two years.

Implementation of this law is highly problematic, as many regions prove to be logistically (and to a lesser extent financially) incapable of implementation.

(*cont.*)

Table 5.4. (Continued)

Development of immigration policy since 1992

February 1992 Law No. 91 Reform of the 1912 Italian citizenship law that allowed applications for citizenship after 5 years of legal residence; TCNs need to demonstrate 10 years of residence before being permitted to apply for naturalization, process is entirely discretionary.

By contrast, facilitation of applications by "ethnic" Italians that can claim second- or even third-generation Italian ancestry and have resided legally in Italy for a minimum of three years, citizens of other EU countries (recognized refugees) can apply for citizenship after only four (five) years of legal residency, but need to surrender their original citizenship.

March 1998 Law No. 40 ("Turco Napolitano Law"), later merged into legislative Decree No. 286 of July 1998 (Consolidated Text (*testo unico*) "concerning immigration matters and standards concerning the condition of the alien"): revives the quota system (Art. 3, para. 4): "In one or more decrees issued by the Prime Minister, having first received the opinions of the interested ministers and parliamentary commissions, formulation is made, on an annual basis, and in accordance with the criteria and other indications contained in the planning document referred to under para. 1, of maximum quotas for the number of foreigners to be allowed to enter the territory of the State for salaried employment, eventually to meet demands of a seasonal nature, or for self-employment, with consideration being given to measures of family reunification and temporary protection, as stipulated under the provisions of article 20. Entry visas for salaried employment, on a seasonal basis, and for self-employment, are issued within the limits of the above mentioned quotas. Should the annual planning decrees not be published, the quotas shall be set in accordance with the last decrees published, under the provisions of the present unified text for the preceding year."

Ministry of Labor thus makes concrete recommendation to Prime Minister based on consultation with social partners and regional labor offices.

Creation of "sponsoring system" (*prestazione di garanzia*): employers, unions, but also NGOs or individuals (including "self-sponsoring") may sponsor individual foreigners who are granted a one-year residency permit to look for employment, sponsor is legally liable for cost of accommodation, maintenance, health insurance, and deportation (if applicable); approximately 15,000 individuals enter Italy under this system.

Special annual quotas for seasonal workers are created, permitting employment for up to six months that may be extended up to nine months, past seasonal workers receive preferential treatment and may receive a residency permit for up to one year if they are being offered an unlimited employment contract by their employer.

Labor quotas are deliberately used to reward or punish countries for cooperation with the Italian authorities in border control matters: "These decrees also set aside, on a preferential basis, quotas reserved for nations not belonging to the European Union, and with which the Ministry of Foreign Affairs, acting in concert with the Ministry of Internal Affairs and with the Ministry of Labor and Social Security, has signed accords designed to regulate entry flows and procedures for reentry." (Art. 21, para. 1).

Foreigners who lose their jobs may not be consequently deported: "Loss of employment does not represent a valid motive for rescinding the residence permit of non-European workers or their family members residing on a legal basis." (Art. 22, para. 9).

Specifies criteria for family reunion (Art. 30) granted to spouses or children of Italian citizens or legal long-term residents.

Creation of permanent residency and working permits (*carta di soggiorno*) for long-term residents that can prove a minimum of five years of residency.

Permits forceful detention of undocumented migrants or individuals entering the national territory illegally for up to 30 days, creates detention centers, referred to as "centers of temporary stay and assistance" (*Centri di permanenza temporanea e assistenza*; CPTAs); deportation decisions are hitherto made by local authorities with possibility to appeal once against the decision made by the civil judge (*giudice ordinario*) permits tougher penalties for traffickers.

Though this law aims to end the "vicious cycle" of legalizing undocumented migrants and thus seemingly encouraging undocumented migration, in actual fact another legalization wave follows the passage of the law.

Government is obliged regularly to issue policy planning action plans for the next three years.

Creation of a Commission for Integration Policy, reporting to the Prime Minister's Office.

July 30, 2002 Law No. 189 ("Bossi–Fini Law") introduces *mandatory* fingerprinting for all foreign residents and the creation of a central database; abolishes sponsoring system, adds provisions for a central database of labor requirements based on input from regional and provincial labor offices, and even private agencies, creates one-stop shop office for working permit applications linked to provincial labor offices (*sportello unico*) that issue a "residency contract," rendering employer legally responsible for any costs associated with the foreigner's presence, including deportation measures where applicable, permits deportation of foreigners who have lost their employment after six months, residency and working permits are now only issued for a maximum of two years, period of legal residence required to apply for a permanent residency permit is being increased to six years; the annual labor quotas are no longer automatically renewed and may even be cancelled at short notice from year to year.

Family reunion rights are no longer automatically granted; family reunion based on marriage presupposes couple physically living together.

The central commission for the recognition of refugees is being abolished and replaced with seven regional commissions (Arts. 31–32); asylum seekers are first interrogated at the border and, if permitted entry, required to lodge their application with the regional administration (*questura*), if judged questionable or if asylum seekers have eluded police controls they are forced to remain in so-called identification centers (*centri di identificazione*); the aim is to cut the time required for processing of asylum applications from an average of 12–18 months to only 35 days, first appeals against negative decisions are dealt with by the same regional committee already responsible for the first verdict, second appeals do not prejudice deportation decisions, deportation orders can be executed immediately and usually are accompanied by bans on re-entry valid for 10 years; a number of additional measures apply to the falsification of documents, "trafficking," employment of undocumented migrants, re-entry despite applicable ban.

Following the implementation of this law on September 10, another legalization campaign covers 650,000 and thus more than the previous three waves combined (645,000).

Development of Immigration Policy Since 1990

Since 1990, immigration policy in Italy has been characterized by a three pillar approach, consisting of increasingly "tough" border controls, integration efforts towards existing migrant communities, and regulated labor migration. This general framework is set forth in the Left's 1990 Martelli Law and has proved remarkably stable, the major modifications contained in the 2002 Bossi–Fini Law notwithstanding. In practice, however, there is a considerable implementation gap at the grassroots level. All major legislative packages have been accompanied by legalization campaigns. In 2006, the Prodi government announced a major overhaul of the restrictive Bossi–Fini framework and has pre-empted such legislative changes by a major legalization program (*Le Monde*, May 25, 2006). The Martelli Law also marked an advance in refugee policy, as it ended the previously limited application of the Geneva Convention.

The 1998 Turco Napolitano Law finetuned earlier legislation and further elaborated labor recruitment policy. It consolidated and clarified existing legislation, specifying procedures for family reunion, long-term residency and deportation, and addressing the ad hoc tendency of immigration law development by institutionalizing a Commission for Integration Policy at the Ministry of Social Affairs (later renamed the Ministry of Labor and Social Policy). This institution finalizes the labor quotas immediately prior to authorization by the Prime Minister, and is also responsible for monitoring immigration, including permits, quotas, and legalization. In addition, a National Coordinating Body at the Labor and Economics Council CNEL was established, along with an advisory council (*consulta*) reporting to the Prime Minister's Office directly. Finally, local migration councils (*consiglio territoriale per l'immigrazione*) were set up in each of the provinces, often comprising representatives of NGOs, trade unions, employers, and professional or artisanal associations. A Commission headed by academic expert Professor Giovanna Zincone and comprising other academics and representatives of various ministries published two major reports on the "integration of immigrants in Italy" in 1999 and 2000,[23] while the *consulta* represents a forum for representatives of non-governmental organizations, ministries and local government. Finally, the CNEL acts as a neocorporatist plenum, uniting representatives of the social partners and local and national governments. Both the Commission and the Consulta were abolished in the 2002 Bossi–Fini Law; the CNEL tellingly remained active. The 1998 law also mandated the issuance of a policy planning action plan for the next three years, a remarkably vague document stressing the need for further "integration" of immigrants and venturing not far beyond simply reiterating the basic parameters of existing policy.

Henceforth, annual labor recruitment quotas were set forth (Art. 3, para 4), developed within the Ministry of Labor in consultation and based on the input both from the social partners and from regional labor offices throughout the country. The three key categories comprise salaried employees, self-employed, and seasonal employees, the latter receiving temporary working permits for sojourns of up to nine months. Given the remarkable amount of power the unions and employers can wield, all social partners established special departments and appointed spokespeople on migration. The social partners are enthusiastic about the possibility actively and tangibly to influence labor migration policy design (interview IT-GOV-1). Most controversially and irksome to the Right, the law also created a sponsorship system (*prestazione di garanzia*), permitting social partners, NGOs, Italian residents, and even applicants themselves to sponsor applications for one-year residency permits as the basis for employment search. During this period, the sponsor assumed full financial responsibility for the applicant's cost of living.

The Italian quota system is deliberately used as a foreign policy tool to reward or punish non-EU countries for migration control efforts, including not only accepting deportees but also active measures to detain transit migration from sub-Saharan Africa and South Asia. Albania, Tunisia, Romania, and Morocco were thus rewarded and in the case of the latter punished for efforts at arresting trans-Mediterranean immigration (interview ITA-GOV-1). In return, these "privileged countries" (*paesi privelegati*) were granted in 2000 annual quotas of 6,000 labor migrants each, including one category for individuals seeking "insertion into the labor market." That same year, the annual quota for non-EU labor migrants was set at 45,000. Egypt, Moldova, Nigeria, and Sri Lanka have been added since. Cooperation with third countries has proceeded apace; bilateral training programs with Libya and the Maghreb countries entail the joint establishment of job training programs with considerable input from Italian companies who are subsequently free to recruit the graduates.

The Right had pointed to immigration as one of the many purported failures of Romano Prodi's 1996–2001 "Olive Tree" (*Ulivo*) coalition during the 2001 electoral campaign, criticizing a purportedly excessively liberal stance (Andall 2007). The far right parties composing Silvio Berlusconi's "House of Liberty" (*Casa della Liberta*) coalition, the "post-fascist" National Alliance (*Alleanza Nazionale*) with its outspoken leader

Table 5.5. Legalization campaigns in Italy (source: Caritas di Roma 2000, 160, own research)

Legislative basis	Implementation	Date	Number of applicants	Accepted
Circulare Ministro di Lavoro December 17, 1979; March 8, 1980, March 2, 1982, September 9, 1982		December 31, 1980	5,000	5,000
Lege 943/1986	Lege 81/1988	December 31, 1986	118,349	118,349
D. L. 416/1989	Lege 39/1990	December 31, 1989	234,841	217,700
D. L. 19/1995	Lege 617/1996	November 19, 1995	258,761	147,900
D. P. C. M. October 16, 1998	D. lgs. 113/1999	March 27, 1998	250,747	214,421
Lege 189–2002		November 11, 2002	700,000	634,728

Gianfranco Fini and the radical Northern League (*Lega Nord*) with its populist figurehead Umberto Bossi, were particularly vociferous regarding immigration and pushed for immediate restrictive intervention. Some of its discourse was overtly xenophobic, highlighting the purported cultural, demographic, and religious threat to the Italian nation. The legislative result of all this clamor was the 2002 Bossi–Fini Law that sought to "toughen" immigration policy, yet left in place the basic parameters initially set forth by the Left. A more restrictive approach surfaces in the detailed regulations on long-term residents, rights to family reunion, and especially asylum and refugee processing procedures. Detention and deportation were facilitated, border controls stepped up. However, in the immediate aftermath of the law the hitherto largest legalization campaign regularized the status of some 650,000 individuals (see Table 5.5). This was all the more remarkable as by then all mainstream parties opposed further legalization programs and not even all NGOs advocated them. Even the trade unions were somewhat divided over the issue (Casadio 2002). The law also abolished the sponsoring system, a thorn in the side of the Right, and streamlined the working permit application procedures, creating a one-stop shop office (*sportello unico*) (Calavita 2005). The new residency contract that labor migrants were obliged to sign did maintain an element of the old sponsorship system, however, by rendering the employer legally liable for all costs associated. Despite rendering the labor migration quotas more contingent by permitting their immediate abolishment and ending the practice of using the previous year's figures as a template, in practice and despite some tinkering with the figures, they were maintained, owing not least to organized business advocacy (interview ITA-GOV-1; ISMU-Cariplo 2001, 26; Zuccolini 2002) Berlusconi proved unwilling to ignore. In fact, for all the rhetorical grandstanding, the law proved a lot less radical than its architects had intended. This moderation was not so much due to the pressure of NGOs and trade unions that organized several major demonstrations (Casadio 2002). Rather, within the moderate Right, both Berlusconi's own Forza Italia and the successor parties to the Christian Democrats, such as the Union of Christian and Center Democrats (*Unione dei Democratici Cristiani et di Democratici dei Centro*), several MPs criticized the first harsh draft of the bill, emphasizing the humanitarian values the Catholic heritage ought to entail. Such reference to Catholic social values was hard to ignore in the lower house Chamber of Deputies. The final result still entailed some of the more radical initial proposals, notably the mandatory fingerprinting of all (documented) foreign residents. But it is a very long way from "zero immigration" and conforms to the pan-European trend towards distinguishing between burdensome undesirables and useful labor migrants. The system of labor migration was modified, but not abolished. In fact, the law sought to strengthen this element by creating the legislative basis for a central database of open positions, based as a novelty also on the input of private employment agencies. In light of the deteriorating economic situation, expanding the quotas would have been difficult to defend politically. The advocacy of the social partners and especially the employers to maintain the quota system was successful (interview ITA-GOV-1). The Far Right encountered an ultimately complex reality—many of northern Italy's prosperous businesses supported active labor migration, as did the National Alliance's wealthy northern clientele, itself not averse to employing the domestic services of foreign employees, legal or not. Tellingly, the "toughest" provisions are thus reserved for "undesirable" refugees and asylum seekers. For labor migrants, the door was not opened any further, but it remained open.

The Impact of Europeanization

Given the relatively recent nature of most legislation, it is unsurprising that the Italian government has not been particularly active in shaping AMP. At the domestic level, immigration emerged as a major public policy issue only in the early 2000s and the nascent AMP seemed to imply relatively little top-down impact at first, except for political pressure from other Schengen member states on Italy and other southern European states to impose more stringent external border controls as a precondition to join the Schengenzone (Whitaker 1992). But such demands largely coincided with national policy developments and were thus easy to accommodate (interview IT-GOV-1). The Italian government had historically supported the movement of migration from the third to the first pillar and the strengthening of the binding nature of legal instruments (Joint Declaration of the German and Italian Foreign Ministers concerning the 1996 Intergovernmental Conference, July 15, 1996). But interest in AMP began to grow only when Italy emerged as a major destination of entry immigration to the EU, especially trans-Mediterranean migration.

In some issue areas, especially asylum law, the government accepted passive top-down Europeanization, given the rudimentary state of development of national legislation. Some of the Bossi–Fini provisions were inspired by what the government anticipated becoming mandatory AMP in the near future; thus the government adopted a stance of pre-emptive obedience regarding the two major EU asylum directives. The establishment of reception centers for asylum seekers is another instance of "downloading" EU policy ideas. The Italian government also found inspiration from policy approaches in other member states, including the electronic transfers of asylum seeker dossiers as in the Netherlands (interview ITA-GOV-1).

Regarding labor migration, the Italians were notably more reluctant to permit AMP interfering with the national quota system, strongly supported by unions and employers, and its use as a foreign policy tool, hoping instead to present this approach as a model that other European countries might seek to emulate (interview ITA-GOV-1). Since these quotas are linked to readmission agreements and general cooperation in "managing" migration, it would be possible to imagine the EU establishing similar agreements, though this may prove difficult in practice, as such treaties might be easier to administer bilaterally and member states have proven extremely reluctant to surrender the power to set quotas autonomously and individually as became evident during the unhappy abortive launch of the EU labor migration directive in 2001. The Italian initiative to introduce at the EU level a similar link between migration quotas and "cooperative" behavior on the part of third countries during the EU presidency in 2003 encountered fierce resistance, especially from Germany.

As a relative newcomer to immigration, Italy responded somewhat ambiguously at first, and did not develop a comprehensive legislative approach until the late 1990s. Since then a three-tier approach has emerged that combines relatively strict border controls, aided by the EU's Neptuno Project for sea border control and joint border controls with Austrian and Slovenian border guards, efforts at integrating existing migrant communities, unfortunately often marred by lack of funding and capacities or indeed political will at the local and regional level, and the active soliciting of labor migrants. By contrast, asylum is a relatively recent area of activity, in which legislation and procedures were still enough in flux to be seriously affected by the restrictive 2002 Bossi–Fini Law. The NGO community has generally not been particularly successful in influencing the agenda due not least to organizational pathologies, while the unions and employers have been active comanagers and coadministrators in influencing quantitative and qualitative annual recruitment targets.

Conclusion: Late Discovery, Top-Down Europeanization Trends

While these three countries have radically overhauled their often antiquated legislation only very recently, they have embraced relatively similar trajectories. More actively managed migration has included more rigorous border control measures, new and generally less comprehensive definitions of citizenship, the (re)definition of access to political asylum, and various schemes to channel actively solicited labor migration. Governments of all political colors have been sympathetic to actively communicated employer concerns about labor shortages in Ireland and Italy, while in Poland high unemployment and the continuing emigration of highly skilled migrants ("brain drain") create a more complex scenario, in which undocumented low-skill low-pay migrants are often tolerated, but legalization seems unlikely and is not in the interest of employers, while recently modified regulations permit high-skilled migrant recruitment.

Regarding asylum policy, humanitarian NGOs have been considerably less successful in shaping policy, though an indirect influence on MPs in Italy with invoking of Catholic social values has helped tone down more restrictive legislative proposals. In Ireland, despite formal consultation procedures, the actual impact of NGOs is often not clearly discernible, and there is ground for suspicion that such procedures may be merely ritualistic, without leading to tangible policy input.

Europeanization is of considerable importance in new immigration countries. Top-down "downloading" has been of particular prominence in Poland, given the eagerness to join the EU, the relatively weak bargaining position even of the largest CEE country and the geographically prominent position with respect to *cordon sanitaire* functions. In light of the rudimentary and often anachronistic nature of migration and asylum policy in these countries, the top-down impact, especially in asylum and refugee policy, is highly significant. Where previous national approaches deliberately obstructed asylum applications like in Italy or did not entail clear procedures as in Poland, top-down Europeanization will have a fundamental, but also potentially liberalizing, impact. Ireland stands apart somewhat due to the "opt-out" of AMP, which leads to selective top-down Europeanization and clever rhetorical marketing of policy initiatives as European inspirations. EU policy developments are both of considerable interest to Irish policymakers and seek to inspire national solutions, motivated by the desire to design mutually compatible migration policy.

Unsuccessful bottom-up Europeanization has arisen out of the Italian bilateral initiatives in labor migration control. The suggestions contained in the Seville resolutions suggest that such link between labor migration quotas and cooperation in border control and deportation is highly representative of the *zeitgeist* of European migration policy and may inform future AMP design.

Notes

1. National frameworks proved widely recognized benchmarks, accepted even by the United States and by multinationals loath to recognize trade unions—since the mid-1980s, only 15 percent have been willing to do so (EIRO 2004*a*). By 2000, the economic boom had unleashed significant inflationary pressures, so that the emphasis shifted to assuring wage restraint, a union concession sweetened by tax reductions. This carrot could no longer easily be offered in 2003, as personal taxation rates were already minimal. Meanwhile, rank and file union members displayed discontent over wage restraint behind a backdrop of high inflation and a real estate boom, while employers were not prepared to accept wage growth above inflation levels (EIRO 2004*b*). While a compromise level was found (EIRO 2004*c*), this issue is likely to delay future negotiations.
2. The data collected by the Department of Industry responsible for the work permits indicates that fewer non-EU citizens are employed in highly skilled

professions such as managers, professionals, and technicians, while central statistics office data would indicate that about one-third of all non-EU citizens work in such occupations.

3. In addition, it specified a legal professional background for members of the Refugee Appeals Tribunal.

4. Interestingly, in the Senate debate on July 7, 2003, the minister of justice, equality, and law reform explained the rationale for the new bill with reference to an obligation arising from Europeanization: "In the context of the Amsterdam treaty and in line with our policy of participation in the Schengen convention to the greatest extent possible consistent with maintaining the common travel area arrangements between us and the UK, we have opted into Articles 26 and 27 of the convention and thus the various Council directives which supplement those articles. Article 26, in particular, concerns itself with the operation of entry controls, as does the associated Council Directive 2001/51/EC. The provisions at Sections 2 and 3 of the Bill fulfill Ireland's obligations under these two instruments as far as carrier liability is concerned, and this new section will implement our remaining obligations under the instruments" (http://www.irlgov.ie/debates-03/s3Jul/Sect2.htm#7).

5. Thus, the total number of Polish citizens in Germany alone increased from 171,500 in 1988 to 220,400 the next year and a total of 285,553 by 1992. The numbers of asylum seekers and ethnic German *Aussiedler* from Poland increased accordingly throughout the 1980s, but levelled off in 1989 and decreased thereafter (Statistisches Bundesamt 1992).

6. The negotiations proceeded in five stages. First, conformity of Polish legislation with the EU *acquis* was assessed ("screening") between April 1998 and November 1999; second, both sides prepared their negotiation positions between September 1998 and December 1999; third, on the basis of these negotiation papers, the actual negotiations unfolded between November 1998 and December 2002; and fourth, the accession treaty was settled, including negotiations on the most difficult issues between December 2002 and April 2003. Finally, the signing and ratification occurred between April 2003 and May 2004 (Leiber 2005).

7. An examination of the Polish government's negotiation position (available in English at www.negocjacje.gov.pl/neg/stne/pdf/stne24en.pdf) is highly revealing. The government is keen to point out its full compliance with the *acquis* in migration, asylum, and border control matters since 2000, with a somewhat later compliance regarding the issue of visa. There is no evidence whatsoever of any reserve vis-à-vis the EU position, despite the adverse impact that the imposition of visa requirements and stricter border controls along the eastern border will have both on relations with the eastern neighbors and indeed on small-scale commerce between the border regions, including some of Poland's poorest regions.

8. A representative of the Office quoted an even lower recognition figure for Geneva Convention refugee status of 3 percent (interview PL-GOV-2).
9. The NSZZ Solidarność argued—not entirely convincingly—that this may lead to a "deepening of the social dumping by inflow of investments aimed at exploitation of cheap work force before the eventual liquidation of barriers."(NSZZ Solidarność 1999).
10. Thus, Ekiert and Kubik (1997) report:

    In 1989, as a result of the "Round Table Agreements," Solidarity was relegalized in its trade union formula. The OPZZ and Solidarity became the two major competitors within a highly pluralistic, competitive, but politically divided trade union sector. Solidarity had 1.7 million members, while the OPZZ boasted a membership of around 4 million; it was, however, a decentralized organization with both largely independent industrial/professional unions and regional structures (WPZZ). The OPZZ lost some 2 million members since 1989 and several unions left the organization, including the powerful Federation of Miner Unions with some 350 thousand members. [...] In sum, the new postcommunist labor sector, that emerged as a result of organizational competition and several splits of old and new organizations, is the best example of the continuity with the communist past.

    During the first few years of democratic consolidation, Solidarity was not able to regain its pre-1989 status and strength. Its membership was a fraction of what it had been in 1980/81 and its staff were mainly newcomers. In the National Committee, only 30 percent of the members had been trade union activists in 1980/81 and those who had were mostly at the factory level. Solidarity was organized in 38 regions, 16 national industry secretariats, and nearly 100 industry branch secretariats. [...]

    Even though the Polish labor sector was dominated by two powerful federations, it too was fragmented. In 1993, there were 1,500 trade unions and some 200 nation wide federations. Polish trade union law adopted in June 1991 set the framework for preserving a fragmented and decentralized union structure. It was not unusual for the employees of one factory or firm to be represented by more than 10 different union organizations. [...] Another example of high fragmentation is provided by the mining sector. Polish miners were represented by 19 unions.

11. (Dziennik Ustaw, No. 27, items 236–239 of March 11, 2004 and the April 20 Act on the Promotion of Employment and Labor Market Institutions, Dzienne Ustaw 2004, No. 99, item 1001).
12. In addition, the April 10, 1974 Law on the Census and Personal Identification Documents specified the obligation to carry personal identity documents, while the December 23, 1977 Decree of the Ministry of Interior Affairs regarding the Rules, Processing, and Forms of Documentation regarding foreigners provided additional regulations concerning noncitizens.

13. That same year, readmission agreements were also signed with the Czech Republic, Slovakia, Ukraine, Romania, and Bulgaria. Exemplary of these agreements, Art. 6.1 of the Agreement on the Legal regime on the Ukrainian–Polish State Boundaries, Cooperation and Mutual Support on Border Issues of January 1993 states: "Each Party shall readmit citizens of third states or persons without citizenship who have illegally crossed the common state border from its territory. If less than 48 hours have elapsed from the time of the illegal crossing by this person of the common state border, the readmitting Party shall readmit such a person without prior notification and unnecessary formalities."
14. Between 2004 and 2006, the Commission had provided €380 million to the new member states to reinforce their administrative capacity to implement and enforce the *acquis*, while more than €900 million for 2004–2006 has been established to help seven of the new member states to finance initiatives at the new external borders of the Union (http://europa.eu.int/comm/justice_home/fsj/enlargement/wai/fsj_enlarge_intro_en.htm). Poland's share has been a total of €45.5 million until 2001, while another payment by the German government amounting to €100 million was made in 2000.
15. Twinning involves cooperation and the posting of preaccession advisors from pre-2004 EU member states to EU-10 ministries or administrative subunits. Polish–German cooperation focused on border control along the eastern border, a 2000 trilateral Dutch–German–Polish project focused also on visa policy, while cooperation with Austria was aimed at migration and visa policy more broadly, encompassing not only the border police but also the Ministry of Foreign Affairs, and the Office for Repatriation and Foreigners. Another cooperation partner in training border guards has been the UK.
16. This requirement was later struck down by the Supreme Administrative Court *Naczelnz Sad Administracyjny*, as it would have de facto resulted in *refoulement* and thus violated the Geneva Convention.
17. At the time, the following relevant nonbinding EU-level resolutions existed: Resolution of November 30, 1992 on manifestly unfounded asylum applications; November 30, 1992 on a harmonized approach to questions concerning host third countries; November 30, 1992 on countries without real risk of prosecution; June 20, 1995 on minimum guarantees for asylum procedures (Kicinger 2005, 13).
18. Thus the spokesman of the Polish border police told Gazeta Wyborcza on October 29, 1998: "We are implementing the provisions of the Aliens Law. The aim of this *akcja* is to demonstrate the credibility of our country prior to admission to the EU. After all our eastern border will be the eastern border of the united Europe"(quoted in TRANSODRA 1999).
19. But due to the noted problems with the reliability of Italian data, these figures should perhaps be best regarded as indicative of broad trends. There are divergences between the figures the Ministry of the Interior itself reports

and those offered by the national bureau of statistics Istat. Caritas' data tend to indicate higher numbers. It should be noted that the number of registered foreigners tends to be lower than the number of residency permits in circulation (cf. Currle 2004, 310, Chaloff 2005b).

20. Thus, in 2000, 850,715 (of which 782,041 non-EU) of the total 1,388,153 (68,674 EU) residence permits awarded were for work purposes (Annuario Sociale figures, quoted in Calavita 2004, 351).
21. The first foreign migrants to arrive came from former Italian colonies Somalia and Ethiopia. They were followed by arrivals from Albania and Yugoslavia. Only over the past few years has Italy become a transit and target country for refugees from the Middle and Far East (China, Sri Lanka), the Indian subcontinent, the Maghreb, and sub-Saharan Africa, as well as Latin America (Peru, Brazil, Dominican Republic). Major source countries of immigration include Albania (142,066), China (60,075), the Philippines (65,353), Egypt (32,841), Yugoslavia (36,823), Marocco (159,599), Tunisia (45,680), and Romania (68,929) out of a total foreign population of 1,388,153 million, including some 151,798 EU citizens (absolute figures as of December 31, 2000, collected by the Ministry of the Interior).
22. He pointed out that such measures were necessary, as the "second generation of immigrants will have diverse problems and possibly larger ones than the first generation, as they will be individuals born on our territory and thus fairly possessing all the legal rights and they will no longer be willing to accept only those jobs refused by Italians." (*La seconda generazione di immigrati porrà problemi diversi e forse maggiori della prima, perché costituita da persone nate sul nostro territorio, che vorranno giustamente avere tutti i diritti e che non si accontenteranno solo dei posti di lavoro rifiutati dagli italiani.*)
23. Premiero Rapporto sull'integrazione degli immigrati in Italia November 30, 1999, Secundo Rapporto sull'integrazione degli immigrati in Italia December 13, 2000.

6
Managed Migration, Populism, and Pragmatism

Whoever claimed that the state is "retreating" has obviously never studied migration policy. Control over access, in the sense of both territory and entitlement, remain central state functions, even true of the radically redesigned neoliberalized twenty-first century competition state. The often forceful and militarized display of state power in this process of policing access control functions is congenial with, not contradictory to, enhanced and facilitated avenues for business-friendly labor migration. The new paradigm of managed migration, mastering (*maitriser*), and guiding (*steuern* or *gestire*) migration flows, entails the active solicitation and encouragement of human resource potentials on the one hand, perceived as a scarce commodity, access to which is subject to fierce competition from other European destinations alongside the more established countries of emigration, and more restrictive procedures and administration of humanitarian migration channels on the other. The latter are increasingly portrayed as a burden, a potential drain on social benefit transfer systems and potentially more serious sinister social pathologies, exacerbating existing social problems related to integration failures of previous migrant generations and their descendants. No mainstream political party in contemporary Europe wants to reverse immigration or even halt it altogether, regardless of how xenophobic public opinion in some EU member states may be. Instead, a bipartisan consensus has emerged to open up tightly constrained "tradesmen's entrances." But such "select pathways" (Menz 2002) are correlated with less liberal administration and regulation with respect to the reception, recognition, and treatment of asylum seekers and refugees and conditions for family reunion related to these humanitarian channels. Though there is no compelling rationale behind this observed correlation, the reasoning in government circles appears informed by a waning commitment to the Geneva Convention and the often erroneous presumption that asylum seekers cannot be integrated into the labor market and thus constitute a drain from an economistic perspective and a menace to societal and social cohesion in the long term.

The strong contention informing the analysis in this book is that policy and politics matter strongly. Trade unions and especially employer associations have been pivotal actors in lobbying, shaping, and in some instances even co-administering economic migration policy. Structural changes to European economies, notably trends towards transnationalization, tertiarization, more flexible, individualist and post-Fordist production patterns and the specialization of political economies inherent in different corporate production and competition strategies usefully highlighted in the varieties of capitalism literature (Hall and Soskice 2001) entail the need for broadened and ameliorated entry channels for labor migrants, a claim submitted by employer associations across Europe, skillfully linked to mellifluous competition state rhetoric falling on fertile ground in government circles keen to accommodate. Different organizational characteristics, notably degree of centralization, internal cohesion, and representation among clientele facilitate or impede lobbying strategies, while divergences of systems of political economy across Europe account for different labor recruitment strategies by employers that in turn spawn distinct economic migration policies. Nongovernmental organizations similarly attempt to influence governmental regulation of migration flows, especially humanitarian access channels, but are hampered by organizational pathologies, often feeble finances and resources and little political clout. They find their task much more challenging and generally affect much less tangible change.

While the key emphasis of this book has been on nonstate actors and their activities in shaping governmental migration regulation, there are obviously other actors who exert powerful currents, notably the media and far right parties. Capitalizing on fears and anxieties arising from rapid societal and economic change, the Far Right has often successfully cast migrants as the personified aliens around whose rejection the increasingly disenfranchised globalization losers can rally. Political apathy and voter abstention have emerged as significant trends, not least as a reaction to the curious blandness that a neoliberal consensus among the major parties of the Right and Left produces. In this climate, the Far Right appeals as the politically incorrect "uncensored" and highly colorful purveyor of an agenda that may be utterly wrong-headed, but sets itself apart from the uninspiring dictate that neoliberal economic and social policy mean for all spheres of public policy and to which the mainstream parties have succumbed. The depressing result is the *lepenisation* of mainstream political parties, where the Far Right successfully colors not only the rhetoric employed towards "undesirable" migrants and migration policy but to some extent the policy agenda as well. Past patterns of migration regulation, sketched in Chapter 2, also continue to influence policy design, but a current critical juncture permits significant momentum for change. Family reunion, in quantitative terms easily the largest immigration channel, is an issue that deserves by far more scholarly attention than it has thus far, similarly the newly emerging nexus between migration and development, especially relevant for African countries, ought to inspire future academic inquiry; however, neither is at the center of this study.

Europeanization and Migration Policy

Tangible AMP is emerging at last, but its nascence is not proceeding anywhere near as quickly or ambitiously as some of its advocates had hoped or its detractors had feared. The jealously guarded national veto power, concerns over adjustment costs to top-down Europeanization, national legacies and traditions in migration policy, and serious concerns over communautarizing this policy domain in general, prevalent among employer associations, conspire to impede rapid and comprehensive progress in this domain, notwithstanding rhetorical commitments on the part of member state governments.

Carefully pre-empting and considering member state concerns through consultation in the CIA, the Commission had proceeded steadily and relentlessly, despite often fierce and protracted battles with individual member states or coalitions. Between 1999 and 2004, the Commission shared the right to initiate policy proposals with member states, but bottom-up Europeanization, despite its promise to minimize transaction costs for successful architects of agenda-setting coalition-building, has proven an arduous, contingent, and extremely difficult process to manage. Thus the Italian proposal for explicit EU level migration quotas, linked to foreign policy objectives vis-à-vis third countries and modelled on the national blueprint model, failed to garner support among governments skeptical of EU labor migration initiatives, notably Germany and Austria, but to some extent also France. But despite the apparent difficulties associated with seeking to "upload" or transfer a certain national regulatory model to the European level, bottom-up Europeanization initiatives, including unsuccessful ones, can have long-term effects in shaping language and ideas.

In the often protracted and embattled politics of decision-making, national governments will often seek to minimize the adjustment cost of top-down Europeanization and sustain status quo ante national arrangements by negotiating for exceptions, abrogations, and loopholes. As the empirical analysis has demonstrated, Europeanization also gives rise to two-level games, where national governments encounter nonstate actors seeking to influence national policy, while at the European level attempting to represent the accumulative national interest position vis-à-vis other national delegations. Some governments display remarkably sly strategies in delaying European decision-making until home battles have been resolved, including tactical concessions to nongovernmental actors, as the German position regarding political asylum motives demonstrates. Other delegations successfully upheld nonintrusive EU level regulation to maximize national room for maneuver as the Austrian resolve to adhere to restrictive national quota systems for family reunion aptly illustrates. Despite the formal opt-out, Irish policymakers carefully monitor EU level developments and cunningly portray top-down Europeanization as an alleged necessity, as the case of the implementation of the two key EU asylum directives highlights.

Generally speaking, governments of new immigration countries have been less skillful in playing such two-level games, however, and top-down Europeanization along with pre-emptive policy learning processes of anticipatory obedience have been particularly pronounced. Where migration regulation is skeletal, incoherent, antiquated, nascent, infantile, or nonexistent, top-down Europeanization cannot be easily absorbed, but will engender paradigmatic and comprehensive changes. The impact of Europeanization has thus been formidable in recasting southern and eastern European migration policy. In the second contention, the influence of domestic actors in this two-level game has been emphasized, but the empirical analysis demonstrates strongly that unions and employers are far more successful and privileged in this process.

The politics surrounding more ambitious movements towards harmonization on asylum, refugee, and family reunion policies will undoubtedly be similarly characterized by national delegations seeking to defend national particularities to prevent costly adjustment processes and proposing national regulation patterns as possible European models, as argued earlier. Some bottom-up Europeanization proposals make a reappearance by stealth: thus the Italian carrot-and-stick approach has spawned the "mobility partnerships" with African countries, while the ill-fated British proposal to erect detention camps for asylum seekers in source countries has informed the pilot camps in Tanzania.

NonState Actors and National Migration Policy: Revisiting the First Contention and the VoC and Sectoral Hypotheses

Unions and employers are pivotal, if commonly neglected actors in the politics of migration. The first contention submitted in this book is that the different models of political economy shape distinct strategies for labor recruitment from abroad. Employers seek access to a steady pool and ideally an unimpaired flow of labor migrants to fill shortages that cannot be recruited for locally, due either to skill shortages or to labor market shortages that may be related to the lack of appeal particularly low-wage service sectors exert. They couch political demands in the rhetoric of competition for scarce and valuable "best brains" that are in demand globally and petition ministries of the interior to create amenable and unbureaucratic access channels. CME production patterns, to some extent mirrored in geographical subregions of MME, including in France and Italy, require mainly highly skilled well-trained labor migrants that can easily be integrated into a high value-added production pattern, with contributions both to the secondary and tertiary sectors. LME production patterns necessitate a steady supply of labor migration into both low-wage low-skill service sector positions where poor working conditions and wages combined with structural flexibility requirements lead to low staff retention. But LME employers also seek to attract highly skilled migrants, as high-skill shortages cannot always be successfully addressed in a generalist education system, while the significant advantage of such a generalist training system lies in the facilitated integration of high-skill migrants into the labor market. The first hypothesis therefore helpfully and accurately indicates the divergence in labor recruitment advocacy strategies.

CME employers are most interested in labor migrants in the tertiary, but to some extent also the secondary sector, while LME employers very clearly focus almost exclusively on service sector employees. In countries in which the primary sector still accounts for a more sizable component of the economy, employers will advocate liberalized labor migration into these sectors, either under the auspices of bilateral treaties as in Italy, in the form of EU-10 nationals as in Ireland or through a laissez-faire approach and liberal visa policy regarding Ukraine as in Poland. The second hypothesis is thus confirmed.

Worth mentioning, though for obvious reasons not central to this analysis, is the role of undocumented migration, which in some countries dampens the need for regulated formalized low-skill migration channels. Deregulated labor markets, feeble union representation at the grassroots level, and a lack of capacity or motivation to impose adherence to standard working conditions all combine to render reliance on undocumented migrants a feasible and even tempting proposition for employers in search for a well-motivated and acquiescent workforce. Where undocumented economic activities assume substantial proportions, "black in black" employment is easier to undertake. Widespread lack of adherence to standard wage and working conditions by French SMEs thus has curbed enthusiasm for employer demands for low-skill migration channels. Ultimately speculative, as difficult to substantiate, is the allegation that facilitated visa access for Ukrainians and minimal enforcement of working conditions are functional equivalents for low-skill migration programs. It is both politically difficult to demand labor migrants for positions that do not require specialist skills and financially more lucrative to position certain jobs within the undocumented and largely unregulated segment of the labor market.

But if calls for unskilled migration are politically difficult to sustain or perhaps not worth pursuing due to the availability of alternative strategies, advocacy of skilled migration is no easy feat, either. Organizational faults, including ideological and organizational subdivision, low centralization, poor internal cohesion, and a feeble membership base often compromise unified lobbying strategies. Constructing new formal and informal avenues of access to ministries of the interior is similarly daunting, as even existing neocorporatist networks tend to connect with ministries of labor. Compounding the organizational problems identified in this study is the current political and economic climate in Europe that is anything but conducive to demanding legislation that facilitates additional labor migrants, with relatively high unemployment, lackluster economic growth, and strong popular antipathy to additional immigration. Advocacy proceeds regardless, of course, but it often assumes somewhat covert formats, advancing through petitions, regularly revived contacts with amiable parliamentarians, "informational events," which may involve think tanks such as Germany's *Initiative Neue Soziale Marktwirtschaft* or the French *Institut Montaigne* and similar lobbying activities through formal and informal channels. In countries with an existing legacy of neocorporatist governance, labor market interest associations are particularly likely to be consulted over issues that impact upon their core domain, namely, labor market and social policy. Thus the Italian social partners are not only consulted but indeed submit requests for new labor migrant quotas and categories in the abstract and petitions for individual cases in the more concrete sense.

Less decisive perhaps, but still significant, was the involvement of the German social partners in the two expert commissions on migration that produced major policy recommendation agendas. Immigration features prominently on the agenda of Irish social partnership meetings. Similarly, in countries with no such neocorporatist tradition, employers and unions need to exert more influence to establish access to apposite ministries, as is apparent in France, to a lesser extent the UK, and with particular vehemence in Poland. But the British CBI was consulted, deriving its position from a poll of member companies regarding new migration regulation, and the French MEDEF was consulted with respect to "chosen" migration and is content with the facilitation of skilled labor migration under the auspices of the Sarkozy Law. The empirical evidence suggests that employer associations have been successful in influencing liberalized labor migration policy conducive to their interests. Organizationally strong employers stand a better chance of influencing governments, as is apparent in Germany and to some degree in France, Italy, and Ireland.

Trade unions support managed labor migration. They have long abandoned the more reticent and in some cases decidedly restrictive stance towards labor migration that pervaded among labor unions in France, Italy, and to a lesser extent the UK and (West) Germany in the 1960s and early 1970s (Haus 2002; Penninx and Roosblad 2000; Watts 2002). This orientation is ideologically legitimated with a rediscovered emphasis of notions of international solidarity, antiracism, and equality. On a more practical level, the reorientation can be attributed to concerns over the negative effects the emergence or persistence of undocumented labor market segments will have on the negotiation position and indeed wages and working conditions. Trade unions are certainly not averse to managed labor migration at all, though they do not as actively and eagerly pursue this goal as employers and expend much less effort on lobbying. The notable exception of the French left-wing CGT union demonstrates that at least in some sections of the labor movement there is concern over exploitative guest worker-style recruitment. Reaching out to labor migrants—and even more so to the second and third generations of descendants of migrants—becomes a crucial component of the quest to organize a clientele that is quantitatively increasingly relevant, but has traditionally been neglected. Italian trade unions are particularly active in this respect, organizing even undocumented migrants.

If labor market interest associations clearly constitute active and important players in shaping national migration policy, the same cannot be said of humanitarian NGOs. These groups commonly face considerable institutional hurdles from a state apparatus that regards them with skepticism, if not open hostility. Where NGOs are not involved in the delivery of services to migrants the state cannot or will not provide, a common pattern among those oriented towards religious values or even directly funded by religious organizations, and conducive to co-option, relations are often characterized by mutual distrust and aloofness. Impaired by limited financial means and thus personnel and outreach capacity, undermined by ideational tensions between more cooperative and dialogue-minded organizations on the one hand and more confrontational and anarchist-oriented groups on the other, NGOs encounter significant hurdles in liaising with governments. Successful lobbying is additionally impeded through encountering ministries of the interior responsible for overseeing law enforcement and being highly influenced by a "securitization" agenda that conflates immigration with crime, drugs, terrorism, or similar real or constructed threats to national security. Even where more formalized consultation fora for NGOs exist, such as in the UK and Ireland, they seem to be merely of symbolic significance with no readily discernible impact on policymaking. Underfunded, overworked, and with little or no established links to ministries, NGOs face the ungrateful task of finding creative ways of lobbying for more liberal asylum policy. Lobbying might target sympathetic parliamentarians, as in the wake of the Italian Bossi–Fini Law or Germany's 2004 legislation. Though informal consultation with ministries of the interior occurs in the UK, Ireland, France, Germany, and much less frequently in Italy and Poland, serious doubts about the actual consequences these exchanges occasion are entertained by actors on both sides (interviews PL-NGO-1, PL-GOV-1, DE-GOV-1, DE-NGO-1, FR-GOV-2, FR-GOV-2, FR-NGO-1, IT-GOV-1, IRL-GOV-1, IRL-NGO-1, UK-GOV-1, UK-NGO-1). The impact of lobbying by NGOs thus appears severely constrained. However, more confrontational tactics, employed by the French *sans papiers* movement and its supporters along with the antideportation movement frequently involved in direct action against airlines and the state apparatus, demonstrate that organizations willing and able to pursue more nontraditional means of shaping policy at the grassroots level can be more successful than might be assumed. The underdevelopment of civil society actors in Poland deserves special mention.

The Political Economy of Non-state Actors' Preferences: Revisiting the Second Contention

European employer associations have (re)discovered labor migration for three principal reasons. First, structural change to the European economy implies rapidly changing and quickly developing sectors that cannot as easily and readily recruit locally. There is a greater incentive to free-ride on foreign educational systems by recruiting skilled labor migrants, who could not be easily substituted with locally trained personnel given the time lag involved. Such new production systems occasion labor demands at short notice and difficult to forecast, rendering the option to recruit internationally even more attractive. Semi-permanent free-riding does entail the danger of structural neglect of educational and training system faults and institutionalized artificially depressed wages in affected sectors. Even if some of the demand for personnel can be satisfied locally, *flexibility* in personnel management can be gained that permits temporary limited recruitment or recruitment at short notice depending on the seasonal extension of production, for example, in gastronomy, tourism, construction, domestic services, care for the elderly, and agriculture. But such flexibility is cherished also in high-skill sectors, such as information technology, medicine, pharmaceuticals, and biotechnology.

Second, employers might prefer labor migrants to domestic applicants for reasons that are more difficult both to publicize and to defend politically. Migrants may be more willing—or desperate enough—to undertake the "dull, dangerous and dirty" work associated with the secondary tier of the labor market (Piore 1979). Employers may well prefer to have certain jobs carried out by employees working illegally—whether of migrant origin or not—or at least knowingly subcontract subcomponents of production processes out to companies that tender bids calculating on the use of substandard working conditions. This is the more unpalatable rationale behind "tolerating" undocumented migration that the Marxist literature of the 1970s highlighted: "the ruling class gains both through the possibility of utilizing cheap labour, and through giving privileges to indigenous workers in order to encourage the development of false consciousness" (Castles and Kosack 1973, 481), pointing to the use of immigrants as a reserve army of workers in Marx's sense. Recent welfare state restructuring and especially the odious active labor market policy implemented across Europe have attempted to force former recipients of welfare state transfer payments into the labor market, causing a deterioration of wages and working conditions. This policy, unsuccessful and costly as it has been, has not, however, spelled the end much low-skill low-wage work being carried out by migrants for several reasons. First, many transfer payment recipients are outside of the labor force for sound reasons and simply cannot be cajoled back in. Employers are reluctant to employ individuals clearly unfit for whatever reason to work. Second, unless wages are brought down to the exploitative levels rendered possible through radical welfare reform in some countries, such as an hourly wage of €1 for certain groups of welfare recipients in Germany, employers may still prefer to employ less demanding, more productive, and more easily disposable employees with foreign roots.

Third, as has been emphasized in this book, the production strategy and the structural composition of the economy influence the profile of migrants employers seek to recruit and the policy they advocate in doing so. Thus the relative weight of the tertiary versus the secondary sector influences employers' recruitment strategies, though labor recruitment in the twenty-first century focuses primarily on the service sector. Labor demand for the primary sector is sometimes satisfied through undocumented recruitment channels, for example in Poland, the UK, Germany, France, and Italy. Even where it is considered a component of official recruitment policy, for example in Italy's bilateral and sector-specific recruitment quotas, it does not figure prominently, reflecting the ultimately minor share of this sector as a percentage of gross domestic product. The infusion of labor recruitment policy with competition state ideology and its concurrent rhetoric certainly has a role to play as well. The competition state can sell the need for new labor recruitment strategy more easily in pointing to modern high tech industries rather than the dull harvesting of grapes.

In addition, individual sectors and in some instances even individual companies will formulate specific demands for policy, reflecting their personnel needs, and coordinate these demands under the auspices of the employer associations. This may spawn internal conflicts and jeopardize a united business position: smaller and medium-sized companies may perceive labor migrants as a menace or a distortion to market structures, unfairly benefiting larger companies. Certain sectoral associations may prefer to satisfy their labor needs nationally and regard recruitment from outside the EU unnecessary. A combination of these factors accounts for the only recently rekindled interest in labor migration in France and Poland.

Different systems of political economy entail structural features that lead embedded labor market interest associations to lobby for a certain profile of migrants. LME employers in the UK and Ireland are interested in low-skill migrants, reflecting the wide differentiation of the labor market in terms of wages and skill levels. However, they also seek to attract skilled migrants in select economic sectors (McLaughlan and Salt 2002). This emphasis on skills is reflected in recent UK and Irish migration policy; explicit low-skill migration recruitment programs have been replaced by the free mobility of labor for EU-10 nationals. Though not an LME, Italy copies aspects of this migration model, accepting low-skill migrants in all main sectors of the economy, whether recruited actively, legalized post hoc or tolerated. But Italian active recruitment efforts also focus on highly skilled migrants, as reflected in specific professional quotas, for example in health care and information technology.

CMEs place much greater importance on skills and close their doors almost entirely to low-skill migration, with extremely limited exceptions, such as temporary agricultural workers. In Germany, the hurdles for labor migrants are set extremely high and skills and high income are pivotal in being granted a working permit. France follows this lead: the facilitation of labor migration contained in the 2006 Sarkozy Law is exclusively geared at highly skilled migrants. To the extent that Poland will develop an active labor migration policy—and already has—it follows the CME model: highly skilled migrants, currently extremely limited in numbers and concentrated in managerial positions, are welcomed. Persistent staff shortages in health care may necessitate sector-specific recruitment programs in this field. But there is no appetite for the recruitment of unskilled migrants. To the degree that Czech labor recruitment programs can be interpreted as indicative of an emerging "eastern" model, the approach there further substantiates the conclusion of CME-style labor recruitment in Central and Eastern Europe.

Quo vadis, AMP?

The politics of managed migration remain hotly and fiercely contested. In a rapidly Europeanized policy domain, national governments are engaged in two-level games, encountering humanitarian NGO calls for more lenient and measured asylum policy and business demands, backed by trade unions, for liberalized labor migration, peppered with well-targeted competition state rhetoric that links labor supply availability with economic success and sustainability. At the second and European level, national delegates in the Council face an activist Commission armed with draft directives that would often impose significant transaction costs in implementation and adaptation. Top-down Europeanization in a politically highly sensitive policy domain, where traditional concerns over sovereignty are now joined by anxieties over achieving the nebulous goal of "global competitiveness," necessarily engenders significant political conflict. The competition state rhetoric entailed in the Lisbon Agenda is also found in documents outlining EU migration policy. In reifying the purported necessity to pursue business-friendly migration policy, the procurement of human resources becomes one of the added responsibilities of the supply-side focus of the lean neoliberalized competition state, whose key tasks are limited to creating an investment-friendly setting. The exact profile of desirable labor migrants is conditioned by the structural particularities of individual systems of political economy, which is why national business associations regard plans for EU level high skill migrant recruitment with considerable hostility. Consequently, the EU will compete globally for skilled (and unskilled) migrants with the established immigration countries. It remains to be seen how well it can do.

Nonstate actors play important and in some instances decisive roles in influencing managed migration policies and informing liberalized provisions for select groups of labor migrants. Managed migration also entails more restrictive approaches towards unsolicited forms of migration in all its formats. Whether this new paradigm can prove successful is not entirely apparent, but given the fierce competition over economic migrants with traditional destinations of immigration on the one hand and ongoing push factors for emigration in Europe's troubled periphery due to political instability, demographic pressures, and increasingly the consequences of environmental degradation on the other, some doubts may well be raised.

Bibliography

Angenendt, Stephan (1999) (ed.) *Asylum and Migration Policies in the European Union*, Berlin: Europa Union Verlag

Amable, Bruno (2003) *The Diversity of Modern Capitalism*. Oxford: Oxford University Press.

Amnesty International (2002) "Stellungnahme von amnesty international zu dem Entwurf eines Gesetzes zur Steuerung und Begrenzung der Zuwanderung und zur Regelung des Aufenthaltes und der Integration von Unionsbürgern und Ausländern (Zuwanderungsgesetz)—BT 14/7387," Amnesty International: Bonn, 14 January 2002.

—— (2003) "UK/EU/UNHCR: Unlawful and Unworkable: Amnesty International's Views on Proposals for Extraterritorial Processing of Asylum Claims," AI Index: IOR 61/004/2003, 18 June 2003.

—— Arbeiterwohlfahrt, Arbeitsgemeinschaft Ausländer- und Asylrecht, Deutscher Caritasverband, Pro Asyl (2007) "Geminsame Stellungnahme zu dem Entwurf des Gesetzes zur Umsetzung aufenthalts- und asylrechtlicher Richtlinien der Europäischen Union in der Fassung vom 8. Februar 2007," Amnesty International: Berlin, March 2007.

ANAFE—Association Nationale d'Assistance aux Frontières aux Etrangers (April 2001) "Bilan des visites en zone d'attente a Roissy: campagne de novembre 2000 à mars 2001," available at: http://www.anafe.org/doc/rapport/bilanaudience.html.

—— (November 2004) "La frontière et le droit: la zone d'attente de Roissy sous le regard de l'ANAFE: bilan de six mois d'observation (avril-ottobre 2004)," available at: http://www.anafe.org/download/rapports/.

—— (January 2005) "Guide théoretique et pratique: La procédure en zone d'attente," available at: http://www.anafe.org/download/rapports/guide-anafe-janvier-2005.pdf.

Andall, Jacqueline (2002) "Second-Generation Attitude? African-Italians in Milan," *Journal of Ethnic and Migration Studies* 28 (3): 389–407.

—— (2007) "Immigration and the Italian Left Democrats in Government (1996–2001)," *Patterns of Prejudice* 41 (2): 131–53.

—— and Russell King (1999) "The Geography and Economic Sociology of Recent Immigration to Italy," *Modern Italy* 4 (2): 135–58.

Bibliography

Anderson, Benedict (1983) *Imagined Communities: The Origins and Spread of Nationalism*. London: Verso.

Angenendt, Stephan (2002) "Einwanderungspolitik und Einwanderungsgesetzgebung in Deutschland 2000–2001," in Klaus Bade and Rainer Münz (eds.) *Migrationsreport 2002*, Frankfurt: Campus.

Aniol, W (1996) *Poland's Migration and Ethnic Policies: European and German Influences*. Warsaw: Friedrich Ebert Stiftung.

Assemblée Nationale (2005) "Rapport d'Information...sur le livre vert sur une approche communautaire de la gestion des migrations économiques," No. 2365, Paris: 8 June.

Aust, Andreas (1999) *The Celtic Tiger and its Beneficiaries: Competitive Corporatism in Ireland*, paper presented at the ECPR Joint Sessions, Mannheim, Germany.

Bache, Ian (2008) *Europeanization and Multi-Level Governance: Cohesion Policy in the European Union and Britain*. Lanham, MD: Rowman and Littlefield.

Bade, Klaus (ed.) (1992) *Deutsche im Ausland, Fremde in Deutschland: Migration in Geschichte und Gegenwart*. Munich: C. H. Beck.

—— (1994) *Ausländer, Aussiedler, Asyl: eine Bestandsaufnahme*. Munich: C. H. Beck.

Bagnasco, A. (1977) *Tre Italie: La problematica territoriale dello sviluppo italiano*. Bologna: Il Mulino.

Baldwin-Edwards, Martin (November 2002) "Southern European Labour Markets and Immigration: A Structural and Functional Analysis," Mediterranean Migration Observatory, MMO Working Paper No. 5, Athens: MMO.

—— and Martin Schain (eds.) (1994) *The Politics of Immigration in Western Europe*, Portland, OR/Ilford, Essex, UK: Frank Cass.

Barrett, Alan, Adele Bergin and David Duffy (2006) "The Labour Market Characteristics and Labour Market Impacts of Immigrants in Ireland," *The Economic and Social Review* 37 (1): 1–26.

Basso, Pietro and Fabio Perocco (2000) (eds.) *Immigrazione e Trasformazione della Societa*, Milan: Franco Angeli.

Baumgartner, Frank and Bryan Jones (1991) "Agenda Dynamics and Policy Subsystems", *The Journal of Politics* 53 (4): 1044–74

—— —— (2002) (eds.) *Policy Dynamics*. Chicago: University of Chicago Press.

BBC News (2000) 4 August—"Cash Offer to Recruit Teachers," available at: http://www.news.bbc.co.uk/1/hi/education/866012.stm.

BDA—Bundesvereinigung deutscher Arbeitgeber (BDA 1983) "Das Ausländerproblem: Die Grundauffassung der Arbeitgeber," 10 March 1983, Cologne: BDA.

—— (2001*a*) "Gemeinsame Stellungnahme von BDA, BDI, DHK und ZDH zum Vorschlag der Europäischen Kommission für eine Richtlinie...über die Bedingungen..für die Ausübung einer selbständigen oder unselbständigen Erwerbstätigkeit", 11 July 2001, Berlin: BDA

—— (2001*b*) "Gemeinsame Stellungnahme von BDA, BDI, DHK und ZDH zum Vorschlag der Europäischen Kommission für eine Richtlinie...betreffend den

Status der langfristig aufenthaltsberechtigten Drittstaatsangehörigen", 13 March 2001, Berlin: BDA
—— (2002) "Stellungnahme zum Zuwanderungsgesetz", 16 January 2002, Berlin: BDA
—— (2005) "Gemeinsame Stellungnahme des BDA, BDI und BDH zum Grünbuch der Europaeischen Kommission zur Verwaltung der Witschaftsmigration," Berlin: BDA.
—— (2007a) "Newsletter: Diskussion um Fachkräftemangel gewinnt an Dynamik," Berlin: BDA.
—— (2007b) "Arbeitgeberpräsident Dr. Dieter Hundt: Einführung des Punktesystems ist ein längst überfälliger Schritt," Press Release 46/2007, Berlin: BDA.
—— (2007c) "Arbeitgeber begrüßen Beschluss des Bundeskabinetts zu kurzfristigen Maßnahmen gegen Fachkräftemangel," Press Release 67/2007, Berlin: BDA.
—— (2007d) "Arbeitgeberpräsident Dr. Dieter Hundt: Gezielte Zuwanderung ja, undurchdachte europäische Gesetzgebung nein!," Press Release 105/2007, Berlin: BDA.
Bendix, John and Niklaus Steiner (Summer 1998) "Political Asylum in Germany. International Norms and Domestic Politics," *German Politics and Society* 16 (2): 32–49.
Berger, Suzanne and Michael Piore (eds.) (1980) *Dualism and Discontinuity in Industrial Societies*, Cambridge/New York: Cambridge University Press.
Berliner Zeitung (1 February 2002) "Die Zuwanderung und das Kalkül der Parteien," [Immigration and the Parties' Strategies].
—— (10 February 2003) "Beim Zuwanderungsgesetz setzt die Union auf Konfrontation," [CDU Chooses Confrontational Tactics Regarding the Migration Bill].
Betz, Hans-Georg (1994) *Radical Right-wing Populism in Western Europe*. New York: St. Martins Press.
Biffl, Gudrun (2005) "Zur Niederlassung von Ausländern und Ausländerinnen in Österreich," Studie des Österreichischen Instituts für Wirtschaftsforschung im Auftrag des Bundesministeriums des Inneren, Vienna: WIFO, 2005/214.
Bigo, Didier (1992) *L'Europe de la sécurité intérieur*. Paris: Institute des hautes études de la sécurité intérieur.
—— (1998) "Europe passoire, Europe fortresse. La sécurisation et humanitarisation de l'immigration," in Anrea Rea (ed.) *Immigration et racisme en Europe*, Bruxelles: Complexe: 203–41.
—— (2002) 'Security and Immigration: Towards a Critique of the Governmentality of Unease.' *Alternatives* 27: 63–92.
—— (2005) 'Frontier Controls in the European Union: Who is in Control?' In Bigo, D. and Guild, E. (eds.) *Controlling Frontiers: Free Movement Into and Within Europe*, Aldershot: Ashgate.
Bloch, Alice (2002) "Refugees' Opportunities and Barriers to Training and Employment," Research Report 179, Leeds: Department for Work and Pensions.

Bibliography

Bloch, Alice (2008) "Refugees in the UK Labour Market: The Contention Between Economic Integration and Policy-Led Labour Market Restriction," *Journal of Social Policy* 37 (1): 21–36.

Blyth, Mark (2003) "Same As it Never Was? Typology and Temporality in the Varieties of Capitalism," *Comparative European Politics* 1 (2): 215–25.

Boesche, Monika (2003) "Trapped Inside the European Fortress? Germany and the European Union Asylum and Refugee Policy," paper delivered at the International Studies Association Annual Conference, Portland, OR, February 25–March 1, 2003.

Bohle, D. and B. Greskovits (2004) "Ein Sozialmodell an der Grenze. Kapitalismus ohne Kompromiss", *Osteuropa* 5–6: 372–86.

Bommes, Michael and Holger Kolb (2005) "Immigration as a Labour Market Strategy: Germany," in Jan Niessen and Yongmi Schibel (eds.) *Immigration As a Labour Market System—European and North American Perspectives*, Brussels: Migration Policy Group.

Borjas, George (December 1994) "The Economics of Immigration," *Journal of Economic Literature* 32: 1667–717.

——(1995) "The Economic Benefits from Immigration," NBER Working Paper Series No 4955, Cambridge, MA: NBER.

——(1999) *Heaven's Door: Immigration Policy and the American Economy*, Princeton: Princeton University Press.

——Richard B. Freeman, and Lawrence Katz (1992) "On the Labor Market Effects of Immigration and Trade," in George J. Borjas and Richard B. Freeman (eds.) *Immigration and the Work Force: Economic Consequences for the United States and Source Areas*, Chicago, IL: University of Chicago Press, 213–44.

Börzel, Tanja (2002) "Member State Responses to Europeanization," *Journal of Common Market Studies* 40 (2): 193–214.

——(2006) "Participation through Law Enforcement: The case of the Europe Union", *Comparative Political Studies* 39 (1) 128–52.

——and Thomas Risse (2000) "When Europe Hits Home: Europeanization and Domestic Change", *European Integration online Papers* (EIOP) 4 (15), 2000.

——(2003) "Conceptualising the Domestic Impact of Europe," in Kenneth Featherstone and Claudio Radaelli (eds.) *The Politics of Europeanization*, Oxford/New York: Oxford University Press, 57–82.

Boswell, Christina (2003) *Europoean Migration Policies in Flux Changing Patterns of Inclusion and Exclusion*, London: Blackwell.

——and Thomas Straubhaar (2004) "The Illegal Employment of Foreigners in Europe," *Intereconomics* January–February: 4–7.

——(2007) "Migration Control in Europe After 9/11: Explaining the Absence of Securitization", *Journal of Common Market Studies* 45 (3): 589–610.

Bourdieu, Pierre (1990) *Logic of Practice*. Stanford, CA: Stanford University Press.

Bibliography

Boyer, Robert (1997) "French Statism at the Crossroads," in Colin Crouch and Wolfgang Streeck (eds.) *Political Economy of Modern Capitalism: Mapping Convergence and Diversity*, London: SAGE.

Brand, Ulrich (2000) *Nichtregierungsorganisationen, Staat und ökologische Krise: Konturen kritischer NRO-Forschung*. Münster: Westfälisches Dampfboot.

Briguglio, Serguo (1993) "Linee per una nuova politica dell'immigrazione," *Affari Sociali Internazionali* 21: 73–82.

Brochmann, Greta and Tomas Hammar (eds.) (1999) *Mechanisms of Immigration Control: A Comparative Analysis of European Regulation Policies*, Oxford: Berg.

Brubaker, Rogers (1992) *Citizenship and Nationhood in France and Germany*. Cambridge: Harvard University Press.

Bundesgrenzschutz (2002) *Jahresbericht 2002*. Berlin: BGS.

Bundesinnenministerium (2006) "Harmonisation of the Asylum Law," available at: http://www.bmi.bund.de/nn_148248/Internet/Content/Themen/Auslaender_Fluechtlinge_Asyl/Einzelseiten/Harmonisation_of_the_asylum_law_Id_57713_en.html.

Bundesregierung (2005) "Stellungnahme der Bundesregierung zum Grünbuch über ein EU-Konzept zur Verwaltung der Wirtschaftsmigration," Berlin: Bundesregierung.

Buzan, Barry, Ole Waever, Morten Kelstrup, and Pierre Lemaitre (eds.) (1993) *Identity, Migration, and the New Security Agenda in Europe*, London: Pinter.

Calavita, Kitty (2004) "Economic Realities, Political Fictions, and Policy Failures," in Wayne A. Cornelius, Takeyuki Tsuda, Philip Martin, and James F. Hollifield (eds.) *Controlling Migration: A Global Perspective*, 2nd edn., Stanford, CA: Stanford University Press.

—— (2005) *Immigrants at the Margins: law, Race and Exclusion in Southern Europe*, Cambridge: Cambridge University Press.

Caritas (2004) *Immigrazione: Dossier statistico 2004, XIV Rapporto*. Roma: IDOS.

Caritas di Roma (2000) *Immigrazione: Dossier statistico 2000*. Roma: Edizione Anterem.

Casadio, Giovanna (2002) "Immigrati, 100,000 a Roma: No alla Legge Fini-Bossi," *La Republica*, 20 January 2002: 10–1.

Castells, Manuel (1975) "Immigrant Workers and Class Structure in Western Europe," *Politics and Society* 5 (1): 33–66.

Castles, Stephen and Gundula Kosack (1973) *Immigrant Workers and Class*. Oxford: Oxford University Press.

—— and Mark J. Miller (2003) *The Age of Migration: International Migration Movements in the Modern World*. 3rd edn. Basingstoke: Palgrave-Macmillan.

Caviedes, Alexander (2004) "The Open Method of Coordination in Immigration Policy: A Tool for Prying Open Fortress Europe?," *Journal of European Public Policy* 11 (2): 289–310.

Bibliography

Caviedes, Alexander (2006) "Chipping Away at Fortress Europe: How Sectoral Flexibility Needs Shape Labor Migration Policy," PhD thesis, Department of Political Science, Madison, WI: University of Wisconsin.

CBI—Confederation of British Industry (2006) "Business Summaries: Immigration and Illegal Working," London: CBI.

CEC—Commission of the European Communities (1977) *Freedom of Workers within the Community*. Brussels: Office for the Publication of the European Community (OPEC).

Cerny, Phil (October 1995) "Globalization and the Changing Logic of Collective Action," *International Organization* 49 (4): 595–625.

—— (1997) "Paradoxes of the Competition State: The Dynamics of Political Globalization", *Government and Opposition* 32 (2): 251–74

CGIL (2006) *Sintesi del documento congressuale: 15 congresso Rimini 2006*. Rome: CGIL.

Chaloff, Jonathan (2005a) "Italy," in Jan Niessen and Yongmi Schibel (eds.) *Immigration as a Labour Market Strategy: European and North American Perspectives*, Brussels: Migration Policy Group.

—— (2005b) "Italy," in Jan Niessen, Yongmi Schibel, and Cressida Thompson (eds.) *Current Immigration Debates in Europe: A Publication of the European Migration Dialogue*, Brussels: Migration Policy Group.

Chiuri, Maria Concetta and Giovanni Ferri (2001) "Where Do They Come from? What Are They? Where Are They Going? Unveiling Features and Expectations of Illegal Migrants in Italy Via a Direct Survey," Mimeo, University of Bari.

CISL—Confederazione Italiana Sindicati Lavoratori (2006) "L'immigrazione in Italia nel contesto europeo," available at: http://www.cisl.it/SitoCISL-Migratorie.nsf/PagineVarie/Immigrazione%5Etesto1.

Clift, Ben (2007) "French Corporate Governance in the New Global Economy: Mechanisms of Change and Hybridization Within Models of Capitalism," *Political Studies* 55 (3): 546–67.

Coates, David (2005) (ed.) *Varieties of Capitalism, Varieties of Approaches*. Basingstoke: Palgrave Macmillan

Codini, Ennio (2001) "Gli Appetti Normativi," in *ISMU Sesto Rapporto sulle migrazioni*, Milan: FrancoAngeli, 25–37.

Cohen, Robin (1987) *The New Helots: Migrants in the International Division of Labour*, Aldershot: Gower

Cole, Mike and Gareth Dale (1999) (eds.) *The European Union and Migrant Labour*. Oxford/New York: Berg.

Collier, R. B. and D. Collier (1991) *Shaping the Political Arena: Critical Junctures, the Labor Movement and Regime Dynamics in Latin America*. Princeton, NJ: Princeton University Press.

Commission of the European Communities (2002) "Green Paper on Community Return Policy of Illegal Migrants," COM 2002, 175 final.

Bibliography

Confindustria (2001) "Disegno di legge recante 'modifiche alla normativa in materia di immigrazione e di asilo A. A. 795'," Rome: Confindustria.

—— (2002) "Migrazioni, la sfida delle inclusioni nell'Italia degli immobilismi: Tesi del Presidente Annamaria Artoni," 17 June, Rome: Confindustria.

—— (2005) "Assemblea 2005 Intervento del Presidente," Rome: Confindustria.

Conseil économique et sociale (2003) "Avis adopté par le Conseil économique et social au cours de sa séance du mercredi 29 octobre 2003," Paris: CES.

Conseil européen (2003) "Conclusions de la Présidence," Bruxelles: 4–5 novembre 2003.

—— (2005) "La commission européenne lance une débat public sur les migrations économiques"; Brussels: Conseil européen, available at: http://europa.eu/rapid/pressReleasesAction.do?reference=IP/05/16&format=HTML&aged=1&language=FR&guiLanguage=fr.

Contel, M. and R. De Biase (1999) "Italy," in S. Angenendt (ed.) *Asylum and Migration Policies in the European Union*, Berlin: DGAP.

COORDEUROP (6 October 2003), Letter to the President of the European Parliament.

—— (10 November 2003), Letter to the Members of the EP Legal Affairs and Internal Market Committee.

Coppel, J., J. -C. Dumont, and I. Visco (2001) "Trends in Immigration and Economic Consequences," OECD Department of Economics Working Paper 284, ECO/WKP 2001/10, Paris: OECD.

Cornelius, Wayne, Philip L. Martin, and James F. Hollifield (eds.) (2004) *Controlling Immigration: A Global Perspective*, Stanford, CA: Stanford University Press.

Council of the European Union (2003) "Draft Initiative of the Italian Republic for a Council Decision on the Shared Organisation of Joint Flights for Group Removals of Third Country Nationals Illegally Present in the Territory of Two or More Member States," Doc. 10910/03, LIMITE MIGR61 COMIX, 413.

Cowles, Maria Green, James Caporaso, and Thomas Risse (2001) "Europeanization and Domestic Change: An Introduction," in Maria Green Cowles, James Caporaso, and Thomas Risse (eds.) *Transforming Europe: Europeanization and Domestic Political Change*, Ithaca, NY: Cornell University Press.

CRE (Commission for Racial Equality) (2003) "Capital can't Afford Racism," *Catalyst Magazine*, Winter 2003/2004.

Crouch, Colin and Wolfgang Streeck (1997) (eds.) *The Political Economy of Modern Capitalism*, London Sage.

Crowley, S. (2004) "Explaining Labor Weakness in Post-Communist Europe: Historical Legacies and Comparative Perspective", *Eastern European Politics and Society* 18 (3): 394–429

Crul, Maurice and Hans Vermeulen (2006) "Immigration, Education, and the Turkish Second Generation in Five European Nations: A Comparative Study,"

Bibliography

in Craig A. Prasons and Timothy M. Smeeding (eds.) *Immigration and the Transformation of Europe*, Cambridge: Cambridge University Press, 235–50.

Culpepper, Pepper (2001) "Employers' Associations, Public Policy and the Politics of Decentralized Coordination in Germany and France" in Peter Hall and David Soskice (eds.) *Varieties of Capitalism: The Institutional Foundations of Comparative Advantage*, Oxford: Oxford University Press: 275–306.

——(2003) *Creating Cooperation: How States Develop Human Capital in Europe*, Ithaca, N.Y.: Cornell University Press.

——(2006) "Capitalism, Coordination and Economic Change: The French Political Economy Since 1985," in Pepper Culpepper, Peter Hall, and Bruno Palier (eds.) *The Politics that Markets Make*, Basingstoke: Palgrave Macmillan, 29–49.

——and David Finegold (eds.) (2001) *The German Skills Machine: Sustaining Comparative Advantage in a Global Economy*, New York, NY: Berghahn Books.

Currle, Edda (ed.) (2004) *Migration in Europa: Daten und Hintergründe*, Stuttgart: Lucius und Lucius.

Cyrus, Norbert and Dita Vogel (2005) "Germany," in Jan Niessen, Yongmi Schibel, and Cressida Thompson (eds.) *Current Immigration Debates in Europe: A Publication of the European Migration Dialogue*, Brussels: Migration Policy Group.

Czommer, Lars and Georg Worthmann (2005) "Von der Baustelle auf den Schlachthof: Zur Übertragbarkeit des Arbeitnehmer-Entsendegesetzes auf die deutsche Fleischbranche," IAT Report 2005–03, Gelsenkirchen: IAT.

Debendetti, Sara (2006) "Externalization of European Asylum and Migration Policies," paper presented at the Robert Schuman Centre Summer School on Migration, June 2006, San Domenico di Fiesole: RSC, European University Institute.

Department of Justice, Equality and Law Reform (2003) *Strategy Statement 2003–2005*. Dublin: Department of Justice, Equality and Law Reform.

——(2005a) *Immigration and Residence in Ireland: Outline Policy Proposals for an Immigration and Residence Bill: A Discussion Document*. Dublin: Department of Justice, Equality and Law Reform.

——(2005b) *Strategy Statement 2005–2007*. Dublin: Department of Justice, Equality and Law Reform.

Dictionnaire Permanent du droit des étrangers (2004), January 2004.

Deutsches Rotes Kreuz (2003) "Europäische Asyl-und Migrationspolitik: Dokumentation einer Fachtagung," Berlin: Deutsches Rotes Kreuz.

DGB (2001a) Deutscher Gewerkschaftsbund, *Grundsätze des DGB für eine Regelung der Einwanderung*, 03/2001, Berlin: DGB.

——(2001b) Deutscher Gewerkschaftsbund, *Deutschland braucht Einwanderung*, 08/2001, Berlin: DGB.

——(2001c) Deutscher Gewerkschaftsbund, *Stellungnahme zum Referentenentwurf des BMI zum Zuwanderungsgesetz*, 10/2001 Berlin: DGB.

——(2002) "Stellungnahme zum Entwurf für...ein...Zuwanderungsgesetz", 9 January 2002, DGB: Berlin.

—— (2007) "Stellungnahme zum Entwurf des Gesetzes zur Umsetzung aufenthalts- und asyrechtlicher Richtlinien der Europäischen Union...", 15 May 2007, BDA: Berlin

—— (2003) Deutscher Gewerkschaftsbund, *Kenforderungen des Deutschen Gewerkschaftsbundes für einen Perspektivwechsel in der Einwanderungs- und Integrationspolitik*, 19 March 2003, Berlin: DGB.

—— and BDA (2004) "Gemeinsame Erklärung von...DGB und...BDA: Miteinander statt Nebeneinander: Integration durch Fördern und Fordern", DGB/BDA: Berlin

Die Zeit (9 November 2000) "Sie kommen, keine Angst".

Dimitrova, Antoeneva and Bernard Steunenberg (2000) "The Search for Convergence of National Policies in the European Union: An Impossible Quest?," *European Union Politics* 1 (2): 201–26.

Dolvik, Jan (1999) *An Emerging Island? ETUC, Social Dialogue and the Europeanisation of Trade Unions in the 1990s*. Bruxelles: ETUI.

Duchrow, Vera (2004) "Flüchtlingsrecht und Zuwanderungsgesetz unter Berücksichtigung der sog. Qualifikationsrichtlinie," *Zeitschrift für Ausländerrecht und Ausländerpolitik* 10: 339–47.

Dyson, Kenneth and Stephan Padgett (eds.) (2005) *The Politics of Economic Reform in Germany*, *German Politics* 14 (2), Special Issue.

Ebbinghaus, Bernhard and Jelle Visser (2000) *Trade Unions in Western Europe Since 1945*. Basingstoke: Palgrave Macmillan.

Eckstein, Harry (1975) "Case Study and Theory in Political Science," in Fred Greenstein and Nelson Polsby (eds.) *Handbook of Political Science*, Reading: Addison-Wesley, Vol. 7: 79–123.

ECRE (17 March 2003) "Statement of ECRE on the European Council Meeting", London/Brussels: ECRE

—— (2003) "Country Report: Ireland," Bruxelles: European Council on Refugees and Exiles.

EIRO (2004a) "Unions Fail to Penetrate Multinational Sector," available at: www.eiro.eurofound.eu.int/print/2004/03/inbrief/ie0403201n.html.

—— (2004b) "2003 Annual Review for Ireland," available at: www.eiro.eurofound.eu.int/print/2004/01/feature/ie0401203f.html.

—— (2004c) "Social Partners Formally Ratify National Deal," available at: www.eiro.eurofound.eu.int/print/2004/09/feature/ie0409203f.html.

—— (2005) "Irish Ferries Dispute Finally Resolved After Bitter Stand-off," available at: www.eurofound.europa.eu/eiro/2005/12/feature/ie0512203f.htm.

Ekiert, Grzegorz and Jan Kubik (1997) "Post-Totalitarian Legacies, Civil Societies, and Democracy in Post-Communist Poland 1989–1993," Working Paper, Ithaca, NY: Institute for European Studies, Cornell University.

Ensor, Jonathan and Amanda Shah (2005) "United Kingdom," in Jan Niessen, Yongmi Schibel, and Cressida Thompson (eds.) *Current Immigration Debates in Europe: A Publication of the European Migration Dialogue*, Brussels: MPG.

Bibliography

Epstein, Gerald (1996) "International Capital Mobility and the Scope for National Economic Management," in Robert Boyer and Daniel Drache (eds.) *States Against Markets: The Limits of Globalization*, London/New York: Routledge, 211–27.

Eurasylum (2007) "Eurasylums's Monthly Policy Interviews: Jonathan Faull, Director-General for Justice, Freedom and Security," June 2007, Brussels: EurAsylum.

European Commission (2003) Communication (2003/15) "Towards More Accessible, Equitable and Managed Asylum Systems".

European Communities (1999) *European Union: Selected Instruments Taken from the Treaties. Book I*, Vol. I, Luxembourg: European Communities. www.europa.eu.int/eur-lex/en/treaties/dat/treaties_en.pdf.

Evrensel, Astrid and Cordula Höbart (2004) "Migration im Österreichischen Roten Kreuz: Gesamtstudie," Vienna: Ludwig Boltzmann Institut für Menschenrechte.

Eyal, Gil, Ivan Szeleny, and Eleanor Townsley (1998) *Making Capitalism Without Capitalists*. New York, NY: Verso.

Faist, Thomas and Andreas Ette (2007) (eds.) *The Europeanization of National Policies and Politics of Immigration*, Basingstoke: Palgrave Macmillan.

Falkner, Gerda, Oliver Treib, Miriam Hartlapp, and Simone Leiber (2005) *Complying With Europe: EU Harmonization and Soft Law in the Member States*, Cambridge/New York: Cambridge University Press.

Fassmann, Heinz and Rainer Münz (1994) *European Migration in the Late Twentieth Century: Historical Patterns, Actual Trends and Social Implications*, Aldershot: Edwards Elgar.

Favell, Adrian (1998) "The Europeanisation of Immigration Politics," *European Integration Online Papers (EIOP)* Vol. 2.

—— (2001) *Philosophies of Integration: Immigration and the Idea of Citizenship in France and Britain*. 2nd edn. Basingstoke/New York: Palgrave.

—— (September 2004) "London as Eurocity: French Free Movers in the Economic Capital of London," *Global and World Cities Research Bulletin* 150.

—— (forthcoming) *Eurostars and Eurocities: Free Moving Urban Professionals in an Integrating Europe*. Oxford: Blackwell.

—— and Randall Hansen (2002) "Markets Against Politics: Migration, EU Enlargement and the Idea of Europe," *Journal of Ethnic and Migration Studies* 28 (4): 581–601.

FAZ (7 February 2002) "Die große Welle ist schon vorüber".

Featherstone, Kevin and Claudio Radaelli (2003) eds. *The Politics of Europeanization*, Oxford: Oxford University Press.

Feldblum, Miriam (1999) "Reconstructing Citizenship: The Politics of Immigration in Contemporary France," Albany, NY: State University of New York Press.

Ferner, Anthony and Richard Hyman (1997) (eds.) *Changing Industrial Relations in Europe*, Oxford: Blackwell

Ferrera, Marurizio (1996) "The 'Southern' Model of Welfare in Social Europe," *Journal of European Social Policy* 6 (1): 17–37.

Bibliography

Fioretos, Orfeos (2001) "The Domestic Sources of Multilateral Preferences: Varieties of Capitalism in the European Community," in Peter Hall and David Soskice (eds.) *Varieties of Capitalism: The Institutional Foundations of Comparative Advantage*, Oxford/New York: Oxford University Press, 213–46.

Fletcher, Mark (2003) "EU Governance Techniques in the Creation of a Common European Policy on Immigration and Asylum," *European Public Law* 66 (5): 769–80.

Foley, Michael (1993) *The Rise of the British Presidency*. Manchester: Manchester University Press.

Force Ouvrière (2006) "Immigration: les travailleurs ne sont pas 'une merchandise'," Press Release, 13 April 2006.

—— (2007) "Immigration: contre la propagande trompeuse," Press Release, 12 March 2007.

Franz, Mariella (2006) "Familienzusammenführung in der Einwanderungspolitik der Europäischen Union," IMIS Beiträge, Edition 30/2006, Osnabrück: Universität Osnabrück.

Freedman, Jane (2004) *Immigration and Insecurity in France*. Aldershot: Ashgate.

Freeman, Gary (1986) "Migration and the Political Economy of the Welfare State," *Annals of the American Academy of Political and Social Science* 485: 51–63.

—— (1995) "Modes of Immigration Politics in Liberal Democratic States," *International Migration Review* 19 (4): 881–908.

—— (2001) "Client Politics or Populism? Immigration Reform in the United States," in Virginie Guiraudon and Christian Joppke (eds.) *Controlling a New Migration World*, London: Routledge, 65–96.

—— (2002) "Winners and Losers: Politics and the Costs and Benefits of Migration," in Anthony Messina (ed.) *West European Immigration and Immigrant Policy in the New Century*, Westport, CT: Praeger, 77–96.

—— (2006) "National Models, Policy Types and the Politics of Immigration in Liberal Democracies," *West European Politics* 29 (2): 227–47.

The Guardian (30 October 2007) "Labour plans migrants points system."

Gamble, Andrew (2002) *Between Europe and America: The Future of British Politics*. Basingstoke: Palgrave Macmillan.

Geddes, Andrew (December 2000*a*) "Lobbying for Migrant Inclusion in the European Union: New Opportunities for Transnational Advocacy?," *Journal of European Public Policy* 7 (4): 632–49.

—— (2000*b*) *Immigration and European Integration: Towards Fortress Europe?* Manchester: Manchester University Press.

—— (2003) *The Politics of Migration and Immigration in Europe*. London/Thousand Oaks/CA/New Delhi: SAGE.

—— (2005) "United Kingdom," in Jan Niessen and Yongmi Schibel (eds.) *Immigration As a Labour Market Strategy—European and North American Perspectives*, Brussels: MPG.

Bibliography

Geddes, Andrew and Virginie Guiraudon (2004) "Anti-Discrimination Policy: The Emergence of a EU Policy Paradigm Amidst Contrasted National Models," *West European Politics* 27 (2): 334–53.

George, Stephen (1994) *An Awkward Partner. Britain in the European Community.* 2nd edn. Oxford: Oxford University Press.

Geyer, Robert (2000) *Exploring European Social Policy.* Cambridge: Polity.

Goetz, Klaus (2002) "Four Worlds of Europeanization," paper prepared for Workshop "Europeanisation and National Political Institutions," ECPR Turin.

—— and Simon Hix (eds.) (2001) *Europeanised Politics: European Integration and National Political Systems.* London: Frank Cass.

Goodin, Robert (2003) "Choose your Capitalism?," *Comparative European Politics* 1 (2): 203–13.

Gordon, D. M. (1972) *Theories of Poverty and Underemployment: Orthodox, Radical and Dual Labor Market Perspectives.* Lexington, MA: D.C. Heath.

—— Richard Edwards, Michael Reich. (1982) *Segmented Work, Divided Workers.* Cambridge: Cambridge University Press.

Gott, C. and K. Johnston (2002) "Migrant Population in the UK: Fiscal Effects", London: RDS Home Office Occasional Paper No. 77.

Gourevitch, Peter (1978) "The Second Image Reserved: The International Sources of Domestic Politics", *International Organization* 32: 881–911.

—— (1986) *Politics in Hard Times: Comaparative Response to International Economics Crises.* Ithaca, NY.: Cornell University Press.

—— (1996) "Squaring the Circle: The Domestic Sources of International Cooperation," *International Organization* 50 (2): 349–73.

Grabbe, Heather (2001) "How Does Europeanization Affect CEE Governance? Conditionality, Diffusion and Diversity," *Journal of European Public Policy* 8 (6): 1013–31.

—— (2003) "Europeanization Goes East: Power and Uncertainty in the EU Access Process," in Kevin Featherstone and Claudio Radaelli (eds.) *The Politics of Europeanization,* Oxford: Oxford University Press, 179–202.

—— (2005) "Regulating the Flow of People Across Europe," in Schimmelfennig Frank and Ulrich Sedelmaier (eds.) *The Europeanization of Central and Eastern Europe,* Ithaca, NY: Cornell University Press, 112–34.

Grant, Wyn (1999) *Pressure Groups and British Politics.* New York, NY: St. Martin's Press.

Graziano, Paolo and Maarten Vink (eds.) (2007) *Europeanization: New Research Agendas,* Basingstoke: Palgrave Macmillan.

Green, Simon (2004) "The Politics of Exclusion; Institutions and Immigration Policy in Contemporary Germany," Manchester/New York: Manchester University Press.

Grimblat, J. A. (December 2003) "Des scenarios d'immigration pour une Europe viellissante," *Esprit*: 199–272.

Groenendijk, Kees (2004a) "Legal Concepts of Integration in EU Migration Law," *European Journal of Migration and Law* 6 (2): 1388–364X.

—— (2004b) "Rechtliche Konzepte der Integration im EG-Migrationsrecht," *Zeitschrift für Ausländerrecht und Ausländerpolitik* 04/2004: 123–9.

Gross, D. (1999) "Three Million Foreigners, Three Million Unemployed? Immigration and the French Labour Market," IMF Working Paper WP 99/124, Washington, DC: IMF.

Guidi, Gianfranco, Alberto Bronzino, and Luigi Germanetto (1974) *Fiat: Struttura Aziendale ed Organizzazione della Sfruttamento.* Milan: Mazotta.

Guild, Elspeth (2007) "EU Policy on Labour Migration: A First Look at the Commission's Blue Card Initative," CEPS Policy Brief No. 145, Brussels: CEPS.

Guiraudon, Virginie (2000a) "European Integration and Migration Policy: Vertical Policy-Making As Venue Shopping," *Journal of Common Market Studies* 38 (2): 249–69.

—— (2000b) "The Marshallian Tryptich Reordered: The Role of Courts and Bureaucracies in Furthering Migrants' Social Rights," in Michael Bommes and Andrew Geddes (eds.) *Immigration and Welfare: Challenging the Borders of the Welfare State*: 72–89.

—— (2001) "European Courts and Foreigners' Rights: A Comparative Study of Norms Diffusion," *International Migration Review* 34 (4): 1088–125.

—— (2002) "Logiques et pratiques de l'Etat délégateur: les compagnies de transport dans le contrôle migratoire à distance," *Cultures et conflits* 45.

—— and Gallya Lahav (2000) "The State Sovereignty Debate Revisited: The Case of Migration Control," *Comparative Political Studies* 33 (2): 163–95.

Haas, Ernst (1958) *The Uniting of Europe.* Stanford, CA: Stanford University Press.

—— (1964) *Beyond the Nation-State: Functionalism and International Organization.* Stanford, CA: Stanford University Press.

Habermas, J. (1992) "Citizenship and National Identity: Some Reflections on the Future of Europe," *Praxis International* 12 (1): 1–19.

Hainsworth, Paul (2000) *The Politics of the Extreme Right: From the Margins to the Mainstream.* London: Pinter.

Hall, Peter (1986) *Governing the Economy: The Politics of State Intervention in Britain and France.* Cambridge: Polity Press.

—— and David Soskice (eds.) (2001) *Varieties of Capitalism: The Institutional Foundations of Comparative Advantage.* Oxford/New York: Oxford University Press.

Hall, Peter A. (1986) *Governing the Economy: The Politics of State Intervention in Britain and France.* New York, NY: Oxford University Press.

Hammar, Tomas (ed.) (1985) *European Immigration Policy: A Comparative Study.* Cambridge: Cambridge University Press.

Hancké, Bob (2002) *Large Firms and Institutional Change: Industrial Renewal and Economic Restructuring in France.* Oxford/New York: Oxford University Press.

Bibliography

Hancké, Bob, and Martin Rhodes and Mark Thatcher (2007) *Beyond Varieties of Capitalism: Conflict, Contradictions and Complementarities in the European Economy*, Oxford: Oxford University Press.

Hanf, K. and B. Soetendorp (eds.) (1998) *Adapting To European Integration: Small States and the European Union*, London/New York: Longman.

Hansen, Randall (2000) *Citizenship and Immigration in Post-War Britain*. Oxford/New York: Oxford University Press.

—— (April 2002) "Globalization, Embedded Realism, and Path Dependence: The Other Immigrants To Europe," *Comparative Political Studies* 35 (3): 259–83.

Hardiman, Niamh (October 2002) "Economic Governance and Political Innovation in Ireland," *West European Politics* 25 (4): 1–24.

Harding, Rebecca and William Paterson (eds.) (2000) *The Future of the German Economy: An End To the Miracle?*, Manchester/New York: Manchester University Press.

Hargreaves, A. (1995) *Immigration, 'Race' and Ethnicity*. London/New York: Routledge.

Hassel, Anke (1999) "The erosion of the German system of industrial relations", *British Journal of Industrial Relations* 37 (3): 484–505.

—— (2007) "The Curse of Institutional Security: The Erosion of German Trade Unionism", *Industrielle Beziehungen* 14 (2): 176–191.

Hathaway, James C. (2004) "Review Article of Niraj Nathwani 'Rethinking Refugee Law'," *American Journal of International Law* 98 (3): 616–21.

Haus, Leah (2002) *Unions, Immigration, and Internationalization: New Challenges and Changing Coalitions in the United States and France*. New York, NY: Palgrave Macmillan.

Hauschild, Christoph (2003) "Neues europäisches Einwanderungsrecht: Das Recht auf Familienzusammenführung," *Zeitschrift für Ausländerrecht und Ausländerpolitik* 23 (8): 266–73.

Hay, Colin (2005) "Two Can Play at that Game... or Can They? In Coates, David (2005) (ed.) *Varieties of Capitalism, Varieties of Approaches*. Basingstoke: Palgrave Macmillan: 106–21.

Heinisch, Reinhard (1999) "Modernization Brokers—Austrian Corporatism in Search of a New Legitimacy," *Current Politics and Economics of Europe* 9 (1): 65–94.

—— (2003) "Success in Opposition—Failure in Government: Explaining the Performance of Right-Wing Populist Parties in Public Office," *West European Politics* 26 (3): 91–130.

Heisler, Martin (1986) "Transnational Migration as a Small Window on the Dimenished Autonomy of the Modern Democratic State," *The Annals of the American Academy of Political and Social Science* 485 (1): 153–166.

Herbert, Ulrich (1986) *Geschichte der Ausländerbeschäftigun in Deutschland: 1880–1980—Saisonsarbeiter, Gastarbeiter, Zwangsarbeiter*. Berlin: Dietz.

—— (2001) *Geschichte der Ausländerpolitik in Deutschland*. Munich: Beck.

Héritier, Adrienne (1996) "The Accommodation of Diversity in European Policy-Making and its Outcomes: Regulatory Policy As Patchwork," *Journal of European Public Policy* 3 (2): 149–67.
—— and Dieter Kerwer, Christoph Knill, Dirk Lehmkuhl, Michael Teutsch, Anne-Cécille Douillet (2001) (eds.) *Diffrential Europe: The European Union Impact on National Policymaking*, Lanham, MD: Rowman and Littlefield.
Hirsch, Joachim (1995) *Der nationale Wettbewerbsstaat*. Berlin: ID-Archiv.
—— (1998) *Vom Sicherheitsstaat zum nationalen Wettbewerbsstaat*. Berlin: ID-Archiv.
Hollifield, James (1992) *Immigrants, Markets and States: The Political Economy of Postwar Europe*. Cambridge, MA: Harvard University Press.
—— (2000) "Immigration and the Politics of Rights: The French Case in Comparative Perspective," in Michael Bommes and Andrew Geddes (eds.) *Immigration and Welfare: Challenging the Borders of the Welfare State*: 109–39.
—— (2006) "The Emerging Migration State," *International Migration Review* 38 (3): 885–912.
Hollingsworth, J. Rogers, Philippe C. Schmitter and Wolfgang Streeck (eds.) (1994) *Governing Capitalist Economies*, Oxford: Oxford University Press.
Home Office (2005a) *Controlling our Borders: Making Migration Work for Britain—Five Year Strategy for Asylum and Immigration*. February 2005, London: Home Office.
—— (2005b) *Managed Migration; Working for Britain—A Joint Statement from the Home Office, CBI, TUC*. London: Home Office.
Hooghe, Liesbet and Gary Marks (2003) "Unravelling the Central State, but How? Types of Multi-Level Governance," *American Political Science Review* 97: 233–43.
Hughes, Gerard and Emma Quinn (2004) "The Impact of Immigration on Europe's Societies: Ireland," Brussels/Dublin: European Migration Network.
Human Rights Watch (2003) "An Unjust 'Vision' for Europe's Refugees: Human Rights Watch Commentary on the UK's 'New Vision' Proposal for the Establishment of Refugee Processing Centres Abroad," 17 June 2003.
Hussey, G. (1995) *Ireland Today: Anatomy of a Changing State*. London: Penguin.
Huysmans, Jef (1998) "Security! What Do you Mean? From Concept to Thick Signifier," *European Journal of International Relations* 4 (2): 226–55.
—— (2000) "The European Union and the Securitization of Migration," *Journal of Common Market Studies* 38 (5): 751–77.
—— (2006) *The Politics of Insecurity: Fear, Migration and Asylum in the EU*. London/New York: Routledge.
Hyman, Richard and Anthony Ferner (eds.) (1994) *New Frontiers in European Industrial Relations*, Oxford, UK/Cambridge, MA: Blackwell.
IBEC (2003) "IBEC's Vision for Social Partnership Beyond 2002."
—— (2008) "Immigration, Residence and Protection Bill 2007."
—— Irish Business and Employers Confederation (2003) *Annual Review 2003–2004*. Dublin: IBEC.
Iglicka, Kdfasf, P. Kazmierkiewicz, and M. Mazur-Rafal (2003) *Zarządzanie migracja. Przypadeki doswiadczenia Polski w osniedsienu do dyrektyw Komisji Europejskiej*

Bibliography

[Managing Immigration. The Polish Case and Experience in the Context of European Commission Directives]. Warsaw: Institute of Public Affairs/Institute for International Relations.

IG Metall (2002) *Abschlussdokumentation des Zukunftskongress vom 13–15.05.2002 in Leipzig: Neue Wege Wagen.* Frankfurt: IG Metall.

Imig, Doug and Sidney Tarrow (eds.) (2001) *Contentious Europeans: Protest and Politics in an Emerging Polity*, Lanham, MD: Rowman and Littlefield.

Immergut, Ellen (1992) *Health Politics: Interest and Institutions in Western Europe.* Cambridge: Cambridge University Press.

Initiative Neue Soziale Marktwirtschaft (2002) *Deutschland im Reformstau: Muster-Koalitionsvertrag.* No. 72, Berlin: Stiftung Marktwirtschaft.

INSEE-Institut national de la statistiques et des etudes économiques (2003) "Travail-Emploi-Population active", INSEE: Paris

Institut Montaigne (2003) "Compétitivité et vieillissement," Paris: Institut Montaigne.

ISMU-Cariplo (2001) *Sesto Rappoto sulle Migrazioni in Italia.* Milan: FrancoAngeli.

Jackson, J. A. (1963) *The Irish in Britain.* London: Routledge and Kegan Paul.

Jacoby, Wade (2004) *The Enlargement of the European Union and NATO: Ordering from the Menu in Central Europe.* Cambridge/New York: Cambridge University Press.

Jessop, Bob (1990) *State Theory: Putting the Capitalist State in its Place.* Cambridge: Polity.

Joppke, Christian (1998) "Why Liberal States Accept Unwanted Migration," *World Politics* 50 (2): 266–93.

—— (1999) *Immigration and the Nation-State: The United States, Germany and Great Britain.* Oxford/New York: Oxford University Press.

Jordan, Andrew (2002) *The Europeanization of British Environmental Policy: A Departmental Perspective.* Basingstoke: Palgrave.

—— and Duncan Liefferink (eds.) (2004) *Environmental Policy in Europe: The Europeanization of National Environmental Policy*, London: Routledge.

Julien-Laferrière, François (Automne 1996a) "La situation des demandeurs d'asile dans les zones d'attente et les lieux de rétention administrative," *Cultures et Conflits* 23: 7.

—— (automne 1996b) "La rétention des étrangers aux frontières françaises," *Cultures et Conflits* 23: 7.

Juss, Satvinder S. (2005) "The Decline and Decay of European Refugee Policy," *Oxford Journal of Legal Studies* 25 (4): 749–92.

Kazenstein, Peter (1978) *Between Power and Plenty: Foreign Economic Policies of Advanced Industrial States*, Madison, WI: University of Wisconsin Press.

—— (1987) *Policy and Politics in Germany: The Growth of a Semi-Sovereign State.* Philadelphia, PA: Temple University Press.

Katznelson, Ira (2003) "Periodization and Preferences: Reflections on Purposive Action in Comparative Social Science" in James Mahoney and Dietrich

Rueschemeyer (eds.) *Comparative Historical Analysis: Innovations in Theory and Method*, Cambridge: Cambridge University Press.

Kelly, R., G. Morrell, and D. Sriskandarajah (2005) *Migration and Health in the UK: An IPPR Factfile*. London: IPPR.

Keohane, Robert and Helen Milner (1996) "Internationalization and Domestic Politics: An Introduction," in Robert Keohane and Helen Milner (eds.) *Internalization and Domestic Politics*, Cambridge: Cambridge University Press.

Kicinger, Anna (2005) "Between Polish Interests and the EU Influence—Polish Migration Policy Development 1989–2004," CEFMR Working paper 9/2005, Warsaw: Central European Forum for Migration Research.

—— and Agnieszka Weinar (2007) "State of the Art of the Migration Research in Poland," CEFMR Working Paper 1/2007, Warsaw.

—— —— and Agata Gorny (2007) "Advanced Yet Uneven: The Europeanization of Polish Immigration Policy," in Thomas Faist and Andreas Ette (eds.) *The Europeanization of National Policies and Politics of Immigration*, Basingstoke: Palgrave Macmillan, 181–200.

King, Russell (1993) *The New Geography of European Migrations*, London: Belhaven Press.

Kingdon, John (1984) *Agendas, Alternatives and Public Policies*. London: Pearson.

Knill, Christopher (2001) *The Europeanisation of National Administrations: Patterns of Institutional Change and Persistence*. Cambridge: Cambridge University Press.

—— and Dirk Lehmkuhl (1999) "How Europe Matters: Different Mechanisms of Europeanization," *European Integration Papers* 3 (7): eiop.or.at/eiop/texte/1999-007a.htm.

—— and Andrea Lenschow (1998) "Adjusting To EU Environmental Policy: Change and Persistence of Domestic Administrations," in Maria Green Cowles, James Caporaso, and Thomas Risse (eds.) *Transforming Europe: Europeanization and Domestic Change*, Ithaca, NY: Cornell University Press, 116–36.

—— and Dirk Lehmkuhl (2002) "The national impact of European Union Regulatory Policy: Three Europeanization Mechanisms", *European Journal of Political Research* 41 (2): 255–80.

Kohler-Koch, Beate (1999) "The Evolution and Transformation of European Governance" in Beate Kohler-Koch and Rainer Eising (eds.) *The Transformation of Governance in the European Union*, London: Routledge, 14–36.

Koopmans, Ruud and Paul Statham (1999) "Political Claims Analysis: Integrating Protest Event and Political Discourse Approaches," *Mobilization: The International Journal of Research and Theory About Political Movements, Protest and Collective Behaviour* 4 (20): 203–21.

—— (1999) "Challenging the Liberal Nation-State? Postnationalism, Multiculturalism, and the Collective Claims Making of Migrants and Ethnic Minorities in Britain and Germany", *American Journal of Sociology* 105 (3): 652–696.

Bibliography

Köppe, Olaf (2003) "The Leviathan of Competitiveness: How and Why Do Liberal States (Not) Accept Unwanted Immigration?," *Journal of Ethnic and Migration Studies* 29 (3): 431–49.

Korys, Piotr and Agnieszka Weinar (2005) "Poland," in Jan Noesse and Yongmi Schibel (eds.) *Immigration As a Labour Market Strategy—European and North American Perspectives*, Brussels: MPG.

Koser, Khalid and Charles Pinkerton (2002) "The Social Networks of Asylum Seekers and the Dissemination of Information About Countries of Asylum," *Findings 165*, London: Home Office, DRS Department.

Koslowski, Rey (1998) "European Migration Regimes: Emerging, Enlarging and Deteriorating," *Journal of Ethnic and Migration Studies* 24 (4): 735–50.

Kostakopolou, Theodora (2000) "The Protective Union: Change and Continuity in Migration Law and Policy in Post-Amsterdam Europe," *Journal of Common Market Studies* 38 (3): 497–518.

Kozlowski, Tomasz Kuba (1999) "Migration Flows in the 1990s: Challenges for Entry, Asylum and Integration Policy in Poland," in Krystina Iglicka and Keith Sword (eds.) *The Challenge of East-West Migration for Poland*, London: Macmillan, 45–66.

Krasner, Stephen (1984) "Approaches to the State: Alternative Conceptions and Historical Dynamics", *Comparative Politics* 16 (2): 223–46.

—— (1989) "Sovereignty: An Institutional Perspective" in James A. Caporaso (ed.) *The Elusive State: International and Comparative Perspectives*, Newbury Park, CA: Sage: 69–96.

Kretzschmar, Cyril (2005) "Immigration as a Labour Market Strategy: France," in Jan Niessen and Yongmi Schibel (eds.) *Immigration as a Labour Market System—European and North American Perspectives*, Brussels: Migration Policy Group.

Krugman, Paul (March/April 1994) "Competitiveness: A Dangerous Obsession," *Foreign Affairs* 73 (2): 28–44.

—— (1996) "Making Sense of the Competitiveness Debate," *Oxford Review of Economic Policy* 12 (3): 17–25.

Kühne, Michael (2000) "The Federal Republic of Germany: Ambivalent Promotion of Immigrants' Interests," in Rinus Penninx and Judith Roosblad (eds.) *Trade Unions, Immigration and Immigrants in Europe 1960–1993*, New York/Oxford: Berghahn, 39–64.

Lahav, Gallya (1998) "Immigration and the State: The Devolution and Privatisation of Migration Control in the EU," *Journal of Ethnic and Migration Studies* 24 (4): 675–94.

—— (2004) *Immigration and Politics in the New Europe: Reinventing Borders*. Cambridge/New York: Cambridge University Press.

Lallement, Michel (1999) *Les gouvernances de l'emploi: relations professionnelles et marché du travail en France et en Allemagne*. Paris: Desclée de Brouwer.

Lane, David (2005) "Emerging Varieties of Capitalism in Former State Socialist Societies", *Competition and Change* 9 (3), September: 221–41.

Bibliography

Lavenex, Sandra (1998) "Asylum, Immigration and Central-Eastern Europe: Challenges to EU Enlargement," *European Foreign Affairs Review* 3 (2): 275–94.

—— (December 2001) "The Europeanization of Refugee Policies: Normative Challenges and Institutional Legacies," *Journal of Common Market Studies* 39 (5): 851–74.

Layton-Henry, Zig (1984) *The Politics of Race in Britain*. London: Allen and Unwin.

Lehmbruch, Gerhard and Philippe Schmitter (eds.) (1981) *Patterns of Corporatist Policy-Making*. Beverly Hills, CA: Sage.

Leiber, Simone (2007) "Transposition of EU Social Policy in Poland: Are There Different 'Worlds of Compliance' in East and West?", *Journal of European Social Policy* 17 (4): 349–60

—— (2005) "Implementation of EU Social Policy in Poland: Is There a Different 'Eastern World of Compliance'?," paper presented at the EUSA Ninth Biennial International Conference, Austin, Texas, March 31–April 2, 2005.

Leif, Thomas (2004) "Die politischen Strategien der Initiative Neue soziale Marktwirtschaft," *Schriftenreihe der Hans-Böckler-Stiftung*, Fakten für eine faire Arbeitswelt, Düsseldorf.

Le Moigne, G. (1986) *L'immigration en France*. Paris: PUF.

Levy, Carl (1999) "European Asylum and Refugee Policy After the Treaty of Maastricht: The Birth of a New Regime?," in A. Bloch and C. Levy (eds.) *Refugees, Citizenship and Social Policy in Europe*, Basingstoke/New York: Palgrave, 12–50.

—— (2005) "The European Union After 9/11: The Demise of a Liberal Democratic Asylum Regime?," *Government and Opposition* 40 (1): 26–59.

Levy, Jonah (1999) *Tocqueville's Revenge: State, Society and Economy in Contemporary France*. Cambridge, MA: Harvard University Press.

—— (2005) "Redeploying the State: Liberalization and Social Policy in France," in Wolfgang Streeck and Kathleen Thelen (eds.) *Beyond Continuity: Institutional Change in Advanced Political Economies*, Oxford/New York: Oxford University Press.

Lillie, Nathan and Ian Greer (2007) "Industrial Relations, Migration and Neoliberal Politics: The Case of the European Construction Sector", *Politics and Society* 35 (4): 551–81.

Lindberg, Leon (1970) *Europe's Would-Be Polity: Patterns of Change in the European Community*. Englewood Cliffs, NJ: Prentice Hall.

Lloyd, Cathie (2000) "Trade Unions and Immigrants in France: From Assimilation to Antiracist Networking," in Rinus Penninx and Judith Roosblad (eds.) *Trade Unions, Immigration, and Immigrants in Europe 1960–1993*, Oxford/New York: Berghahn Books, 111–32.

Lodziński, S (2001) "Polish Citizenship—Ethnic Boundaries and Issue of Citizenship in Polish Society," in B. Balla and A. Sterbling (eds.) *Ethnicity, Nation and Culture. Central and East European Perspectives*. Hamburg: Krämer, 149–63.

Bibliography

Lütz, Susanne (2004) "Convergence Within National Diversity: The Regulatory State in Finance," *Journal of Public Policy* 24 (2): 169–97.

Mac Éinrí, Piaras (2005) "Ireland," in Jan Niessen, Yongmi Schibel, and Cressida Thompson (eds.) *Current Immigration Debates in Europe: A Publication of the European Migration Dialogue*, Brussels/Dublin: Migration Policy Group.

Macioti, Maria Immacolata and Enrico Pugliese (1991) *Gli Immigrati in Italia*. Bari: Editori Laterza.

Mac Sharry, R. and P. White (2000) *The Making of the Celtic Tiger*. Dublin: Mercier Press.

Mahoney, James (2001) *Legacies of Liberalism: Path Dependence and Political Regimes in Latin America*. Baltimore: Johns Hopkins University Press.

Mandel, E. (1978) *The Second Slump: A Marxist Analysis of Recession in the Seventies*. London: NLB.

March, James and Johan Olson (1989) *Rediscovering Institutions: The Institutional Basis of Politics*. New York, NY: Free Press.

——— (1998) "The Institutional dynamics of international political orders", *International Organization* 52: 943–69.

Marie, C.-V. (1999) "Emploi des étrangers sans titre, travail illegal, regularisations: des débats en trompe-l'œil," in P. Dewitte (ed.) *Immigration et intégration: l'état des savoirs*, Paris: La Découverte.

Marks, Gary and Liesbet Hooghe (2002) *Multi-Level Governance and European Integration*. Lanham, MD: Rowman and Littlefield.

Marshall, Barbara (2000) *The New Germany and Migration in Europe*. Manchester/New York: Manchester University Press.

Matthews, Gareth and Martin Ruhs (2007) "Are You Being Served? Employer Demand for Migrant Labour in the UK's Hospitality Industry," COMPAS Working Paper 51, Oxford: COMPAS.

McLaughlan, G. and J. Salt (2002) "Migration Policies Towards Highly Skilled Foreign Workers: Report to the Home Office," London: Home Office.

McMenamin, Iain (2004) "Varieties of Capitalist Democracy: What Difference Does East-Central Europe Make?," *Journal of Public Policy* 24 (3): 259–74.

MEDEF (2000) "Attirer la matière grise," Debate at the MEDEF Summer School, 1 September 2000.

——— (2006) "Intervention de Nicolas Sarkozy," Speech at the MEDEF Summer School, 31 August 2006.

Mény, Philip, Pierre Muller and Jean-Louis Quermonne (eds.) (1996) *Adjusting to Europe: The Impact of the European Union on National Institutions and Policies*, London: Routledge.

Menz, Georg (August 2001) "Beyond the Anwerbestopp? The German-Polish Labor Treaty," *Journal of European Social Policy* 11 (3): 253–69.

——— (2002) "Patterns in EU Labour Immigration Policy: National Initiatives and European Responses," *Journal of Ethnic and Migration Studies* 28 (4): 727–42.

—— (2005a) *Europeanization and Varieties of Capitalism: National Response Strategies to the Single European Market*. Oxford/New York: Oxford University Press.

—— (June 2005b) "Old Bottles and New Wine? The New Dynamics of Industrial Relations," in Kenneth Dyson and Stephan Padgett (eds.) *The Politics of Economic Reform in Germany*, *German Politics* 14 (2), Special Issue.

—— (2005c) "Auf Wiedersehen, Rhineland Model: The Internalization of Neoliberalism in Germany," in Susanne Soederberg, Georg Menz, and Philip Cerny (eds.) *Internalizing Globalization: The Rise of Neoliberalism and the Decline of National Varieties of Capitalism*, New York/Basingstoke: Palgrave.

—— (2006) "'Useful' Gastarbeiter, Burdensome Asylum Seekers, and the Second Wave of Welfare Retrenchment: Exploring the Nexus Between Migration and the Welfare State," in Craig Parsons and Timothy Smeeding (eds.) *Immigration and the Transformation of Europe*, Cambridge: Cambridge University Press.

Milanaccio, Alfredo and Luca Ricolfi (1976) *Lotte Operaie e Ambiente di Lavoro: Mirafiori, 1968–1974*. Turin: Giulio Einaudi Editore.

Miles, R. and D. Kay (1992) *Refugees or Migrant Workers? European Voluntary Workers in Britain 1946–1951*. London: Routledge.

Miller, Mark J. and Philip L. Martin (1982) *Administering Foreign-Worker Programs; Lessons from Europe*. Lexington, MA: Lexington Book.

Milner, Helen (Spring 1992) "International Theories of Cooperation of Nations: A Review Essay," *World Politics*, 44 (3): 466–96.

—— (1997) *Interests, Institutions and Information: Domestic Politics and International Relations*. Princeton: Princeton University Press.

Ministère de la Justice (December 1999) "Le travail illégal et sa répression," *Infostat Justice*, No. 54.

Minkenberg, Michael (2000) "The Renewal of the Radical Right: Between Modernity and Anti-Modernity," *Government and Opposition* 35 (2): 170–88.

[Italian] MinofInt (2001) *Rapporto del Ministro dell'Interno sullo Stato della Seurezza in Italia*, Bologna: Il Mulino.

Monar, Joerg (2005) "Justice and Home Affairs," *Journal of Common Market Studies* 43: 131–46.

Moravcsik, Andrew (1993) "Preferences and Power in the European Community: A Liberal Intergovernmentalist Approach", *Journal of Common Market Studies* 31 (4): 473–524.

—— (1998) *The Choice for Europe: Social Purpose and State Power from Messina to Maastricht*. Ithaca, NY: Cornell University Press.

Morice, Alain (November 2000) "De l'immigration zero aux quotas," *Le Monde diplomatique*: 6–7.

Morris, Lydia (2002) *Managing Migration: Civic Stratification and Migrants' Rights*. London: Routledge.

Mottura, Giovanni (2000) "Immigrati e Sindacato," in Enrico Pugliese (ed.) *Rapporto Immigrazione: Lavoro, Sindacato, Società*, Rome: Ediesse.

Bibliography

MRCI—Migrant Rights Centre Ireland (2008) "Immigration, Residence and Protection Bill—Policy Response," www.mrci.ie, internet accessed on February 25, 2008.

Murphy, T. V. and W. K. Roche (eds.) (1997) *Irish Industrial Relations in Practice*. Dublin: Oak Tree Press.

Mykhnenko, Vlad (September 2005) "What Type of Capitalism in Eastern Europe? Institutional Structures, Revealed Comparative Advantages, and Performance of Poland and Ukraine," CPPR Discussion Paper Series, No. 6.

Nathans, Eli (2004) *The Politics of Citizenship in Germany: Ethnicity, Utility and Nationalism*. Oxford/New York: Berg.

Nolan, B. and P. J. O'Connell (2000) *Bust to Boom? The Irish Experience of Growth and Inequality*. Dublin: Institute of Public Administration.

Nolte, Paul (2001) "Die Krise des Konservatismus," *Die Zeit* 31.

Notizie Ansa (2002*a*) "Immigrazione: +15% Annuo Presenza Stagionali Agricultura," available at: http://www.stranieriinitalia.com.

——(2002*b*) "Lavoro: Extracomunitari, Poco Sindacato al Nord, Piu' al Sud in Campania 'Sindicalizzazione' Superiore alla Media Regionale," available at: http://www.stranieriinitalia.com.

NSZZ Solidarnosc (12 October 1999) "Statement on Freedom of Movement After the Enlargement of the European Union,".

Ohmae, Kenichi (2005) *Next Global Stage: The Challenges and Opportunities in Our Borderless World*, Philadelphia: Wharton School Publishing.

O'Keeffe, D. (1999) "Can the Leopard Change its Spots? Visas, Immigration and Asylum Following Amsterdam," in David O'Keeffe and Patrick Twomey (eds.) *Legal Issues of the Amsterdam Treaty*, Oxford: Hart, 271–88.

[Polish] Office for Repatriation and Foreigners [Urząd do Spraw repatriacji i cudzoziemców] (2006) "Statistics," available at: http://www.uric.gov.pl.

Okólski, Marek (1994*a*) "Migracje zagraniczne ludnosci Polski w latach 1980–1989," *Studia Demograficzne* 40 (3).

——(1994*b*) "International Migration in Poland: Characteristics, Magnitude, Causes," in *Migration as Socio-Economic Phenomenon in the Process of Poland's Transition Within the Context of European Transition*, Paris: OECD, 75–117.

——(2000) "Polen—Wachsende Vielfalt von Migration," in Fassmann Heinz and Rainer Münz (eds.) *Ost-West Wanderung in Europa*, Vienna: Böhlau, 141–62.

——(2006) "Costs and Benefits of Migration for Central European Countries," CMR Working Papers, 7 (65), Warsaw.

Olsen, Johan (2002) "The Many Faces of Europeanization," *Journal of Common Market Studies* 40 (5): 921–52.

Olson, Mancur (1971) *The Logic of Collective Action*. Cambridge, MA: Harvard University Press.

Ostrom, Elinor (1990) *Governing the Commons: The Evolution of Institutions for Collective Action*, Cambridge: Cambridge University Press.

Paul, Kathleen (1997) *Whitewashing Britain: Race and Citizenship in the Postwar Era*. Ithaca, NY: Cornell University Press.
Peach, Ceri (1968) *West Indian Migration to Britain*. London: Oxford University Press.
Peck, Jamie (2001) *Workfare States*. New York, NY: Guilford Press.
Penninx, Rinus and Judit Roosblad (2000) *Trade Unions, Immigration and Immigrants in Western Europe 1960–1993*. New York/Oxford: Berghahn Books.
Perrineau, Pascal (1997) *Le symptôme Le Pen. Radiographie des électeurs du Front National*. Paris: Fayard.
Peters, B. Guy (1998) *Comparative Politics: Theory and Methods*. Basingstoke: Macmillan.
Pierson, Paul (1994) *Dismantling the Welfare State? Reagan, Thatcher, and the Politics of Retrenchment*. Cambridge/New York: Cambridge University Press.
—— (2000) "Increasing Returns, Path Dependence and the Study of Politics", *American Political Science Review* 94 (2): 251–67.
—— (2004) *Politics in Time: History, Institutions, and Social Analysis*, Princeton: Princeton University Press.
Piore, Michael (1979) *Birds of Passage: Migrant Labor and Industrial Societies*. Cambridge: Cambridge University Press.
—— and Charles Sabel (1984) *The Second Industrial Divide: Possibilities for Prosperity*. New York, NY: Basic Books.
Polska Akcja Humanitarna (2003) *Annual Report 2003*. Warszawa: PAH.
Pontusson, Jonas (2005) "Varieties and Commonalities of Capitalism" in In Coates, David (ed.) (2005) *Varieties of Capitalism, Varieties of Approaches*. Basingstoke: Palgrave Macmillan: 163–88.
Porter, Michael (1990) *The Competitive Advantage of Nations*. New York: The Free Press.
ProAsyl (2004) "Europäische Asylpolitik: Minimale Standards—Maxiamle Abschottung," Frankfurt: ProAsyl.
Putnam, Robert (1988) "Diplomacy and Domestic Politics: The Logic of Two-Level Games," *International Organization* 42: 427–60.
Quinn, Emma and Gerard Hughes (2004) "The Impact of Immigration on Europe's Societies: Ireland", Report Prepared for the European Commission, Dublin: Economic and Social Research Institute.
Radaelli, Claudio (2000) "Whither Europeanization? Concept Stretching and Substantive Change," available at: http://eiop.or.at/eiop/texte/2000–008.htm.
—— (2003) "The Europeanization of Public Policy," in Kenneth Featherstone and Claudio Radaelli (eds.) *The Politics of Europeanization*, Oxford/New York: Oxford University Press, 27–56.
Rapport Annuel au parlement sur la Securité sociale (September 1999), chapter 12.
Recchi, Ettore, Damian Tambini, Emiliana Baldoni, David Williams, Kristin Surak, and Adrian Favell (2003) *Intra-EU Migration: A Demographic Overview*. Pioneer

Bibliography

Working paper No. 3, State of the Art Report, available at: http://www.obets.ua.es/pioneur.

[British] Refugee Council (May 2003) "Unsafe Havens, Unworkable Solutions." London: Refugee Council.

Regini, Marino (2000) "Between Deregulation and Social Pacts: The Responses of European Economies to Globalization", *Politics and Society* 28 (1): 5–33.

—— (2003) "Work and Labour in Global Economies: The Case of Western Europe", *Socio-Economic Review* 1: 165–84.

Reich, Robert (1991) *The Work of Nations: Preparing Ourselves for 21st Century Capitalism*. New York, NY: Knopf.

Rhodes, Martin (1998) "Globalization, Labour Markets and Welfare States: A Future of 'Competitive Corporatism'?," in Martin Rhodes and Yves Meny (eds.) *The Future of European Welfare: A New Social Contract?* London: Macmillan, 178–203.

—— (2000) "Desperately Seeking a Solution: Social Democracy, Thatcherism and the 'Third Way' in British Welfare," *West European Politics* 23 (2): 161–86.

Ribas-Mateos, Natalia (2004) "How Can we Understand Immigration in Southern Europe?," *Journal of Ethnic and Migration Studies* 30 (6): 1045–65.

Richard, Jean-Luc (2004) *Partir our rester? Les destinées de jeunes issus de l'immigration étrangère en France*. Paris: PUF.

Richardson, Jeremy (ed.) (1993) *Pressure Groups*. Oxford: Oxford University Press.

Robinson, Vaughan and Jeremy Segrott (July 2002) "Understanding the Decision-Making of Asylum Seekers," *Home Office Research Study 243*, London: Home Office.

Rogowski, Roger (1989) *Commerce and Coalitions*. Princeton, NJ: Princeton University Press.

Rose et al. (1969) *Colour and Citizenship: A Report on British Race Relations*. London: Oxford University Press.

Rudolph, Christopher (2003) "Security and the Political Economy of International Migration", *American Political Science Review* 97 (4): 603–20.

—— (2006) *National Security and Immigration*, Stanford, CA: Stanford University Press.

Rühl, Stefan and Edda Currle (2004) "Deutschland," in Edda Currle (ed.) *Migration in Europa: Daten und Hintergründe*, Stuttgart: Lucius und Lucius, 17–80.

Ruhs, Martin (2003) "Emerging Trends and Patterns in the Immigration and Employment of Non-EU Nationals in Ireland: What the Data Reveal," Policy Institute Working Paper No. 6, The Policy Institute at Trinity College Dublin.

—— (2005) "Managing the Immigration and Employment of Non-EU Nationals in Ireland," *Studies in Public Policy 19*, Dublin: The Policy Institute at Trinity College Dublin.

Ryan, Bernard (2001) "The Common Travel Area Between Britain and Ireland," *Modern Law Review* 64: 855–74.

Sabatier, Paul (1988) "An Advocacy Coalition Framework of Policy Change and the Role of Policy-Oriented Learning Therein," *Policy Sciences* 21 (2–3): 129–68.

Sachverständigenrat (2004) *Sachverständigenrat für Zuwanderung und Integration, Erfahrungen nutzen, Neues wagen: Jahresgutachten 2004*. Nuremberg: BFL.

Salt, John (1992) "Migration Processes Among the Highly Skilled in Europe," *International Migration Review* 26: 485–505.

Samers, Michael (2003) "Invisible Capitalism: Political Economy and the Regulation of Undocumented Immigration in France," *Economy and Society* 32 (4): 555–83.

—— (2004) "The 'Underground Economy,' Immigration and Economic Development in the European Union: An Agnostic-Skeptic Perspective," *International Journal of Economic Development* 6 (2): 199–272.

Sarkozy, Nicholas (2003) *Libre*. Paris: Edition Pocket.

Sassen, Saskia (2001) *The Global City*. Princeton, NJ: Princeton University Press.

Schain, Martin, Aristide Zolberg and Patrick Hassay (eds.) (2002) *Shadows over Europe: The Development and Impact of the Extreme Right in Western Europe*, Basingstoke: Palgrave Macmillan.

—— (1987) "The French Party System and the Rise of the National Front in France," *West European Politics* 10 (2): 229–52.

Scharpf, F. (1996) "Negative and Positive Integration in the Political Economy of European Welfare States," in G. Marks, F. Scharpf, P. Schmitter, and W. Streeck (eds.) *Governance in the European Union*, London: Sage, 1–14.

Schibel, Yongmi (2004) *Monitoring and Influencing the Transposition of EU Immigration Law: The Family Reunion and Long Term Residents Directive*. MPG Occasional Papers Series, Brussels: Migration Policy Group.

Schierup, Carl-Ulrik, Peo Hansen and Stephen Castles (2006) *Migration, Citizenship and the European Welfare State*, Oxford: Oxford University Press.

Schimmelfennig, Frank, Stefan Engert, and Heiko Knobel (2003) "Costs, Commitment and Compliance: The Impact of EU Democratic Compliance on Latvia, Slovakia and Turkey," *Journal of Common Market Studies* 41 (3): 495–518.

—— and Ulrich Sedelmaier (eds.) (2005) *The Europeanization of Central and Eastern Europe*. Ithaca, NY: Cornell University Press.

Schmidt, Vivien (1996) *From State to Market? The Transformation of French Business and Government*. Cambridge/New York: Cambridge University Press.

—— (2002) *The Futures of European Capitalism*. Oxford/New York: Oxford University Press.

Schmitter, Philippe (1979) "Still the Century of Corporatism?" in Philippe Schmitter and Gerhard Lehmbruch (eds.) *Trends towards Corporatist Intermediation*, New York: Sage.

Schuster, L. and J. Solomos (1999) "The Politics of Refugee and Asylum Policies in Britain: Historical Patterns and Contemporary Realities," in A. Bloch and C. Levy (eds.) *Refugees, Citizenship and Social Policy in Europe*, Basingstoke/New York: Palgrave, 51–75.

Schwartz, Herman (undated) "Down the Wrong Path: Path Dependence, Increasing Returns and Historical Institutionalism", mimeo, University of Virginia.

Bibliography

Sciortino, G. (1999) "Planning in the Dark: The Evolution of Italian Immigration Control," in G. Brochmann and T. Hammar (eds.) *Mechanisms of Immigration Control*, Oxford/New York: Berg.

Sénat (2005) "Rapport d'Information fait au nom de la délégation pour l'Union européenne sur la politique européenne d'immigration," *Session ordinaire 2004–2005*, No. 385.

Sewell, William (1996) "Three Temporalities: Toward an Eventful Sociology" in Terrance J. MacDonald (ed.) *The Historica Turn in the Human Sciences*, Ann Arbor: University of Michigan: 245–80.

Shonfield, Andrew (1965) *Modern Capitalism: The Changing Balance of Public and Private Power*, London: Oxford University Press.

Siaroff, Alan (1999) "Corporatism in 24 Industrial Democracies: Meaning and Measurement", *European Journal of Political Research* 36: 175–205.

Silvia, Stephen (1999) "Every Which Way But Loose: German Industrial Relations since 1980" in Andrew Martin and George Ross (eds.) *The Brave New World of European Labor*, New York/Oxford: Berghahn Books: 75–124.

Siméant, Johanna (1998) *La Cause des Sans-Papiers*. Paris: Presse de Sciences Po.

Slany, K. (1997) *Orientacje Emigracjne Polakow*. Cracow: Kwadrat.

Smith, Anthony (1991) *National Identity*. London: Penguin.

Snyder, Glenn (1977) *Conflict Among Nations: Bargaining, Decision-Making and System Structure in International Crisis*. Princeton, NJ: Princeton University Press.

Soederberg, Susanne, Georg Menz and Philip Cerny (eds.) (2005) *Internalizing Globalization: The Rise of Neoliberalism and the Decline of National Varieties of Capitalism*, New York/Basingstoke: Palgrave.

Soskice, David (2007) "Varieties of Capitalism and Macroeconomic Institutions", in Bob Hancké, Martin Rhodes and Mark Thatcher, *Beyond Varieties of Capitalism*, Oxford: Oxford University Press:

Soysal, Yasemin (1994) *Limits of Citizenship: Migrants and Post-National Membership in Europe*. Chicago, IL: University of Chicago Press.

Staniszkis, Jedwiga (1991) *The Dynamics of Breakthrough*. Berkeley, CA: University of California Press.

Stark, David (1996) "Recombinant Property in East European Capitalism," *American Journal of Sociology* 101 (4): 993–1027.

—— and László Bruszt (1998) *Postsocialist Pathways: Transforming Politics and Property in East Central Europe*, Cambridge: Cambridge University Press.

—————(January 2001) "One Way or Multiple Paths? For a Comparative Sociology of East European Capitalism," *American Journal of Sociology* 106 (4): 1129–37.

Statham, Paul (2001) "Zwischen öffentlicher Sichtbarkeit und politischem Einfluß: Mobilisierung gegen Rassismus und für Migranten in Großbritannien," *Neue Soziale Bewegungen Forschungsjournal* 14 (1/1): 72–86.

—— and Andrew Geddes (March 2006) "Elites and the 'Organised Public': Who Drives British Immigration Politics and in Which Direction?," *West European Politics* 29 (2): 248–69.

Statistisches Bundesamt (1992) *Statistisches Jahrbuch der Bundesrepublik Deutschland.* Wiebaden: Statistisches Bundesamt.

Steinmo, S., K. Thelen and F. Longstreth (1992) *Structuring Politics: Historical Institutionalism in Comparative Analysis.* Cambridge: Cambridge University Press.

—— (27 February 2004) "Deutschland braucht qualifizierte Zuwanderer,".

Stola, D. (2001) "Two Kinds of Quasi-Migration in the Middle Zone: Central Europe as a Space for Transit Migration and Mobility for Profit," in D. Stola and C. Wallace (eds.) *Patterns of Migration in Central Europe,* Basingstoke: Palgrave Macmillan, 84–104.

Storper, Michael (1997) *The Regional World: Territorial Development in a Global Economy.* New York, NY: Guilford Press.

Strange, Susan (1996) *The Retreat of the State: The Diffusion of Power in the World Economy.* Cambridge: Cambridge University Press.

Streeck, Wolfgang (1992) "Productive Constraints: On the Institutional Conditions of Diversified Quality Production," in Wolfgang Streeck (ed.) *Social Institutions and Economic Performance,* London: SAGE, 1–40.

—— (1997) "German Capitalism: Does it exist? Can it Survive?," in Colin Crouch and Wolfgang Streeck (eds.) *The Political Economy of Modern Capitalism,* London: Sage.

—— and Anke Hassel (2004) "The Crumbling Pillars of Social Partnership," in Herbert Kitschelt and Wolfgang Streeck (eds.) *Germany: Beyond the Stable State,* London: Frank Cass, 101–24.

—— and Martin Höpner (eds.) (2003) *Alle Macht dem Markt? Fallstudien zur Abwicklung der Deutschland AG.* Frankfurt: Campus.

—— Jürgen Grote, Volker Schneider, and Jelle Visser (eds.) *Governing Interests: Business Associations Facing Internationalization,* London/New York: Routledge.

—— and Kathleen Thelen (2005) (eds.) *Beyond Continuity: Institutional Change in Advanced Political Economies,* Oxford: Oxford University Press.

Terray, Emmanuel (1999) "Le travail des étrangers en situation irrégulière ou la delocalisation sur place," in E. Balibar, M. Chemillier-Gendreau, J. Costa-Lascoux, and E. Terray (eds.) *Sans-Papiers: L'archaïsme fatal,* Paris: La Découverte.

Thelen, Kathleen (1999) "Historical Institutionalism in Comparative Politics", *Annual Review of Political Science* Vol.2., Palo Alto, CA: Annual Reviews, Inc.

—— (2001) "Varieties of Labor Politics in the Developed Democracies" in Peter Hall and David Soskice (eds.) *Varieties of Capitalism: The Institutional Foundations of Comparative Advantage,* Oxford: Oxford University Press: 71–103.

Bibliography

Thelen, Kathleen (2004) *How Institutions Evolve: The Political Economy of Skills in Germany, Britain, the United States and Japan.* Cambridge: Cambridge University Press.

Thielemann, Eiko (forthcoming) "The 'Soft' Europeanisation of Migration Policy: European Integration and Domestic Policy Change," *Journal of Ethnic and Migration Studies.*

Thomas, Graham (2000) "Has Prime Minister Major Been Replaced by President Blair?," in Lynton Robbins and Bill Jones (eds.) *Debates in British Politics Today,* Manchester: Manchester University Press, 13–26.

Thraenhardt, Dietrich and Simone Wolken (eds.) (1988) *Flucht und Asyl: Informationen, Analysen und Erfahrungen aus der Schweiz und der Bundesrepublik Deutschland,* Freiburg: Lambertus.

Thurow, Lester (1999) *Creating Wealth: New Rules for Individuals, Companies and Countries in a Knowledge-Based Economy.* London: Nicholas Brealay Publishing.

TRANSODRA (1999) *Polnische Flüchtlings- und Migrationspolitik.* Potsdam, Germany: Deutsch-Polnische Gesellschaft Brandenburg.

Traxler, Franz, Sabine Blaschke and Bernhard Kittel (2001) *National Labour Relations in Internationalized Markets: A Comparative Study of Institutions, Change and Performance.* Oxford: Oxford University Press.

TUC (2003) *Overworked, Underpaid and Over Here: Migrant Workers in Britain.* London: TUC.

—— (2005) *Forced Labour and Migration to the UK.* London: TUC.

—— (2006) *Press Release: TUC Demands Law Change to Prevent Exploitation of Migrant Workers.* London: TUC, 26 January.

Ucarer, Emek (1997) "Europe's Search for Policy: The Harmonization of Asylum Policy and European Integration," in Emek Ucarer and Donald Puchala (eds.) *Immigration into Western Societies,* Washington, DC: Pinter.

UIL (5 February 2003), Press Release, Rome: UIL.

UK Government (2005) *European Commission's Green Paper on an EU Approach to Managing Economic Migration: The Response of the United Kingdom.* London: UK Government.

UK Home Office (2006) *A Points-Based System: Making Migration Work for Britain.* London: HM Stationery Office.

UK Parliament (1992) *Official Report: Home Department: Immigration Ministers Meeting.* Column 481, 7 December, available at: http://www.publications.parliament.uk/pa/cm199293/cmhansrd/1992-12-07/Writtens-3.html.

—— (2005) *Green Paper on a European Union Approach to Managing Economic Migration.* Select Committee on European Scrutiny, Twelfth Report, 12 April 2005.

Unabhängige Kommission (2001) Unabhängige Kommission Zuwanderung, *Zuwanderung gestalten, Integration fördern,* Berlin.

UNHCR (2002) *Stellungnahme zum Zuwanderungsgesetz vom 14.1.2002, BT-Durcksache 14/6741.* Berlin: UNHCR.

UNICE (13 May 2005) *Commission Green Paper on an EU Approach to Managing Economic Migration: UNICE Response.* Brussels: UNICE.

—— (10 May 2006) *UNICE Position on the Commission Policy Plan on Legal Migration.* Brussels: UNICE.

Unioncamere (2006) "In cinque anni raddoppiate imprese straniere in Italia," available at: http://www.uil.it/immigrazione/focus.htm.

Vink, Maarten (2005) *Limits of European Citizenship: European Integration and Domestic Immigration Politics.* Basingstoke: Palgrave Macmillan.

Vitols, Sigurt (2001) "Varieties of Corporate Governance: Comparing Germany and the UK" in Peter Hall and David Soskice (eds.) *Varieties of Capitalism: The Institutional Foundations of Comparative Advantage*, Oxford: Oxford University Press: 337–60

Waever, O. (1993) "Societal Security: The concept" in B. Buzan, O. Waever et al. (eds.) *Identity, Migration and the New Security Agenda in Europe*, London: Pinter.

Wallace, Helen (2000) "Europeanisation and Globalisation," *New Political Economy* 5 (3): 369–82.

Walraff, Günter (1988) *Ganz unten.* Hamburg: Kiepenheuer and Witsch.

Watson, Matthew (2003) "Ricardisn Political Economy and the 'Varieties of Capitalism' Approach: Specialization, Trade and Comparative Institutional Advantage", *Comparative European Politics* 1 (2): 227–40.

Watts, Julie R. (2002) *Immigration Policy and the Challenge of Globalization: Unions and Employers in Unlikely Alliance*, Ithaca, NY: Cornell University Press.

Weil, Patrick (1991) *La France et ses étrangers: L'aventure d'une politique de l'immigration.* Paris: Calmann-Lévy.

—— (2002) *Qu'est-ce qu'un français ? Histoire de la nationalité française depuis la révolution.* Paris: Bernard Grasset.

—— (2005) *La France et ses étrangers: L'aventure d'une politique de l'immigration de 1938 à nos jours.* Paris: Galimard.

Weiner, Myron (1993) *International Migration and Security.* Boulder, CO: Westview Press.

Weiss, Linda (1998) *The Myth of the Powerless State*, Ithaca, N.Y.: Cornell University Press.

Whitaker, E (1992) "The Schengen Agreement and its Portent for the Freedom of Personal Movement in Europe," *Georgetown Immigration Law Journal* 6: 191–214.

Woll, Cornelia (2006) "National Business Associations Under Stress: Lessons from the French case," *West European Politics* 29 (3): 489–512.

Wrench, John (2000) "British Unions and Racism: Organisational Dilemmas in an Unsympathetic Climate," in Rinus Penninx and Judith Roosblad (eds.) *Trade Unions, Immigration and Immigrants in Europe 1960–1993*, New York/Oxford: Berghahn Books, 133–56.

Bibliography

WSI—Wissenschafts- und Sozialwissenschaftliches Institut der Hans Böckler Stiftung (2005) *Entsendegesetz: Hohe Hürden in 34 von 40 Wirtschaftsbereichen.* 11 May, Düsseldorf: WSI, available at: www.boeckler.de.

Zubek, Radoslaw (December 2001) "A Core in Check: The Transformation of the Polish Core Executive," *Journal of European Public Policy* 8 (6): 911–32.

Zuccolini, Roberto (January 20, 2002) "Colf e Lavoratori Agricoli: Un Esercito di Irregolari," *Corriere della Sera*, 4.

Zysman, John (1983) *Governments, Markets and Growth: Finance and the Politics of Industrial Change*, Ithaca, N.Y.: Cornell University Press.

Index

Absorption, and Europeanization 79, 81
Accommodation, and Europeanization 13, 79, 81
Acquis communautaire 20, 85, 86
Agenda-setting 80–5
Asylum qualification directive 107–12

Blue Card program 49–50, 53
Börzel, T. and Risse, T. 79–84

Capital 92
Capitalism
  Varieties of Western European 94–5
Cerny, Philip 30
Competition state 29–35, 94, 97, 116, 121–2
Coordinated market economies 93, 94–5, 172

Dirty, dull and dangerous ("3 D") jobs 34, 265
Dual labor markets 34, 92–4
Dublin Convention 42, 51

Emerging market economies 94–6
Employer organisations 93–5, 262
European Court of Justice 87, 101
European Union
  And immigration policy 6
Europeanization
  And immigration 40–55, 77–8, 80
  In France 150–2
  In Germany 185–8
  In Ireland 215–16
  In Italy 249–51
  In Poland 225, 228–32
  In the United Kingdom 164–7
  In a bottom-up fashion 80–5, 115, 167, 187
  And Central and Eastern Europe 85–6
  And theoretical approaches 13, 77–9
  In a top-down fashion 77–9, 151, 188, 252

Family reunion directive 100–6
Far Right wing parties 91, 103, 133–4, 168
France
  And employer organizations 89, 114, 136, 139, 146, 148–9
  And humanitarian NGOs 129–32, 139, 142–6, 149
  And immigration policy 57–61, 126–35, 140–50
  And political economy 135–6
  And structure of interest intermediation 139–40
  And trade unions 89, 138–9, 149
  Preference formation 129–49
Freeman, G. 90–1

Germany
  And employer organizations 89, 95–6, 109, 114–15, 175–7, 181, 184–5
  And humanitarian NGOs 102, 109–10, 179, 181, 184
  And immigration policy 61–4, 167–72
  And political economy 172–8
  And structure of interest intermediation 178–9
  And trade unions 89, 95–6, 109, 177–8, 181, 184
Guestworker 62

Hague Program 47–8, 107
Highly skilled labor 5, 94–6, 146, 157, 163
Hirsch, Joachim 32–3
Humanitarian nongovernmental organizations (NGOs) 3, 6, 81

Immigration
  And courts 135, 153
  And the media 201
Ireland
  And employer organizations 89, 203, 205
  And humanitarian NGOs 208, 211, 213

299

Index

Ireland (*cont.*)
　And immigration policy 68–70, 199–202
　And political economy 202–7
　And trade unions 89, 203, 207
　Preference formation 205–9
Italy
　And employer organizations 89, 236, 240–1
　And humanitarian NGOs 242
　And immigration policy 66–8, 232–6, 243–9
　And political economy 236–9
　And trade unions 89, 239
　Preference formation 241–2

Labor migration directive (EU) 112–19
Liberal market economies 93, 94–5, 156, 202
Lobbying 8, 88–92, 101, 178–9
Low-skill labor migration 10, 153, 169
　In agriculture 148, 238

Managed migration 1, 147–8, 163–4
Mixed market economies 94–6
　As applied to France 135–6
　As applied to Italy 236–9

Nongovernmental actors 4, 88–91, 101–2, 264

Organizational power 89–91, 97

Path-dependency 26
　As applied to migration policy 25–9

Pierson, Paul 26, 28
Poland
　And employer organizations 89, 96, 220
　And humanitarian NGOs 221, 226–7
　And immigration policy 70–1, 216–18, 222–32
　And political economy 218–21
　And trade unions 89, 220
　Preference formation 221
Policy learning 86–7, 198
Prüm Treaty 48–9, 53
Punctured equilibrium 25

Schengen Treaty 40–1
Securitization of migration 5, 8, 35–7, 39–40, 108
Seville, European Council meeting 46–7, 98, 101

Tampere. European Council meeting 44–5, 97–9, 119
Third country partnerships 120–1
Trade unions 93–4, 96–7, 189, 263–4
Two-level games 12–13, 80, 102, 186

United Kingdom
　And employer organizations 89, 95–6, 118, 158–9, 163
　And humanitarian NGOs 160–1, 165–7
　And immigration policy 64–6, 152–6, 161–4
　And political economy 156–60
　And structure of interest intermediation 160–1
　And trade unions 89, 159